International Political Economy Series

General Editor: Timothy M. Shaw, Professor of Political Science and
International Development Studies, Dalhousie University, Nova Scotia

Robert Boardman
PESTICIDES IN WORLD AGRICULTURE

Inga Brandell (*editor*)
WORKERS IN THIRD-WORLD INDUSTRIALIZATION

Richard P. C. Brown
PUBLIC DEBT AND PRIVATE WEALTH

Bonnie K. Campbell (*editor*)
POLITICAL DIMENSIONS OF THE INTERNATIONAL DEBT CRISIS

Bonnie K. Campbell and John Loxley (*editors*)
STRUCTURAL ADJUSTMENT IN AFRICA

Jerker Carlsson and Timothy M. Shaw (*editors*)
NEWLY INDUSTRIALIZING COUNTRIES AND THE POLITICAL
ECONOMY OF SOUTH–SOUTH RELATIONS

David P. Forsythe (*editor*)
HUMAN RIGHTS AND DEVELOPMENT
THE UNITED NATIONS IN THE WORLD POLITICAL ECONOMY

David Glover and Ken Kusterer
SMALL FARMERS, BIG BUSINESS

William D. Graf (*editor*)
THE INTERNATIONALIZATION OF THE GERMAN POLITICAL
ECONOMY

Betty J. Harris
THE POLITICAL ECONOMY OF THE SOUTHERN AFRICAN PERIPHERY

Steven Kendall Holloway
THE ALUMINIUM MULTINATIONALS AND THE BAUXITE CARTEL

Matthew Martin
THE CRUMBLING FAÇADE OF AFRICAN DEBT NEGOTIATIONS

James H. Mittelman
OUT FROM UNDERDEVELOPMENT

Paul Mosley (*editor*)
DEVELOPMENT FINANCE AND POLICY REFORM

Development Finance and Policy Reform

Essays in the Theory and Practice of Conditionality in Less Developed Countries

Edited by

Paul Mosley
*Professor of Development Economics and Policy
and Director, Institute for Development Policy and Management
University of Manchester*

St. Martin's Press

First published in Great Britain 1992 by
THE MACMILLAN PRESS LTD
Houndmills, Basingstoke, Hampshire RG21 2XS
and London
Companies and representatives
throughout the world

A catalogue record for this book is available
from the British Library

ISBN 0–333–56967–9

Printed in Great Britain by
Antony Rowe Ltd,
Chippenham, Wiltshire

First published in the United States of America 1992 by
Scholarly and Reference Division,
ST. MARTIN'S PRESS, INC.,
175 Fifth Avenue,
New York, N.Y. 10010

ISBN 0–312–07915–X

Library of Congress Cataloging-in-Publication Data
Development finance and policy reform : essays in the theory and
practice of conditionality in less developed countries / edited by
Paul Mosley.
p. cm.—(International political economy series)
Includes bibliographical references and index.
ISBN 0–312–07915–X
1. Loans, Foreign—Developing countries. 2. Economic
stabilization—Developing countries. I. Mosley, Paul. II. Series.
HJ8899.D495 1992
336.3'435'091724—dc20   91–42578
                                                    CIP

Contents

List of Figures & Tables

FIGURES

TABLES

List of Acronyms

ADB	Asian Development Bank
AID	(US) Agency for International Development
BoP	balance of payments
CA	current account
CFA	Communaute Financiere d'Afrique (franc zone)
EC	European Community
ECA	UN Economic Commission for Africa
EIAL	early intensive adjustment lending
ESAF	enhanced structural adjustment facility
GDP	gross domestic product
IBRD	International Bank for Reconstruction and Development (World Bank)
IDA	International Development Association
IDS	Institute of Development Studies, University of Sussex
IFIs	international financial institutions
IIE	Institute of International Economy, Washington, DC
ILO	International Labour Organisation
IMF	International Monetary Fund
LDCs	less developed countries
NBER	National Bureau of Economic Research
ODA	official development assistance *or* Overseas Development Administration (UK)
ODC	Overseas Development Council (US)
OGL	open general licence
PBL	policy-based lending
PPR	Policy, Planning and Research (World Bank)
PRE	Policy, Research and External Affairs (World Bank)
SAL	structural adjustment loan
SDR	special drawing rights
SECAL	sectoral adjustment loan
SPA	special programme of assistance
SSA	sub-Saharan Africa
UN	United Nations
UNDP	UN Development Programme

UNESCO	UN Educational, Scientific and Cultural Organisation
UNICEF	UN Children's Fund
USAID	US Agency for International Development
WHO	World Health Organisation

Notes on Contributors

John Cameron is Senior Lecturer in Economics, School of Development Studies, University of East Anglia.

Vittorio Corbo is Professor of Economics, Pontificia Universidad Nacional de Chile, and until April 1991 was Chief, Macroeconomics and Debt Division, World Bank.

Stanley Fischer is Professor of Economics, Massachusetts Institute of Technology, and until September 1990 was Vice-President and Chief Economist, World Bank.

David F. Gordon is Regional Economic Policy Adviser, USAID, Nairobi, on leave from the University of Michigan.

Anne Henderson is Assistant Professor of Political Science, College of William and Mary, Williamsburg, Virginia.

Paul Mosley is Professor of Development Economics and Policy, and Director, Institute for Development Policy and Management, University of Manchester.

Joan M. Nelson is Senior Fellow, Overseas Development Council, Washington, DC.

Alessandro Pio is Professor of Economics, Instituto di Studi Latino-americani, Bocconi University, Milan.

Moeen Ahmad Qureshi recently retired from the post of Senior Vice-President (Operations), World Bank.

Peter Sandersley is Senior Economic Adviser, ODA, London.

Frances Stewart is Senior Research Fellow, Queen Elizabeth House, Oxford.

John Toye is Director, IDS, University of Sussex.

1 Introduction

Paul Mosley

As an instrument of international economic policy, conditionality is on the increase. Already practised by the International Monetary Fund (IMF) for nearly half a century, it has in the last decade been applied by both the World Bank and by most bilateral agencies to that growing proportion of their expenditure which goes in the form of programme assistance, or general balance-of-payments support. In recent years, the scope of conditionality has widened further: both the established development agencies and new ones such as the European Bank for Reconstruction and Development have committed themselves to tie their disbursement not only to an improvement in the recipient's economic policy but also to evidence of multi-party democracy, respect for human rights and other components of 'good government'.

It would, however, be wrong to say that this rapid spread of conditionality was a response to evidence demonstrating it to be effective. The question of effectiveness breaks down into a political question (does conditionality cause the governments of developing countries to change their economic policies?) and a consequential economic question (if it does, do their economies improve as a result?). Ten years ago, when the last major studies of IMF conditionality appeared (Williamson, 1983; Killick et al., 1984) the first question had not received an answer, whereas the second had been answered in distinctly sceptical terms. On the available evidence (see also Khan and Knight, 1985; Goldstein, 1986) IMF programmes had achieved some (but often transient) improvement in the balance of payments of recipient countries, reduced their rate of growth and influenced inflation in an insignificant manner. The new wave of conditional development finance of the 1980s was thus launched in a spirit of hope rather than experience. Was the hope justified? The essays in this book address that question. Many of them were first presented at a conference held at Hulme Hall, University of Manchester, on 10 and 11 September 1990, which brought representatives of recipient countries and major agencies involved in policy-based lending together with independent observers of the process.

1

The first part of the book contains presentations of the rationale of policy-based lending by senior staff of three of the major agencies which have become heavily involved in the process during the 1980s: the World Bank (IBRD), USAID and the UK Overseas Development Administration (ODA). In principle, this rationale is clear and simple: after the IMF has established macro-economic stability in a borrower country through the application of its own policy conditions such as devaluation and monetary restrictions, the World Bank and bilateral donors will seek to enforce a move towards micro-economic efficiency through liberalisation of price controls and the structure of protection against foreign trade. The practice has not been so straightforward. As is pointed out by Moeen Qureshi, the Senior Vice-President (Operations) of the World Bank (Chapter 2), the latest extension of conditionality has taken place against a background of widespread and protracted debt crisis, and where the objective of quick disbursement to contain this crisis conflicts with the enforcement of conditionality, it tends to be the quick disbursement objective which wins. The slippage on conditions to which this has given rise is described by both David Gordon (Chapter 3) and Peter Sandersley (Chapter 4); the former in addition shows that the award of the World Bank and IMF 'seal of approval' to developing countries attempting a programme of economic reform has by no means, in most cases, persuaded private banks and multinational companies to resume the flow of investment towards those countries which was interrupted by the world recession and debt crisis of 1980–3. What began as a temporary expedient, exemplified by the continuing use of the word 'adjustment loans' to describe the programme lending of the international financial institutions, has turned into a long-term policy dialogue as those institutions seek to plug the financing gap of developing countries more or less unaccompanied. This has plunged them into the political complexities of attempting to assemble and sustain a coalition in favour of economic reform, a problem which they never foresaw.

Part II of this book focuses on these complexities, which hold the key to the first major research question described above: do the policy reforms requested under conditionality get implemented or not, and if so under what circumstances? John Toye (Chapter 5) argues, with particular reference to sub-Saharan Africa, that since the losers from any policy reform are well-organised and articulate, whereas the potential gainers are scattered and often doubting – a 'knife-edge' first described by Machiavelli – the wonder is not that conditionality often fails but that it sometimes succeeds – in 60 per cent of cases, according to World Bank data, although Toye notes that burdensome conditions have often been circumvented rather than openly breached, for example by imposing new controls on the economy while removing others in fulfilment of the terms of a conditionality agreement. Joan Nelson, in Chapter 6, identifies a number of the conditions which appear to be necessary to negotiate the political knife-edge, including recent experience of economic decline, a new government, and effective measures to neutralise the opponents of reform. However, such opposition has been disarmed through the ballot box at least as frequently as through dictatorial measures, and Nelson further argues that the sustaining of reform requires a broader-based coalition in support than the initiation of reform. In Chapter 7, I bring this domestic political battle in the borrowing country together with pressures on the lender's side in a theoretical model which suggests that the costs of enforcing conditionality, in terms of a reduced probability of loan repayment, may often exceed the benefits, and that in consequence the lender's threat of punishment for breach of conditionality will often not be very credible.

Part III of the book assesses the results of conditional programme lending – both the intended results on competitiveness, exports and growth, and the unintended effects on investment and the quality of life. The essay by Corbo and Fischer (Chapter 8) reports on World Bank surveys of the macro-economic effects of its conditional programme lending: the good news is that they have improved exports and the balance of payments, but the bad news, at a time when the Bank is seeking to re-focus its attention on long-term growth, is that they appear to have depressed investment. The effects on GDP growth are mildly positive. These results have been broadly confirmed by Harrigan and Mosley (1991) using a different methodology, but when the effects of policy conditions and loan money are examined separately, the former show up positive and the latter negative, which suggests that the Bank's reform proposals *if implemented* may be supportive of growth but that conditional lending packages are being used by some countries to postpone rather than to facilitate reform, thereby perpetuating their state of macro-economic crisis.

Frances Stewart (Chapter 9) and Alessandro Pio (Chapter 10) examine the social impact of adjustment; their analysis thus goes beyond the narrow confines of conditional adjustment *lending*. Stewart's essay is empirical, and constitutes an extension and an update of her work with UNICEF on *Adjustment with a Human Face* (Cornia, Jolly and Stewart, 1987). The findings are that the deterioration in health and education standards noted in that book for the early 1980s persisted throughout the decade in much of Africa and Latin America; programmes in mitigation of these effects introduced into the donors' conditionality late on in the decade, such as PAMS-CAD in Ghana, have so far been urban-biased and confined to a very small number of 'losers'. Pio's main thesis is that these social consequences of adjustment should not be seen purely as damage to the consumption standards of low income groups but also as a depletion of the human capital of those countries which will feed back into their future growth potential.

Part IV, finally, assesses the prospects for conditionality in the 1990s in the light of the experience of the 1980s and previous decades. Anne Henderson (Chapter 11) assesses the prospects for the new wave of conditional lending to Eastern Europe in the light of the IMF's experience there to date. Noting that in some regimes (such as Yugoslavia) the process of compensating the losers from reform went so far as to 'sabotage the whole thrust of the adjustment effort', she concludes that cold turkey is now, in the view of the international financial institutions, the only way to cut through the tangle of distortions which hold the Eastern European economies back and that programmes such as Poland's which seek to carry out all the necessary reforms in a short space of time represent the way forward. (Interestingly, this approach contrasts with that of the World Bank elsewhere, which in its most recent report [1990a] argues for greater gradualism.) John Cameron (Chapter 12), having described how conditionality was extended in the mid-1980s to embrace social welfare under the stress of 'civil disturbance and political instability', criticises this process as incomplete, and argues that until the structure of policy-making in developing countries is amended to put power in the hands of the powerless, conditionality will not be in a satisfactory state. The idea of extending conditionality into the political realm has recently become common ground between left and right, of course, in spite of its shortcomings as a tool of economic policy reform. Joan Nelson, in the concluding Chapter 13, examines the possibilities for bringing about 'good government' through policy dialogue, and concludes that, even more than in the purely economic sphere, there is ample scope for countervailing action as well as overt slippage; hence, by a paradox which the reader will encounter throughout the book, conditionality is only truly effective where the borrower is already committed to reform and where conditionality as a consequence is not required.

The high failure rate for conditionality revealed by these studies is not an original insight: in 1975, Klaus Knorr argued that in twenty-five cases where the United States had attempted to influence the policy of other countries by cutting off economic aid, twenty-two had failed or yielded indeterminate results (Knorr 1975, pp. 180–3, 337–9). But if conditionality yields so little, it is interesting that its use, so far from being on the wane, is being taken up all the time by new agencies (e.g. the European Community (EC)) and being extended by existing agencies to new policy purposes, such as reforms in environmental policy, social policy and structures of government. Of course, a high failure rate in itself means little: as David Baldwin has reminded us (Baldwin, 1985, pp. 22–3, 310–19) the test of an instrument of foreign policy is not what it achieves in absolute terms, but what it would have achieved in relation to the best alternative. But an alternative does exist, namely for the lender to demand that the change in policy s/he wishes to see be implemented *in advance of* any disbursement. The cost of doing this is that the advantages of quick disbursement, which may include the preservation of the recipient's solvency, are lost. For one instrument of policy to be expected to chase two or more objectives at the same time is to condemn it to inevitable failure in chasing at least one of those objectives, whatever the potency of the instrument.

The essays in this book provide ample evidence of the frustrations which suppliers of conditional aid have suffered through their obligation to pursue other policy objectives at the same time, and suggest that as the number of objectives multiplies in the 1990s, the effectiveness of conditionality as an instrument of foreign policy may be further diluted. This conclusion in no sense contradicts the need for economic adjustment in developing countries or denies the magnitude of the adjustment which has already taken place; rather, it suggests that it is the governments of developing countries, for all their economic weakness, who hold the trump cards in determining what the speed and pattern of adjustment will be.

Part I
Rationale and Donor Perspectives

2 Policy-Based Lending by the World Bank

Moeen Ahmad Qureshi

INTRODUCTION

This chapter has two main objectives. The first is to present the basic logic of quick-disbursing adjustment lending by the World Bank.[1] The second is to assess some of the broader implications of the experience with policy-based lending for the Bank's other, and still dominant, form of project lending.

The Bank became involved with policy-based lending in the early 1980s when it felt that changes in the world economy were having long-lasting repercussions on the economies of many developing member countries, and that adjusting to changes that had occurred in oil prices, interest rates and trade conditions would require massive structural change, particularly in highly indebted countries. In these circumstances, the attainment of balance of payments equilibria, compatible with medium-term growth and the satisfaction of basic human needs, was considered to be a strong priority. To facilitate its fulfillment, it was felt necessary by the Bank to complement traditional short-term balance of payments financing extended by the International Monetary Fund with longer-term financial support for sustaining the needed policy changes and structural reforms at the country level.

Strictly speaking, the Bank had always lent resources for structural adjustment. Its project loans went to support either productive activities or to create the necessary conditions for growth, and thus change, in the economies of the member countries. The Bank also maintained a dialogue with its member countries on economic policy issues. What happened in the 1980s is that, in consideration of the size and extent of the structural change needed in the economies of many member countries, a much closer linkage between country policy objectives and Bank lending was established, and the policy objectives being supported became more general than those previously addressed through project and sector lending.

9

The development of policy-based lending has nonetheless affected Bank thinking and Bank operations in many ways. One of its principal lessons has been the heightened appreciation of the need to seek and maintain the closest possible integration between the support of external and internal policy objectives at the country level, and thus between Bank lending for broad structural goals and the lending for specific, micro- and sector objectives. Another lesson has been that lending and dialogue over medium-term policies with member countries need to proceed in close coordination, possibly in unison, for without viable medium-term external equilibria economic growth become unsustainable and lending is unproductive, while the pure and simple pursuit of short-term macrobalances can become too costly in social and political terms, and thus make lending redundant. Learning the conditions for this type of policy equilibrium in specific country situations and helping them to remain in place through appropriate combinations of lending and other types of assistance is a necessary, if daunting, task. The Bank is continuously gaining new experience in this area, and learning by doing it.

The chapter will start by presenting the basic logic of policy-based lending: why it makes sense in certain contexts and why Structural Adjustment Loans (SALs) and their close relative Sectoral Adjustment Loans (SECALs) are structured as they are. The role of 'conditionality' will be considered in this context, as there are still considerable misconceptions over what 'conditionality' means. Based on this analysis, the chapter will then turn to the logic of the Bank's *non*-adjustment lending in order to consider how other Bank lending operations are being affected in their design and implementation by the current experience of policy-based lending.

THE LOGIC OF ADJUSTMENT LENDING

Reduced to its core, the basic logic of quick-disbursing adjustment lending is simple and straightforward. A country has a balance of payments problem which, if nothing is done, is expected to be permanent or at least not short-term. Whether the cause is internal or external (or, most commonly, a combination of both) is not the issue here; rather, the key is that, for some reason, the country needs balance of payments support and the reasons for such need go beyond the economic cycle. They have to do instead with lack of basic competitiveness of the tradable goods sector whose underlying causes may be simple or complex, but almost always necessitate fundamental policy changes. The mere supply of balance of payments finance would not help solve the problem. Resumption of medium-term, sustainable growth depends on successfully dealing with the structural causes of the external imbalance.

With such type of balance of payments requirements, the country that comes to the World Bank for help must be pursuing basic objectives that go well beyond short-term financing of the existing gap. If no policy measures were being taken by the country that would be expected to lead to an eventual resolution of the type of balance of payments difficulties at hand, loans from any lending institutions would do nothing but postpone the resolution of the problem for a period while adding to the country's debt, while loans from a development institution such as the Bank would possibly be misplaced from both the standpoint of effectiveness and purpose. After the funds ran out, the country would in fact have to return again to the international community requesting more funds (and hence debt) and the process would be repeated *ad infinitum* or, rather, until the international community refused to lend more.

In such circumstances it therefore only makes sense for the Bank to provide finance in the context of an adjustment programme that the country has adopted, which is expected to resolve the underlying medium-term balance of payments difficulties and create the condition for a resumption of growth and for its sustainability over time. The country should develop this programme and be willing, to implement it. In today's jargon, it must 'own' the adjustment programme. But for the lender to follow its proper fiduciary responsibilities, the programme being supported must be one that in its judgement has a good chance of success. Only with such a programme in place, can the Bank responsibly lend funds to meet some of the immediate balance of payments needs of the country in question. 'Responsibility' here is both towards the supplier of the capital and the users of such capital. In the case of the Bank, part of this capital is supplied by the market.

One immediate question that arises is: why should funds be lent at all in these circumstances? One could argue that, if the country adopted a sufficiently strong adjustment programme, this could obviate the need for balance of payments support. It is, of course, true that a country can always proceed without external finance for balance of payments purposes after some shock; the real question is at what cost. A sufficiently severe austerity programme, exchange

rate devaluation, and/or set of import controls can conceivably restrict foreign exchange demand to the supply available, but generally
at a large cost in terms of reduced output and incomes. Outside
support in case of balance of payments difficulties is designed to
reduce this fall in output *relative to what would otherwise follow.* The
provision of external funds to meet some of the foreign exchange
needs can cushion the immediate negative impact of balance of
payments readjustment. But more importantly, as the reform programme being implemented should lead to a situation where eventually there will be no need for special balance of payments assistance,
external funds provide time for policy changes to have their desired
effect. External funding, therefore, can help to ease the pains from
the time of the implementation of the new policies to the time at
which they produce results. One can think of these 'pains' as losses of
household consumption or investments. One can also think of them
as reductions in the supply of essential public services due to the loss
of output and government revenue.

The general case is that countries facing structural balance of
payments difficulties have to go through an adjustment process that
implies substantial losses in output levels. The real issue that such
countries face is that the loss would be much greater were balance of
payments support not provided. Bank support in these cases, helpful
as it is in reducing these losses, cannot eliminate them. Neither can
Bank support eliminate the social and political problems that often
accompany structural change wherever implemented. It can only try
to alleviate them and attack directly their most disruptive consequences, supporting, for example, minimum levels of consumption
by the most affected groups.

Since the early 1980s Bank support for countries facing structural
balance of payments problems has been greatly expanded. If one
examines the quantitative contribution of the Bank to one group of
countries in need of support of this type – the highly indebted
countries – one sees that the Bank, through both its quick-disbursing
adjustment loans and its continuing project lending operations, has
been an important source of funds to them since the onset of the debt
crisis. Although only one part of the whole in the financial programmes followed, the Bank has been the largest single contributor
of funds to them. The basic figures are shown in Table 2.1 for
countries categorized as 'severely indebted' and, more broadly, as
'debt distressed' (which includes also the 'moderately indebted'
category of countries) (World Bank 1989c). The results are basically
similar for whichever broad category of countries is used. Since 1982,

TABLE 2.1 *Growth of debt*

| | *All severely indebted countries* | | | *Shares of debt* | | |
	End 1982	*End 1989*	*Change 1982–89*	*Stock 1982*	*Stock 1989*	*Share of Change 1982–89*
	- - - (millions of US $) - - -					
Creditor:						
IBRD + IDA	16,265	49,817	33,552	3.7%	8.0%	17.8%
IMF	8,422	22,749	14,327	1.9%	3.6%	7.6%
Other multilateral	10,441	26,805	16,364	2.4%	4.3%	8.7%
Bilateral	46,122	133,156	87,034	10.6%	21.3%	46.1%
Private sources,						
MLT debt	240,620	310,768	70,148	55.3%	49.8%	37.1%
Short-term debt	113,394	80,866	(32,528)	26.1%	13.0%	–17.2%
Total debt	435,264	624,161	188,897	100.0%	100.0%	100.0%
Memo: Total private sector	354,014	391,634	37,620	81.3%	62.7%	19.9%

| | *All debt distressed countries* | | | *Shares of debt* | | |
	End 1982	*End 1989*	*Change 1982–89*	*Stock 1982*	*Stock 1989*	*Share of Change 1982–89*
	- - - (millions of US $) - - -					
Creditor:						
IBRD + IDA	30,534	87,659	57,125	5.0%	9.4%	17.9%
IMF	15,770	27,846	12,076	2.6%	3.0%	3.8%
Other multilateral	17,652	51,726	34,074	2.9%	5.6%	10.7%
Bilateral	102,595	235,099	132,504	16.8%	25.3%	41.6%
Private sources,						
MLT debt	303,249	408,849	105,600	49.7%	44.1%	33.2%
Short-term debt	139,757	116,731	(23,026)	22.9%	12.6%	–7.2%
Total debt	609,557	927,910	318,353	100.0%	100.0%	100.0%
Memo: Total private sector	443,006	525,580	82,574	72.7%	56.6%	25.9%

SOURCE World Bank, figures for 1989 are preliminary estimates. Country categories are defined as in World Bank, *World Debt Tables 1989–90* (Washington, DC: World Bank).

the World Bank Group (including IDA) has accounted for almost 18 per cent of the net disbursement of funds to these countries. The IMF contributed for 7.6 per cent of the total net disbursements to the severely indebted countries, and for 3.8 per cent to all debt distressed countries. Bilateral government creditors, to a large extent through

Paris Club reschedulings, have provided 46 per cent and 42 per cent of the net disbursements, respectively. As a group, the bilateral creditors have been the largest source of funds, but they are, of course, a grouping of many separate governments.

However, in evaluating recent lending trends, be they sectoral or global, one should not forget that the Bank has, since its founding, provided balance of payments support to its borrowers through what has been referred to as 'programme loans'. In fact, the first loan it made in 1947, for $250 million, was a programme loan to provide balance of payments support for France's reconstruction efforts. Programme loans were provided through the 1950s, 1960s and 1970s to countries as diverse as Bangladesh and Turkey. These loans provided balance of payments assistance, although they were often linked to the importation of some basic group of commodities such as fertilizers or raw materials and spare parts for industry. Yet, programme loans, as then prepared and implemented, were still aimed at meeting relatively short-term payment difficulties. Such loans did not sufficiently address directly the overall policy environment and did not, therefore, always provide an adequate basis for long-term balance of payments sustainability. They ran the risk, in other words, that recipient countries could remain dependent on them.

SAL lending, introduced in 1980, was designed to address some of the concerns that had previously emerged over programme loans. These loans addressed explicitly the policy environment within which lending was taking place, where a government presented to the Bank a programme of policy reform specifically designed to adjust the economic structure over the medium-term, and the provision of external finance was aimed at facilitating the implementation of the programme. In practice, of course, such programmes were worked out jointly with the Bank. To be successful, however, the programme must be one in which the government believes and which the Bank also believes has a reasonable chance of success.

Briefly, for the programme to succeed, there is a need for the country and its lenders to reach agreement in three basic areas (Please, 1984). These are: (a) the ultimate objectives; (b) a medium-term programme (of probably five years or more) designed to achieve those objectives; and (c) the specific next steps (or, at the beginning, the initial steps) necessary to implement this medium-term programme.

In the Bank's practices and procedures, the ultimate objectives and the medium-term programme are presented by the government in a

'Letter of Development Policy' addressed to the Bank. The specific next steps then form the basis for decisions to release funds in support of the programme, where most SALs and SECALs provide the funds in two tranches (although there are some operations with three tranches and some with just one). Each of the tranches is released when the specific policy steps agreed to have been completed. In reality, the SALs and SECALs provided to a country should not be treated as individual and isolated operations, but rather are normally part of a series of such operations, with the individual loans focused on different aspects of the reform programme. SALs are generally broad-based, where agreement has been reached on reforms in a broad range of sectors, but usually on a 'shallow' basis in a relative sense. SECALs, in contrast, focus on just one sector (such as international trade policy, the financial sector, agriculture, or energy), but treat these sectoral issues in much greater depth. A common approach is to start a country programme with a SAL, touching on a range of priority issues, and then follow with a series of SECALs that deal with individual sector issues in depth.

THE ISSUE OF 'CONDITIONALITY' IN ADJUSTMENT LENDING

SALs and SECALs have been somewhat controversial lending instruments since they began to be used in 1980. Much of the controversy has centered on the issue of 'conditionality', both in terms of what it means and how it is applied. This section will discuss some of the issues that have raised questions about Bank lending policies and practices. (World Bank, 1988d and 1989a)

It is not at all surprising that there should be controversy over what specific conditions should be required by the Bank or other lenders in providing a SAL or a similar loan. Controversy over what should be considered the 'proper policy environment' has been at the centre of economics since the discipline was born. It is hardly likely that such controversies could be settled here, and this chapter will therefore not get into them. However, even though economists might disagree over what specific conditions the Bank should require before providing a SAL, it is difficult to see why anyone would disagree with the principle that a lender should ensure its loans are provided in an environment (in this case a policy environment) where it believes they have a chance of fulfilling their objectives. This distinction is important. The policy environment considered appropriate by one economist is likely to differ from that considered appropriate by another depending, *inter alia*, on their respective political leaning and value systems, but both should agree that a development bank should lend into a situation only when it believes the environment is appropriate.

There has also been confusion over the nature of the conditionality associated with Bank SALs (or SECALs). Some appear to believe the conditionality is simply the legal conditions presented in the legal documents, which list what policy actions need to be taken before certain portion (usually the second) of the loan will be released. For some SALs and SECALs (not all), there may also be certain legal conditions on policy actions that must be undertaken before the first tranche will be released. But this is a narrow and legalistic view of the conditionality associated with a SAL, and is focussed on what is indeed normally the least important aspect. 'Conditionality' is in fact not a good term for the factors that the Bank takes into account in deciding whether to proceed.

The basic decision by the Bank on whether to proceed or not in support of a government's programme in fact takes place much earlier, at the time when the government decides to proceed with a major policy reform programme and takes the initial important actions. At that time, basic agreement is reached between the government and the Bank over what the objectives are, what the basic medium-term program will be to achieve those objectives, and the outline of the Bank's financial support to that programme, through a series of adjustment loans as well as through more traditional lending operations. SALs or SECALs are then developed with links to specific, identifiable, actions to implement the government's medium-term programme, but the basic 'conditionality' for proceeding at all must be considered the reform programme in its entirety. In a broad sense Bank loan conditions aim at increasing savings and improving resource allocation; they try to help channel expenditure towards purposes from which long-term benefits to the country can be maximized (de Vries, 1987).

This is, of course, somewhat an idealisation of a process, which in reality is much more complex and at times messier. Medium-term plans and objectives are never completely clear; a government does not speak with one mind – there are usually competing factions within it; and plans change over time. However, the distinction between this broader (but often less precise) 'conditionality' and the narrow (if more precise) legal conditions of the loan documents is important. The ideal adjustment programme would be one where the government has developed and implemented all of the necessary reform measures prior to approaching the Bank for financial support. The Bank would then provide the financial support, and with the actions already implemented, there would be no need to specify specific 'tranche release' conditions in the legal documents. For those who view such legal conditions as the only 'conditionality' associated with the operation, such a loan would thus be viewed as one having no conditionality. In fact, one should view such an operation as having very strong conditionality, where all of the conditions have been implemented prior to the release of any funds. There are important advantages to such an approach for political reasons as well, in addition to the economic.

There is also an argument put forward by some that if the government truly believes in the reform programme (as is necessary for its success) then there should be no need for any explicit legal conditionality in the loan agreements. Under this view, such legal conditionality is, by its nature, forced on a reluctant government. If the government believed in it, it would not have to be there and if it does not believe in it, it should not be there. Such an argument misses the point, however, on why these legal conditions are specified. The SAL funds are provided only if there is agreement between the government and the Bank on the specific steps of what needs to be done. Writing down these actions in the form of legal conditions in the loan agreement, and in a more general way in the Letter of Development Policy, is important as it crystallises and makes concrete the understandings between the government and the Bank on what needs to be done. This helps to ensure that there are no misunderstandings (or at least fewer misunderstandings). Of course, writing down such understandings in a few simple phrases often leaves out much that is important. It also focusses attention on actions which by their nature are specific or quantifiable, which are not always the most important elements of the government's programme. Finally, it should be remembered that what is written down may be primarily for the benefit of an outside audience (the Board of Directors of the Bank, for example), since those actually involved, both in the Bank and in the government concerned, may be well aware of other intangible and unwritten intentions and understandings, which might well cover a wider area than can be summarised in a brief legal statement. Focussing simply on the legal conditions can produce a skewed view of what are in fact the most important aspects in the decision to proceed.

Finally, it is important that the conditions agreed are on *policy* actions and not economic results. That is, agreement is reached on policy actions the government can carry out directly, such as the removal of certain administrative restrictions on imports or the end of some subsidy. The conditions would *not* be of the nature such as: 'inflation will be reduced to less than 10 per cent per annum' or 'the current account deficit will be brought to zero'. These are economic results which the policy actions might be designed to achieve, but there can be no assurance that such results will be achieved. The government does, in contrast, have direct control over policy actions and therefore the conditions agreed between the government and the Bank are defined in terms of such actions.

THE RELATIONSHIP BETWEEN ADJUSTMENT AND NON-ADJUSTMENT LENDING BY THE WORLD BANK

The extensive use of SALs and SECALs by the Bank in the 1980s has also helped to focus attention on the conditions for effectiveness of its traditional lending instruments. There has been, as a consequence, an increased recognition of the importance of the policy environment within which a traditional project is carried out.

The Bank had long recognised the close linkages that exist between projects and policies. Project financing was generally made conditional upon the implementation of specific policy changes. Yet, the required policy changes were most often project-related, or internal to the project or to its immediate environment. Policy-based lending has, instead, helped the Bank and its borrowing members focus on another set of relationships: those that link the project to its general economic context. As a consequence, greater attention than in the past is paid in Bank financing decisions to the external conditionality that maximises the benefits of the project.

A project, though technically excellent in a narrow sense, when carried out in a poor policy environment, may fail in achieving some of its key development objectives. The Bank could, for example, finance the construction for an irrigation scheme, which might be implemented in a technically excellent way, and which, in the proper economic environment, would make a significant contribution to the country's development. However, in a poor economic environment the project could fail to make such a contribution. If, for instance, crop prices were too strictly controlled by the government or too heavily taxed at the export stage, the benefits of the scheme in raising farm output might be very limited. Similar effects would occur if the exchange rate were kept overvalued.

The basic question, then, is how best to ensure the existence of an appropriate policy environment in which all types of Bank lending to a country would fit, and how to link specifically the requirements for the maintenance of such an environment to the specific forms of Bank (and other external) lending for development that focus on specific projects. Again, as in the discussion above on SALs, this chapter will not deal with the question of *what* is the appropriate policy environment for project lending, but will rather focus on what the Bank's involvement should be in ensuring that a proper policy environment materialises, assuming there is agreement on it. It should also be remembered that the Bank's traditional projects (as those of other lending institutions) have always carried loan conditions attached to them. Traditionally, these project conditions have been rather strictly related to the project, as, for example, a condition that requires that project implementation or auditing units be established or that the supply of adequate support services be ensured by the government of the borrowing country. Sometimes the conditions have been broader as, for example, a condition that power tariffs be raised to some minimum level or farm marketing system changed.

However, the broader the conditions are, the less related they are likely to be to the specific project being financed and the less appropriate it generally is for them to be attached to such projects. If the broader policy conditions have an important impact on the project, the project managers in the government will generally not have adequate authority to make decisions concerning them. Indeed, the managers of the irrigation projects being financed by the Bank may fully agree with the Bank staff on the need to raise support prices for crops or to lower export taxes, so as to create adequate demand for the irrigation facilities that they are building, but the discussion will be rather one-sided and ineffective when those that would be opposed to such policy changes are not involved in them.

The Bank's traditional investment projects may, therefore, often have had an *excess* of conditionality, and have ineffectually tried to deal with changes in the economic policy environment by trying to add more conditions to the specific investment operations. (Please,

1984: 24–8) Whenever broader policy issues are involved, SALs or SECALs are generally better avenues through which government authorities can be helped to tackle them. Yet, though SALs and SECALs do focus on policy issues, they are also vehicles for quick-disbursing balance of payments support, and thus may not always represent the appropriate avenue for policy changes. It is important, therefore, to keep in mind that SALs and SECALs have two distinct dimensions: one that focuses on the requirements for policy changes and another that privileges the goal of providing balance of payments support. It is quite possible that, in fact, the need to improve a certain policy environment may not be accompanied by a parallel requirement for quick disbursing funds. It may also occur that the balance of payments problem may vanish, while the need to change certain aspects of economic policies continues to exist.

For the Bank, the incentive to develop approaches by which the necessary policy focus can be made a central element in its lending operations has always been there. Recent experience with adjustment lending has made it even clearer that several alternative approaches may be needed. These range from the definition and scope of individual project operations, through operations with a broader sectoral focus, to decisions on groups of operations in a sector.

For individual lending operations, it is perhaps easiest to describe what is being done by presenting a caricature of the 'old way' and the 'new way' of doing things. Take, as an example, an urban water supply project. Under the 'old way' of doing things, the Bank may have worked only with a reasonably well run water agency, and financed some large, discrete, project such as construction of a reservoir and associated water lines. Not much attention would have been paid to existing operations (such as those for maintenance). Concerns over the tariff structure would probably have centred on conditions to ensure that the water agency had sufficient funding and financial independence. To supervise construction of the large discrete project, the Bank might have insisted that a special project implementation unit be set up, which would have possibly been staffed by drawing on the best people in the agency. This caricature is, of course, an exaggeration, but there are elements of truth in it.

In the 'new way' of doing things, the Bank would focus much more on the state of the water agency, and any need for restructuring of it. Such restructuring might involve a decentralization from one national-level agency to individual municipal-level agencies. There would probably be changes in staffing levels, and a focus on training

and staff development. Close attention would be paid to the development of a capacity *within* the agency to design and carry out a
reasonable investment programme, as well as an operating and
maintenance programme. The Bank would provide financial assistance to the restructured water agency, but not necessarily (or normally) for a few large, discrete, projects. Rather, attention might be
focussed on maintenance and repair, where the returns are often
high, as well as on breaking bottlenecks and possibly the development of low cost distribution networks (in particular to under-served
low-income areas). There would be a large set of such individually
small sub-projects, and the Bank might provide finance for a set of
them (within the context of the overall investment plan of the
agency). In certain cases the Bank might finance a so-called 'time-
slice' of the agency's investment programme, which would be some
fixed percentage of the agency's total investments in each year over
some period of time (say five years). This description of the 'new
way' of doing such projects is an idealisation in many respects, but
serves to emphasise differences with the 'old way' of approaching
such projects. These new-style loans are sometimes referred to as
'sector investment' operations.

Another method being developed to introduce a stronger policy
focus in the Bank's lending operations, is to incorporate a mid-term
review of policy developments at some mid-point in the operation.
This approach is most relevant to operations such as when the Bank
provides funds for some financial intermediary in a country, for
on-lending to a large set of individually small sub-borrowers. It is also
relevant for sector investment loans, but would not be as appropriate
for a loan provided for some large discrete project such as a hydro-
electric dam, where there would be major costs to stopping the
project half-way through. The purpose of the mid-term review would
be to review progress on policy issues where it had been agreed
before that change was necessary, but where immediate changes
were considered inappropriate or too much of a shock. For example,
for a loan providing funds to a financial intermediary, there might be
agreement on a programme to phase out government subsidies
gradually. If progress by the time of the mid-term review had not
been as planned, then the Bank would withhold further funds under
the operation.

The Bank is also paying closer attention to overall sectoral reform
needs before deciding whether to proceed with a set of individual
projects in the sector. For example, in agriculture the government

may be following policies that discriminate against farmers, lowering the prices they receive for their crops. The Bank might indicate that in such a situation it would not make sense for it to finance an irrigation scheme or the construction of roads, as farmers would not produce to true potential in any case. However, with reforms enacted, then a series of agriculture operations financed by the Bank over several years might be possible. An individual Bank operation in agriculture would be inappropriate as a vehicle for such policy conditionality, but as a group they could be. By extension, the approach applies not simply to individual sectoral issues, but in certain cases more broadly to the Bank programme in its entirety in a country.

Finally, the Bank has used on occasions so-called 'hybrid loans' in recent years, as a vehicle for introducing policy reforms along with the financing of specific project expenditures. The instrument has been used relatively infrequently, mostly in Africa where the government budgetary situation is often especially tight. Hybrid loans combine a quick-disbursing component linked to specific policy reforms, and a traditional project component linked to the financing of a specific project.

THE ROLE AND FUTURE OF POLICY-BASED LENDING IN THE BANK

There are therefore a variety of instruments that have been developed or are being developed through which a focus on policy issues can assume a more central role in the Bank's lending operations. SALs and SECALs should, therefore, be viewed as part of the range of lending instruments available to the Bank, as needed and as appropriate, to address specific issues in a specific country context. In this regard, there is confusion in the arguments made by some that the Bank will now shift from a lending phase that (in the 1980s) focussed on SALs and SECALs, to another (in the 1990s) where operations such as the sector investment loans described above predominate.

SALs and SECALs became important in the 1980s to meet a demand for adjustment in the structure of the economies of many member countries that should not continue to exist indefinitely. To the extent that adjustment lending was successful in achieving the objectives that it had, demand for it should decline at least in the countries where it was strongest during the 1980s. Therefore, one can expect that, other things being equal, the relative importance of this type of operations in total Bank lending should diminish over time. While one should not generalise too easily from what may be true for individual countries to what is true for the whole set of Bank borrowers, and should not extrapolate lightheartedly from the trends observable in the countries now undergoing adjustment, the expectation that, in the absence of large outside shocks, the demand for Bank SALs and SECALs would decline, relative to that for other types of lending, seemed reasonable until quite recently. Another oil shock, the likelihood of which has now unfortunately increased, could of course change this expectation. Even if one discounts such an outcome, it would still be reasonable to expect that SALs and SECALs continue to be a useful tool in certain country situations for quite a while and remain an integral part of the set of instruments which can be drawn on as needed by the Bank and its members.

The increased attention paid to policy issues has also had important implications for the economic and analytical work done by Bank staff. This work is now being oriented much more than in the past to the Bank's borrowers as an audience. This redirection of focus also leads to a need for increased flexibility in deciding when to undertake work and in what area. In the area of country economic work, for example, rather than large, formal country reports, produced by major economic missions planned well in advance, the demand has arisen for smaller, more flexible efforts that can respond to the emerging needs of the Bank's borrowing members. This flexibility is especially important as there is often only a narrow period of time when a government may have the political capacity to proceed with major policy changes. Experience has shown that the period when major new changes are possible is often only after a change in government, when the new government has been installed in part because of economic deterioration under the old. Bold measures can then be politically possible. However, as it takes time to prepare such measures, there is often a risk that by the time the measures are technically ready, the political opportunity for their adoption has passed. Perhaps even worse, the political leadership may try to implement only partially-developed measures, which then fail and discredit the whole programme. It is important, therefore that reform measures be prepared ahead, and, when this was not possible, that specific capacity to assist quickly and efficiently in the preparation process be in existence inside the Bank.

CONCLUSION

The development problems of the 1980s have forced a re-thinking of some of the approaches that had previously been used by the Bank and other lenders in providing financial assistance to developing countries. The experience made has also been useful in underscoring on the one hand the importance of the policy environment in which lending takes place, and on the other the need to have available at all times an array of lending instruments capable of meeting the changes in demand that arise. Experience with adjustment lending has also helped the Bank to adapt traditional lending instruments to new realities and to improve their effectiveness in certain situations. New lending instruments have also been added to the Bank 'tool box'.

In an environment where the need for fundamental policy changes to ensure long-term growth became paramount for many developing countries, Bank lending could not but become more focused than in the past on meeting these needs. Thus, in a fundamental sense, all Bank lending became more focused on the macro-policy requirements for economic growth. Yet, in some other critical sense, the basic orientation of Bank lending remained the same as in the past. It aimed, as it always did, at augmenting the supply potential of the economies of its members, by helping them to change policies through the supply of medium-term balance of payments assistance where policy changes were needed, or the supply of direct investment finance when an injection of external capital for specific purposes was deemed useful and could be productively utilised, or by doing both of these. In this sense Bank lending in all its various forms has remained oriented towards the promotion of growth in its member countries.

NOTES

1. This will often be abbreviated to simply the 'Bank' in the text below when the context is clear. Also, unless otherwise noted, the World Bank's concessionary loan affiliate, the International Development Association (IDA), is included when reference is made to the Bank.
2. The specific countries included in these categories are listed in World Bank (1989c).
3. This is the breakdown proposed by Stanley Please (1984).
4. The record of Bank conditionality has been extensively examined in the two reviews of adjustment lending prepared by Bank staff. See World Bank, 1990.
5. See on this point Barend A. de Vries, (1987) pp. 59–61.
6. Stanley Please *op. cit.*, pp 24–28.

3 Conditionality in Policy-Based Lending in Africa: USAID Experience

David F. Gordon

INTRODUCTION

In sub-Saharan Africa, the international financial institutions (IFIs) and the donor community have been at the forefront of efforts to promote economic restructuring in order to restore sustainable economic growth. Controversy about the role of the IFIs and the bilateral donors has focused on their use of conditionality to promote policy change. While conditionality has dominated discussions of IFI and donor activities in Africa in recent years, it is not easy to precisely define the term. In general, conditionality refers to the agreements between donors and recipients that exchange financial transfers (either grants or loans) by the donors for policy changes by the recipients. But the specific relationship between the resource transfers and the policy changes is a source of disagreement among observers of conditionality.

Donors themselves tend to portray this relationship as *reinforcement*, i.e. that the resource transfer provides an added incentive for the recipient government to implement policy changes to which it is already committed. Critics of the IFIs have viewed the relationship as *imposition*, i.e. that the donors utilise financial dependence to impose inappropriate policy changes on otherwise unwilling governments. Finally, academic analysts have tended to conceptualise the relationship as one of *purchase*, i.e. that the donors 'buy' reforms that governments, for one reason or another, would otherwise hesitate to make.[1]

The predominance of conditionality in Africa in the 1980s has generated the widespread misperception that external actors have been virtually the only source of economic policy change. While the donor community has taken the leading role in setting the agenda within which African governments have responded to the continent's economic crisis, other factors have also motivated economic reform. The very fact of economic decline has weakened the political payoffs from existing policies in many nations, thus serving as a spur to reform. Reform in Africa has also been promoted by the general re-orienting of global strategies for growth – a new belief in the efficiency of markets, a more open stance towards the international economy, a larger role for entrepreneurship – that has affected other areas of the developing world as well as Eastern Europe. *Glasnost* and *perestroika* in the Soviet Union, the remarkable changes transpiring in Eastern Europe, and the economic dynamism achieved by the 'four tigers' of East Asia are capturing the imagination of African intellectuals today much as the Cuban revolution and the Chinese Cultural Revolution did a generation ago. A young generation of economic technocrats imbued with the belief in economic reform is emerging all over the continent.[2]

But, while the need for economic reform in Africa has been almost universally proclaimed, it remains a bitterly contested terrain of public policy.[3] The economic and technical problems of reform are far more complicated than many thought. The politics of implementing adjustment are similarly difficult and unpredictable. Equally problematic are the social and political ramifications of reform, often touching on basic elements of the social fibre of African societies.[4] Almost invariably, the specifics of reform programs lie firmly in the intellectually sticky realm of 'second-best' solutions. A recent World Bank Working Paper by Harvard economist Dani Rodrik argues that the economic theory behind liberalisation efforts in developing countries is embarrassingly weak.[5] Similarly, Toronto economist G.K. Helleiner, a long-time observer of Africa, has argued that there is little common meaning attached to 'structural adjustment' in the African context.[6]

In this chapter I will review the international response to Africa's economic crisis, examining the origins of the use of conditionality and its evolution in the past decade. I will then explore the analyses of conditionality and offer some explanations for why its influence has been more apparent than real. I will examine the validity of the critiques of conditionality made from the left, i.e. that it threatens the sovereignty of African states, and from the right, i.e. that it actually impedes adjustment by providing African governments the leeway to continue 'business as usual'. I will then explore some of the lessons that can be garnered from USAID's experience in policy-based non-project assistance in Africa. Finally, I will begin to categorise the actual impact of donor conditionality in Africa and look at some of the reasons why the process in general has been a frustrating experience for both the donors and the recipients. While attempting to gain a region-wide perspective, specific examples will be drawn upon to illustrate the analytical themes and empirical trends.

BACKGROUND

Africa's economic crisis is now entering its second decade. While a handful of countries have avoided serious economic difficulties, and the level of distress among the crisis countries varies widely, the general picture as expressed in aggregate data is bleak indeed. After experiencing reasonably good levels of economic growth in the 1960s, performance began to lag in the 1970s. But it was not until the end of the decade that fears emerged that even those slower growth levels of the 1970s were fast becoming unsustainable. Largely on the basis of dramatically increased external flows, gross domestic investment in sub-Saharan Africa in the 1970s had risen to over 20 per cent of gross domestic product (GDP). But the productivity of investment was sharply diminishing. In the 1960s, an aggregate investment level of roughly 15 per cent of GDP had generated average annual growth in per capita income of almost 2 per cent. In the 1970s, despite higher levels of investment, per capita income for sub-Saharan Africa as a whole stagnated. Worse still, the data in the late 1970s possibly overstates real growth achieved, since in many countries the most rapidly growing sector was 'government services', all too often non-productive expenditures.[7]

While the international environment certainly contributed to Africa's downturn in the 1970s, the fact that other regions of the developing world did not experience the same trends weakens explanations based predominantly on external factors. During the 1970s, Africa's share of non-fuel exports of developing countries fell by more than half, from 19 per cent to 9 per cent, a sign of the specificity of the African malaise.[8] In agriculture, per capita output declined by more than 1 per cent per year. Africa's external debt rose at an ever-increasing rate. Between 1973 and 1977, total external debt increased from $9 billion to $27 billion. By 1982, the total reached close to $70 billion.[9] On the basis of these trends, the World

Bank's *World Development Report 1980* stated that sub-Saharan
Africa 'has the most disturbing outlook' of any region and foresaw
further decline in per capita income.'[10]
The Bank's prediction proved all too correct. By the mid-1980s,
most of the sub-Saharan states found themselves in a vicious economic cycle of low exports, high debt service, insufficient imports and
stagnating growth. Under the impact of weakening export performance and the collapse of non-concessional flows (for most of the
1980s, non-concessional flows and export earnings generated well
under one-half of Africa's foreign exchange inflows), and despite
rapidly expanded flows from the IFIs, import levels were forced to
contract, dropping 40 per cent in per capita terms between 1980 and
1986.[11] Investment, without which growth is impossible, dropped by
20 per cent between 1980 and 1986. The efficiency of investment,
moreover, continues to be substantially lower in Africa than in other
areas of the developing world. New non-concessional capital flows,
an indicator of the continent's international financial reputation, fell
from a yearly level of about $8 billion in the early 1980s to virtually
zero by 1985. Concessional capital inflows in the 1980s were directed
substantially to debt service and the maintenance of minimal import
levels; very little has supported investments that would enhance debt
service capacity.[12] As a result, real per capita income levels in
sub-Saharan Africa are lower today than they were twenty years ago;
in many countries they are lower now than at the time of independence. In these circumstances, the social and political infrastructures
of many countries began to unwind. In at least a half-dozen countries,
parallel economies came to dwarf the official economy.[13]
    Until the Eastern European upheavals of late 1989, the political
origin of Africa's economic crisis was considered too 'impolite' an
issue to be raised explicitly in the international debates about Africa's
crisis and appropriate responses. Nonetheless, it loomed heavily in
donor thinking and became an important dimension of the international relations of economic reform in Africa. In the 1980s, Afri-
canist political scientists such as Robert Bates, Richard Sandbrook
and Thomas Callaghy powerfully argued that African 'policy problems' originate less in mistaken strategic and technical judgments and
more in Africa's politics.[14] While these analysts differ among themselves, all emphasise Africa's tragic paradox, whereby the politically
rational became economically irrational and vice versa. According to
Callaghy, Africa became dominated by

a crony statism consisting of three interrelated characteristics: (1) clientelist networks used to build support through the extraction and distribution of rents, (2) the expansion of the size of the state, including the creation of an extensive parastatal sector, and (3) the purchase of primarily urban support via state welfare services and subsidies.[15]

In the aftermath of events in Eastern Europe and in the context of increasing domestic pressures for political reform in many African nations, the political concomitants of economic reform have been put more explicitly on the agenda of donor debates concerning Africa and there is increasing pressure to expand the scope of conditionality. In the US, especially, there are calls for the use of pluralism and democratisation criteria in determining aid levels for African countries. More radical proposals have called for the use of 'political conditionality' in addition to economic policy conditionality as part of individual loan and grant agreements. Calls to expand the scope of conditionality have also been sounded by supporters of expanded debt forgiveness for Africa who see more conditionality as a means of reducing the 'moral hazard' problems involved in debt relief. Most of these various proposals to expand conditionality assume that the leverage it gives to donors is very great indeed. Later in this chapter, I will critically explore that assumption, through examining the analytics of conditionality, looking at its actual impact in Africa, and discussing some of the lessons from USAID's efforts at bilateral policy-based foreign assistance.

DONOR CONDITIONALITY IN AFRICA IN THE 1980s

As a result of the economic crisis, African governments became increasingly dependent upon the IFIs and other donors to provide foreign exchange needed to finance both debt service and continued imports of goods and services. Conversely, in the early 1980s, Africa's economic crisis emerged as an issue for the international community. The initial stage of the international response to Africa's crisis, which comprised the first half of the 1980s, was marked by sharp debate and conflict between the donor agencies (led by the IMF and the World Bank) and African governments over both the causes of Africa's crisis, and strategies to respond to it. African governments perceived the roots of crisis to lie in a hostile external environment, but lacked any coherent strategy to respond to these perceptions. Donors perceived the roots of crisis to largely lie in African governments' policies and sought more influence over those policies as a strategy for resolving the crisis.[16]

The donor perspective was most forcefully presented in a 1981 World Bank document entitled *Accelerated Development in Sub-Saharan Africa: An Agenda For Action* (commonly known as the Berg Report, after its primary author, Elliot Berg). The Berg Report located the roots of Africa's poor economic performance in a confluence of factors (high rates of population growth, the legacy of colonialism, vulnerability to bad weather, adverse trends in the international economy), but paid special attention to policy problems as a source of economic distress. Critical among these problems were poor public sector management, a bias against agriculture, and trade and exchange rate biases against exports.[17] The report's focus on domestic policy problems, initially very controversial, has been widely (if often grudgingly) accepted. The report argued that growth and development in Africa could be reignited only through a process of 'structural adjustment' centred on realigning overvalued exchange rates, improving price incentives (especially in agriculture), limiting the role and improving the performance of the public sector, and energising entrepreneurship in the private sector.

The strategy that the donor community (especially the IFIs) generated for addressing Africa's economic crisis was based on the use of external financial flows (concessional and non-concessional) to both leverage 'structural adjustment' policy changes and to support them until a growth trajectory was restored. The process by which donors attempt to implement this strategy is commonly referred to as conditionality. Under conditionality, external resources are made contingent upon the recipient government's undertaking a set of (in principle) mutually agreed-upon policy changes.

Conditionality-based lending and donor assistance is designed to enhance growth in three ways: by improving the policy environment, by directly increasing the availability of foreign exchange, and by catalysing other foreign exchange flows, both private and public, concessional and non-concessional. These increased foreign exchange flows ease the import constraint which, in turn, is supposed to facilitate a quickened response to the reforms undertaken. Conditionality was seen by the IFIs as particularly important in sub-Saharan Africa since international capital markets had essentially declared the region non-creditworthy. Conditionality was intended to decrease the likelihood that external finance would play the role that so much of it had in the 1970s: allowing countries to escape the imperatives of adjustment, providing 'rents' for privileged groups, and ending up as capital flight.

During the early 1980s, global efforts to respond to Africa's crisis through conditionality were dominated by the IMF, whose approach focused on short-term, sharp programmes of demand restraint. By 1983, some twenty 'stand-by' or 'extended fund facility' agreements between African governments and the IMF had been undertaken, whereby the governments committed themselves to currency devaluation, reducing government expenditure, limiting domestic credit creation and limiting expansion of the money supply. In return for these commitments, the IMF disbursed foreign exchange at nearly commercial terms. These programmes were generally only partially implemented, and in no case led to their intended result of restored balance-of-payments stability precluding the need for further IMF loans.[18] Given the failure of their programmes and the continued deepening of the economic crisis, the IMF became a major creditor in sub-Saharan Africa, with real assets at risk and its own financial interests at stake in Africa's emerging debt crisis.

The second stage of the international response to Africa's economic crisis, roughly from the mid-1980s until 1989, appeared much more consensual and saw the beginning of concerted international action to reverse Africa's economic deterioration. The consensus centred around the UN Program of Action for African Economic Recovery and Development, adopted at an extraordinary special session of the General Assembly in 1986. The Program, agreed to by African nations and the international community, affirmed the necessity for African governments to undertake a wide range of difficult economic reforms, and the equal necessity of an increased flow of new international financing.

Institutionally, the World Bank increasingly replaced the IMF as the lead international agency dealing with the African crisis. The Bank increased its own policy-based lending operations through the vehicle of the Structural Adjustment Loan (SAL) mechanism it had introduced in the early 1980s. World Bank SALs are similar to IMF mechanisms in that they involve the disbursement of foreign exchange in response to commitments on policy reform. One difference is that the conditionality in SALs concerns the policy changes themselves rather than aggregate targets such as the rate of inflation as in

IMF programmes.[19] In return for agreement to a set of policy reforms by the recipient country, SALs offer non-projectised foreign exchange usually disbursed in a series of tranches.

The typical SAL of the mid-1980s sought a range of policy changes: improvement in producer prices, especially in agriculture; the reduction or elimination of consumer subsidies; the liberalisation of international trade through shifting from quotas to tariffs and lowering the overall level of protection; the liberalisation of domestic trade through reducing of licensing and price controls; the reorganisation and streamlining of government agencies, including reducing the size of the public service; the restructuring of education and health services and the introduction of cost-recovery schemes; the restructuring and sometimes privatisation of state-owned enterprises; and the development of multi-year public investment programmes.

The Bank later initiated Sectoral Adjustment Loans (SECALs), a SAL-like instrument that sought a more narrow focus for individual adjustment operations rather than attacking a very broad range of policy issues as is done under SALs. In the mid-1980s, policy-based lending rapidly increased to 30 per cent of all Bank lending to Africa. At the same time, the Bank encouraged bilateral donors to co-finance Bank programmes. A number of major donors have done this, while the US and France have, in addition, undertaken their own conditionality-based policy programmes.

The use of conditionality in Africa by the World Bank and other donors has been driven by a range of factors. The Berg Report's focus on the policy roots of Africa's economic crisis was consistent with several large cross-national studies that argued that a country's international trade regime was an important source of differential growth in the Third World. Countries with 'open' trade regimes consistently outperformed those with more 'closed' regimes, both in times of international economic stability and in times of international shocks.[20] Africa was seen as the prime example of a region where efforts to promote import-substituting industrialisation led to adverse economic outcomes.[21] Within the World Bank, a series of project assessment reports concluded that the relatively poor outcome of Bank projects, particularly in the agricultural sector, had been due to inappropriate overall economic policies that thwarted even the best designed projects. The implication of this was that the Bank needed to design lending instruments that could improve the quality of projects by enhancing Bank influence over general policy environments in African countries.

Many of the bilateral donors, for their part, were concerned that traditional foreign assistance activities (focusing on projects) were not working. A series of empirical studies suggested that foreign assistance, in theory intended to supplement investment, was slipping over to support increased consumption.[22] This, combined with a more generalised 'aid fatigue', led several of the bilateral donors to be interested in new forms of assistance that focused more directly on policy issues. Coincidentally, the onset of the economic crisis led African governments to also seek different forms of funding from the World Bank and the bilateral donors. Countries sought resources that were flexible, not tied to particular projects, were fast-disbursing, and could be used to maintain import capacity. They sought non-project assistance. Thus, at the same time as donors sought influence over policy, recipients sought more flexible resources. The basis was laid for a new foreign assistance instrument: the non-project, policy-based loan or grant.

The World Bank and the bilateral donors' use of conditionality in Africa was also influenced by critics of the IMF 'demand management' approach to Africa's external payments crisis. Critics argued that Fund programmes were inappropriate to the problems of African countries for two reasons: first, their timescale was unrealistically short; second, their approach was too narrowly focused on the financial sector rather than on the 'real economy', the supply-side issues of enhancing responsiveness and growth.[23] The failure of IMF programmes in the early 1980s lent weight to these critics. While their views never gained support at the IMF, (despite the stretching of IMF programs to include 'supply-side' issues), they did find a sympathetic ear among policy-makers at the World Bank.[24] Rather than propose an alternative to IMF programmes, the Bank developed an instrument to supplement the demand-restraint and external balance-oriented IMF programmes with 'supply-side' measures.

In the wake of the rise of policy-based lending, the IFIs' financial stake in Africa increased dramatically in the 1980s. In 1982, IMF credits made available to sub-Saharan Africa already totalled $4 billion. By 1988, they were over $7 billion. The multilateral banks' stake (of which the World Bank comprises the bulk) increased from $14 billion in 1982 to almost $30 billion in 1988. As the 1980s wore on, the IFIs' role in Africa substantially evolved. In the early 1980s, they were primarily catalysts for economic reform. By the latter part of the decade, they had become major creditors whose assets and reputation were at risk; in addition, the international community gave the IFIs, especially the World Bank, the task of providing much-needed financial resources to the continent, lest it fall irrevocably behind the rest of the developing world.

In retrospect, the consensus of the second phase of the international response to Africa's economic crisis was more apparent than real. Frequent media reports notwithstanding, laissez-faire notions have not run rampant in Africa, especially not among politicians and bureaucrats. While there is broad agreement about the need for economic reform in Africa, there is little consensus about the specifics involved, about the pace and sequencing of such reform and the plausible speed of recovery, about the social and political implications of reform, about the relationship between adjustment and debt relief, and about the role of the international community, specifically the use of conditionality, in the process.

In the spring of 1989 the World Bank and the UN Economic Commission for Africa (ECA) each issued reports on economic adjustment in Africa.[25] The two reports reached quite different conclusions. The Bank argued that donor-supported economic reform programmes had begun to help African countries improve their economic performance, while the ECA argued that inappropriate donor-imposed programmes were actually exacerbating Africa's economic crisis. In late 1989, the World Bank issued a report, *Sub-Saharan Africa: From Crisis to Sustainable Growth*, which was an explicit effort to move beyond this debate and focus on longer-term issues of African development.[26] While the Bank consulted widely with African intellectuals and policy-makers in preparing the report, its emphasis on the importance of political and administrative reforms and its call for a renewed commitment to equitable development, far from dampening donor-recipient conflict, is more likely to exacerbate it.

THE ANALYTICS OF CONDITIONALITY

Conditionality in Africa presents the following paradox: while in the course of the 1980s there has been an ever-expanding set of conditions placed upon donor resource flows to Africa, evidence suggests that there has been increasingly less donor influence over policy outcomes. In other words, we have witnessed ever more conditions, but less and less effective conditionality. While the IMF has sometimes been able to achieve policy reform on narrow stabilisation measures, including devaluation, and the World Bank and the bilateral donors have been able to use their leverage to initiate broader programs of structural reform, I will argue that the use of financial leverage on the part of the Fund, World Bank and the bilateral donors is a blunt instrument and a wasting asset in promoting broader economic reform. While it can be effective in placing the issue of policy reform on the agenda of African governments, it is able to play a far less positive role in implementing and sustaining reform.

In order to begin to understand the paradox of more conditions but less conditionality, consider a simplified economic model of conditionality.[27] In the model, economic growth is constrained by a lack of efficient investment, which in turn is a result of government policy. The indirect, but primary, goal of conditionality is to catalyse the restoration of external financial flows from private sources. Foreign investors refuse to lend because they fear that their loans will not be repaid. They believe this because they (correctly) recognise that governments have a strong preference for present consumption (including, for the purpose of simplicity, rent-seeking investment) over future consumption. Thus, financial inflows will inevitably go to such consumption rather than investment. The direct goal of conditionality is to bind government to alter its consumption/investment preference function towards investment. Thus, conditionality functions not only to enhance the viability of the loans to which it is attached but also improves the investment climate for all creditors, thus catalysing restored external private flows. Similarly, conditionality promotes a context in which assumptions about foreign aid as additional to domestic savings become realistic, thus promoting increased foreign assistance.[28]

This simple model of conditionality is consistent with a series of real-world attitudes and behaviours. On the one hand, it provides a basis for the widely-held belief that conditionality involves ceding sovereignty to the IFIs. On the other hand, it provides the theoretical underpinning for the widespread notion that an IMF agreement is akin to the Good Housekeeping Seal of Approval for government policy, increasing the attractiveness of a country to foreign investors. It also helps explain IFI optimism about the potential for policy reform in Africa and frustration that recipient countries generally didn't believe that conditionality is in their interests.[29] Finally, the model explains the IFI and donor beliefs that conditionality enhances the credit-worthiness of countries.

But, as the 1980s have evolved, conditional agreements became decoupled from increases in private external flows, especially in Africa. This suggests that conditionality has become less credible in the eyes of international capital markets and that there might be flaws in the economic model of conditionality presented above. The model sinks or swims on the assumption that conditionality is, in practice, binding; that is, that governments will implement conditional agreements. How valid is that assumption? While African states have a powerful incentive to *enter into* conditionality-based agreements – their desperate need for the foreign exchange that accompanies such agreements – they have much weaker incentives to *implement* the conditions that they have agreed to, nor do they always have the technical or political capacity to do so. These disincentives derive from several different sources: characteristics of the international system, incentives in the IFIs and donor agencies, and politics in African countries.

The most important disincentive to implementing conditionality is the understanding that non-implementation will often not be sanctioned. In the 'anarchic' international system, the legal constraints upon sovereign nation-states are minimal. In theory, the IFIs and the bilateral donors should be able to ensure complicity by threatening to withhold *future* funding if the conditionality attached to existing programs is not implemented. But, are the IMF and the World Bank really the tough financial 'cops' that they are often made out to be?

Here is where the multiple roles of the IFIs – promoters of reform, major creditors and 'financiers of last resort' – come into conflict. Once would-be promoters of reform develop large stakes as creditors in a situation in which repayment is problematic, their reform goals are in danger of becoming subordinated to their creditor interests. Similarly, since the IFIs and the donor agencies have assumed the task of providing a financial cushion for Africa in the context of an unsustainable debt situation, the conditionality that is attached to their financial transfers over time has lost much of its credibility. Thus, the pressures on the IFIs and the donors to continue to supply financing to African states undermine their ability to sanction non-compliance with conditional agreements. Moreover, given that the IFIs' own debt repayments may be put at risk if programmes are cancelled, the IFIs themselves have a disincentive to enforce conditionality. The situation is worse for bilateral donors such as USAID who often have more obvious political stakes that preclude sanctioning.

This bias against sanctioning non-compliance is reinforced both by the difficulty in monitoring compliance and by the bureaucratic incentives within donor agencies. SAL conditionality, often involving dozens of specific items, provides a nightmare for monitoring, with the possibility that reforms enacted might be countermanded by other policy initiatives outside of the scope of programmes. The resources provided for monitoring and evaluation of conditional programmes are miniscule compared to the task involved. It is no exaggeration to say that the Bank often does not really know if governments are complying with their conditions. Partly for this reason, Fund staff are often openly disdainful of the World Bank's claim to be effective in applying conditionality.

In the 1980s, the path to career success in the IFIs, especially the World Bank, has been through participation in the design and implementation of successful policy reform programmes. IFI staff members have a strong incentive to portray the conditional lending activities in which they have been involved in the best light possible. Similarly, at an institutional level, given the controversy attached to conditionality, the IFIs have a broad institutional interest in enunciating the positive. This is particularly true of countries that have good relations with the IFIs, repay their debts, and have been described as successful adjusters, such as Kenya. In such contexts, recipient governments gain a good deal of flexibility in how (or whether) they implement conditionality-based programmes.

Evidence from recent studies supports this interpretation. Several comparative studies agree with Tony Killick that 'the Fund has experienced considerable difficulty in ensuring that its programmes are implemented'.[30] Bienen and Gersovitz note that 'the penalties for partial compliance are not great'.[31] If anything, the World Bank and the bilateral donors are even more flexible. Gates, in a study of Bank and USAID conditionality, found minimal risks for recipients despite non-compliance.[32] Both IMF, World Bank and bilateral programmes are continually renegotiated.

This is not to imply that there are never sanctions for non-implementation of conditionality nor that the IFIs are nothing more than 'paper tigers'. IMF programmes are sometimes discontinued, and World Bank SALs are generally only undertaken in the context of an IMF programme. But discontinuance, in and of itself, has not heavily damaged a country's ability to re-approach the IMF and the World Bank later and renegotiate a new programme. The point of this discussion is that recipient governments are aware of the very limited sanctions for non-implementation and are thus less likely to implement conditions that they have agreed to. The stop-go nature of the implementation of conditional agreements presents a picture quite different from the theoretical model of conditionality, in which it is assumed to be binding. It is thus not surprising that conditionality has lost credence with global financial markets and has not had the 'catalytic' role of generating other external resource flows that it was designed to have.

Within the IFIs, there has been a growing recognition that the limited likelihood of sanctioning non-compliance substantially weakens the financial leverage of conditionality. This is expressed empirically in the growing emphasis in donor discussions of economic reform on ascertaining recipient government 'commitment' *before* initiating policy-based programmes. If conditionality was more binding, this would not have become such a pressing concern. The World Bank and USAID have begun to engage political scientists as staff members and consultants to work on policy-based programmes. But, as will be discussed later in the essay, judging commitment is very difficult indeed, largely because of the incentives generated by the very lack of sanctioning.

The limited likelihood of sanctioning creates a context where recipient governments have an interest in expressing a commitment to reform even where one does not exist. Generally, the policies attached to conditionality challenge the interests of key components of the coalition behind 'crony statism'. For example, devaluation hurts anyone who has had privileged access to undervalued foreign exchange. This gives rise to what Miles Kahler has labelled the 'orthodox paradox' of conditionality: how can external actors convince governments to change policies that are economically damaging but politically rational? While dominant political coalitions produce many of the distortions that conditionality seeks to change, external actors must nonetheless work through the instruments of the state.[33] A growing literature has argued that economic restructuring programmes have not been more effective because dominant elites have a vested interest in the status quo and thus don't want them to work.[34] In Africa, the cases of aborted adjustment in Liberia, Zaire, and Somalia are examples in which entrenched elites gained access to considerable conditionality-based external resources without moving beyond the initial stages of implementation of reform packages.

But ruling elites who don't implement structural adjustment programmes are motivated by a range of factors in addition to commitment to the status quo. Recall the 'time consistency' problem that is the rationale for conditionality. The root of African governments' preference for immediate consumption over investment is the political fragility of African states. The imperative of regime maintenance often clashes with conditionality's effort to shift government expenditure (and societal incentives) from consumption to production. The classic empirical example of this is the risks attached to removal of consumer subsidies on basic goods, such as bread or flour. African politicians, like all others, have difficulty looking beyond the short term.

Parallel to the 'time consistency' problem is the 'coalition problem', the fact that while the benefits of adjustment tend to be marginal but broad-based, the costs are sharp and focused. The theory of collective action suggests that, in such circumstances, 'losers' will politically mobilise against the reform to a much greater degree than 'winners' will mobilise in its favour. The empirical record of the politics of economic reform in Africa supports this. With the possible exceptions of Madagascar, Tanzania and Kenya, nowhere in Africa has economic restructuring developed any widespread popular support.

Even those elites who want economic restructuring to work – and their numbers are increasing in the face of the collapse of alternative Marxist models and the success of the East Asian NICs – do not always have the ability to ensure implementation, nor do they wish to pay the inevitable cost of implementing such programmes.[35] In several instances, conditionality-based agreements entered into in good faith by governments were not implemented because of a combination of limited technical skills and bureaucratic blockage. This is an especially difficult problem in complex institutional reform efforts such as privatisation and budget and tax reform. Implementing structural adjustment is an inherently difficult task; it involves changing standard operating procedures, challenging vested interests in the bureaucracy, and establishing new relations with the private sector and non-governmental organisations.

Finally, ruling elites do not necessarily accept the technical analysis upon which the policy conditionality is based. They may not believe that their undertaking the policy changes indicated will achieve the intended outcomes. The record of IFI programmes in Africa during the economic crisis suggests that this analytical scepticism is justified. Many governments have completed one stabilisation programme only to have to return to the IMF in a year or two to undertake a new programme, having failed to achieve the balance-of-payments stability that is the goal of Fund programmes. If anything, the technical analysis behind World Bank and bilateral donor 'structural adjustment' programmes is weaker still; and the Bank is still unable to point out a single example of sustained, effective 'structural adjustment' in Africa.

This entire analysis suggests that the incentives for implementing conditionality-based agreements are not particularly strong, and that the ability of IFIs and other donors to 'buy' economic reform through the instrument of conditionality is very limited. At the same time, it challenges the notion that conditionality has diminished the sovereignty of African states by allowing the IFIs to assume control over economic policy. While donor financial leverage, in the context of Africa's economic deterioration, could put the issue of economic restructuring on the agenda of African governments, it was incapable, by itself, of generating more than initial stabilisation measures. Given these realities, conditionality has taken on many attributes of a 'game', in which donors attempt to 'buy' as much reform as they can with a given amount of money, while recipient governments try to get as much money from the donors as they can for as little reform as possible.

The 'game' element in conditionality actually has a negative effect on economic reform, drawing government attention away from the serious need for economic restructuring by creating a context in which the benefits of reform became identified as increased donor resources rather than improved economic performance. Decisions concerning economic reform became responses to external pressures and attempts to maximise external resource flows, rather than efforts to grapple with imperative domestic problems.

Nonetheless, in a large number of African countries, economic reform activities have been quite substantial. How can we explain the extent of reform initiatives in Africa in recent years, if, as we have discussed, the financial leverage of donors is really quite limited, and, as appears to be the case, the political base of support for such activities is so limited? It is here that we need to make a distinction between the financial leverage of conditionality and the broader instruments of donor influence that are involved in conditionality agreements. While financial leverage as an instrument of donor influence is indeed limited, other forms of donor influence, especially when combined with financial leverage, have played a significant role in promoting economic reform in Africa.

The IFIs have been the main conduit of the diffusion of the ideas behind economic reform in Africa. This has taken place through a number of mechanisms, some linked to conditionality, others independent of it. Directly linked to conditionality are the formal 'policy dialogues' that the IFIs engage in with all recipient governments both over individual programmes and concerning the broader overall economic policy context. The extensive training programmes which the IFIs conduct are attended by both middle- and senior-level government technocrats. In addition, many senior African policy-makers have actually worked in the IFIs. Finally, the IFIs and the other donors involved in policy reform have provided extensive technical assistance support, especially to core economic ministries such as central banks, ministries of finance and ministries of planning. Taken together, these amount to a tremendous intellectual impact on the way in which economic policy is perceived and acted upon, especially by technocrats.

Another, and more sensitive, form of influence by the IFI and donors is political influence. According to their charters, the IFIs are supposed to be strictly apolitical. They have never really been apolitical; but the rise of conditionality in Africa forced them inexorably into an even more active political stance. Increasingly, as the 1980s wore on, the donors most directly engaged in policy reform coordinated closely with domestic reformist elements, especially at the highest technical levels of the bureaucracy. In many policy reform efforts, a key political role was played by 'credible technocrats', individuals having the ear of both senior government officials and respected by the donor agencies as well. Such technocrats have been crucial to reform efforts in Tanzania, Madagascar, Kenya and Nigeria among other countries. In several countries, the most prominent being Nigeria, IFI representatives have played an important role in coordinating and enhancing the political influence of these technocrats. In other countries, such as Malawi, while the IFI political role was less direct, a central aim of policy reforms proposed was to enhance the political influence of senior technocrats.

Thus, while *financial* leverage is the tangible form of IFI and donor conditionality, *intellectual* and *political* influence have also been important components of donor efforts to promote economic reform through conditionality. While in theoretical terms, conditionality is generally analysed as the exertion of financial leverage, in practice, it has involved varying mixes of financial, intellectual and political influence. As I have argued, the influence that derives to donors from financial leverage alone is quite limited and is highly unlikely to form the basis for successful efforts to promote economic reform. Unfortunately, it does not appear that the designers of early conditionality programmes in Africa seriously explored the question of the practicality of the leverage generated by conditionality. While donors were motivated by a rudimentary economic theory – that of economic liberalism – they did not have a parallel political theory of how reform would work domestically nor of how donor influence, in the form of conditionality, would have its desired effects. In recent years, donors have been forced to deal with these questions much more realistically. Paradoxically, this new realism is in danger of being undermined by rising calls for yet more conditionality, especially regarding democratisation. Those who now call for expanding conditionality in Africa to promote political democratisation goals would do well to ponder the lessons of donor role multiplication in the past decade. The evidence strongly suggests that as donor roles multiply, donor influence actually decreases.

SOME LESSONS FROM USAID'S EXPERIENCES

In the 1980s, a number of bilateral donors became actively involved in the promotion of policy reform efforts in Africa. Most bilateral involvement took the form of co-financing of World Bank policy-based operations. But both the United States and France undertook a more serious and independent approach, while still working within the broad framework that had been generated by the IFIs. In this section, I will focus on some of the issues that have arisen for American foreign assistance and some of the lessons that can be garnered from AID's efforts in policy-based donor assistance in Africa.

The factors behind AID's growing involvement in economic policy reform activities in Africa closely parallel those of the World Bank, with the added impetus of the coming to power of the conservative Reagan Administration in early 1981.[36] In the early 1980s, AID became involved in several macro-economic policy reform activities through conditionality-based cash transfers under the mechanism of the Economic Support Fund (ESF).[37] AID also played a leading role in early efforts at agricultural marketing reform, building on the agency's long experience, at the project level, in this sector. In the middle 1980s, AID introduced the African Economic Policy Reform Program (AEPRP), designed to be a more flexible instrument to encourage economic reform and to deepen AID's own institutional incentives in the direction of policy-oriented activities.

In 1987, the US Congress created the Development Fund for Africa (DFA) in order to increase development resource flows to Africa and to give AID increased flexibility in its African operations. Currently, two of the four strategic objectives of the DFA refer directly to economic reform themes. The first of these is to 'improve the management of African economies by reducing the role of the public sector and increasing its efficiency'. The second is to 'strengthen competitive markets to provide a healthy environment for private sector growth.'[38] Under the DFA, AID has defined its niche in policy reform activities as that of 'sector adjustment'. Since that time, the agency has been actively involved in the design and implementation of non-project assistance (NPA) activities in agriculture, health care financing, private sector development, public sector restructuring, and export promotion. What are some of the lessons of these activities? How does AID conditionality differ from that of the IFIs? What might be the future direction of AID's NPA activities?

While AID has defined its niche as 'sector adjustment', it has become clear that the line between sectoral and macro issues is quite blurred. The success of most sectoral adjustment programs depends, in large part, on the existence of a stable and appropriate macroeconomic framework. Nonetheless, in practice, there is not a sharp temporal distinction between macro-level adjustment and sectoral adjustment. In most African countries, sectoral adjustment programs have been undertaken in the absence of a fully stabilised macro environment.[39] Nor is there a sharp distinction between policy issues at the macro-level and those at the sectoral level. The classic example of this overlap, of course, is the exchange rate. In such contexts, AID has inevitably become involved with macro-economic issues. Its approach to those issues, however, tends to be informed more by their sectoral implications than their macro implications.

One difficult issue in the design of AID's policy-based activities has been how to determine whether a degree of stabilisation has been achieved that will allow the intended sectoral reform activity to be viable. A related issue is the potential vulnerability of sector reform efforts to deterioration of the macro environment. A special problem, in this regard, has been AID's efforts in export promotion activities in CFA countries, where there is increasing evidence of substantial overvaluation but the use of exchange rate depreciation as a policy instrument is not open to governments.

Another issue for AID has been conceptualising the purpose of the cash transfers involved in NPA. Recall that in macro-level adjustment, the official purpose of the cash transfer has been to stimulate a supply response to policy change and to maintain consumption levels until the supply response takes hold. Analytically the transfer has often been seen as the 'price' of purchasing the desired policy change. In AID's sector adjustment efforts, the cash transfers are both too small to maintain consumption and too 'distant' from the policy reforms to stimulate a supply response.[41] While some AID officials have viewed the cash transfers as a means of 'buying' reform, the analysis presented earlier suggests that such an approach is quite unrealistic.

What then is the role of the cash transfer in AID non-project assistance? There are two, I believe. First, the cash transfer does 'buy' influence for AID; not the influence to make policy, but the ability to undertake analytical work and policy dialogue that will allow a technocratic consensus concerning the reform to be developed. The cash transfer also enhances the likelihood that this technocratic consensus will be seriously considered by the recipient government because of the possibility of subsequent non-project assistance. It provides AID the opportunity to become involved in the policy process, to work jointly on a particular issue with senior government technocrats, to engage both expatriate and local researchers to study important issues of policy.

Secondly, the cash transfer provides a resource to offset the risks that governments face, or perceive themselves to face, about a particular policy reform. These risks might be financial or they might be political. Risk reduction might take the form of partial compensation for 'losers', such as public employees who are made redundant.[42] It might take the form of additional foreign exchange to balance the almost inevitable increase in imports following trade liberalisation. It might provide the recipient Treasury with reassurance against a fall in revenues in the immediate aftermath of a tax reform programme. In each of these examples, the transfer facilitates the policy change by reducing government risk in undertaking the reform.

Related to the problem of the purpose of the cash transfer in non-project assistance is the issue of the size of the cash transfer. While in theory, AID undertakes a rate-of-return analysis in NPA programmes, in practice the size of the cash transfer is a function of other factors: overall country programme financial commitment, sectoral priorities of the Mission, commitments undertaken at Bank-sponsored Consultative Group meetings, and judgments related to the programme size needed to 'buy a seat at the table' and to offset the specific risks that have been identified as constraining government willingness and ability to undertake the particular reform programme. Unfortunately, the latter considerations are not always consistent with the former.

One of the most important lessons of AID's activities in sectoral adjustment is the absolute need for a solid analytical base behind policy reform programmes. It is during this phase that the consensus-building process between AID and senior government technocrats is begun. As was discussed earlier, the analytical base behind structural adjustment efforts has all too often been very weak. While AID broadly favours a market-oriented economic strategy, there is no single set of pre-identified specific adjustment policies in any sector. In general, AID is dealing in reform areas in which maximalist options (pure market solutions) are neither possible nor necessarily desirable. The world of sector adjustment tends to be the world of second-best choices, and these choices are technically quite complex and demand solid analysis.

In addition, the data upon which such choices are made tends to be of poor quality. In particular, our knowledge of informal economies, which in many Third World countries are quite extensive, and their connections to the formal economy, is very limited. Yet the impact of basic policy reforms, such as devaluations, will vary significantly depending on the extent of and nature of the informal sector. In the future, successful AID sector adjustment programmes will have to be driven by a solid analytical base that is best developed through cooperative research and technical analyses undertaken by joint teams of AID and other American researchers and local research staff and institutions. Of particular importance here will be gaining a better understanding of the relationship between the formal and informal economies and how that affects different policy options.

A second lesson for AID is that there is not a sharp distinction between non-project policy-based assistance and more traditional project assistance. The success of any particular policy reform depends not only on gaining influence over the choice of policy, but also on ensuring that implementation of the reform is effective and that the response to the reform is achieved. The latter two outcomes are directly in the realm of traditional project assistance. More broadly speaking, the success of economic restructuring programmes (including their political viability) will depend upon donors maintaining a judicious blend of 'new style' adjustment programmes with more traditional development projects.

As an illustration of this, consider briefly the politics of adjustment in agriculture. For decades, many African countries attempted to supply cheap food to urban consumers by paying low prices to agricultural producers. One of the foci of AID sector reform efforts in agriculture has been to raise the prices paid to producers in order to stimulate greater production. While appropriate in the short-term, this does little to resolve the political dilemma that African governments face of a trade-off between cheap food and good producer prices. But, by improving agricultural productivity, a country can have both cheap food *and* good producer prices. Such improvements cannot come about by policy reform alone, but need a blend of appropriate policies *and* improved farming systems, relevant agricultural research, and effective extension and other services, i.e. the kinds of activities undertaken under the traditional foreign assistance project mode.

A final lesson from AID experience is the importance of recipient government commitment to the specific sector reform programme. The risk of lack of commitment can be minimised in policy reform programmes that involve a 'one time only' set of policy changes. These can be made preconditions to the disbursement of the cash transfer. But most of the sector adjustment programmes involve a series of policy and institutional changes that can only be implemented over a period of time. In such circumstances, the issue of political commitment becomes more problematic. One purpose of the analytical preparation for sector assistance and the policy dialogue around the specific interventions is to enhance recipient government commitment. But these efforts can only have a limited impact. In general, commitment is overwhelmingly a function of factors over which AID has little influence. There is now almost universal recognition that in the absence of such commitment, economic reform endeavours will not succeed. But while the importance of commitment is recognised, it is not easy to tell whether or not it is there. As discussed earlier, recipient governments have powerful incentives to express commitment to reform but then not to fulfill their commitments.

While government commitment can never be precisely predicted, there are some signposts and analyses that can assist in the determination of the level of government commitment. The first is past actions by government in adhering to commitments undertaken with various donors. The second is the consistency of government's public statements regarding the specific policy reform issues. The third is the level of government scapegoating of the donors. While limited government recourse to scapegoating can be a useful means of deflecting the political cost of policy reform, continuous scapegoating is a signal of a hostile political climate and often precedes the demise of reform programmes. Finally, two analytical undertakings can assist the assessment of political commitment. The first is a 'mapping' of the distributional consequences of the specific policy reform, laying out 'winners' and 'losers' in both the short and long term. The second is a 'decision analysis' of how outcomes are determined in the particular policy area. These analyses are useful both for predicting the politics of the particular reform effort and also for designing programme elements that can counteract the potential negative political fallout.

CONCLUSIONS: THE IMPACT OF CONDITIONALITY IN AFRICA

What, then, has been the impact of conditionality on the process of economic reform in Africa? Evaluating the impact of conditionality is never an all-or-nothing exercise. Within countries, it is likely to look ambivalent at any given point in time, with effective reforms occurring in one sector, little change occurring in another, and perhaps even backtracking in a third. In Africa the impact of conditionality has varied widely by country. There appear to be several patterns that are emerging and allow us to begin to categorise the impact according to particular characteristics of recipient countries. In the following section, I discuss three such patterns, realising that this does not capture the range of variation in African experiences.

Conditionality, broadly defined, has been especially influential in initiating economic restructuring in countries with new political regimes, not encumbered by the baggage of poor past performance. In these countries, the combination of widespread institutional disintegration, a dire need for foreign exchange, a widely-held perception of the need for change, and a new regime creates a context conducive to external influence in favour of economic restructuring. Entrenched interests are limited and the political risks of reform are quite small. In this category are the broad-based externally-supported adjustment efforts in Ghana and Guinea, and the reform programme in Tanzania under President Mwinyi.

In these countries, external influence on adjustment has been largely positive, but not without its downside. In most of these cases, the entire reform process has been heavily identified with foreigners and highly dependent on continuing centralised political contexts. Ironically, as initial restructuring efforts in these countries begin to bear fruit, the politics of adjustment is likely to become much more contentious. There is evidence of this already taking place in Ghana. Tanzania is an exception to these trends, and may have the basis for a more sustainable restructuring programme because of the lower visibility of foreign actors.

Conditionality has been less successful in promoting even limited reform in countries in which severe economic decline has been combined with the persistence of political regimes. In these countries the donors have tended to enter into agreements too soon, before the domestic basis for even short-term sustainability had been achieved. In Tanzania, the hiatus between the aborted reform of the early 1980s and the adoption of a reform package in 1987, allowed a much broader technical and political consensus in favour of reform to emerge. Zambia, Liberia and Somalia are examples of premature, non-credible and aborted reform, clearly illustrating the limits of external influence. Madagascar and Mozambique are interesting exceptions, where external influence played an important role in policy change despite the lack of political change. In the latter case, this was driven by the dire situation generated by the South African-supported MNR insurgency. It is no exaggeration to say that the government of Mozambique could not have continued to exist without the donor support of the past several years.

While the international donors have also been successful in putting economic restructuring on the agenda of African countries that did not witness severe economic deterioration, it has been much more difficult, in those countries, to generate comprehensive economic restructuring programmes. Interests opposing restructuring tend to be much more entrenched and there is generally less of a widespread perception of the need for change. In these countries, the 'game' elements of conditionality, whereby the benefits are defined in external resource terms rather than in improved economic performance, have been the strongest.

In a number of such countries there have been real, but limited, reform efforts that have been able to generate substantial external balance-of-payments support. There is evidence that such levels of support might be slowing the restructuring process. In Kenya, generous balance-of-payments support levels in the late 1980s unduly strengthened the exchange rate, keeping domestic costs too high to provide much of a supply response to reforms that were instituted. Also, in a number of countries, including Uganda and Senegal, there is a growing dependence on balance-of-payments support to sustain import levels and government expenditures in a context in which the investment response is too weak to create increased export earnings and public revenues.

This raises the question of the relevance to Africa of the conservative critique of conditionality. This perspective charges that conditionality-based external resource transfers enable governments to continue to avoid necessary reforms by providing them with 'breathing space' that they would otherwise not have.[43] Clearly, some elements of the analysis that I have presented, especially the limited sanctions for non-compliance and the counter-productive impact of large volumes of balance-of-payments financing discussed in the previous paragraph, are consistent with such an interpretation. But what about the larger picture? Does conditionality lubricate reform or does it offer an escape from it?

The evidence from Africa does *not* offer broad support to the conservative critique.[44] The recent World Bank report on adjustment in Africa compares the evolution of policy in countries with sustained restructuring programmes supported by the IFIs with those in countries with either no programmes, recent ones, or only sporadic efforts. In the areas of reduction of currency over-valuation, lowering of inflation, improvement of fiscal balance and improvement of agricultural production incentives, the policy performance of countries with sustained conditionality-based programmes with the IFIs has been stronger than those countries without such sustained programmes.[45] While hardly definitive, this suggests that the overall role of conditionality has not been to promote an escape from the imperatives of adjustment.

Nonetheless, given the high expectations of the early and mid-1980s, the record for externally-supported economic restructuring efforts in Africa has been disappointing. To summarise the analysis presented, I think we can focus on three mutually-reinforcing reasons why this has been the case. The first is that the multiple roles that IFIs and donors played – as promoters of reform, major creditors, and financiers of last resort – make it extremely difficult for these external actors to catalyse policy change. The financing role and the reforming role rub against each other, limiting the actual leverage that donors have over policy change. The evidence suggests that external finance can *either* be an instrument for cushioning the debt burden or a lever for promoting economic restructuring; it is very difficult to do both simultaneously. The second is that, given limited donor leverage, their influence depended upon the political commitment of recipient country governments. Studies of economic restructuring more generally have concluded that external influence is greatest and most successful when it is 'pushing against an open door'; that is, when government inclination and commitment is already present.[46] In Africa, despite much rhetoric to the contrary, the commitment to economic restructuring is still very limited.

Finally, donor-supported reform efforts have been seriously hampered by the weak technical capacities of African states. Again, studies of global economic restructuring have stressed the key role of high levels of technocratic competence.[47] While the external donors are able to substitute for such expertise in the early phases of reform programmes, their ability to do so diminishes over time. External donors promoting economic restructuring in Africa are presented with the paradox of having to *strengthen* the capacity of states in order to undertake reforms that *limit* state intervention in the economy. Unfortunately, for much of the 1980s, this paradox was not perceived and acted upon.

The interplay of multiple donor goals, limited African commitment to reform, and weak technocratic capacity served to frustrate efforts by the IFIs and the donor community more generally to promote economic restructuring in Africa. While I believe that the donors are learning the appropriate lessons from the limited impact of their activities in the 1980s, they face the unpleasant reality of a very difficult task. In a larger perspective, the case of policy reform in the 1980s reinforces a basic theme of the continent's history: the fundamental intractability of the African terrain to external manipulation.

NOTES

1. For a recent re-statement of the 'reinforcement' position by senior World Bank staff see Vittorio Corbo and Stanley Fischer, 'Adjustment Programs and Bank Support: Rationale and Main Results', Chapter 8 in this volume. For an example of the 'imposition' perspective, see Robert Browne, 'Conditionality: A New Form of Colonialism' in *Africa Report*,

September, 1984. For the 'purchase' argument, see Paul Mosley, *Conditionality as Bargaining Process: Structural Adjustment Lending 1980–1986* (Princeton, NJ: Princeton University Press, 1987).

2. Thomas Callaghy has argued that perception of having fallen into an economic 'trough' has been a crucial motivator for reform in Africa. See Callaghy, 'Lost Between State and Market', in J. Nelson (ed.), *Economic Crisis and Policy Choice: The Politics of Adjustment in the Third World* (Princeton, NJ: Princeton University Press, 1990).

3. In several African countries, including Ethiopia, Angola and Mozambique, Soviet and Eastern European advisers had urged the adoption of market-oriented adjustment programmes on these friendly 'socialist' regimes.

4. See the critique in G.A. Cornia, R. Jolly, F. Stewart, *Adjustment with a Human Face* (Oxford: Clarendon Press, 1987).

5. Dani Rodrik, 'How Should Structural Adjustment Programs Be Designed?', *World Politics*, July, 1990.

6. G.K. Helleiner, 'Structural Adjustment and Long-Term Development in Sub-Saharan Africa', unpublished paper, 1989.

7. For an influential discussion of Africa's performance in the 1970s see World Bank, *Accelerated Development in Sub-Saharan Africa* (Washington, DC: World Bank, 1981).

8. Rupert Pennant-Rea, *The African Burden* (New York: Twentieth Century Fund, 1986) pp. 22–4.

9. Percy S. Mistry, *African Debt: The Case For Relief For Sub-Saharan Africa* (Oxford: Oxford International Associates, 1988) p. 4.

10. World Bank, *World Development Report 1980* (Washington, DC: World Bank, 1980).

11. Charles Humphreys and John Underwood, 'The External Debt Difficulties of Low-Income Africa', in I. Husain and I. Diwan (eds), *Dealing With the Debt Crisis* (Washington, DC: World Bank, 1989).

12. Op. cit., Pennant-Rea.

13. The parallel economy in Africa has yet to be the focus of much detailed research. An exception is Janet MacGaffey, *Entrepreneurs and Parasites: The Struggle for Indigenous Capitalism in Zaire* (Cambridge: Cambridge University Press, 1987).

14. To get a flavour of these analyses, see Thomas Callaghy, 'The State and the Development of Capitalism in Africa', in D. Rothchild and N. Chazan (eds), *The Precarious Balance* (Boulder, Colorado: Westview Press, 1988); Robert Bates, *Markets and States in Tropical Africa* (Berkeley, Calif.: University of California Press, 1981); and Richard Sandbrook, 'The State and Economic Stagnation in Tropical Africa', *World Development*, 14, 3, 1986.

15. Op. cit., Callaghy, 'Lost Between State and Market'.

16. For a discussion of the early debates concerning Africa's economic crisis see David F. Gordon and Joan C. Parker, 'The World Bank and its Critics: The Case of Sub-Saharan Africa', *Rural Africana*, Spring, 1984.

17. Op. cit., World Bank, *Accelerated Development in Sub-Saharan Africa*.

18. See Stephan Haggard, 'The Politics of Adjustment: Lessons From the

IMF's Extended Fund Facility', in M. Kahler (ed.), *The Politics of International Debt* (Ithaca, NY: Cornell University Press, 1986).

19. See Pierre Landell-Mills, 'Structural Adjustment Lending: Early Experience', *Finance and Development*, January, 1981.
20. See Anne Krueger, *Foreign Trade Regimes and Economic Development* (Cambridge: Ballinger Press, 1978); and Max Corden, *Trade Policy and Economic Welfare* (Oxford: Clarendon Press, 1974).
21. Op. cit., World Bank, *Accelerated Development in Sub-Saharan Africa*; also see Michael Roemer, 'Economic Development in Africa: Performance Since Independence and a Strategy For the Future', *Daedalus*, Spring, 1982.
22. For the economic theory of development assistance see H. Chenery and A. Strout, 'Foreign Assistance and Economic Development', *American Economic Review*, 56, 4, 1966. For a review of the empirical studies on the impact of aid see Paul Mosley, 'Aid, Savings and Growth Revisited', *Oxford Bulletin of Economics and Statistics*, 42, 1980. For a recent overview see A. Krueger, C. Michalopoulos, V. Ruttan, *Aid and Development* (Baltimore: The Johns Hopkins University Press, 1989).
23. See Tony Killick et. al., *The Quest for Economic Stabilization: The IMF and the Third World* (London: Heinemann, 1984).
24. Op. cit., Mistry.
25. World Bank and UNDP, *Africa's Adjustment and Growth in the 1980s* (Washington, DC: World Bank, 1989). UN Economic Commission for Africa, *African Alternative Framework to Structural Adjustment Programs for Socio-Economic Recovery and Transformation* (New York: United Nations, 1989).
26. World Bank, *Sub-Saharan Africa: From Crisis to Sustainable Growth* (Washington, DC: World Bank, 1989).
27. This model is heavily influenced by the recent work of Jeffrey Sachs, published both by the National Bureau of Economic Research and the World Bank. See, for example, 'Conditionality and the Debt Crisis: Some Thoughts for the World Bank', unpublished manuscript, 1986; and *Efficient Debt Reduction* (Washington, DC: World Bank, 1989).
28. For a theoretical discussion of the broader issue of which this is a subset see Robert Putnam, 'Diplomacy and Domestic Politics: the Logic of Two-level Games', *International Organization*, Summer, 1988.
29. Comparative studies include K. Remmer, 'The Politics of Stabilization: IMF Standby Programs in Latin America, 1954–1984', *Comparative Politics*, 1986; and J. Zulu and S. Nsouli, *Adjustment Programs in Africa: The Recent Experience*, Occasional Paper No. 34 (Washington, DC: IMF, 1985).
30. Op. cit., Killick, pp. 251–5.
31. Henry Bienen and Mark Gersovitz, 'Economic Stabilization, Conditionality and Political Stability', *International Organization*, 39, 4, 1985.
32. Scott Gates, 'Micro Incentives and Macro Constraints on Development Assistance Conditionality', unpublished Ph.D. dissertation, University of Michigan, 1989.
33. Miles Kahler, 'International Actors and the Politics of Adjustment', in Joan Nelson (ed.), *Fragile Coalitions: The Politics of Economic Adjust-*

ment (New Brunswick, NY: Transaction Books, 1989).

34. Op. cit., Callaghy, 'Lost Between State and Market'; and Gates. For a discussion of the Zambia case see Kenneth Good, 'Debt and the One-party State in Zambia', *Journal of Modern African Studies*, 27, 2, 1989.

35. Within the World Bank there is an increasing focus on the problems of implementing policy reform programmes. For discussions of the issues involved see John Nellis, *Public Enterprise Reform in Adjustment Lending* (Washington, DC: World Bank, 1989); and Barbara Nunberg, *Public Sector Pay and Employment Reform* (Washington, DC: World Bank, 1988).

36. For a discussion of the impact of the World Bank's 1981 Report on USAID, see James Mudge, 'Implications of the Agenda for AID Policies and Priorities in Agriculture', *Rural Africana*, Spring, 1984.

37. Op. cit., Gates, for a detailed discussion of USAID's difficulty of influencing policy through the use of ESF funds in both Africa and Asia.

38. Agency for International Development, *US Assistance for Africa: The Development Fund for Africa – An Action Plan* (Washington, DC: Agency for International Development, 1989).

39. Op. cit., Rodrik, for a discussion of the design of adjustment programmes in the absence of economic stabilisation.

40. See James Boomgard, *AID Microenterprise Stocktaking: Synthesis Report* (Washington, DC: Agency for International Development, 1989).

41. See Brandon Robinson, 'Collaborative Sector Analysis: A Foreign Assistance Technique for Improving LDC Sector Management', *World Development*, July, 1990.

42. See Jeffrey Herbst, 'Labor in Ghana Under Structural Adjustment: The Politics of Acquiescence', unpublished manuscript, 1990.

43. James Bovard, *The Continuing Failure of Foreign Aid*, Washington, Cato Institute, 1986. Doug Bandow, 'What's Still Wrong With the World Bank', *Orbis*, Winter, 1989.

44. An earlier essay that agrees with some elements of the conservative critique while rejecting its ultimate validity is E. Berg and A. Batchelder, 'Structural Adjustment Lending: A Critical View', (Washington, DC: World Bank, Country Policy Department, 1985).

45. Op. cit., World Bank and UNDP.

46. See the country case studies in Joan Nelson (ed.), *Economic Crisis and Policy Choice: the Politics of Adjustment in the Third World* (Princeton, NJ: Princeton University Press, 1990).

47. Ibid. For a discussion of Korea, see Larry Westphal, 'Industrial Policy in an Export-Propelled Economy: Lessons From South Korea's Experience', *Journal of Economic Perspectives*, Summer, 1990.

4 Policy-Based Lending: an ODA Perspective

Peter Sandersley

This chapter examines experience with policy based lending (PBL) in Africa from the perspective of the UK Overseas Development Administration (ODA). We start by examining the scale and nature of ODA PBL and how these have changed over time. The next section reviews African adjustment programmes in terms of country coverage and the design process. We then consider performance in implementation and some issues arising. The next section briefly reviews recent economic performance while the final section looks ahead to some possible changes in emphasis.

EVOLUTION OF UK POLICY-BASED LENDING

For the purposes of this chapter, *policy-based lending* (PBL) is defined as the provision of balance of payments support (quick disbursing aid in World Bank terminology) in the context of a World Bank and IMF supported adjustment programme. In UK terminology (and aid statistics) the term used to denote this form of assistance is programme aid.

The growth of bilateral UK programme aid has been very rapid: from £37m in 1984 to £190m in 1989 (All aid figures, unless otherwise stated, are in annual disbursement terms). Of the £190m, all but £28m went to sub-Saharan Africa (SSA) where it rose from £16m to £159m over the same period; this is a ten-fold increase in nominal terms and nearly eightfold increase in real (OECD) terms, equivalent to 48 per cent per annum. All such aid is on grant terms.[1] UK programme aid outside Africa is currently limited to Bangladesh, Bolivia, Guyana and Jamaica. Because of the concentration of UK programme aid in Africa, the rest of this chapter focuses on experience there. Moreover, within Africa such aid is directed towards a restricted group of countries. The comments and views offered should be understood with these limitations in mind.

The growth of programme aid to Africa is in the context of a virtual doubling of total UK aid to SSA over the same period in nominal terms, so that the share of programme aid in the total has risen from 7 per cent in 1984 to 33 per cent in 1989. It now accounts for almost half of 'country programmes' expenditure – that is, that part of the Africa aid programme which is managed directly by the geographical departments of the ODA and which may be said to constitute the primary focus of year-to-year aid planning. (Country programmes exclude such items as debt relief; investments by the Commonwealth Development Corporation; food aid; disaster relief; and miscellaneous other items.) The result of this trend is that programme aid now dwarfs capital project aid to SSA which has fluctuated around an average of £45m since 1984.

British programme aid in Africa is, for obvious reasons, heavily concentrated in the anglophone countries (83 per cent of programme aid going to Commonwealth countries between 1984 and 1989). Recipients of substantial amounts of such aid (in UK relative terms) and which currently have adjustment programmes in place include Ghana, Tanzania, Nigeria, Mozambique, Uganda, Zambia, Malawi, Kenya and The Gambia (in order of amounts disbursed). Other beneficiaries in recent years have included Senegal, Somalia, Sudan, Zaire and Zimbabwe (not linked to an IMF/Bank adjustment programme – see Table 4.1).

Over 75 per cent of UK programme aid since 1984 has gone to countries currently benefitting under the World Bank's Special Programme of Assistance (SPA) for low-income debt-distressed countries of SSA launched in December 1987. These countries account for a bit less than half the total population of SSA and about one-third of its GNP. The major potentially eligible economies which have not yet qualified are Sudan and Ethiopia. Another 11 per cent of programme aid has gone to Nigeria which, although poor, debt-distressed, and having an adjustment programme in place, continues to receive loans from the World Bank on IBRD terms as well as (for the last two years) some IDA credits, and is therefore not eligible on current SPA criteria.

Under the first phase of the SPA the UK pledged £250m in commitment terms over the three years 1988/89–90/91, of which half was untied as part of a multilateral untying initiative agreed among SPA donors. These amounts have been nearly fully committed and are expected to be reflected in a broadly equivalent level of disbursements over the same period.

TABLE 4.1 UK aid to sub-Saharan Africa allocable by country (in £m)*

	(1) Total Aid	(2) Project Aid	(3) Programme Aid	(4) TC	(5)† 'Country Programmes'	(6) ATP	(7) Debt Relief	(8)‡ Other NPA	(9) CDC	(10) Pensions	(11) Other TC
1984	241.1	59.8	16.4	67.5	143.7	5.5	17.5	14.0	49.3	10.3	0.8
1985	284.8	49.6	29.1	72.7	151.4	1.3	25.9	55.1	35.0	13.5	2.6
1986	258.4	40.7	43.2	78.9	162.8	7.1	19.0	23.0	29.9	12.4	4.2
1987	281.1	32.3	53.0	87.0	172.3	8.8	15.6	21.3	34.9	18.7	9.5
1988	380.9	48.6	99.8	107.0	255.4	9.8	23.8	26.7	31.6	11.3	22.3
1989	465.4	43.0	161.7	120.5	325.2	9.6	14.9	32.1	59.7	10.7	13.2

Ratios	1984	1985	1986	1987	1988	1989
Programme aid % of country programmes	11.4	19.2	26.5	30.8	39.1	49.7
TC % of country programmes	47.0	48.0	48.5	50.5	41.9	37.0
Programme aid % of total aid	6.8	10.2	16.7	18.8	26.2	34.7
TC % of total aid	28.0	25.5	30.5	30.9	28.1	25.9

* Differs from total aid to SSA by small amounts, e.g. £2.0 million in 1989.
† (5) = Columns 2+3+4. Country programmes exclude pensions and miscellaneous TC included in Column 11 under Other TC. 'Country programmes' approximate to desk programmes but may exceed the latter marginally.
‡ 'Non-projected' (Budgetary aid; food aid; disaster relief).

SOURCE *British Aid Statistics 1984–1988* (London: Central Statistical Office, 1989) table 18, excluding St Helena and dependencies.

TABLE 4.2   UK programme aid to sub-Saharan Africa, 1984–9

Country	(£ '000)
Ghana	88,619
Tanzania	55,938
Nigeria	55,275
Mozambique	32,665
Uganda	28,469
Zambia	24,466
Zimbabwe	22,604
Malawi	21,722
Sudan	20,926
Kenya	19,332
Gambia	14,884
Somalia	7,836
Zaire	4,564
Senegal	2,000
Mauritius	1,088
Seychelles	243
Total	400,631

Note: Includes provisional figures for 1989; all figures in disbursements.

SOURCE   British Aid Statistics 1984–1988 (London: Central Statistical Office, 1989).

The growth of programme spending has had implications for financial management of the aid programme. UK public expenditure operates on an annual disbursement basis. Since the mid-1980s, a block provision for programme aid to sub-Saharan Africa has been made each year. Before the start of the financial year allocations are made to particular countries for in-year spending; these allocations may sometimes have been provisionally earmarked a year or two ahead in accordance with a planned level of spending in particular countries or for co-financed operations with the World Bank. Nevertheless, in broad terms UK programme aid is effectively tranched on an annual basis. In-year switching within the block disbursement ceiling may be made should a country go off track.

The gradual dismantling of administrative mechanisms of foreign exchange allocation in the context of trade liberalisation and taxation/tariff reform has required the adaptation of UK programme aid disbursement procedures. Under the traditional approach a list of specified end-users or eligible sectors for British programme aid was agreed with the recipient government based on detailed end-user appraisal, physical importation of the goods being undertaken by a designated procurement agent. The procedures were time-consuming and expenditure targets were sometimes not met.

More liberalised foreign exchange markets (such as the open general licence or auction) and the increased fungibility that they imply, has led our programme aid to be increasingly provided in the form of direct support for such systems. This normally requires ex-post reimbursement by the donor for goods in respect of which orders have either already been placed or are in process. Though subject to the conditions of the grant agreement, the aid thus provided becomes equivalent to untied free foreign exchange.

Untying of balance of payments support by source and usage thus finds its rationale as a necessary complement to the recipient's own liberalisation efforts ('symmetric liberalisation' to adapt Cassen's phrase). It has also had the side effect of accelerating disbursement of UK programme aid.

Commitments of UK programme aid to SPA countries have been divided roughly fifty-fifty between co-financed operations with the the World Bank and 'coordinated' actions. In the latter case, the programme aid grant is not linked to specific Bank actions but is generally conditional on the progress of the adjustment programme. Increasingly for both the Bank and ourselves, this is normally defined by an IMF arrangement being in place and staying on track. This is in recognition of the importance of an appropriate macroeconomic framework if supply-side reforms are to work. Depending on timing considerations, however, the trigger for UK disbursements under a coordinated grant will frequently be a Bank first or second tranche release.

Once an annual allocation of co-financing or coordinated financing has been committed and spending triggered in the way just described, it is not normally subject to further tranching linked to Bank or Fund conditionality; most programme aid grants are too small to justify tranching.

The choice between coordinated and co-financing is determined partly by timing considerations and partly by whether the particular Bank operation (including its related conditions) is deemed of critical importance in intrinsic adjustment terms, or co-financing is deemed desirable to give impetus to the adjustment process as a whole.

In neither case – co-financing or coordinated financing – does the UK currently seek to impose its own policy conditions beyond those agreed by the recipient with the Fund and Bank, though specific procurement-related conditionality may be added. Through active participation in co-financing missions with the Bank we may, however, bring our views to bear on particular macro-economic or sectoral issues. We also often contribute through technical assistance to detailed examination of policy issues as the precursor to policy actions.

Co-financing has one other important advantage. When the donor involvement is an active one, it encourages a better-informed donor constituency and can enhance the effectiveness of bilateral technical assistance.

The trends described demonstrate a very strong commitment by the UK to the adjustment process. This commitment is not confined to bilateral aid. About half of the UK's aid programme is spent through multilateral channels. Much of this is disbursed as balance of payments support for adjustment – through the EC, the World Bank, and the regional development banks as well as through the IMF. A measure of our commitment to the adjustment process is that the UK is the largest contributor to the ESAF subsidy account, to the tune of approximately £327 million over fourteen years. We and other donors also regard debt relief through the Paris Club as a form of financing for adjustment: Paris Club rescheduling agreements are conditional on pursuit of an IMF programme.

It can confidently be stated that a doubling of total bilateral UK aid to Africa would not have occurred if growing numbers of African countries had not been prepared to adopt formal adjustment programmes. This growth in aid volume, and its provision in the form of programme aid conditional on economic reform, have thus been two sides of the same coin.

EXTENT AND DESIGN OF PROGRAMMES

Adjustment is a continuous process and takes place willy-nilly: it may, however, be either 'orderly' or 'disorderly' (i.e. more 'costly' in economic efficiency cum social welfare terms). Fund and Bank programmes represent time slices of (attempted) orderly adjustment. Although World Bank lending for structural adjustment proper began in 1980, Fund adjustment attempts (mainly centred on stabilisation) have been going on for very much longer. There were over 100 Fund arrangements in sub-Saharan Africa between the mid 1970s and mid 1980s. The current wave of comprehensive Fund- and Bank-supported adjustment programmes mainly dates from 1985. The Fund and the Bank come at adjustment from different starting points. The Fund's traditional role has been to support short-term stabilisation programmes. The Bank's mandate has been for longer-term development concerns. But the Fund has found that, particularly in the context of the poorest countries, stabilisation cannot sensibly be divorced from the need for longer-term structural reforms. The Bank has found that developmental goals cannot sensibly be pursued without an adequate macroeconomic framework. Fund and Bank objectives have thus been growing steadily closer. For the poorest countries a Policy Framework Paper agreed by both Fund and Bank is now the basis for lending operations by both institutions.

To put some numbers on this:[2] comparing the two five-year periods 1980–4 and 1985–9, fourteen SSA countries received commitments of Bank policy-based loans (PBLs) during 1980–4. This had risen to nineteen by 1986 and thirty-four by 1989 in cumulative terms (including countries which dropped out between the two periods). In financial terms, World Bank PBL commitments of adjustment credits approved in SSA averaged $336m per year during 1980–4 and over $1 billion during 1985–9, a three-fold nominal increase. By 1989 annual commitments had reached $1.5 billion, representing about 38 per cent of Bank commitments to SSA in 1989.

Although IMF commitments rose only marginally between the two periods, from an average of $1.3 billion during 1980–4 to $1.5 billion during 1985–9, the number of SSA countries which had entered into IMF arrangements rose from eighteen to thirty-five. Also, lending has increasingly been on concessional terms for *structural* adjustment under SAF/ESAF arrangements: as of mid 1990, there were five SBAs but twenty-three SAF and ESAF programmes in sub-Saharan Africa (including interrupted arrangements).

Considering only the group of currently eligible SPA countries as at end 1989, only seven had received PBLs during 1980–4, but eleven had had IMF arrangements during this period. Bank PBL commitments for this group rose from $138 million per year during 1980–4 to $685 million during 1985–9 (a five-fold rise) while IMF commitments rose from $650 million pa to $960 million (a 50 per cent rise).

Two points may be noted in passing. Not all commitments of the Bank or Fund were disbursed during these periods because of the on-again-off-again nature of some of these programmes; some commitments were cancelled. Second, Fund commitments were much higher than Bank commitments in both periods. Taking the whole ten-year period 1980–90, Fund commitments were virtually double those of the World Bank, both for the SPA group separately ($8 billion versus $4.1 billion) and for SSA as a whole ($14.1b versus $6.8b).

These figures are encouraging in one sense and sobering in another. It is undeniably encouraging that in the last five years over half of SSA countries have been willing to adopt comprehensive reform programmes. On the other hand, the figures remind us of the substantial resources (especially of the Fund) which have gone into failed or largely failed attempts, leaving a large burden of debt to the IMF, much of it (from the early 1980s) on non-concessional terms. The IMF's arrears problem can partly be seen as a legacy of these failed programmes.[3]

The commitment figures cloak an uneven process in which some countries come on and off track for varying periods, or a hiatus occurs between disbursements of consecutive tranches, as conditions fail to be met or programme targets are missed which require redesign or rephasing of programme elements. Sierra Leone, Sudan and Zambia embarked on programmes then dropped out completely over the period, although Zambia has recently embarked on a new Fund-monitored programme under the recently agreed 'rights approach' for countries in IMF arrears. Ghana has enjoyed the longest uninterrupted flow of both Bank PBL commitments and disbursements (dating from 1983), while The Gambia, Mozambique and Tanzania programmes in their current form date from 1986–7. Within the group of currently eligible SPA countries two (Somalia and Zaire) have come off track, with Fund and Bank adjustment financing suspended (these programmes have been more off-track than on over the past several years), while several have had their programmes interrupted for varying lengths of time.

No-one expects the process of negotiating or implementing programmes to be a smooth one. Successful design in the broadest sense encompasses good technical design and political feasibility, and the two interact. It does not follow that because every programme is to some extent politically constrained, it is 'optimal' in a design sense. Some programmes are weak and insufficiently demanding in adjustment terms: this applies to some arrangements for countries in IMF arrears where it could be argued that acceptance of a relatively weak programme has been used as a device to reduce exposure (through the drawing-in of aid flows). Others have been agreed where the *ex ante* chances of successful implementation were known to be low at the time of Board approval, either because of institutional weaknesses, specific design constraints (e.g. absence of the exchange rate instrument resulting in excessive emphasis on demand-reducing policies e.g. in CFA countries), or lack of sufficient political will; although the proximate technical causes of breakdown or slippage may have been failure to meet monetary or fiscal targets or agreed structural measures.

Donors must, of course, share the blame where programmes with low chances of success are approved for political reasons. For countries with a poor record of policy implementation based on earlier adjustment efforts (which tends to include those in arrears to the IFIs) stronger prior actions and time to re-establish a track record are now generally accepted principles for new arrangements.

Adjustment programmes are the products of a negotiating process in which the political commitment of governments and stance of the Fund and Bank are obviously of crucial importance. In this process an enormous responsibility devolves on the Fund and Bank staff charged with the negotiations. The aim is to obtain the degree of adjustment required to achieve stabilisation with growth in a medium term perspective, within the likely availability of external financing, and consistent with implementation capacities including political and social feasibility. In the case of the Fund, specific objectives for the ESAF at the outset were the achievement of medium term viability, defined as eliminating the need for 'exceptional' financing (i.e. debt rescheduling and other non-sustainable flows), and ensuring repayment of Fund purchases. It soon became apparent that for some countries (e.g. Mozambique) no feasible set of policies could be devised which would meet the viability objective; in such cases 'progress towards viability' has become a second-best target.

Donors rely on the Fund and Bank to do the running and make the important judgements as to when the time is ripe for a programme to be brought to their Boards, and that the resulting package is sufficiently substantial and the 'best' one available in the circumstances. In this process, the staffs of both institutions – and we are mainly talking about economists – are inevitably drawn into judgements about the political feasibility of programmes or particular measures, or into accepting the political constraints implicit in the negotiating limits. Also, as suggested earlier, the adequacy of the institutional arrangements in place for implementation have sometimes not received the prior attention they deserved. This can be exacerbated for sectoral adjustment credits by a lack of co-ordination within a borrowing country which can lead the core ministries to overstate the implementation capacity of line ministries.

All this is no more than to say that it would be wrong to attribute a degree of technical optimality to programmes – in terms of relative priorities, depth and pace of implementation of reforms – which the political and negotiating realities do not support, though a minimum threshold of adjustment needs to be achieved to warrant donor support. Differences emerge among countries in solutions adopted and relative strength of actions proposed which cannot convincingly be explained on the grounds of the *sui generis* features of the particular economy or the 'stage' of adjustment reached, but reflect differences in negotiating outcomes. These 'random' differences tend to support the view that the process of adjustment could be significantly accelerated in some countries and in some key areas of adjustment given stronger political commitment.

Underlying this is the fact that the process still so often works against the political grain, so that countries would much prefer less adjustment to more. This has embedded a gradualist approach to adjustment in Africa which, though unavoidable and even desirable in many institutional and non-price areas of reform, is less obviously desirable and effective in areas of pricing and administrative controls of all sorts on economic activity. But in the face of the resistance still encountered, the process is obviously a wearing one for Fund and Bank staff as well as donors – to say nothing of the reasonably small group of recipient country officials at the heart of the process of negotiations.

The notion of gradualism links up with an apparent paradox of aid-supported adjustment: that on the one hand most adjustment measures are supposed to work to reduce the need for aid by improving the external account; while on the other, more aid is justifiable on poverty grounds *tout court*. Ensuring consistency requires that adjustment assistance should help (through the concomitant reorientation of public expenditures at the margin) to cushion the human impact of adjustment in the transitory phase (e.g. through short term compensatory mechanisms where necessary), while balance of payments support provides a 'shot in the arm' for the productive sectors through the injection of working capital inputs (but which may include consumption goods). This should not, however, undermine the essential reallocative processes at work, i.e. prolong economic activities which ought to fall by the way if adjustment is 'successful'. Thus adjustment assistance is fully consistent with more resources for the social sectors and direct poverty alleviating measures, and the reallocation of public expenditures to these ends is a crucial part of the process.

In practice the separation of objectives can become confused. Adjustment assistance continues to support uneconomic activities for prolonged periods as pricing and other reforms are implemented gradually (for example, the activities of certain public enterprises); while reorienting public expenditures in the ways desirable to support poverty alleviation objectives proceeds at a much slower pace. Undoubtedly getting the balance right is difficult and is influenced by political and institutional considerations (see further below) including, for instance, the feasibility of substituting consumption subsidies for production subsidies. *Ex ante* we may not know precisely which industries will go to the wall and it may be a matter of waiting to see which of the fittest survive. The strategy endorsed by donors and the IFIs is, generally speaking, that more aid should support stronger adjustment, but it is not clear that the principle can always be intelligibly applied in practice: generous aid levels have in some cases slowed adjustment down or created an incentive to eke out reforms – an aspect of the potentially addictive nature of adjustment-related balance of payments support.

PROGRAMME IMPLEMENTATION

How do the achievements of adjustment appear at the individual programme level and across a sample of commitments (including those on which UK aid has been mainly concentrated)? The following is a very selective overview, touching only on some of the key reform indicators and problem areas common to many programmes, and which continue to occupy the foreground of the adjustment agenda. Some of them are also areas which impinge directly on programme aid modalities.

Over-Valued Exchange Rates

Looking at reform indicators first, there has been substantial progress in reducing over-valued exchange rates although this is, of course, limited to anglophone Africa. For the SPA group of countries, real effective exchange rates (REER) depreciated by 25 per cent on average between 1985–9. For Tanzania, the depreciation was 75 per cent, Ghana 60 per cent, Kenya 33 per cent, the Gambia 25 per cent and Malawi 10 per cent. The only case of significant appreciation (Uganda) has since been reversed.

Many countries have recently been willing to move to a more explicit market-oriented basis of exchange rate determination which takes greater account of the parallel market and has unification of the official and parallel rates as an objective. Following the example of Ghana, foreign exchange bureaux trading in a kerb parallel market for foreign currency have been licensed in Nigeria and Uganda, and Zambia has adopted a 'second window' for financing imports on an open general licence list at an exchange rate determined by the parallel market (a multiple currency practice that the Fund has been willing to live with). The Gambia has operated a successful inter-bank system since 1987.

Although spreads between official and parallel market rates have been reduced substantially, less than half of the SPA countries outside the franc zone have yet achieved what comes closest (in the presence of residual controls on capital outflows) to a fully market-based regime. One of the prime reasons is the politically contro-versial nature of exchange rate policy.

Political sensitivity stems from two main factors. First, in the absence of strong supportive monetary and fiscal policies, devalua-tion will not produce exchange rate stability and may be counterpro-ductive (Zambia 1985–7); this is of course more an argument for ensuring devaluation is coupled with such policies. Fear of adding to inflationary pressures and/or of hurting the poor is obviously an element, but in the presence of flourishing parallel markets may be exaggerated. (It partly depends on the nexus of food price controls and/or subsidy policies in place and their effectiveness, the size and efficiency of parallel markets and related transactions costs, and price formation.)

Secondly, vestigial ideological bias, partly linked to a distaste for parallel markets, viewed as the province of profiteers, has no doubt played a contributory role. It is hard, however, to avoid concluding that, coupled with administrative (i.e. discretionary) mechanisms for allocating foreign exchange, the rents accruing to those receiving allocations and those making them have in some cases been import-ant factors in retarding faster progress to market based exchange rates. Urban and/or 'elite' groups which benefit from cheap imports represent, of course, another type of vested interest in slow reform.

The speed of exchange rate adjustment thus remains an important issue. There seems, however, to be a gathering disillusionment in the Boards of the IFIs with the step-wise gradualist model of devaluation followed by inflation, with one rate chasing the other down in the hope of eventual convergence to the equilibrium. Rather there is a leaning towards the 'Polish' model – overshoot on the exchange rate and hold it there with tough financial policies – although, admittedly the Polish experiment remains under the watchful gaze of the international community with more hope than certainty at this stage.

Import Liberalisation

A second (closely related) area of significant progress in reform programmes has been import liberalisation and the associated shift to non-discretionary mechanisms for allocating foreign exchange. (Although the two are not synonymous, progress in both spheres has tended to be complementary.) A few countries have virtually completed the transition to effectively full import liberalisation or are well on the way to doing so (e.g. Ghana, The Gambia, Malawi, Kenya, Nigeria among the anglophone group), with official foreign exchange purchased in an inter-bank pool or auction at a market determined rate or one reasonably close to this.

As a transitional mechanism, several countries have adopted the open general licence (OGL) system, under which foreign exchange for imports of commodities on the OGL list is guaranteed on demand. Priority OGL treatment is normally given to spares, raw materials, intermediate inputs etc, or through a sectoral ordering (e.g. agriculture, transport etc.) according to general criteria or notions of what constitutes 'essential imports', with consumption goods tending to receive lower priority. However, in a situation of widespread scarcities and distortions such an ordering may not be meaningful in economic terms. During the transition, the OGL operates alongside traditional rationing mechanisms to finance imports not on the free list.

Because meeting all foreign exchange demand in the OGL import categories is the key, rationing demand is achieved by widening the categories only as free foreign exchange (including aid) resources permit, and/or by allowing a differential (i.e. market related) exchange rate to play the equilibrating role in the OGL. Zambia has adopted the latter approach but in other countries (e.g. Uganda, Tanzania and Mozambique) OGL imports are purchased at the same, substantially overvalued, official rate. (In Mozambique a second window may soon, however, be introduced.)

The OGL thus helps to solve the problem of rent seeking prevalent in traditional discretionary arrangements of foreign exchange allocation, but it perpetuates allocative inefficiency where exchange rates remain substantially overvalued or in the presence of other distortions (e.g. the absorption of OGL imports by inefficient public enterprises). (The OGL does not necessarily eliminate all opportunities for rent seeking since it still has to be determined which items will be put on the OGL list.)

Nevertheless, the OGL provides a framework for accelerating the process of import liberalisation and exchange rate adjustment. In this, aid can play an important role. Channelling balance of payments support through such arrangements not only assists adjustment in these areas directly. By helping to 'homogenise' the disparate types of balance of payments support on offer by donors and effectively converting them into free foreign exchange, it facilitates exchange and reserve management as well as the financing of the adjustment programme as a whole. While numbers of donors have adapted their programme aid modalities accordingly, more need to do so as part of the *quid pro quo* of more rapid adjustment in this area.

Stabilisation Problems

Stabilisation problems continue to dog many adjustment programmes and managing inflationary pressures remains a priority concern. High rates of inflation have contributed to exchange rate disequilibrium, done little to provide the stability necessary to encourage private investment, and have retarded progress towards positive real interest rates. This is despite a reduction in fiscal deficits (as a proportion of GDP) in several countries when aid grants are added in. (When aid grants are excluded there has been little trend improvement in the overall budgetary position, reflecting continuing public expenditure distortions in some countries and poor revenue mobilisation.)

Controlling excessive monetary expansion in these countries remains a problem. Putting public enterprises off budget in order to have their excessive financing needs met by the banking system substitutes one problem for another. Other causes of excessive monetary expansion require tackling the root causes: for example, excessive or 'unrequited' crop financing related to pan-territorial pricing policies, export marketing problems or the still dominant role of institutions in the agricultural marketing and cooperative sectors (e.g. Tanzania, Zambia, Uganda recently).

As a consequence, for the anglophone group of SPA countries average inflation rates are higher than elsewhere in Africa. During the period 1985–9 inflation for this group averaged slightly less than 50 per cent per annum. If Uganda (with triple digit inflation) is excluded, the average was slightly more than 20 per cent. Only Kenya managed single digit inflation. In Ghana, seven years into the adjustment programme inflation has proved stubbornly difficult to bring down and remains in the 15–20 per cent range.

Interest Rates

As mentioned, high inflation – linked to a fixed interest rate regime – has slowed progress towards positive real commercial interest rates, prolonging allocative distortions and discouraging financial savings and intermediation, as well as (with over-valued exchange rates) abetting capital flight. Few non-franc zone countries have progressed to a completely liberalised interest rate regime, preferring to rely on gradual reductions in inflation and upward adjustment of nominal rates to bring about less negative real rates. As a consequence, real interest rates remained negative in a number of countries several years into adjustment, though by 1990 most anglophone SPA countries had attained positive real rates.

Agricultural Pricing and Marketing Reforms

In other areas of the adjustment agenda, reforms of agricultural pricing and marketing have been fairly widespread. Food crop prices have been decontrolled and trade liberalised in many countries, with benefits in terms of real producer prices for farmers and a reduction in implicit taxation; though given the thriving parallel market existing in many countries the extent of change should not be overstated. Though key export crops tend to remain subject to controls, producer price incentives have been improved. However, national marketing agencies and/or cooperatives in numerous cases remain a severe constraint on marketing efficiency and a drain on resources, as well as constituting a threat to monetary stability in some. A key question remains as to whether Africa can regain comparative advantage in traditional crops and capture substantial net benefits, or whether growth of these crops will simply drag prices down.

Public Enterprise Reform

Progress on public enterprise reform has on the whole been slow, with some 'action programmes', diagnostic studies and rehabilitation measures buying time in the absence of coherent or willing policies of divestiture. They often also put the cart before the horse: it is doubtful, for example, that physical rehabilitation is justified with a view to privatisation given the discount likely to be applied by private investors to such investments. Where prices have been decontrolled, imports liberalised, and tariffs reformed the restructuring should encourage a reduction in protectionism to the parastatal sector; however, the dominant market positions of some parastatals means they are likely to continue to enjoy effective oligopoly benefits for some time to come unless broken up (e.g. in distribution).

Full privatisations and liquidations have been very few relative to the total number of enterprises, and few countries are willing to divest their profitable enterprises, even to reduce debt overhang. However more are prepared to offer equity participations to the private sector. Given the small size of internal capital and savings markets privatisation policy needs to be integrated with capital markets development as well as policy towards foreign direct investment.

A lingering ambivalence in attitudes to private, including foreign direct, investment, along with red tape, remains in a number of countries which even favourable investment codes cannot dispel (e.g. Ghana). Fear of U-turns in policy makes foreign investors particularly cautious. So long as such attitudes prevail, the necessary investor confidence required to promote a surge of private investment will remain elusive. However, other elements of the adjustment agenda will need to have been completed for private investment to respond in the ways hoped, including completion of the macroeconomic reforms discussed earlier, and infrastructure rehabilitation.

Most programmes have slipped because of institutional weaknesses in the public sector. A particular problem has been the inability of some central banks to discharge their responsibilities, whether in the conduct of monetary policy, managing the foreign exchange account or even maintaining their own accounts. More generally, the absence of adequate and transparent accounting-cum-auditing systems and controls on the disposition of resources in some countries, including budgetary controls required to underpin programme agreements, constitutes an issue of public accountability which has almost certainly not been sufficiently seriously addressed to date in the process of formulating and approving reform programmes.

At a wider level, reform of the civil service has been slow. Progress, albeit delayed, has been made in decompressing salary structures and shedding surplus labour. However, control on manpower numbers remains weak (the initial focus on redeployment targets in Ghana overlooked substantial simultaneous recruitment) and little progress has been made in developing the institutional capacity to streamline the service and improve procedures.

Summing the process up, there has been significant progress in the general area of pricing reforms and administrative decontrol in important segments of the economy: these reforms economise on administrative resources and therefore cannot be said to be demanding in such terms, although they make claims on high level analytical skills during the preparatory stages of reform. In institutional areas (e.g. public enterprise management, financial and banking sector reform, civil service restructuring), progress has been generally much patchier and slower within and across the sample of adjusting countries. These are also areas more demanding of scarce administrative capacities, specialist skills and hard preparatory work, and where a process of gradual improvement is likely to be unavoidable.

A central issue for future programmes is to accelerate the process of adjustment in certain key macro-economic areas: e.g. further liberalising markets and eliminating price controls and the dominating role of certain parastatals; exchange rate reform including market-based allocation of foreign exchange; trade liberalisation; and reducing government direct control in most areas of the economy. Many countries are still grappling with these basics at the cost of continuing economic distortions (providing opportunities for rent seeking), postponing genuine adjustment, and tying up scarce high-level resources in ministerial and senior officials time devoted to defending or administering existing arrangements; this has high opportunity costs also in terms of distracting attention from other priority development tasks. (Zambia provides a recent example of how the exchange rate has been substantially demythologised and taken off the political boil.)

Recent evidence from IMF, SAF and ESAF programmes worldwide is that where an improvement in the external current account position and export diversification has occurred, rapid adjustment on the exchange rate and trade fronts, supported by strong financial policies, have been crucial factors. Dealing with the macro-economic-cum-stabilisation basics is the first priority of adjustment. Addressing deeper-seated institutional reforms is bound to have to be spread over a longer period and some might be more properly categorised as developmental rather than short-medium term adjustment issues. The list of reforms included in policy matrices is invariably long, with generally no prioritisation of activities within it (as distinct from the sequential timing of some actions).

The risk with prioritisation is that it may merely *invite* policy slippage. Given a generally overloaded adjustment agenda, this may be only an academic difference. A deeper (though partly related) reason for reluctance to prioritise is the linkage among issues, so that the benefits of reforms in Priority 1 areas (e.g. cutting the fiscal deficit and rationalising expenditure patterns) might be significantly diluted by failure to implement complementary reforms placed under Priority 2 (e.g. improving public expenditure planning and control procedures). Nevertheless, priorities have to be established and more careful attention to these may improve the effectiveness of policies in individual areas where efforts are otherwise dispersed over too broad a front.

A related question concerns the number of conditions in Bank PBLs and the record on implementation. Following the World Bank's first report on adjustment lending in 1988, there was agreement among donors that the number of conditions should be fewer but that they should be more stringently enforced (i.e. fewer waivers). This does not yet seem to be reflected in Bank PBLs. That said, the performance of SSA countries on Bank conditionality has generally been good in aggregate terms. The latest Bank review of adjustment lending shows that the proportion of loan agreement conditions 'at least substantially implemented' at the time of final tranche release was 80 per cent for SSA compared with 84 per cent for all loan agreements. If other actions not included in loan agreements but listed in the President's reports are added, the proportion is 75 per cent (77 per cent world wide). These figures are based on PBLs covering all of the 1980s. For SSA the conditions involved are mainly those falling under the heading of supply side, growth oriented policies, i.e. trade and sectoral policies (industry, energy, agriculture), public enterprises, financial sector reforms, foreign exchange allocation, fiscal policy, etc. Implementation appears to have improved during the 1980s. One question is whether conditionality has been softened to accommodate more gradualism. Another is whether the easiest, least significant conditions have been met, whilst the more crucial conditions have not, as some studies have suggested. Implementation of IMF conditionality has been less good in aggregate terms. On average, two-thirds of SAF and ESAF *financial benchmarks and performance criteria (PC)* were observed.[4] The countries which met all of their criteria were Kenya, Mozambique, Ghana, Malawi. Lesotho met none. Observance was significantly worse for *monetary and fiscal* benchmark indicators averaging only 42 per cent: only the four countries just mentioned met all of these. Less than half the countries met the *inflation* target. More than half, however, met the *external current account* objective although *ex post* this indicator is, of course, determined by unanticipated external financing, terms of trade movements and other exogenous influences.

There has been significant slippage also of IMF *structural benchmarks*. For the same countries as above, these covered mainly fiscal reforms, public enterprises and financial sector reforms, accounting for over 60 per cent of all structural benchmarks. Some of the benchmarks were also Bank conditions. The fact that they slipped in IMF terms does not necessarily mean the equivalent Bank conditions would not be 'substantially met' by the time of Bank second tranche release, allowing for delays in the latter. The sample base is also different, however.

Although the record on IMF conditionality is worse than that for the World Bank, some caveats are in order. By their more quantitative nature, IMF targets are more difficult to fudge and therefore the proportion of conditions set is a more demanding measure. Second, IMF conditions are more closely correlated with each other than Bank conditions, so that failure in one area (e.g. fiscal deficit) might be expected to be reflected in failure in another (e.g. monetary expansion). Third, the tendency to systematically underestimate inflation may reflect weaknesses in the Fund's financial programming model or in programme implementation; it is possible that programmes actually negotiated are not always consistent with assumptions underlying model projections.

Causes of IMF programme shortfalls include terms of trade shocks, civil disturbances and financing difficulties. Policy slippages have, however, been important contributory factors, and have sometimes had a feedback effect on financing shortfalls through conditionally linked BoP support. The different conditionalities imposed by the Fund and Bank can mean that while IMF resources flow, Bank (and co-financed) resources are held up, with consequences for the financing of the programme as a whole: an example of the need for close collaboration and understanding among all donors (and recipients) on what constitute the key adjustment and public expenditure policy issues. Also, as indicated earlier, donors need to adapt their own financing modalities to ensure both that the aid is quick disbursing and that it helps directly to support adjustment objectives.

Suggestions have been made for slower disbursing Bank PBLs which relate disbursements more closely to implementation of policies. The issue arises from the fact that implementation in some areas extends beyond the normal interval between first and second tranche release. It is desirable that disbursements should, so far as possible, relate to substantive policy actions rather than promises of these as provided in action programmes and the like. However, slower disbursing loans would imply either larger 'unit' disbursements or an increase in the number of PBLs if underfunding of short-term financing gaps is to be avoided. Sectorally focussed PBLs help to address the issue, but too many PBLs have administrative implications for the Bank and recipients alike, as well as implying more conditionality. A somewhat different point is that some large PBLs of the SAL variety cover too wide and disparate a range of issues (the so-called 'Christmas tree' phenomenon), augmenting the risk of slippage and clouding priorities.

RECENT ECONOMIC PERFORMANCE

How far we should assess adjustment progress on the basis of expected improvements in macro-economic aggregates in the short to medium term has been one of the main issues of debate. Given its starting point, as a short-term stabilisation organisation the Fund has tended to place greater weight on them than other players. It is worth recalling some of the difficulties.

Everyone is agreed that in the long run successful adjustment *must* show up in faster growth of GDP associated with higher (and more productive) investment rates, higher savings rates and a lower external current account (CA) deficit to GDP ratio reflecting faster export growth relative to import growth. Higher private investment must be part of higher investment. Higher real consumption per capita, along with improved food security and progress in poverty alleviation including improving social indicators, must also in the long term be considered necessary criteria of adjustment success.

In the short-medium term (three years, but perhaps much longer) some or all of the quantifiable macroeconomic indicators may move in either direction, even with 'good' adjustment and in an ex-ante planned away. Following the adoption of a programme the external CA deficit (and GDP) may be planned to rise as a consequence of higher aid-financed imports following a period of severe import compression and pending export growth. A rise in the CA deficit need not necessarily reflect 'weak' adjustment vis-a-vis another case where the CA deficit was reduced: it depends on what efforts a government was making to reduce imports/expand exports before balance of payment support was offered. In any case, variability in ex-ante CA deficits partly reflects differences in relative aid endorsements (donors' preferences/biases), which bear no obvious relationship to strength of adjustment (see pp. 58–9 above).

On the same lines, the investment ratio may be high and rising, but a poor indicator of future growth potential as a result of an inflated or inefficient public investment programme containing large numbers of poor projects: reducing it in the first instance, pending a rise in private investment may be desirable. On the other hand, both GDP and investment may fall in the short term in the face of the required fiscal and monetary restraint and pending aid flows and/or lagged responses to supply side reforms. Conversely, higher inward investment may permit a higher current account deficit on a sustained basis for many years.

For undiversified, primary producing African economies, an ex ante or ex post rise in GDP and exports in the short-medium term may reflect good weather, terms of trade influences or simply the effects of higher imports permitting increases in capacity utilisation and yields, and hence not be attributable to policy reform as such (though no less desirable). Or it may partly reflect the switching of trade from unofficial to official markets and statistics which, though also desirable, could reflect the effects of improved price incentives without implying a corresponding rise in net output. In some cases, output growth has not been reflected in commensurate exports owing to transport and infrastructural bottlenecks (Uganda, Tanzania). Finally, to the extent that growth of output during the adjustment 'transition' occurs in highly protected sectors, and in the face of continuing distortions in key prices (including exchange and interest rates) there will be some continuing 'bad' growth.

Inflation – an intermediate indicator – poses some analogous problems given the need to separate the effects of price decontrols, real exchange rate depreciation and other exogenous influences from persistent underlying inflationary pressures. On top of all this, of course, is the uncertainty of outcomes inherent in programme design – against the background of no agreed detailed model of how adjustment works – and the effects of political disruption and civil strife in some countries, with repercussions on their neighbours. Lastly, the quality of much of the statistics used is such that the margin of error can mask any trends. All or some of the effects described earlier have been and are at work among the current sample of African adjusting countries including the UK's aid recipients. There are, therefore, pitfalls in relying on the use of 'outcome' indicators as monitors of adjustment progress or strength of adjustment in the current stage of development of many African programmes. Careful analysis is required in each case, with an emphasis on the strength of the underlying policy, structural and institutional measures.

For all these reasons, along with the statistical problems in specifying the counterfactual scenario, and the fact that comprehensive adjustment in Africa in its modern guise has become widespread mainly since the mid 1980s, one ought not to be surprised that econometric studies based on such outcome indicators tend to show very little significant association between implemention of programmes and improvements in these indicators over the short-medium term. Some recent Fund work based on Fund programmes in Africa during the 1970s and early 1980s shows some significant effects on inflation in the year or two following adoption of programmes, but in fact reducing inflationary pressures has proved one of the difficult areas in non-franc zone African countries (see pp. 67–8 above).

With these caveats, there has been a general improvement in the economic performance of the SPA countries since 1985. On an unweighted average basis, GDP growth has averaged around 3.5 per cent, compared with less than 1 per cent, during 1981–4. For other IDA-only countries growth has averaged about 3 per cent per annum throughout the 1980s. A strong *relative* improvement in growth between the two periods for SPA countries is what one would wish to see if adjustment has made any contribution. However, it is impossible from this alone to say how much of the relative improvement in SPA growth is attributable to adjustment policies, to better weather in some parts of Africa, and/or to relatively faster growth of aid flows to SPA countries.

Disaggregated data show that among the 'strong reformers' in

Bank/Fund terms (defined by the record on policy implementation), some enjoyed a big increase in growth between 1981–4 and 1985–9 (Kenya, Ghana, Madagascar, Togo). Though The Gambia merely maintained above average growth throughout the 1980s, it was on a more sustainable basis at the end of the 1980s (with concessional replacing non-concessional flows). Malawi has only in the last year or two shown a significant step-up in GDP growth compared with 1981–4. In some of these countries part of the improvement can reasonably be attributed to improved supply side policies, e.g. from improved agricultural pricing and marketing policies, often linked to the impact of exchange rate reform on export crops. In nearly all cases a key factor has been increasing concessional flows. However, some 'average' reformers (Tanzania, Uganda, Mozambique) as well as 'weak' ones (Somalia, Mauritania) have also shown strong improvement in GDP growth between the two periods.

The recovery in export volume growth since 1985 for the SPA group (again on an unweighted average basis) has been significantly stronger than for other IDA-only countries, with growth averaging about 5 per cent per annum in 1985–9 compared with negative growth in 1981–4. Here again, performance is variable among SPA countries with strong recoveries in Ghana, Kenya, Tanzania and Togo but little overall growth in Malawi (all 'strong' reformers). However, many countries, reforming and non-reforming alike, enjoyed a large increase in exports in 1989, reflecting favourable rains. Ugandan exports have suffered from infrastructure bottlenecks.

SPA countries have shown a markedly stronger recovery in investment than other countries, and within this group stronger reformers have performed best. However in both cases, recovery followed a period of greater decline. Increased investment has not been associated with any improvement in domestic savings, where no clear trends have been evident. Both savings and investment rates remain low (13 per cent and 16 per cent respectively in 1987) in terms of what is required to achieve sustainable GDP growth of 5 per cent a year, and compared to the rates achieved in the 1970s (21 per cent for investment). Per capita consumption has witnessed a very modest recovery in IDA countries since 1985, but this has been more marked in non-SPA countries.

There is as yet little evidence of any significant restructuring of production in SPA countries. Growth has been very largely concentrated in traditional sectors. Non-traditional export growth has still to make a significant impact. New industrial activities and foreign direct investment have been slow to materialise. Parastatals still dominate the industrial and distribution sectors of most economies.

Partly as a consequence, progress towards external viability – defined as a reduction in the external resource gap as a proportion of GDP – remains a distant prospect for most countries, implying no let-up in the need for aid. For SSA as a whole, the Bank feels able to project no better than a 5 per cent GDP growth rate and equivalent growth of exports which, coupled with unitary import elasticity, implies no reduction in the resource gap ratio over the next decade; a combination of continuing real terms growth of ODA and concessional debt relief would be required to fill the gap. Within these aggregates some countries will, of course, do much better than others. It is, however, desirable that everything possible should be done to raise growth rates if significant progress towards poverty reduction is to be made. Given some question marks over the likelihood of aid flows growing on the scale envisaged, faster growth would need to be achieved on the basis of a lower import elasticity such as that achieved during the late 1960s to early 1970s (i.e. less than 0.5 for the region as a whole).

LOOKING AHEAD

Can the process in its present form be improved? Much has been made, and understandably so, of the Washington-driven nature of present arrangements and the need for recipient countries to be in the lead in the formulation of adjustment strategy. There is a genuine issue here, but it would be wrong to view it merely as a question of power politics (and economics). Part of the problem is the dearth of African capacities in policy analysis and formulation – not an absolute dearth (there are many highly qualified Africans in their own countries) but a dearth where these functions are most needed, i.e. at the heart of the policy formulation process in governments.

The issue is bound up with wider questions of 'good government'. Conditions of service are only part of the problem. A genuine demand for improved capacities in the areas of economic policy analysis demonstrated by their integration in the policy making process right up to the top echelons, and backed up by an intellectual climate which encourages genuine debate and unbiased discussion of important issues of public policy, is necessary if countries are to play the much fuller part in the adjustment process which all donors want to see. The recently launched Africa Capacity Building Initiative addresses this issue along with related proposals being developed for improving graduate economics teaching in Africa.

The record on implementation of Bank conditionality, subject to earlier caveats, suggests that conditionality 'works' (see above). However, there is a feeling that the often fraught nature of the current process is not a suitable basis for international economic cooperation, and proposals have recently been made (e.g. in the World Bank's Long Term Perspective Study) for delinking ex ante Bank conditionality from adjustment support, presumably dropping the second tranche conditions and policy matrices typical of Bank PBLs. Under these proposals, which have not been elaborated in detail, balance of payments support would continue so long as countries continued to implement reforms. But the amount of support would come to depend on how well a country was doing on adjustment in an ex-post way, analogous to the prior actions currently required before programmes are approved. (Presumably, a 'base' level of BoP support would be established at the start based on a notional 'index' of adjustment progress, from which increases or decreases would be measured).

The proposals are linked to two others: a *more selective approach* to adjustment support which would exclude bad performers altogether; and a gradual reduction over time in BoP support and shift to *direct funding of sectoral programmes* ('time slices') in key areas (e.g. health, education, infrastructure). Such sector aid would retain a quick disbursing, fungible character and include provision for local cost financing, so helping directly to raise the volume and/or quality of public expenditures while transferring resources in a form suitable also for supporting adjustment efforts.

On the issue of conditionality, we do not think the time is ripe to ditch the present arrangements, although it is clearly desirable that the aid-giving process should mature to a stage where there is need for less conditionality, at least in certain areas or as countries 'complete' their structural reforms. In principle, however, conditions should be few and more resolutely enforced. Properly focussed and selective conditionality, sensibly applied, provides a discipline which, apart from encouraging implementation, ought to sharpen the design of programmes and the identification of key priorities among all parties – Fund, Bank, donors and recipients.

The risk with *ex post* arrangements in Africa today, coupled with the suggested more selective approach (which, however, is desirable in itself), is that a number of countries would slip back or that the process would move even more slowly in important areas. This might tend to erode the principle of selectivity unless donors were prepared to withhold significant amounts of aid. Assessment of adjustment progress might become even more subjective with the demise of some objective tests. Finally, it would risk significantly diluting the intensive Bank-recipient policy dialogue which present arrangements permit.

The British government has welcomed the proposals in the Long Term Perspective Study for a significantly enhanced emphasis on human resources development, including the social sectors, and a gradual shift from an excessive reliance on balance of payments support. Part of the 'theory' of balance of payments support is that the resources so transferred finance appropriate forms of public and private expenditures. While creation of an enabling environment for the private sector through structural adjustment reforms helps towards the second objective, improvements in public expenditure have been very slow to achieve despite the public expenditure reviews (PERs) carried out by the World Bank.

It is evident that the public expenditure dialogue with the Bank has frequently not, or only very slowly, helped to reorient public spending in the ways necessary for faster and more efficient growth with greater emphasis on poverty alleviation and human resources development. It is important that balance of payments support should not finance wasteful public expenditures which can undermine the case for aid in donor countries. The growth of such support – both in financial terms and in terms of the administrative resources in staffing and senior management time devoted to this high profile activity among donors and recipients – may have tilted the balance too much away from the public expenditure programme as a key focus of the aid relationship. Given the number of separate occasions on which macroeconomic and adjustment issues are discussed in the boards of the Fund and Bank over an eighteen-month cycle – for approval of Policy Framework Papers, SAFs/ESAFs and Bank PBLs – there is a need for consultative groups to devote more time to public expenditure (including sectoral) issues. The shift to direct sectoral funding could help to rectify this.

Certainly, there is room for improvement in the process of designing and negotiating programmes: by continuing improvements in Fund/Bank collaboration; better prioritisation and related conditionalities clearly defined and focussed on the key areas (including more sectorally focussed PBLs); incorporating contingency financing mechanisms in Fund programmes; integrating social dimensions and poverty policy in the design of programmes (important for 'accelerated' adjustment in the areas of pricing and the exchange rate); a better understanding of institutional processes and realities (in which social and political scientists can provide valuable insights); better dissemination of experiences from one country to another including more 'horizontal' interaction among African policy makers engaged in the process; and by drawing lessons from previous programmes. In the latter context, it would be desirable for an independent evaluation unit to be established within the Fund along the lines of the Bank's Operations Evaluation Department. Donors, too, have a contribution to make to this process, through detailed sectoral and institutional knowledge as well as – importantly – through their understanding of local political situations.

NOTES

I am grateful to colleagues in and outside ODA for discussion and comment on issues raised in this chapter, especially Suma Chakrabarti, Charles Enoch, Neil Gregory, Richard Manning, Craig Pickering, Richard Teuten and Sam Sharpe. The views expressed do not necessarily reflect official HMG views or policy on all matters commented on.

1. Three broad types of assistance dominate UK aid: project aid (including various sectoral forms of aid akin to project aid); programme aid; and technical cooperation. These three forms accounted for about 70 per cent of total UK bilateral aid in 1989. In organisational terms, spending under these headings constitutes the bulk of the managed aid programme at country level ('country programmes'). See table below for Africa.
2. Financial commitments in support of reform by the World Bank and IMF between 1980–9 and related number of countries receiving assistance were as follows:

TABLE 4.3 *IMF and World Bank financial commitments to Africa,*
1980–9

| | World Bank | | IMF | |
	1980–4	1985–9	1980–4	1985–9
SPA 22				
Number	7	22	11	22
US$ billion	0.7	3.4	3.2	4.8
Other SSA				
Number	7	9	7	11
US$ billion	1.7	5.1	6.6	7.5
Total SSA				
Number	14	31	18	33
US$ billion	2.4	8.5	9.8	12.3

Note: countries receiving assistance in both periods are counted twice. In some cases commitments were not fully disbursed and remaining amounts may have been cancelled. World Bank sectoral loans and credits may include some financing that is not quick disbursing.

SOURCE World Bank, Review of the SPA and Proposals for a Second Phase.

3. For a discussion of these arrears problems, see M. Faber, 'Debt: New hope for the chronic but repentant', *Journal of International Development*, 2, April 1990, pp. 232–42.
4. The sample covers sixteen arrangements for which a full programme year had been completed between July 1988 and December 1989. The countries were: Burundi, Central African Republic, Chad, Equatorial Guinea, Kenya, Lesotho, Mali, Mozambique, Niger, Tanzania, Togo, Uganda, The Gambia, Ghana, Malawi, Senegal. *Source*: IMF, *Structural Adjustment Facility – Review of Operations*, June 1990 (Washington, DC: IMF).

Part II
The Politics of Conditional Lending

5 Interest Group Politics and the Implementation of Adjustment Policies in Sub-Saharan Africa

John Toye

INTRODUCTION

When at the very beginning of the 1980s international agencies like the IMF and the World Bank suddenly started to advocate policies of structural adjustment to the governments of developing countries, discussions of the political aspects of structural adjustment were very much *sub rosa*. They were not on the formal agenda of debate. To the extent that politics was discussed clandestinely, however, a clear conventional wisdom existed about how the politics of adjustment would work – what the political problems would be, what challenges these would pose to politicians who sought structural adjustment and how donor agencies could assist the successful meeting of those challenges.

In this chapter, a sketch of this conventional wisdom is given below. In the following section, a summary is given of the findings of the recent study by Mosley, Harrigan and Toye (1991) as they relate to the politics of implementing adjustment policies in three developing countries in sub-Saharan Africa – Ghana, Malawi and Kenya. Finally, the implications of these findings are examined in the context of current calls for greater democratisation of political life in developing countries.

THE POLITICS OF STRUCTURAL ADJUSTMENT: A SKETCH

The most powerful and comprehensive analysis of the political economy of development available to influence thinking about structural adjustment at the end of the 1970s was *Why Poor People Stay Poor* by Michael Lipton, which was published in 1977. This influential book codified and rationalised the concept of urban bias, and eloquently denounced its malign effects on policies designed to promote development. Many other people had, from the 1960s, onwards, examined parts of the urban bias story – excessive industrialisation, distorting trade regimes, the failure of redistributive taxation strategies, the neglect of agricultural investment or the virtues of primary health care compared with modern curative medicine. Lipton's book tied all these things (and more) together and created a powerful polemic against the 'urban coalition' which was undermining development and efforts to alleviate poverty. After structural adjustment policies had been launched, Bates (1981) made an even sharper statement of this polemic and the 'Berg Report' identified persistent anti-agriculture bias as African governments' chief policy error (World Bank, 1981).

Not surprisingly, the politics of structural adjustment were interpreted with the concept of urban bias in mind. The need for structural adjustment had arisen, it was believed, because governments in developing countries had been 'captured' by workers and industrialists to form an urban coalition (Bates, 1986: 6–8). Captive governments had legislated their economic policies to advance urban interests at the expense of rural interests. The whole dirigistic apparatus of trade and exchange control, state-owned banks and industries, trading corporations with monopolies of agricultural export crops, food procurement agencies and so on was seen as a single great scheme to exploit the rural hinterland and grow rich on a variety of artificially created rents in the cities and towns. A new Gestalt had arrived. Instead of a series of isolated 'policy mistakes', developing countries were seen to be in the grip of a syndrome, in which dirigisme and rent-seeking were mutually reinforcing, and of which the perpetrators and the beneficiaries were the urban coalition. The academic public choice theorists expressed this more clearly than officials of the World Bank, but the latter were also strongly influenced by this idea.

From this new Gestalt, the problems and paradoxes of the politics of structural adjustment proceeded. Taken together, they can be described as 'the politics of the knife-edge'. This starts from the *distributional* proposition that stabilisation and structural adjustment reduce the rents accruing to urban interest groups and benefit rural interest groups whom dirigisme has systematically disadvantaged. To this is added a proposition about *timing* – that the negative effects on urban interests will be felt almost immediately, as the prices of imported consumer goods rise and subsidies on food, transport and other utilities are withdrawn, while the positive effects on rural interests will not accrue until new crops are planted, harvested and sold at the new, more favourable prices. A third proposition concerned *expectations*. The benefits of stabilisation and structural adjustment would not accrue at all unless people believed that the government would persist with the policies of reform. Yet it was difficult for people to believe in government persistence because of the paradox of reform, first enunciated by Niccolo Machiavelli. In *Il Principe*, Machiavelli noted that the innovator 'has for enemies all who had done well under the old order of things, and lukewarm defenders in those who may do well under the new' (Machiavelli, 1968, p. 29). Thus during the first year or two of an adjustment programme, the situation was expected to be highly unstable. To push ahead strongly might be the path to success as the government's resolve persuades people to adjust their behaviour to the new economic environment. But it also might not, if opposition proved stronger than the government expected and was capable of surmounting. If the government were to lose confidence in its ability to persist, the programme of adjustment would quicky collapse. Hence the metaphor of the knife-edge.

This kind of political analysis informed the international financial institutions' understanding of their own role in the adjustment process. It was to provide much-needed foreign credits to ease the difficult first year or two by re-filling the shops and rehabilitating essential infrastructure which had been allowed to deteriorate. This would help to bridge the gap between the arrival of the bad news (rising prices, heavier taxes, loss of subsidies) and the good news of higher producer prices and the relaxation of the underlying import strangulation. The ability to deploy resources for the purposes of bridging the bad news/good news gap was seen as the source of the IFIs' political leverage. Where opinion was divided evenly between pro- and anti-reform camps within a government, the Fund and Bank could throw their weight behind the pro-reform group and carry the day for stabilisation and structural adjustment.

Such in sketch form were the political ideas which underpinned the move to adjustment lending in the 1980s. I have not laboured to document precise instances. Many were in confidential documents. But in any case the aim here is not to convict particular individuals or institutions of error. It is merely to remind ourselves of lines of thinking that were popular at the time, as a background to presenting the results of case studies of the implementation of adjustment reforms. Before doing so, however, some further observations may be helpful in elaborating aspects of the basic political understanding of the time.

(1) The urban bias theme itself, though capturing something important about the exploitation of rural exporters, especially in Africa, ran into much criticism. Two problems relevant here are the loose and fluctuating definition that is given to the 'urban coalition', and the absence of clear evidence of the ways in which urban people operate politically as an interest group (Moore 1984; Toye 1987, pp. 127–30). This was unsatisfactory in itself, but especially worrying for those intending to intervene to counter-balance the urban coalition's influence.

(2) The concept of an interest group (apart from rural interest groups which were supposed to be a distant gleam in the eye of the external actors) came in the new Gestalt to bear an unambiguously *negative* connotation. They were divisive and parasitic; if successful they caused social rigidities or were otherwise socially destructive. This was a considerable reversal of the earlier view that their activities were analogous to a competitive process within the political arena, blunting the extremism of each other's political demands and ultimately promoting compromises and social consensus (see Toye, 1990(a), p. 6).

(3) The negative connotation given to interest groups combined with the dilemma of the bad news/good news gap to create a strong presumption in favour of the effectiveness of authoritarian governments in carrying through adjustment programmes, even if they were not regarded as desirable in any wider sense. 'A courageous, ruthless and perhaps undemocratic government is required to ride roughshod over these newly-created special interest groups', wrote Deepak Lal (1983, p. 33) in a pamphlet that was widely acclaimed at the time. Lal was no mere academic scribbler, but an influential figure in the Research Department of the World Bank.

(4) Machiavelli's paradox of reform helped to answer an important question about structural adjustment, namely 'why should fresh foreign credits be released to the reforming government *before* reform takes place rather than *after*?' It provided a

political argument for a course of action that was not, on the face of it, congruent with economic prudence. The arrival of fresh credits could, after all, reduce rather than increase the urgency of economic policy reform in the government's mind. And there was considerable scope for defaulting on promises of reform, once the credits had arrived. 'Facilitating the transition' with IFI finance could just as easily result in delaying it, or even aborting it. But it made sense once given a firm belief in the story of defeating the urban coalition.

(5) Finally, the presumption in favour of authoritarian regimes as managers of adjustment, and the IFIs' support of such regimes with concessional finance, had to be justified. Justification was provided by a three step argument. First, a distinction was drawn between the interests of an authoritarian government and the interests of the people which it governs. Second, that the interests of the people should be defined by the Rawlsian principles of distributive justice, including the proscription of changes which further disadvantage the least advantaged groups in a society. Finally, if stabilisation and structural adjustment programmes do redistribute income from the urban rich to the rural poor, they *are* in the interests of the people because they do not violate this Rawlsian principle. Therefore, it is legitimate for the IFIs to support the adjustment programmes of authoritarian regimes – of whom they may or may not approve on other grounds (Donaldson 1990).

IMPLEMENTATION OF STRUCTURAL ADJUSTMENT IN THREE SSA CASES: THE MHT RESULTS

The Mosley, Harrigan and Toye study of structural adjustment (henceforth MHT) is based in part on case-studies of nine developing countries which borrowed from the World Bank to finance adjustment programmes in the 1980s. In Africa they were Kenya, Malawi and Ghana; in Asia, Turkey, Thailand and the Philippines; in the Caribbean and Latin America, Jamaica, Guyana and Ecuador. The general results obtained reflect obviously the initial selection of countries. The choice was aimed at a wide spread, both geographically and in terms of *ex ante* perceived performance – both Turkey and Guyana are here. One important result, however, does not seem to be particularly sensitive to choice of cases. It is that all countries do not achieve a middling or average performance in implementing the policy conditions of structural adjustment loans – an impression which the Bank fosters by quoting an *aggregate* number for condition fulfilment of 60 per cent while not being willing to provide individual country estimates. Country performances divide quite sharply between the excellent and the very poor. The evidence suggests that countries either seriously commit themselves to the adjustment process, or they do not.

There are various ways of manipulating the indicators of compliance which the World Bank studies, but this is only a way of masking the underlying reality of either strong commitment, or rather little serious interest in pursuing adjustment.

The question then arises: how is the strong commitment which produces excellent implementation generated? The MHT study looks at four distinct (but not mutually exclusive) hypotheses.[1]

(1) that authoritarian regimes are more likely to be strongly committed to adjustment and thus to be better performers at it than are democratic regimes.

(2) that (regardless of regime type) newly-formed governments are likely to be better adjusters than governments of long standing, i.e. that 'new brooms sweep cleanest'.

(3) that a sudden sharp worsening of economic conditions – an economic crisis – triggers a social learning experience (in any regime, in new or old governments) to the effect that adjustment must be undertaken as a conscious policy rather than allowed to happen as the inevitable outcome of inaction and policy paralysis.[2]

(4) that commitment results from a struggle between pro- and anti-reform interest groups, in which pro-reform groups (with Bank/Fund help) become politically dominant.

At a superficial level, it appears that 'authoritarian regimes' are better adjusters than 'democratic' regimes, when the latter are defined as those with regular elections for both the head of state and a representative assembly plus freedom of the press and personal expression. Turkey, Thailand and Ghana are authoritarian on this criterion and they were the best performers on adjustment (see Table 5.1). The two worst performers were Ecuador and Guyana, who come out as non-authoritarian.

If, however, we confine our focus to the three sub-Saharan African cases of Ghana, Kenya and Malawi, the authoritarian regime hypoth-

TABLE 5.1 *Possible explanations of commitment to policy reform*

Country	Authoritarian regime?	New government?	Standard of living 1980–2 more than 25% below average level of 1970s?	Level of implementation (%)
Turkey	Yes*	Yes	No	95
Thailand	Yes*	No	No	70
Ghana	Yes	Yes	Yes	58
Philippines	No (post 1986)	No (yes post 1986)	No	62
Jamaica	No	Yes	Yes	63
Malawi	Yes	No	No	55
Kenya	Yes*	No	No	38
Ecuador	No	Yes	Yes	28
Guyana	No	No	Yes	15

Notes and sources:
A regime is defined as 'authoritarian' if any of the following do not hold: regular elections for representative assembly and head of state; freedom of press and personal expression. In countries marked * there is an elective representative assembly. 'New government' denotes a change in political leadership during the two years preceding the grant of the first World Bank adjustment loan. 'Standard of living' is GNP per capita as set out in successive issues of World Bank *World Development Reports* (Appendix, Table A.1). Levels of implementation for each case-study country are as set out in Table 5.2.

esis does not discriminate between the better performers in the implementation of structural adjustment loan conditions (Ghana, Malawi) and the less good (Kenya). This is because, like so many other countries in SSA, all the three case-study countries fall into the category of dictatorships. The observed variations in their adjustment performances must be the result of something other than the basic nature of their political regimes.

The regime of the Provisional National Defence Council (PNDC) in Ghana, under its Chairman, Flt.Lt. Jerry Rawlings, is best described as bonapartist. Founded by two coups (one failed in 1979 and one successful at the end of 1981), the new regime presented itself as a Marxist revolution and instigated various measures of popular mobilisation. But in its first years it lost legitimacy through its episodic espousal of violence and summary executions, and then split on the issue of whether to call in the Bank and the IMF. Since 1983, a small PNDC rump has ruled without permitted opposition or press freedom, and without any representative institutions until elections for district assemblies were held in 1988.

The Malawian polity has been described as 'a centralised, efficient, personal dictatorship' by Dr Hastings Banda, President – now Life President – since 1964. Coercion and patronage were the original basis of Banda's personal power, which permitted the subversion of the checks and balances in the original Independence constitution. In more recent years, a range of populist and patrimonialist strategies have been used for the ideological and material consolidation of Banda's position (MHT II, pp. 204–5).

The regime presided over by Daniel arap Moi in Kenya is the chosen successor to Kenyatta's original Independence government, and in much the same authoritarian mode. Although Kenya has an elected assembly, dissent is not tolerated and opponents who become too outspoken have met a variety of violent ends. The bureaucracy is manipulated as a direct instrument of presidential power. Little divides Kenya from Malawi and Ghana in the degree of its authoritarianism. If the authoritarian explanation of success in structural adjustment alone were valid, little should separate the performance of the three countries. Since in fact performance was significantly different, we must turn to other hypotheses next for enlightenment.

How relevant is the newness of the government as cause of successful adjustment? Do new leaders enjoy a specially advantageous opportunity for reform when they first come to power – a political honeymoon period? The political honeymoon can be important in some situations, but it is less relevant for authoritarian than for non-authoritarian regimes. The advantages of a new leadership derive from its renewal of popular legitimacy and the willingness of those inclined towards opposition temporarily to hold their political fire. Where the new leadership is authoritarian, such considerations do not so obviously apply. Indeed, as previously noted, the PNDC in Ghana, acting with few constraints, quickly dissipated much of the popular legitimacy which it may have had and provoked internal opposition which produced numerous attempted counter-coups in the first few years of its existence. The fact that Rawlings repudiated all the governments in Ghana, at least since the time of Nkrumah, was not a source of strength. One of these, that of Dr Busia (1969–72) had marked out the path of liberalising economic reform down which Rawlings himself quickly had to walk in 1983.

The three cases of Ghana, Malawi and Kenya provide examples of governments of widely ranging degrees of newness. Banda had been in power for seventeen years already in 1981, when structural adjustment began in Malawi. Moi's tenure of power had been less than half of that when Kenya received its first SAL in 1980. In Ghana, Rawlings initiated Bank-funded adjustment after only eighteen months in power. But Malawi's record of implementation of reforms was only marginally worse than Ghana's. If an elderly government retains (as Banda's did) widespread popular support and an efficient administration, it can reform the economy as successfully as a new government which sets itself up as a 'new broom' – or so the MHT statistics appear to show. However, some caution is called for here. The Ghanaian administrative capacity was probably less than that in Malawi. Ghana's record might well have exceeded Malawi's by more than it did, had both countries had equally competent administrations. If that is so, the hypothesis that recent accession to power assists reformers may still contain an element of truth. We return to this question when we discuss the fourth hypothesis, on interest groups.

What is the role of economic crisis in stimulating successful adjustment? The depth of economic distress does seem to play some catalytic role. As Table 5.1 shows, only in one of the three SSA countries, Ghana, had the standard of living in the early 1980s fallen below the average level of the 1970s by more than 25 per cent. Ghana also had the greatest success in implementing its economic reforms. This association between crisis and the thoroughness of reform may not be causal, but it does not allow us to dismiss the hypothesis out of hand.

The origin of Kenya's economic difficulties was ironically a boom during 1976–7 in coffee and tea prices, which the government allowed to feed through into the private sector, and which was followed by heavy international borrowing (including variable interest rate recycled petro dollars) and expansion of public recurrent expenditure and investment in parastatals. When the coffee price fell sharply in 1979, a balance of payments deficit quickly emerged, which drove Kenya first to the IMF and then in 1980 to the Bank for external finance (MHT II, pp. 271–4). Sudden falls in primary commodity prices (in this case, tobacco and tea) also triggered a substantial balance of payments deficit in Malawi in 1979–80, which was exacerbated (as in Kenya) by rises in international interest rates. In Malawi the crisis was further worsened by drought and the disruption of

Malawi's traditional trade route to the sea through Mozambique. Again, like Kenya, Malawi resorted to the IMF in 1979 and when this proved insufficient, to the Bank in 1981 (MHT II, pp. 210–3).

Serious as these difficulties were, the crisis in Ghana was much more deep-seated, and brought the country to virtual economic collapse in the early 1980s. Whereas both Kenya and Malawi had been regarded as relatively well-managed economies until the second half of the 1970s, Ghana's development strategy had developed fundamental flaws in the 1960s, and Busia's hesitant attempt at correction did not get very far before he was ousted by the military. Ghana then suffered during the rest of the 1970s from military rulers who not only failed to pursue *any* economic policy but who ruthlessly exploited public resources for private gain. Finally, strong exogenous shocks in the form of drought, rising oil prices and the repatriation of almost one million Ghanaians working in Nigeria completed the debacle. Although their crisis had begun much earlier than Kenya's or Malawi's and done much more economic damage, the Ghanaians took longer to apply for help to the Fund and the Bank. All of this may help to explain why, when they did finally do so, they pursued the required reforms with a more thorough commitment – virtually placing the whole task of economic reconstruction under the supervision of the Fund and Bank.

But even if we acknowledge some explanatory power in the relative depth of the economic crisis, this should not be to the exclusion of our fourth hypothesis – the struggle between competing interest groups leading to the emergence of a dominant pro-reform coalition. On this question, the MHT study provides interesting evidence that vested interests do exist, which have the power to frustrate certain types of economic reform. But the way in which those vested interests operate is quite different from the way their operation is conceptualised in the conventional view of the politics of structural adjustment with which we began.

In both Kenya and Malawi, the most central failures of the structural adjustment programmes concerned the liberalisation of agricultural marketing. In Malawi, parastatals and large holding companies were used to create a distortion *within* the agricultural sector, favouring the large estates at the expense of the small holders. In Kenya, a National Cereals and Produce Board had a monopoly on the buying and selling of maize which had originated in the colonial period. This monopoly allowed oligopoly rents to be earned by granting licences for the movement of maize from surplus to deficit areas of the country. Despite the dominance of agriculture in Malawian exports and the economy more generally, the Bank did not set out to tackle the intra-sectoral distortions of agriculture head-on. Instead it prescribed a series of *ad hoc* reforms which disrupted the working of the existing system and which led to the *status quo ante* being partially restored in 1986–7. More focussed pressure was applied by the Bank on the Kenyan government to review arrangements for maize marketing and allow the private sector greater scope therein. Despite agreeing to the decontrol of the maize trade when the second Kenyan SAL was signed, this measure was never implemented by the government.

Both of these failures of Bank-designed reforms have to be understood by reference to the vested interests within the agricultural sector in each of the countries. In Malawi, the President personally owned Press Holdings, a large private company holding equity in most sectors of the economy, including the commercial banks. Press Holdings borrowed heavily at home and abroad, debt that was frequently guaranteed by the government and used to finance the acquisition of tobacco estates by Dr Banda. Press Holdings also encouraged the commercial banks to lend to leading Malawian politicians and bureaucrats so that they too could acquire tobacco estates and benefit from the incentives granted to 'pioneer' tobacco farmers. These incentives for the tobacco estates were paid for by setting the prices of smallholders' export crops (including tobacco) well below export parity prices. The Malawian estate tobacco farmers, with the President at their head, had a substantial vested interest to defend. While it is not clear whether the Bank diagnosed accurately the full ramifications of the intra-sectoral bias in agriculture, it is clear that the adjustment measures required under the SALs in the mid-1980s did not succeed in removing it.

The arrangements for maize marketing in Kenya also constituted a well-established vested interest of large maize farmers, including the President. The maize marketing board's monopoly powers of purchase from farmers and sales to millers have substantially raised the price of maize to the consumer for many years. Farmers licensed to sell maize in deficit regions make inflated profits thereby, and the allocation of licences for inter-regional maize movements is therefore an important source of political patronage. In these circumstances, it is perhaps not surprising that, while those who were negotiating directly with the Bank led it to believe that the major trade would soon be de-controlled, the measure was blocked by the President's

Office throughout 1983, until the 1984 drought removed it from the political agenda on the (specious) pretext of food security (MHT II, p. 290).

A striking similarity characterises the political circumstances of these failures. The general political and ideological climate of both countries at the time was not hostile to liberalisation efforts. Within both governments, a small group of enthusiastic technocrats was making a genuine effort to pursue liberalisation in the areas agreed with the Bank to be desirable. Ultimately, the Bank's good rapport with the Kenyan and Malawian technocrats proved insufficient to procure the agricultural marketing reforms. In both cases, the President of the country had a personal stake in agribusiness, and the 'distortions' objected to by the Bank formed an important part of the mechanism for ensuring political support for the President's party. It is, therefore, an important finding of MHT that some of the most recalcitrant vested interests in the path of economic liberalisation were in the agricultural rather than the industrial sector, whereas the conventional justification for policy reform was the need to remove the urban biases which disadvantage rural producers.

Apart from the two cases from SSA which are discussed in this chapter, the MHT study also identified a very similar failure of adjustment in Ecuador. There the *latifundistas* in the sierra and the agro-exporting oligarchy held the key economic positions, and economic strength had been converted into political influence. The Bank aimed at eliminating subsidies on agricultural credit and permitting free trade in food crops. Neither objective was achieved, despite the enthusiastic cooperation of the talented economic technocrats who appeared to have policy-making in their control, and who themselves strongly favoured liberalisation (MHT II, pp. 431–2).

Let us now review the original four hypotheses on the causes of successful implementation adjustment loan conditions. The question of whether authoritarian regimes are helpful to adjustment cannot be addressed without going beyond the three SSA cases, because all qualify as authoritarian. All that can be said is that other factors are necessary to explain the variation in success between our three SSA dictatorships.

The comparison between reform in Malawi and in Ghana appears to show that some success in adjustment is possible for old and new governments alike – because both showed approximately average success in their performance of loan conditions. But, again, other factors seem to be relevant in this comparison. Ghana, one suspects, would have done better if it had possessed Malawi's level of administrative capacity. Malawi, on the other hand, suffered from one very powerful vested interest – the agricultural estates sector – for which there was no equivalent in Ghana. It would therefore be wrong to dismiss the 'new broom' hypothesis entirely.

The hypothesis that economic crisis promotes social learning is not refuted if only SSA cases are compared. Ghana seems a strong example. But Table 5.1 indicates that, among all nine of the MHT countries, the hypothesis does not stand up. Leaving Ghana aside, the success rates were higher in countries which did not have an especially severe shock to living standards at the start of the 1980s.

Our fourth explanation, at its simplest, looks suspiciously like a tautology: that the strength of the impulse towards reform depends on the outcome of the competitive struggle between pro- and anti-reform interest groups. If 'interest groups' includes interest groups *within* government, the hypothesis is true by definition: obviously the relative progress of reform between countries depends on the relative power of pro- and anti-reform elements. The meaningful questions evidently lie one step back from here. What caused the relative influence of different groups to diverge as between countries? Are there institutional differences which influence the way in which interest group conflicts are played out?

The MHT study suggests four main propositions.

(1) Reform efforts work better *ceteris paribus* if the gainers were organised in support of the proposed reform. But typically farmers as a whole in developing countries do not constitute an organised, let alone a powerful interest group. So far this goes along with the conventional wisdom sketched above, pp. 86–7. But big landowners find it much easier to make common cause than farmers in general, and in Kenya (as in Ecuador) they organised themselves as a 'national farmers' union', whose members were also well represented in parliament. While supporting *price-based* reforms which keep prices above export-parity levels, they frustrated *market-based* reforms which tried to remove the element of rent in the price paid by the government marketing board.

(2) Industrialists do *not* constitute a unified interest group in matters of trade policy. Each industry has its own proposals and its own special pleading for protection. Thus only where a measure will benefit a majority of industrialists will it gain the

backing of an industrialists' lobbying organisation. Most industrialists will benefit from a quick relaxation of restrictions on
importing key inputs. Measures to liberalise imports have been
among the more successfully implemented parts of structural
adjustment packages.

(3) The degree to which groups can mobilise themselves is only
part of the explanation of the effectiveness of an interest group
in influencing structural adjustment. Countries differ in their
formal political institutions and their informal ideological apparatus. The 'thickness' or 'thinness' of such institutions also
determines the extent to which a group with an organised
common interest can influence policy. A country without a free
legislature, a free press or normal liberal civil rights is much
less open to interest group influence than one with 'thicker' or
'denser' institutions of civil society. In Ghana, the sphere of
action available to interest groups was highly circumscribed by
the thinness or absence of civil society. To say this does not
imply that authoritarian regimes will be more effective as
economic reformers, however. *It may simply imply that the
power to subvert economic reform will be monopolised at the
highest levels of the state.*

(4) With only rare exceptions, structural adjustment programmes
were not designed to compensate those who were losers in the
policy changes. This was so even when a compensation change
could be made without introducing any fresh distortions with
the policy mix. Explicit political calculation seemed to be
largely absent from the IFI's programmes, except insofar as
loan credit permitted a generally welcomed easing of import
compression. Perhaps lack of economic sophistication in local
bureaucracies partly accounts for this, too. Certainly, the
administrative skills of the bureaucracy emerged as a visible
factor which determined differences in implementation as between governments who were equally committed in principle
to the philosophy of adjustment. While there was little to
choose in level of commitment between Turkey and Ghana,
the latter, with a weaker administration, achieved only 58 per
cent implementation, compared with Turkey's 45 per cent.

SHOULD IFIs SUPPORT DEMOCRATISATION IN SSA?

If one now looks back on the initial beliefs which were in vogue at the time when structural adjustment programmes were first devised, it is clear that the MHT study suggests some rather far-reaching revisions.

The Rural-Urban Divide and Dirigisme

MHT sees neither rural nor urban interests operating through well-functioning unified interest groups. In the rural areas large farmers can and do organise, but to help themselves rather than small family farms, let alone the landless wage workers who constitute the poor and the very poor.[3] Sometimes, as in Malawi, they help themselves directly at the expense of the poor smallholders. In the urban areas, supporters of industry are too divided to agree on how and where to create rents and can unite mainly to support import liberalisation. It therefore seems implausible that the syndrome of dirigisme could have been the outcome of a struggle between rural and urban unified interest groups, with the urban coalition winning. Rather, it would appear to be the product of a centrally-directed patronage politics. That is to say that dirigisme results from the active search by government leaders for support – which may be built up either in the urban or in the rural sectors. It is a 'top-down' rather than a 'bottom-up' phenomenon (Sandbrook, 1986). This has strong negative implications for any defence of authoritarianism as a catalyst of economic reform.

Knife-Edge Politics and Authoritarianism

The political analysis of structural adjustment has focussed too much on the early period of a programme. Perhaps this was inevitable before the process had got well underway. The knife-edge problem was visible clearly only in the Ghanaian case, where a difficult first year was accompanied by some attempted coups, and in more recent years in the Philippines. Even in Ghana, external factors such as drought were a major cause of the difficulties, and when they reversed themselves started the recovery *before* the adjustment policies had much chance to bite. There was an over-estimation of the importance of policy-induced changes in the economic situation, compared with exogenous factors like drought in Ghana and Kenya.

Although J.J. Rawlings did face a knife-edge and did not lose his nerve, this seems insufficient evidence from which to conclude that authoritarian governments *ipso facto* make a better job of economic adjustment, as Lal had argued in the statement quoted on p. 88 above.

Political Institutions and the Role of Interest Groups

The MHT study also puts the conventional negative connotation of interest groups in developing countries in a new light. As sketched above (p. 88), interest groups are now generally condemned as socially destructive (e.g. by Olson, 1982, pp. 36–73). This condemnation provides the basic justification for authoritarian regimes – i.e. they are socially desirable because they ride roughshod over such groups. But one can look at the matter the other way round. In such regimes, political institutions are 'thin', particularly in developing countries. Nothing much stands between the ruler, his security services and his ministers and their officials and the people who are governed. There may be very few independently organised interest groups at all – no free trade unions, a politically quiescent church, a muzzled press, no producers' associations. But additionally, there may be no representative political institutions, and thus no forum where competition could discipline sectional demands and force them to advance themselves by articulating a conception of the public interest (Rawls, 1972, pp. 224–7). The only politics may be sporadic acts of popular resistance, and it is easy to romanticise the extent to which these embody 'the general will'. Thus where a negative view of the behaviour of interest groups is justified, it may well be (although not necessarily, as the US case indicates) a pointer to the grossly truncated political institutions of authoritarian rule. To plead for more authoritarianism in such circumstances is likely to be self-defeating. This is especially so if the existing interest groups are the creatures of government patronage, rather than autonomous and self-propelled.

The Distributional Argument

An important part of the case for structural adjustment was its claim to improve income distribution. Although some advocates were prepared to say that adjustment was necessary whatever the distributional consequences, many believed that arguments from equity strengthened the case for adjustment. Even with hindsight, it is hard to validate this. The size of the changes were probably exaggerated in advance on both sides of the argument. Factors like the interdependence of formal and parallel markets make it hard to quantify what the distributional effects have been – except in very dramatic cases, such as that of some of the heavily indebted Latin American countries. But in qualitative terms, we are now more aware of the rural groups who will *not* benefit – small food crop farmers, who are often women, and many agricultural labourers who work for wages. We are also aware that the urban losers who are affected by government lay-offs and rising consumer goods prices will be the urban poor, who will often move back silently to join the rural poor rather than benefit from the few public works projects laid on to soften the effects of adjustment.[4]

Effect of IFI Credit

It looks increasingly as if IFI credit may have delayed reform in some countries. The Bank's move away from providing immediate credit in exchange for promises of action later and towards prior performance conditions and ever finer tranching of credit suggests that it learned by experience that the facilitation argument had flaws. Some countries seem to have used the credits to buy more time and postpone action, despite the fact that reform measures (when implemented) seem to have improved exports and the foreign balance, though without doing much for economic growth or increased private foreign investment.

Just as the MHT study was being completed, dramatic changes were occurring in the political scene worldwide. In the autumn of 1989, a veritable liberal revolution occurred in Eastern Europe (Toye, 1990 (b)). There the restoration of human and civil rights and political representation preceded the search for strategies of economic liberalisation. There it was out of the question to propose that the move from dirigisme to a market-based economy could be undertaken successfully only with an authoritarian government. There, too, the delicate moral considerations for giving credits to such regimes have been simply swept aside. The charter of the new European Bank for Reconstruction and Development enshrines its commitment to 'the fundamental principles of multi-party democracy, the rule of law, respect for human rights and market economics' (*Financial Times*, 21 August 1990).

In Africa, disillusion with the one-party states of African socialism had already set in. The unhappy state of affairs in Tanzania had led to criticisms of the African socialism concept of which it was a model, especially the monopoly of power by the ruling party and the absence of free trade unions (Sender and Smith 1990, pp. 129–39). More generally in Africa, various signs have appeared of a pro-democracy movement – the increasing abandonment of one-party rule, the appearance of African efforts to promote political pluralism and the spread of human rights movements organised by Africans (Legum 1990, p. 134). The Organisation of African Unity has after many years adopted a Charter of Human and People's Rights, with a Commission, headquartered in Banjul, The Gambia, whose purpose is to make these rights more effective. These developments are likely to be further encouraged as the ending of the Cold War puts an end to superpower rivalries played out by unpleasant puppet regimes such as Doe's Liberia and Mengistu's Ethiopia.

The great post-1989 question, which has already been raised in political speeches, is whether foreign aid can be used to promote both economic liberalisation *and political liberalisation at the same time.* In answering this question it is important to begin by remembering the limitation on aid conditionality as an instrument to bring about economic liberalisation. It has not been very successful in *inducing* change in economic policy. But when policies had been changed, it often lent valuable support in maintaining or extending the new directions. The same is likely to apply to the inducement of political change. The mechanisms of aid conditionality are likely to be too creaky to exert much leverage over the recalcitrants and procrastinators of political liberalisation.

One of the interesting findings of the MHT study in the economic policy field was the phenomenon of 'countervailing action'. In other words, a government could comply with a loan condition, but at the same time take other actions not specifically prohibited which had the effect of neutralising that compliance. Obviously the same sort of possibilities for countervailing action exist in the political arena as have been demonstrated in the arena of economic reform. That is why it is rather arbitrary to do as is done in Table 5.1, for example, to specify a few simple criteria to distinguish authoritarian from democratic regimes. This can be unreliable, because it is possible to have apparently democratic institutions with representative government, election of representatives and even fairly extensive human rights, and still have a single party maintaining an unchallengeable monopoly of power. Devices such as giving sitting representatives the right directly to disburse public expenditure in their constituencies, plus occasional round-ups of opponents on unspecified security grounds – followed by eventual release without charge – can ensure that democratic institutions remain nothing more than a facade for authoritarian rule.

The problem of countervailing action not only bedevils the task of using aid to induce political liberalisation, it also affects the weaker strategy of rewarding such changes once they have taken place. Even responding *ex post* by allocating aid only to democratic regimes requires some reliable means of discriminating them from their opposite. It would require much research to prevent such judgement being arbitrary, and therefore potentially destructive of international goodwill when the intention of aid is precisely the opposite.

Even if the judgement could be made simply and reliably, an ethical dilemma remains. If it was morally acceptable to channel aid to authoritarian governments in order to benefit their people during the 1980s, why is it not acceptable to do so today? Are those who have the misfortune to live under such a regime to be doubly punished, by being also denied the economic benefits which foreign aid projects can bring? To do so might be acceptable if the refusal of aid were likely to bring down the existing regime and allow a quick move both to democracy and to the resumption of aid. But the implication of all that, as has been said above, is that this is most unlikely to happen.

Thus the process of democratisation will not be much assisted by aid policy. We are therefore likely to see an increasing differentiation in the mode of operation of interest groups in the process of adjustment. In authoritarian regimes, they are likely to remain creatures of the ruler and obstacles to adjustment in selected areas of economic reform. In democratic regimes, political institutions and civil society should both develop, become both more independent of the state and (unparadoxically) more effective in promoting the public interest. That, at any rate, is the challenge which faces the new democracies of the 1990s.

NOTES

I would like to express my thanks to Mike Faber, Joan Nelson and Robert Wade for their helpful comments on earlier versions of this chapter. Useful comments were also given by participants in conferences where early versions were discussed, at Manchester (September, 1990), Bergen (October, 1990) and Leicester (April, 1991).

1. A fifth hypothesis was also examined, that implementation success was determined primarily by the economic factor of the size of the available IFI credit, relative to that available without conditions from alternative sources. As we are concerned with politics here, the findings on this are not reported (but see MHT, I, Chapter 5 for details).
2. Miles Kahler, in a very interesting paper (Kahler, 1990) makes a much stronger contrast than is presented here between external influence over ldcs' domestic policies exercised by conditionality and bargaining, and external influence exercised by social learning and the growth of consensual knowledge. The latter, 'developed primarily as an explanation for international cooperation and the evolution of international institutions . . . focuses . . . on the tacit and explicit alliances across the negotiating table that are created by policy dialogue, technical assistance and other avenues of influence in the policy process' apart from the leverage of conditionality.
3. The Ghana Living Standards Survey of 1987 gives a snapshot of the distribution of annual per capita expenditure in Ghana. Over 80 per cent of the lowest quintile of this distribution live in rural areas. However, 41 per cent of the highest quintile of this distribution *also* lives in the rural areas. This suggests a rural sector that is highly heterogeneous in its economic and social make-up, and casts serious doubt on the notion of the rural sector as a unified interest group (Loxley 1991, p. 41).
4. Commenting on the GLSS results quoted in Note 3, Loxley remarks that 'when combined with other information from the survey, these data caution one against generalising simplistically about the urban/rural distributional impacts of adjustment programs' (ibid).

6 Consolidating Economic Adjustment: Aspects of the Political Economy of Sustained Reform

Joan M. Nelson

INTRODUCTION

Views vary on the potential contribution of policy-based lending to better economic management and longer-term reforms in countries facing economic difficulties. But there is broad agreement that a government's own commitment and capacity to cope with domestic political pressures are crucial to effective economic adjustment and reform. In the past few years the international development community has placed growing emphasis on host country 'ownership' of adjustment programmes, on 'good governance', and more broadly on the political economy of adjustment. This chapter considers some of the factors shaping political commitment and capacity to launch and consolidate adjustment measures. Its focus on internal forces is intended to complement the emphasis on donor-recipient interactions in other studies in this volume.

The discussion draws on recently completed research on the politics of economic stabilisation and structural change, pursued in collaboration with Thomas Callaghy, Stephan Haggard, Miles Kahler, Robert Kaufman, and Barbara Stallings. The group initially analysed and compared experience with stabilisation and reform during the 1980s in thirteen countries under nineteen governments. Our early goal was to better understand the political factors shaping governments' adjustment choices and implementation. More specifically, we sought explanations for the *timing* of adjustment choices – different governments' prompt or delayed responses to emerging economic difficulties; for the *scope* of their decisions – ranging from short-run macro-economic stabilisation measures only to broad structural reform programmes; and for the *content* of their choices – characterised broadly as orthodox or heterodox.[1] We also probed the political reasons behind varied *implementation records*, ranging from rapid collapse to sustained and vigorous pursuit of adjustment programmes.[2]

In later phases we examined a range of cross-cutting issues including the interplay between governments' relations with external agencies (including conditionality) and domestic political factors; the links between distributive effects of adjustment and political sustainability; the effects of regime type and regime transitions (especially transitions from authoritarian to democratic systems) on adjustment; and the role of state capacity.[3]

As the research continued, we became increasingly interested not simply in implementation but in consolidation of reforms. Both macroeconomic stabilisation measures, and some important aspects of structural reform are notoriously easy to reverse or erode. Therefore, while it remains important to understand how and why reforms are adopted, it is equally or more important to analyse how and why improved macroeconomic management and market-oriented reforms become embedded in a country's political and administrative system, and therefore difficult to reverse.

This chapter sketches our lines of thought on consolidating reform. Two themes emerge. First, we suspect that the political requirements for consolidating reforms may diverge from the factors facilitating initiation of adjustment programmes. Second, we believe that administrative and political institutions powerfully channel and shape political incentives and behaviour, and warrant more fine-grained attention than they have received thus far in analyses of the political economy of adjustment.[4]

INITIATION VERSUS CONSOLIDATION: A BRIEF OVERVIEW

Much of the fairly modest body of research on the politics of stabilisation and structural change in developing nations has focussed on the initial stages of reform: the circumstances and forces leading governments to decide on such measures and the immediate political reactions to their choices. The political dynamics of maintaining momentum and consolidating reform have received much less attention.

One reason for the emphasis on initiating reform is self-evident: without initiation there will be no reform, and policy-oriented analysts are understandably preoccupied with getting reforms under way. Moreover, policy choices provide a comparatively sharp focus for research, both in time and with respect to key actors. In contrast, the process of consolidation stretches over a long period, during which expectations, incentives, public and private institutional arrangements, and recognised interests grow up around a reform and make it increasingly difficult to reverse. The process is inherently diffuse and gradual. It is hard to identify its endpoint, that is, the point at which the political and economic costs of reversing the reform are high enough to make reversal highly unlikely. One plausible criterion for judging whether a reform has been consolidated is its persistence through at least one change in administration.

There is a further reason for researchers' relative neglect of consolidation issues. Until recently, while sporadic stabilisation efforts and occasional adoption of structural reforms were common, sustained broad-gauged reform efforts were rare. Such efforts have become much more numerous in response to the extraordinary pressures of the 1980s and the considerable (though still far from complete) convergence of views regarding the importance of prudent macro-economic management and the content of appropriate development strategies. There are now a fair number of countries with track records of five or more years (considerably more in Turkey, Mexico, and Chile among others). Consolidation of reforms (or failure to consolidate) is therefore both more feasible to study, and of growing relevance in many countries.

The political requisites and tasks of initiating reform, including both the decision to proceed and early application, differ from the political tasks of maintaining and consolidating reform.

The thesis regarding initiation can be bluntly stated: given commitment at the highest political level, *the key to initiation is neutralising opposition.* In virtually all cases, governments cannot expect early support from organised and politically potent groups to outweigh potential opposition from those who see their interests threatened. The reason has long been well-recognised: both stabilisation and many market-oriented reforms usually impose costs that are immediate, certain, and often concentrated (or perceived as such) on specific groups, while the benefits of such measures are deferred, uncertain, and diffused. Losers know who they are; gainers are much less certain. Moreover, losers include powerful vested interests (not least from within the state apparatus) that are organised and vocal, while potential winners often are not.

At best there may be a broad public desire for strong economic and political leadership and a widely recognised need for basic reform going beyond improved management. But most groups are nervous about or fear much of the specific adjustment agenda, and will at most acquiesce. As is increasingly evident in Eastern Europe, even desire for fundamental change does not obviate (though it may dampen) protests against specific measures. Neutralising opposition therefore is the initial political task in support of a firm stabilisation programme and/or major structural changes.

Governments' options for neutralising or containing opposition to adjustment have been much analysed. They are discussed in more detail later in this chapter. The crucial point to note for this overview is that *all the techniques available to manage opposition are either intrinsically temporary or costly.* In most circumstances, reforms can be long sustained only if the costs of managing opposition decline.

Both designing reforms and neutralising opposition while reform gets under way usually require concentrated executive authority. In contrast, *consolidation of reforms may require considerable sharing and diffusing of power* – a more participatory and consultative style of governance and some delegation of control over aspects of economic management to impersonal and apolitical agencies and processes. In short, the political tactics and strategy of initiating reform must change to promote consolidation.

Opposition (and the costs of managing it) will decline as old and new groups develop vested interests in the altered policies and arrangements. Consolidation of reforms can be analysed as a three-step process: growing credibility (the spread of confidence that the reforms are feasible and durable, and that their benefits will be shared reasonably equitably); altered economic behaviour in response to new incentives; and conversion of new vested interests into political support for reformed policies and procedures. The process of consolidation can be promoted by skilful government tactics, but is more fundamentally shaped by economic outcomes and by political and administrative institutions. These propositions are examined more closely in the sections that follow.

INITIATING REFORM

A useful definition of 'initiating reform' must go beyond the adoption of an austerity programme. Faced with acute economic difficulties, almost all governments ultimately adopt and at least briefly pursue corrective macro-economic policies, although many relapse promptly. 'Reform' goes beyond stabilisation, to seek to correct weaknesses in incentives and economic structure contributing to the problems. In the 1980s and 1990s, there is a growing consensus on the broad direction of such reforms, despite continuing debate on their speed, phasing, and precise design. Key elements include reduced direct state intervention in economic activity, hence substantial freeing of prices (including interest and exchange rates), reduction of subsidies, and the opening of the economy to international trade.

For this discussion, 'initiation' is also broadly defined to include not only the signing of agreements with external donors and announcement of reform measures, but also the initial phases of implementing such reforms. As it has become increasingly clear that structural reform is a long-term process, the 'initiation' phase can stretch to cover several years.

A Reform Syndrome

Many governments adopted stabilisation measures, often accompanied by some piecemeal reforms, in response to the acute pressures of the 1980s. Far fewer adopted and persisted in pursuing a broader programme of structural reforms. Our comparative studies suggest a pattern or syndrome of factors associated with the vigorous initiation of broad-gauged reform.

Among the nineteen governments in thirteen countries covered in our initial study, five undertook ambitious programmes of structural reforms and pursued them over several years. These included: Pinochet in Chile (from about 1975 on); Seaga in Jamaica (starting soon after his election in 1980 but intensifying in late 1983-early 1984); de la Madrid in Mexico from 1982 (continued by his successor Salinas through to the present); Rawlings in Ghana from April 1983 to the present; and Aquino in the Philippines after 1986, especially during the eighteen months before the convening of the legislature. These cases share a number of features with at least three other strong reform programmes: Sri Lanka from Jayawardene's election in 1977 until rising ethnic conflict increasingly subverted the economic effort in the mid-1980s; Turkey under Ozal's guidance first as economic tzar and later as president from late 1980 to the present; and Bolivia during Paz Estenssoro's administration from 1985 to 1989. With few exceptions, these cases shared the following features:

(1) Reform was preceded by long periods of slow economic growth or actual decline, accompanied by growing and severe political polarization and civil conflict. Mexico was an exception to this aspect of the syndrome, and Turkey and the Philippines had suffered episodic economic troubles and political conflict rather than long-term decline.

(2) As a result, in most cases (again excepting Mexico) there was a widespread popular perception that major reforms were crucial to restore economic progress and political stability – although often no consensus on what reforms were needed.

(3) Reforms were initiated by new governments which had strong support from large parts of the citizenry. This applies not only to the elected governments of Jayawardene, Seaga, and Aquino, but also to those entering office through coups: Pinochet, Rawlings, and the military in Turkey in 1980. Paz Estenssoro, however, had not won a plurality in the 1985 elections and entered office as a result of a fragile Congressional coalition.

(4) Most of these new governments represented a sharp break with the prior regime and the vested interests that had supported it. This was less clear in the cases of de la Madrid and Paz Estenssoro. But de la Madrid and those around him did represent elements within the dominant party different from those dominating the previous administration. And Paz Estenssoro's advanced age and focus on his place in history provided autonomy from his own party's and supporters' concerns and demands.[5]

(5) Moreover, in almost all these cases groups which might have been expected to oppose structural reforms were constrained or disabled. In Chile after 1973 and Turkey in 1980, in Sri Lanka in 1977 and Jamaica in 1980, the parties and unions opposed to the new governments were splintered and in disarray. The same was true of the coalition that had supported Marcos until his fall. In Bolivia, the unions remained powerful but public opinion and the military were frustrated with their obstructionism. In Ghana, there was no major organised opposition to Rawlings' takeover, though some groups in the population had misgivings. In Mexico, opposition groups were not particularly in disarray in 1982, but were in part contained by the broad and powerfully institutionalised coalition that had long supported the PRI. Some of these governments, most obviously in Chile and Turkey during the period of military rule, also used considerable repression.

The net result of these various factors was a high degree of autonomy and freedom of action for the executive. This was clearly true of the new military regimes in Chile, Turkey, and Ghana, and the well-known strong executive built into the Mexican system. But it was not a function of regime type: the democratically elected governments of Jayawardene, Seaga, and Aquino also enjoyed unusually sweeping discretionary authority. Jayawardene and Seaga reinforced the power conferred by their landslide elections by strongly dominating their cabinets and parties. Both also engaged in later manoeuvre that heightened their dominance. In the early 1980s Jayawardene introduced constitutional changes and altered electoral arrangements to extend his tenure. In December 1983 Seaga called a snap election that was boycotted by the opposition and resulted in a single-party legislature. Aquino, while much less dominant within her government, ruled by executive decree for eighteen months before the National Assembly was reconvened.

Among these cases, Paz Estenssoro entered office with the least apparent strength. Yet political acumen and statescraft created at least temporary autonomy. The new president seized the initiative by rapidly announcing a sweeping economic programme and sending leftist party and labour leaders into temporary exile. He then extended his control by negotiating an interparty pact trading changes in electoral laws desired by the major rival party for the promise of support for his economic reforms.[6]

Strong and autonomous executives were in turn able to shield economic technocrats from political pressures. In Bolivia, Paz Estenssoro split his cabinet into two virtually separate entities, assigning non-economic posts to old-line politicians drawn from his party's competing factions, and segregating economic posts for a strong technocratic team. In Chile, Turkey (1980–3) and Ghana, political leaders who themselves had little grasp of economics firmly backed strong economic advisors. In Sri Lanka, Jayawardene and his party had carefully prepared their programme over a period of several years before the 1977 elections, and took office with a coherent and agreed programme of action. In Jamaica, Seaga acted as his own chief economic minister, finessing the issue of relations between technocrats and politicians. Perhaps the least well-shielded from political pressures were the technocrats advising Aquino.

Reform programmes in all of these cases, in short, were initiated and pursued by new executives with strong centralised authority, responsive to and protective of their technocratic advisers, and temporarily fairly free from strong opposition challenges. The pattern was not associated with any one regime type: the characteristics applied to several military governments, several democratic governments, and one dominant-party system (Mexico). The syndrome combined *incentive* for strong action (in most cases, a long history of worsening economic and political difficulties) with institutional and political *capacity* to take strong action.

The syndrome highlights a combination of factors that have clearly facilitated reform in some of the most dramatic adjustment cases. But it is neither a necessary nor a sufficient formula for adjustment. There are cases of significant adjustment without some or most of the elements of the syndrome: Korea, Thailand, Costa Rica, Madagascar and Malawi come to mind. Conversely, in some cases virtually all the elements in the syndrome were present but attempted adjustment failed, as in Argentina under Alfonsin. In that case, however, the military were discredited and in disarray, but opposition unions were not. We can only speculate what might have happened had the unions also been disabled.

The syndrome, then, is not a formula but a heuristic device, calling our attention to critical factors facilitating the initiation of broad reforms, by encouraging commitment on the part of political leaders, and by helping to neutralise the inevitable opposition to reforms.

Neutralising Opposition

Given commitment, the key political task of initiating reforms is neutralising opposition. But a closer examination of the means available for accomplishing that task suggests that all the approaches are either temporary, costly, or both.

As the reform syndrome suggests, major groups likely to oppose structural adjustment are sometimes temporarily disabled by *exogenous events*, such as the death of key leaders. They may also be discredited by poor performance, as in the cases of the parties regarded as responsible for Jamaica's economic debacle in the late 1970s, Sri Lanka's impasse earlier in that decade, or the Communist governments of Eastern Europe; or the Argentine military's disastrous war in the Falklands/Malvinas Islands. Such events provide openings for reform.

Opposition can also be reduced and made more manageable by shrewd *timing and sequencing* of reforms. Depending on the room for manoeuvre permitted by the economic setting and external support, governments can try to avoid affecting several major groups simultaneously, or can seek to spread out over time (rather than bunch) measures that impose costs on particular groups. For instance, most governments confronted with the necessity of cutting wage bills have chosen to maintain public sector employment while permitting real wages to erode dramatically, rather than concentrating costs on redundant workers through severe retrenchment.[7]

It is easier to use such tactics in the launching of structural changes than macro-economic stabilisation programmes. Stabilisation measures usually must be introduced as packages, because their effectiveness depends on interactions. Moreover, stabilisation affects much of the population simultaneously and transparently (that is, in ways the affected groups think they understand, whether or not an economist would agree with the analysis). Structural changes, in contrast, generally unfold as a series of measures announced at different times and carried out on varying timetables, even where they are part of a broader pre-announced strategy. Moreover, the impact of specific structural reforms often is obvious and immediate only for particular groups rather than the broad public.

Persuasion and explanation, directed to the general public and to specific interest groups, can also prolong acquiescence and defuse opposition. The World Bank's most recent assessment of adjustment lending stresses the potential of persuasion, citing government efforts in Bolivia, Mexico, Korea, Ghana, and Thailand to explain the nature and timing of reforms and why they were necessary.[8] Persuasion and explanation are important even in authoritarian settings. For instance, in Chile the privatisation of pension funds and the revising of the labour code were both preceeded by months of explanation and discussion on radio and television. Explanations are more persuasive if there is an obvious crisis. Where ordinary people have not yet felt the repercussions of emerging economic difficulties, they may be quite sceptical of government explanations, as in Tunisia in 1983 where a long record of good growth and rumours of unexploited oil and gas reserves made government warnings of impending problems unconvincing.

Partial compensation is another option for managing opposition. Governments may want to use compensation to defuse potential opposition or to try to maintain coalition partners.[9] Those goals may be at odds with external agencies' pressures on governments to use compensatory or social safety net programmes to protect their poorer and more vulnerable citizens.[10] Sizable and well-administered pro-poor employment and feeding programmes like those in Chile and Costa Rica do help to soften criticism of the government on equity grounds. But the most potent political opposition is unlikely to come from the poorest and most vulnerable groups. The Bolivian Emergency Social Fund sought to serve both political and equity goals by offering special benefits for laid-off miners, plus a broad array of social projects. Recent assessments conclude that very few miners made use of ESF benefits, and many of those employed on ESF projects were not among the poorest.[11] Nevertheless there is a consensus that ESF was an important political asset for the government.

There are strong political pressures to expand the scope of compensatory programmes to reach urban working class and middle strata as well as the very poor and vulnerable. But such expansion increases costs and risks undercutting the objectives of the adjustment programme itself. Current debates regarding the design and scope of social safety net arrangements in Eastern Europe reflect this dilemma.

Social 'pacts' can be viewed as formally negotiated partial compensation in exchange for the promise of co-operation from unions or other interest groups or parties. Fairly stringent conditions are required if social pacts are to be effective. The unions or other societal groups must be sufficiently well-organised and disciplined to guide their own members' behaviour. They must further be persuaded not only that the government can deliver on its immediate promises but that the longer-run prospects warrant their binding their own freedom of action. That is, they must be convinced that the government's broader programme is on the right track, is likely to continue, and will offer their group future gains more than commensurate with current sacrifices. For its part, the government must be convinced the likely gains from the pact will outweigh the immediate costs. It is worth noting, for instance, that the Mexican government entered into a pact with many of the labour unions only as elections loomed a few months in the future.[12]

Reformist governments may need to use partial compensation to mollify interests within as well as outside of the bureaucracy. Reforms that drastically alter or reduce the role of government in economic activity pose multiple threats to government officials and workers. External financing conditioned on reforms usually offers nothing to counter such costs to the agencies and public officials affected by the reforms, although the aid may provide a strong incentive to the central economic officials and agencies responsible for the overall performance of the economy. A number of governments have provided generous severance packages including relocation assistance for workers laid off in the course of administrative reforms. Other types of losses within the bureaucracy are more difficult to compensate.

Governments seeking to neutralise opposition to structural adjustment can also seek to *weaken opposition groups directly*. Co-opting leaders, encouraging rival groups, and encouraging splits in established organisations are all well-recognised tactics. The de la Madrid government, for instance, pursued all three tactics in dealing with trade unions between 1982 and 1987.[13]

Finally, governments have the option of *repressing* opposition groups. Strong authoritarian governments are most prone to use repression, particularly against labour unions, student protests, and opposition parties. But elected governments have also resorted to fairly forceful measures, as for example Jayawardene's breaking of the attempted general strike in Sri Lanka in 1979 and Paz Estenssoro's handling of the Bolivian unions in 1985. The costs to democratic governments of repression are much lower if there is popular demand for strong leadership and economic management, and if the opposition groups involved are widely viewed as irresponsible.

Some of these short-run techniques of managing and containing opposition are intrinsically temporary. Disabled opposition groups are likely to pull themselves together, as did Manley's party in Jamaica after roughly three years of internal debate and restructuring. Persuasion becomes rapidly less effective in the absence of performance. Gratitude for single-shot compensatory measures will predictably fade. Other techniques of managing opposition are inherently costly. This is most obviously true of on-going compensation, and of repression. In democracies especially, while 'firm' handling (within legal limits) directed against particularly extreme or irresponsible groups is acceptable, especially in times viewed as national emergencies, frequent or continued repression is not a sustainable option.

In short, while skilful use of techniques for managing and neutralising the inevitable opposition is crucial for initiating reforms, the task is likely to become harder rather than easier unless support begins to emerge to counterbalance opposition. A clear lesson of the 1980s is that structural adjustment usually takes a long time, unless the initial structural defects were moderate and/or favourable exogenous factors boost recovery. How is reform sustained and consolidated?

CONSOLIDATING REFORM

A reform – that is, a set of new policies, including altered institutions and procedures – may be viewed as consolidated to the degree that it is unlikely to be reversed, dismantled, or eroded. It follows that consolidation is a state that can be approached but never fully achieved. Virtually any set of reforms is reversible under some circumstances. But in any specific case, some reforms can be identified as more consolidated than others. Reforms become consolidated as those groups and interests in a position to reverse or erode them become convinced that the reforms are desirable and should be preserved (or, more minimally, that the costs of trying to alter them are not worth the gains). The groups that have to be convinced vary with the specific reform: those in a position to challenge or erode a new labour code, for instance, are not the same groups in a position to undermine measures establishing an autonomous central bank.

There is no sharp boundary between the process of initiating reforms, and their consolidation. Ideally, the two processes run concurrently. Consolidation begins as implementation is launched, if and to the degree that some groups or interests view the new policies and arrangements as opportunities for gain. But as noted earlier, market-oriented reforms often create far more obvious and immediate self-perceived losers than gainers. That is particularly true if reforms are introduced in the midst of a depression, and implemented simultaneously with macro-economic austerity measures. Few reform measures have an instant constituency; most (if they succeed at all) develop supporters only gradually, as more and more groups come to have vested interests in the new arrangements.

The Process of Consolidation

Three separate elements are necessary for the political consolidation of reforms. The logical first step is the perception that the reforms are credible: that is, the belief that they will in fact be implemented, that they are likely to prove durable, and that they offer some potential for gain. The second step is the conversion of credibility into vested interest, as individuals, firms, or agencies alter their behaviour in accord with new incentives and opportunities and are able to improve their position as a result. The third necessary step is conversion of vested interest into effective political support for the reforms. Sometimes all three steps in the consolidation process occur almost simultaneously. More often they emerge as a sequence. Sometimes that sequence stretches over several years, perhaps even longer. To state the same point slightly differently, the second and third steps do not always follow automatically or easily from the first. The three steps merit a somewhat more detailed discussion, before turning to the ways in which they may play out for different categories of political actors.

Credibility is the prerequisite for reforms to elicit desired changes in the behaviour of economic actors. The credibility of a stabilisation and/or reform package, or of more specific measures, reflects three judgments on the part of the general public and specific interest groups. The government's programme must of course be perceived as both appropriately designed to address the particular economic difficulties, and feasible to implement. A long history of failed stabilisation and reform programmes, as in Argentina or Brazil, generates scepticism from the outset. That scepticism may well feed a cycle of negative self-fulfilling prophecies.

Credibility also reflects the judgment that the government's policies are durable, and not likely to be reversed. Price reforms, including devaluation and altered interest rates, are perhaps particularly open to questions about durability. Precisely because prices are relatively easy to change by centralised fiat, reforms can also be readily reversed. Moreover, even where they are not reversed they can be eroded by failure to pursue some more difficult measures, such as containing inflation. Measures requiring institutional and legal reform are harder to implement; here scepticism focusses on the chances that initial steps will not be followed by the further measures needed to bring about the desired results.

Credibility implies a third and less often discussed criterion: not only must adjustment measures be plausible and likely to endure, but they must hold the promise for key groups of a fair share of future benefits. That criterion is well-recognised as an element in restoring business confidence. Potential investors need to be assured not only that there are real and enduring prospects for profitable investment, but that they will not be deprived of those profits through excessive taxes, restricted convertibility, or other burdens. Analogous considerations apply to organised labour, other interest groups, and the general public. In successful adjustment cases, growing credibility and confidence prompt increasing economic activity responding to the programme's altered relative prices and institutional roles. Over time a growing range of groups and individuals (in the public as well as the private sectors) develop vested interests in the new arrangements. In the case of well-organised and politically active interest groups (such as export sectors in some cases), altered interests translate readily to political support for reforms already in place (though not necessarily for additional liberalising reforms, for instance, further import liberalisation). The translation from perceived vested interest to effective political support is less automatic in the cases of the general public and categories of winners not previously organised. In Ghana, for instance, cocoa producers are a sizable group that benefitted early and substantially from the far-reaching reforms launched in 1983. Yet the Rawlings government has not contrived mechanisms for translating economic gains among cocoa producers into political support, since most of the more obvious political arrangements for doing so run the risk of also mobilising the vocal and numerous urban groups that feel themselves to be relative losers from the reforms.

Complementing the process of creating credibility and eventual support from organised interests and the broader public is a second process that contributes to the consolidation of reforms: *the lowering of expectations*. This complementary process applies particularly to those groups that relied heavily on the regulations, subsidies, and trade protection that are the main targets of market-oriented reforms: firms surviving largely as a result of heavy subsidies and high trade barriers, or public and private sector workers with legally mandated wages and benefits many times the levels prevailing in the larger labour force.

Normally such groups will lower their expectations only when their economic losses are combined with reduced political salience. Retrenched public sector workers lose not only their jobs but their union connections: unless they protest promptly, they are not likely to comprise a coherent political force. In many cases even organised workers who keep their jobs (and union membership) are unlikely to regain their earlier wage growth trajectory, though their wages may gradually recover. If the prospects for effective protest are dim, they may simply come to accept their reduced circumstances. Similarly, in some cases the military may have to accept permanent reductions in force levels. Economic losses may be confirmed and perpetuated by institutional and legal changes reducing such groups' relative power, for instance through altering the constitutional position of the military or the legal rights of unions.[14]

A special type of lowered expectations is the recognition that apparently painless heterodox solutions will not work – although particular techniques such as temporary wage-price freezes may be helpful, under some circumstances, in combination with more conventional stabilisation and structural reforms.

It is useful to consider separately the tasks of building credibility and consolidating reforms as they apply to established interest groups and to the general public.

Building Credibility and Support Among Established Interest Groups

Sustained adjustment requires building credibility, vested interest, and eventually political acceptance or support for reforms among at least some major established interest groups, primarily business associations and labour unions and federations. The key role and the difficulties of restoring business confidence have been extensively studied. Business and manufacturing activities, of course, are heterogeneous and different lines of activity are affected very differently by market-oriented reforms. Some clearly benefit, some clearly lose, and others confront mixed effects from measures such as devaluation, import liberalisation, new export incentives, and deregulation of prices. Reduction or removal of direct and indirect subsidies is always painful; the groups that stand to gain often do not immediately perceive any benefits. Different business interests also have varying capacity to respond to changed incentives, depending on a host of factors such as their liquidity, their technical and commercial sophistication, and their access to infrastructure and a flexible labour force. In a few of the countries that carried out extensive liberalising reforms in the 1980s, important segments of the business community supported the reforms from the outset: Mexico provides one clear example. In others, business support emerged more gradually, but became increasingly important, as in Chile.

There are some fairly direct analogies between the requirements for restored investor confidence and labour union acquiesence or co-operation in adjustment. Workers are asked in the course of adjustment to sacrifice current gains (that is, to accept reduced real wages and benefits, and perhaps also to accept layoffs) for a share in future national benefits. Their at best reluctant acquiescence depends on their perceptions that the government programme can indeed restart growth, that it is likely to endure, and that labour will receive a fair share of benefits of future growth. Expected equity is particularly important since in many or most adjustment programmes workers bear a larger relative share of the costs of adjustment than do elite and upper middle-class groups whose assets are more mobile, and perhaps also than poorer groups that have been less well protected in the past.[15] The experience of some successful adjusters, such as Spain, suggests that both assurances of access and concern for equity, and acceptance of somewhat lowered expectations regarding wage levels and employment protection, may be necessary to gain union acquiescence or support for reforms.

Public sector workers' unions and civil service associations constitute a special problem. The co-operation or active collaboration of many government agencies is essential to effective adjustment. Yet government and parastatal agencies are targets of stabilisation and adjustment programmes. Trimming redundant personnel, increasing efficiency, and privatisation all constitute direct threats. Reducing state economic regulation not only destroys opportunities for rent-seeking, but also challenges long-standing functions and programmes to which some civil servants feel a genuine commitment. On the more positive side, effective reforms may bring higher wages for some civil servants. (Compressed salary schedules and ridiculously low compensation for higher level personnel are major problems in many countries, especially in Africa.) And morale – often shredded by years of inadequate wages, materials, and guidance – may sometimes improve with trimmed work forces and altered programme mandates, especially if these are part of a broader recovery programme. Despite such potential gains, the task of building credibility and support for adjustment within the state machinery itself constitutes a particularly urgent and difficult challenge.

SUSTAINING CREDIBILITY AMONG THE GENERAL PUBLIC

The reform syndrome suggests that prolonged economic stagnation or decline can create a broad public perception that radical reforms are necessary to restart growth – without necessarily implying any general consensus on the exact nature of the reforms required. High inflation (above all, hyperinflation) is particularly likely to prompt strong public desire for firm economic management, as in Bolivia in 1985. Even where earlier economic performance has been good, a sharp and sudden deterioration creates public acceptance of tough emergency measures, as in Costa Rica in 1982–3.

However, continued public acquiescence depends on visible improvements in the economy. Moreover, those improvements must be reflected in at least modest improvements in conditions affecting ordinary people: employment, prices and availability of consumer goods, quantity and quality of public services. Reductions in arrears or narrowed fiscal deficits *per se* are not likely to be reassuring (though well-publicised increases in debt are often alarming to public opinion).

Ironically, perceptible improvements may or may not translate into acceptance or support for further reforms. In Costa Rica, the impressive turnaround during the first eighteen months of the Monge government reassured the public that the emergency was over. Popular opinion shifted to a demand for the rapid restoration of pre-crisis real wages and living standards, complicating reformers' efforts to continue prudent macro-economic management and push through structural reforms. The initial benefits of stabilisation in Argentina in 1985–6 led to complacency that reduced support for a firm attack on the budget deficit. In Bolivia, in contrast, the dramatic halting of hyperinflation strengthened diffuse public support for Paz Estensoro's reform package, to the point that all contending presidential candidates in the 1989 elections pledged to continue the programme. (The extent of real commitment on the part of parties and candidates was of course a separate question.) Improved economic performance can be read two ways: as evidence that the difficulties have been overcome and further sacrifice is not necessary, or as evidence that the government is on the right track and merits support in its further efforts. The depth and duration of previous difficulties may largely determine which interpretation prevails.

The requirements for sustained credibility among the general public highlight two areas of considerable concern to the international development community. The first issue is the adequacy of current adjustment prescriptions and financing to restart growth in varied country circumstances. The second is the importance of attention to distributive issues in the course of adjustment. Both issues are of course receiving on-going attention. But continued negative resource flows and deep doubts (especially in the least developed countries) regarding many aspects of market-oriented approaches suggest that the financing issue cannot be regarded as settled. Nor, despite the proliferation of 'social dimensions of adjustment' projects, can equity concerns be viewed as well addressed. Indeed, there is tension between current emphasis in international circles on poverty reduction, and political demands in Latin America and Africa for relief for the urban middle strata which have been particularly hard-hit by depression and adjustment. Adjustment programmes that are credible in the view of the politically potent popular classes may also need to include plausible evidence that elites are bearing their share of the burden. The corrosive anger feeding popular opposition to continued adjustment in many developing countries flows partly from the perception (probably at least partly accurate) that some or much of the elite have escaped the costs, or have even benefitted, from their nations' economic difficulties.

ADMINISTRATIVE AND POLITICAL INSTITUTIONS AND CONSOLIDATION OF REFORMS

By the beginning of the 1990s, the links between administrative and political institutions and processes, on the one hand, and effective economic reform, on the other, were drawing mounting interest in developing nations themselves and in the international development community. In many Latin American nations, the merits of parliamentary versus presidential systems are being actively debated, and decentralisation of some government activities to provincial and local governments is also under consideration or in train. In much of sub-Saharan Africa the issue of better governance, embracing both administrative and political reform, has suddenly emerged as a crucial element for breaking the economic stagnation that grips much of the continent. In Eastern Europe, of course, political reform is viewed as inextricably entangled with economic restructuring. Yet we know very little about the ways in which political institutions shape the initiation and consolidation of economic reforms. Through the 1980s, most analysts of the politics of adjustment focussed on societal forces – that is, the array of interests opposed to or favouring reforms – and on the tactics governments can use to cope with interest group pressures. Institutional factors – the effects of political and administrative institutions and procedures on political behaviour and on governments' options – were largely neglected. The impact of regime type did indeed receive considerable attention starting in the late 1970s. These studies yielded a fairly clear conclusion: classifying governments into broad categories of democracies and authoritarian systems tells us little about capacity to adjust. Both categories of regimes include examples of effective adjustment and of total failure. Yet it is clear that finer-grained institutional variables, including some associated with and others cutting across regime type, do shape and channel the influence of pressure groups and the political dynamics of adjustment.[16]

Consider, for example, the credibility of reforms. One element affecting credibility is the expectation that reforms will actually be implemented. Such expectations of course are shaped by the overall competence and morale of the civil service. They are also affected by the degree to which central economic authorities in fact exercise control over key variables: for instance, the degree to which the Ministry of Finance has authority over (or even information regarding) the borrowing and expenditures of parastatal agencies.

While concentrated and unencumbered executive discretion is often crucial in facilitating *initiation* of adjustment measures, confidence in the *continuity* of certain reforms (especially regarding prices, exchange rates, and interest rates) may hinge on the relinquishing of executive discretion, the insulation of technical agencies and the delegation of authority from political leaders to impersonal and apolitical agencies and procedures.

For example, a major devaluation calls for bold political initiative. But confidence that exchange rates will be managed thereafter so as to prevent recurrent overvaluation may be bolstered by delegating responsibility for exchange rate management to an agency and procedure governed by apolitical rules: a formula for frequent automatic adjustment, an exchange auction, or some similar mechanism. Similarly, strong central leadership usually is needed to shrink an unsustainable fiscal deficit. But sustained fiscal prudence may well require much greater authority for a technical budget agency with control over wayward ministries and decentralised agencies, and protection from ministerial and legislative demands. Paz Estenssoro put in place a particularly transparent and simplistic version of a mechanism to bind politicians' hands (including his own): the requirement that no expenditure be committed without a corresponding revenue increase. The degree of Central Bank autonomy is well recognised as a key element in prudent and consistent management of monetary policy.

While insulation and delegation of control over such core economic management functions is often seen as conflicting to some extent with responsive and accountable economic policy, these features can play a major role in expectations of predictability and durability of reforms.

Expectations about equity are also affected by specific arrangements for managing aspects of economic policy, and may require not so much the delegation as the *sharing* of executive authority. Consultative arrangements, tripartite wage and price boards, and other devices can help to reassure unions and business associations alike that their concerns and interests will be heard in the course of designing new policies and implementing old ones.

Broader political structure as well as executive branch institutions enter into calculations regarding the durability of reforms. Frequent elections, a one-term limit for the chief executive, and weak control by the executive over the legislature all can prompt scepticism about durability.

The structure of the party system also enters into expectations regarding both the durability and the equity of economic policy. A two-party system where both major parties incorporate a broad cross-section of the population usually tends toward moderation, encouraging both parties to look for support not at the extremes of the political spectrum but toward the centre. Interest groups within each party are under pressure to bargain with other groups and modify their own positions in the interests of a coherent platform and an electoral majority. The effect is to narrow the gap between the platforms of different parties and encourage confidence in broad continuity of policy lines, even if the government should change hands. In contrast, where major parties are largely based on non-overlapping, antagonistic constituencies (whether class, ethnicity, region, or ideology is the base), interest groups worry that today's policies will be sharply reversed by tomorrow's new government.[17]

Institutional arrangements, in short, play major roles in encouraging or undermining expectations about the durability and equity, and therefore the credibility of structural adjustment measures. They also strongly influence the third main stage of consolidating reforms: the translation of new vested economic interests into altered patterns of political support. Again, both formal legal and bureaucratic arrangements and political processes and institutions are relevant. The formation of new interest groups, and the re-orienting of old ones, are affected by the laws and regulations governing the formation and activities of business, labour, and other associations. The channels and nature of relations between interest groups and parties, legislatures, and government agencies will also shape the political expression of new vested interests created by reforms. While appropriate institutions can facilitate economic reform, successful adjustment can in turn legitimise and strengthen those same institutions. Semi-autonomous budget agencies, autonomous central banks, or depoliticised exchange rate adjustment mechanisms can come to be valued by a range of interest groups as institutions promoting their long-run interests, even when today's specific decisions are disadvantageous. Similarly, on the broader political scene, the structure of parties associated with long-term good performance comes to be valued even by the losers in the last election. Reforms are truly consolidated when they are embedded both in the perceived interests of a range of social groups and in institutional arrangements for on-going implementation.

CONCLUDING NOTES

What are the implications of these observations for the growing number of countries simultaneously seeking more democratic political arrangements and market-oriented economic reforms? If initiating adjustment is indeed greatly facilitated by highly concentrated executive authority, this poses special challenges for new democracies. There is an inherent tension between the centralised and unencumbered executive authority required to initiate painful economic reforms, and growing demands for more decentralised and participatory forms of decision-making and governance. When indices of fiscal performance and management of central bank credit are compared across twenty-five countries, including established democracies, established authoritarian governments, and governments in transition to democracy, the transitional governments performed notably less well than the two types of established regimes.[18]

Where democracy is accompanied by intense popular desire for far-reaching economic reform, there may be a period of popular acquiescence in rapid, centrally-directed reform. But that grace period will predictably be brief. Both popular groups and decision-makers will then confront a series of challenges: are they prepared to cede aspects of economic management to insulated technocratic agencies, relying on elections to periodically reassert popular control? Can confidence-building participatory mechanisms be created to honour yet channel demands for equity? The record thus far points to severe tensions between the political requirements for initiating reform, and those required for sustaining democratic processes.[19] The 1990s will test these issues in a growing number of countries.

More generally, countries in process of economic adjustment and those advising and supporting them may need to give more attention to the requisites not only of launching but of sustaining and consolidating reforms. At a minimum, donors need to be sensitive to the changing dynamics of the politics of reform, as governments move from initiation into consolidation phases. That shift may affect the selection and design of conditions attached to aid, and perhaps also the balance between conditions and other techniques of external influence and support for reform. Donors are also likely to focus more attention on the institutional prerequisites for consolidating economic reform, as signalled by the newly energetic discussions on governance in both the World Bank and bilateral donor agencies.

These tentative observations also have implications for the focus of future research on the politics of economic reform. It is time to move away from the preoccupations of the 1980s with stabilisation rather than structural changes, and with initiation rather than consolidation of reforms. There are now many cases of countries with considerable track records that are still in the midst of adjustment efforts: Turkey, Ghana, Jamaica, Mexico, Madagascar, Morocco, and Senegal are only a partial list. We need to examine more closely the changing positions and roles of various groups, the evolving tactics used by governments, and the roles of administrative and political institutions in facilitating or hampering the consolidation of reform.

NOTES

1. The contrast between 'orthodox' and 'heterodox' approaches has become less germane as the parameters of debate on policy options narrowed during the 1980s. Compared to the range of views in 1980, there is now much greater consensus on the importance of monetary and fiscal discipline and realistic exchange and interest rates. Moreover, few governments remain convinced of the value of detailed regulation and direct production by the state, nor of import-substitution as an engine of development. A more useful current shorthand label characterising the content of policy choice might be stronger or weaker orientation towards

private markets and an open economy – issues on which there remains considerable disagreement despite the narrowed parameters of debate.

2. Our case studies and comparative analysis of these issues appear in Joan M. Nelson (ed.), *Economic Crisis and Policy Choice: The Politics of Adjustment in the Third World* (Princeton, NJ: Princeton University Press, 1990).
3. Joan M. Nelson and contributors, *Fragile Coalitions: The Politics of Economic Adjustment* (New Brunswick, NY: Overseas Development Council Policy Perspectives Series 12 Transaction Press, 1989).
4. The discussion here builds on Stephan Haggard and Robert Kaufman's 'Introduction: Institutions and Economic Adjustment', forthcoming in Haggard and Kaufman (eds), *The Politics of Economic Adjustment: International Constraints, Distributive Politics, and the State* (Princeton, NJ, Princeton University Press, forthcoming 1992).
5. James M. Malloy, 'Democracy, Economic Crisis and the Problem of Governance: The Case of Bolivia', unpublished manuscript, University of Pittsburgh, August 1989, p. 21.
6. Malloy, 'Democracy . . .', pp. 20–3.
7. For a more detailed discussion along these lines, see John Waterbury, 'The Political Management of Economic Adjustment and Reform', in Nelson, *Fragile Coalitions*, pp. 39–56; also Laurence Whitehead, 'Democratization and Disinflation: A Comparative Approach', in the same volume, pp. 79–93.
8. World Bank, Country Economics Department, *Adjustment Lending Policies for Sustainable Growth* (Washington DC, World Bank Policy and Research Series No. 14, March 1990) p. 58.
9. For discussions of the potential uses of compensation, see Waterbury, 'Political Management . . .'; Paul Mosley, Jane Harrigan, and John Toye, *Aid and Power: The World Bank and Policy-Based Lending in the 1980s* (London: Routledge, 1991) especially Chapter 9.
10. This point is developed at greater length in Joan M. Nelson, 'The Politics of Pro-Poor Adjustment', in Nelson et. al., *Fragile Coalitions*, pp. 95–113.
11. John Newman, Steen Jorgensen, and Menno Pradhan, 'How Did Workers Benefit from Bolivia's Emergency Social Fund?', World Bank draft staff study, November 1989.
12. For a discussion of the role of organised labor and attempts at social pacts in Brazil, Argentina, and Mexico see Ian Roxborough, 'Organized Labor: A Major Victim of the Debt Crisis', pp. 91–108 in Barbara Stallings and Robert Kaufman (eds), *Debt and Democracy in Latin America*, (Boulder, Colorado: Westview, 1989).
13. Kevin Middlebrook, 'The Sounds of Silence: Organized Labour's Response to Economic Crisis in Mexico', *Journal of Latin American Studies* 21, 1989, pp. 195–220.
14. Laurence Whitehead has argued recently that lowered expectations must play a major role in Latin America in order to simultaneously sustain democratic openings and economic reforms. (Paper prepared for the Inter-American Dialogue meeting, June 1990).

15. On decreased labour shares, see M. Pastor, Jr., 'The Effects of IMF Programs in the Third World: Debate and Evidence from Latin America', *World Development*, 15, 2, February 1987, pp. 254, 258; World Bank, *Turkey Economic Memorandum: Towards Sustainable Growth* (Washington, D.C., 12 October 1988), citing Ozmucur, 'National Income Estimates by Quarters, in Dollar Terms and by Income Types' (Istanbul Chamber of Commerce, 1987).

16. The effects of political business cycles on economic policies have been extensively studied in industrial democracies. But that line of research thus far has produced somewhat conflicting results; moreover, the findings would probably have to be modified considerably to make sense in the context of most developing nations.

17. The effects of party systems and their interaction with underlying political cleavages comprise one major theme of Stephan Haggard and Robert Kaufman's discussion of 'The Political Economy of Inflation and Stabilization in Middle-Income Countries', in Haggard and Kaufman, *The Politics of Economic Adjustment* . . (forthcoming).

18. Stephan Haggard and Robert Kaufman, 'Economic Adjustment in New Democracies', in Nelson and contributors, *Fragile Coalitions*, pp. 57–77.

19. For a vivid discussion of these tensions, see Adam Przeworski, 'The Political Economy of Adjustment', unpublished manuscript, 1990.

7 A Theory of Conditionality

Paul Mosley

DEFINITION OF THE PROBLEM

Since the establishment of a new international economic order at the Bretton Woods conference in 1944, conditionality – that is, the linking of the disbursement of a loan to understandings concerning the economic policy which the government of the borrower country intends to pursue – has been an important component of the mechanism by which international financial institutions attempt to regulate the behaviour of the world economy. Since its foundation the International Monetary Fund (IMF) has attached policy conditions to its stand-by loans, usually involving restriction of public expenditure and domestic credit expansion (Killick, 1984; Williamson, 1983); more recently, from the early 1980s onward, both the World Bank and bilateral donors have committed an increasing proportion of their resources to 'policy-based loans' which are conditional on policy measures intended to build up the supply side of recipient economies. Over 70 per cent of the IMF's lending, at least 30 per cent of the World Bank's, and about 25 per cent of total OECD bilateral aid spending – some $20 billion annually – is devoted to conditional financial loan transfers (OECD, 1991).

These loans all share certain common features (Mosley, 1987: Mosley, Harrigan and Toye, 1991):

(1) no collateral is demanded by the lender;
(2) ostensibly as a substitute for collateral, the lender imposes policy conditions designed to increase the probability of repayment;
(3) the implementation of these conditions – usually involving the removal of a protective shield against market forces such as exchange controls, import licensing, price controls or food subsidies – will have political costs for the recipient government, which naturally has an incentive to escape implementation of

those conditions which are burdensome. This is often feasible, for reasons discussed below, and the decision to implement conditions, like the decision to repay a loan, is therefore subject to moral hazard;

(4) in principle lenders can punish breach of conditionality by refusal of further credit. In practice, as we shall see, they have good reason not always to do so, and do not always do so.

Given the increasing reliance by lenders on conditionality as an instrument for increasing the effectiveness of financial transactions and the suspicion that, because of (3) and (4) above, this may not be an easy thing to do, some analysis of the conditions under which donors and recipients may expect to extract advantage from involvement in such transactions would appear long overdue.

In this chapter I attempt to fill the gap by presenting a simple bargaining model of the conditionality process in the first section. In this model the relationship between borrower and lender is presented as a two-person game; the empirical findings are presented in the following section. It emerges from my analysis that a key element in any solution to the game is the outcome of an internal conflict *within* one of the players (the borrower) between winners and losers from the implementation of conditionality. This conflict is explicitly discussed in the concluding section. My conclusions at this interim stage of the research are that:

(1) some slippage is to be expected on any conditional loan contract, given the donor's need to disburse; the optimal degree of slippage, from the recipient's point of view, depends on when it expects to make an exit from the conditionality relationship;
(2) from the donor's point of view, random punishment of slippage, as a threat strategy, dominates 'punishment according to the size of the crime'.

SIMPLE (TWO-PERSON GAME) FORMULATION

I begin by considering the objectives of lender[1] and recipient. The recipient government has a financial motive to maximise the inflow of finance in support of its balance of payments, and a political motive, as discussed earlier, to resist at least some elements of conditionality. There are, of course, gainers from the reform measures imposed as part of a conditionality package – if there were not, the argument for conditionality would fall at the first fence – but it is our contention that these gains, first of all, accrue to the politically weak rather than the strong – for example, small farmers, importers who lack licences – and second, accrue over the long period rather than the short. The recipient's utility function is therefore

(1) $U_j = f(t, x)$; $f_t < 0$, $f_x > 0$

where j = recipient subscript, t = tightness and number of conditions imposed, x = value of lending. The greater the cost of the political conditions with which the recipient expects to have to comply, the steeper the trade-off between the political costs and financial benefits of receiving conditional finance.

I now consider the motivation of the lender. As a first approximation we may suppose that he will try and extract as much policy reform as he can from a given recipient over a given time period. There are various reasons for supposing this: at the technical level, if government-imposed price distortions are thought to be the major barrier to growth in developing countries, then the more distortions the lender is able to buy out in a given operation, the more successful the operation; and at the level of staff motivation, the more policy-reform conditions a country loan officer is able to negotiate as part of a particular loan agreement, the more impressed his superiors in operational departments of the lending institution are likely to be.

There does exist a constraint on the enforcement of conditionality: which is that a financial institution, whether a quasi-commercial operation such as the World Bank, a revolving fund such as the IMF, or a bilateral agency such as USAID or ODA, needs to spend its budget if it is to maintain its viability. For a bilateral aid agency, the penalty for failing to do this is simply gradual attrition, since the aid agency's inability to spend its budget in a given financial year will weaken its ability to bid for funds from the finance ministry the following year in competition with other government agencies (Wildavsky, 1964; Heclo and Wildavsky, 1974). For a commercial operation such as the IMF or the 'hard windows' of the World Bank and regional development banks the penalty is more immediate, since very many potential borrowers from these institutions are debt-distressed countries who are at risk of defaulting on their obligations to the World Bank and IMF themselves, as well as to commercial banks,[2] and if disbursement of a programme loan is held up because the recipient has failed to implement policy conditions attached to that loan, it may not be able to maintain repayments on that and its other borrowings. In this sense, although the *imposition* of conditionality is intended to be a substitute for collateral, its *enforcement* may have the opposite effect of making loans harder and not easier to repay, and the lender may have to choose between enforcement of the commitment to implement policy conditions attached to a loan and enforcement of the commitment to repay the loan itself, a problem which we describe as the *disbursement dilemma*. In consequence of this conflict between lending and leverage the lender's utility function will be of the form:

$$(2) \quad U_i = g\,(t, x); \, g_t > 0, \, g_x > 0$$

The lender and the recipient, then, have conflicting interests concerning the implementation of conditions and a common interest in spending the donor's budget. The bargaining range within the first stage of the game – the stage at which policy-based lending agreements are concluded – is defined by those possible outcomes which are Pareto-optimal in the sense that they cannot make the donor happier without hurting the recipient, or vice versa. If for the moment we work on the simplifying assumption that the donor begins with a fixed and unalterable planning allocation for programme lending to each recipient country, the possible outcomes all lie between points T_i and T_j on Figure 7.1: that is, the level of programme lending to each country is predetermined by the budget ceiling, and all that is left to argue about is the political price – in terms of conditions implemented – which the recipient must pay.

Before examining what the outcome within this bargaining range is likely to be, it is necessary to consider the likely future course of the game and the information available to the participants, as these will determine the strategy which each player is likely to pursue. For logical simplicity, the conditionality game can be divided into three periods or 'acts':

(1) An initial negotiating process (Act 1) in which lender and recipient try to agree on the conditions that are to be attached to a development loan, as depicted in Figure 7.1. This process culminates in agreement on a set of specific policy actions, some of which may have to be undertaken before the first disbursement is made.

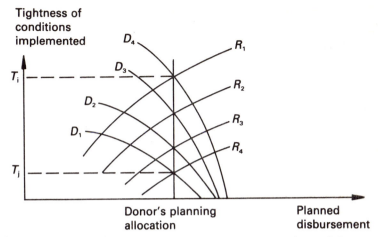

FIGURE 7.1 *Relationship between donor and recipient utility and the bargaining range for 'Act 1'*

(2) An implementation process in which the recipient decides how far to honour the promises it has made during Act 1.

(3) A response by the donor in the following period consisting of a decision to grant or refuse further finance to the recipient in the light of the recipient's performance during Act 2.

If the lender's Act 3 response is positive, there will be subsequent acts to the play – i.e. follow-up loans – but they will have the same logical structure as Acts 2 and 3.

The possible moves which donor and recipient can make are set out in the game tree of Figure 7.2. By the end of Act 1 four outcomes are possible: breakdown of negotiations as the result of an unsuccessful ultimatum by either party, settlement on the recipient's terms (T_j), settlement on the lender's terms (T_i), or something intermediate between the last two possibilities. If one of the last two cases materialises, the recipient may attempt during Act 2 to escape from the political costs which compliance with a 'coercive' deal would impose by failing to implement part or all of the agreed package, balancing these prospective costs against the possible costs of failing to secure repeat finance if the lender decides to punish him for his delinquency by refusing it. In Act 3, the donor must decide, if there has been any slippage on the Act 1 deal, whether to punish or not. This yields, by the end of Act 3, eight possible outcomes, of which empirical examples (for the case of World Bank lending in the 1980s) are cited at the

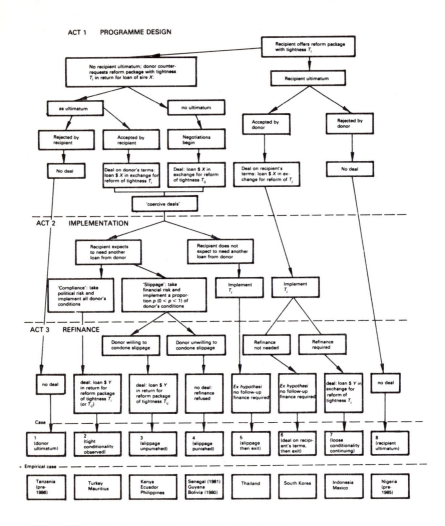

FIGURE 7.2   *The 'tree' of the conditionality 'game'*

bottom of Figure 7.2. Of these eight outcomes, five offer little or no scope for the exercise of strategy by donor or recipient. In cases 1 and 8 a donor or recipient ultimatum, respectively, is rejected by the other party and negotiations break down; but this will be irrational unless they are motivated, respectively, purely by the desire to impose or escape conditions, in other words if loan disbursement has no weight in the utility function. In cases 6 and 7 the donor agrees to disburse a loan on the recipient's terms because his desire to lend overrides his desire to enforce conditionality. In case 5 there is a negotiating process surrounding the determination of conditionality in Act 1, but no mystery surrounding the ultimate outcome since the recipient, by hypothesis, does not expect to need a loan in Act 3 and therefore has no motive to comply with any externally imposed conditions (i.e. conditions in excess of T_j) in Act 2, since to do so imposes political costs which offset the benefit of the loan, and not to do so does not. His optimal strategy is therefore to accept whatever conditions the donor proposed in Act 1, and then in Act 2 to comply only with those conditions which formed part of his original intention, i.e. T_j. This leaves us with cases 2, 3 and 4, in which the donor attempts to exert 'leverage' by extracting from the recipient a set of reforms in excess of those which he would have spontaneously carried out. If such leverage is attempted, the recipient must decide in Act 2 how much of it to accept, and if this is less than the amount agreed the donor must subsequently decide in Act 3 whether and how to punish such 'slippage' by restricting the supply of further finance. Let us now consider the strategies which it may be sensible for each party to pursue in this context.

Let us adopt the notation:

α = subjective utility attached by donor to one extra unit of tightness negotiated with recipient (i.e. if $\alpha = 1$, one extra condition imposed on the recipient adds one unit to the donor's utility)
β = subjective (dis)utility attached by recipient to one extra unit of tightness negotiated by donor (i.e. if $\beta = -2$, one extra condition imposed on the recipient subtracts two units from the recipient's utility)
p = percentage of agreed Act 1 conditions implemented by recipient in Act 2
X = value of finance granted in Act 1

136   *The Politics of Conditional Lending*

Y = value of finance (if any) granted in Act 3
T_{ij} = tightness of package of conditions agreed at end of Act 1

Using this notation the payoffs to be expected by donor and recipient in Acts 2 and 3, depending on the recipient's compliance in Act 2 and the donor's response in Act 3, are as set out in Table 7.1. This is a prisoner's dilemma: donor and recipient are both better off in Act 2 and Act 3 under 'co-operative behaviour' (outcome 2) than in the 'conflict situation' (outcome 4), but for the recipient 'exploitative behaviour' (outcome 3), if it can be got away with, dominates 'cooperative behaviour'. Since the payoff to him from such behaviour is greater in both Act 2 and Act 3, the outcome of the game thus turns on whether such behaviour can be got away with; in other words, on the donor's punishment strategy in Act 3, and the recipient's subjective expectation of such punishment during Act 2. The prisoner's dilemma is asymmetric, since although the recipient has an incentive to exploit the lender in this way, the lender has no incentive to exploit the recipient by breaking off the financial relationship so long as the recipient complies with the conditions.

We now consider the determination of three components of the donor's and recipient's strategies: (1), the initial Act 1 agreement, T_{ij}; (2) the recipient's Act 2 slippage, p; and (3) the punishment imposed by the donor in Act 3, in the sense of the likelihood that any slippage by the recipient in Act 2 will be followed by a refusal by the donor to grant refinance in Act 3. These must be considered in reverse order, because the utility derived by each party from a deal T_{ij} in Act 1 will be determined by awareness that there may be slippage (p) on that deal in Act 2, the likelihood of which is determined by the nature of the donor's punishment in Act 3, which will depend on the costs (to each party) of punishment in relation to its returns, which will depend, finally, on the relationship between observance of conditionality and loan repayment.

The conventional Nash equilibrium solution for the Act 1 bargain, T_{ij}, is the point which satisfies the requirement

(3) $T_{ij}^* = \max (U_i [T_{ij}] - C_i) (U_j [T_{ij}] - C_j))$

where c_i, c_j are the 'conflict points', i.e. in this case the utilities derived by donor and recipient from the situation in which no deal is done. Let $C_i = C_j = 0$, by arbitrary choice of units. And from our previous argument:

TABLE 7.1 Cases 2, 3 and 4 of the game tree: donor and recipient pay-offs

Donor strategies		
Recipient strategies	Offer refinance in Act 3	Do not offer refinance in Act 3
(Outcome 2) Total compliance in Act 2	Donor: $\{X + \alpha T_{ij}$ (Act 2) $\{Y + \alpha T_{ij}$ (Act 3)	
	Recipient: $\{X - \beta T_{ij}$ (Act 2) $\{Y - \beta T_{ij}$ (Act 3)	
(Outcome 3) Partial or zero compliance in Act 2	Donor: $\{X + \alpha p (T_{ij} - T_j)$ (Act 2) $\{Y + \alpha p (T_{ij} - T_j)$ (Act 3)	(Outcome 4) Donor: $\{X + \alpha p (T_{ij} + T_j)$ (Act 2) $\{0$ (Act 3)
	Recipient: $\{X - \beta p (T_{ij} - T_j)$ (Act 2) $\{Y - \beta p (T_{ij} - T_j)$ (Act 3)	Recipient: $\{X - \beta p (T_{ij} - T_j)$ (Act 2) $\{0$ (Act 3)

(3a) $U_i (T_{ij}) = (1 - \pi) \{(X + \alpha T_{ij}) + \dfrac{1}{1 + r} (Y + \alpha T_{ij})$

$+ \pi \{ \gamma (X + \alpha p (T_{ij}^* - T_j) + \dfrac{1}{1 + r}$

$(Y + \alpha p) (T_{ij}^* - T_j)$

$+ (1 - \gamma) (X + \alpha_p (T_{ij}^* - T_j))\}$

and (3b) $U_j (T_{ij}) = (1 - \pi) \{(X - \beta T_{ij}) + \dfrac{1}{1 + r} (Y - \beta T_{ij})$

$+ (1 - \pi) \{ \gamma (X - \beta p(T_{ij}^* - T_i) + \dfrac{1}{1 + r}$

$(Y - \beta p) (T_{ij}^* - T_i)$

$+ (1 - \gamma) (X - \beta p (T_{ij}^* - T_j))\}$

where π = probability that recipient commits slippage during Act 2
  p = level of recipient's slippage during Act 2
  r = discount rate between Act 2 and Act 3
  γ = probability that donor will grant follow-on finance during Act 3
    as foreseen at the beginning of Act 1.

Hence the solution value of T_{ij}^*, for Act 1 is the value which satisfies

(4) $(1 - \pi) \{X + \alpha T_{ij} + \dfrac{1}{1 + r} (X + \alpha T_{ij}) + \pi$

$[\gamma ((X + \alpha_p (T_{ij}^* - T_j) + \dfrac{1}{(1 + r)} (Y + \alpha_p) (T_{ij}^* - T_j))$

$+ (1 - \gamma) ((X + \alpha_p (T_{ij}^* - T_j))]\}.$

$(1 - \pi) \{X - \beta T_{ij} + \dfrac{1}{1 + r} (Y - \beta T_{ij}) + (1 - \pi)$

$$[\gamma \, ((X + \beta_p \, (T_{ij}^* - T_i) + \frac{1}{(1+r)} \, (Y + \beta_p) \, (T_{ij}^* - T_i))$$

$$+ \, (1 - \gamma) \, ((X - \beta_p \, (T_{ij}^* - T_j))]\} = \text{maximum}$$

The tightness of the deal done at the beginning of Act 1, in other words, will be influenced by the shape of the donor's and recipient's preference functions α and β; the probability and extent of expected slippage π and p; and the nature of expected punishment $(1 - \gamma)$, the severity of which, as shown in the Appendix, is likely to be responsive to the recipient's debt-service ratio. This contract is, of course, incomplete: some slippage in Act 2 is foreseen by the donor, but the actual level may depart from this in the light of the recipient's calculations. We now consider these calculations.

In Act 2, the recipient's decision concerning the level of slippage (p) will reflect his assessment of the risks of, and disutilities attached to, future punishment of such slippage in Act 3. In terms of the notation of Table 7.1 these are as shown in Table 7.2. If the probability of punishment, as foreseen by the recipient in Act 2, is $(1 - \gamma)$, then the payoff, as noted in Table 7.1, is

(5a) $Y - \beta \, T_{ij}^*$ if there is no slippage

and

(5b) $\gamma \, (Y - \beta p \, (T_{ij}^* - T_j))$ if there is slippage.

If therefore $\beta((1 - p) \, T_{ij}^* - T_j) > (1 - \gamma) \, Y$, that is to say the avoided utility costs of coercion under slippage exceed the costs

TABLE 7.2   *Payoff to recipient from different Act 2 outcomes*

Recipient strategy \ Donor strategy	Offer refinance in Act 3	Do not offer refinance in Act 3
No slippage on conditions	$Y - \beta T_{ij}^*$	
Some slippage on conditions	$Y - \beta_p(T_{ij}^* - T_j)$	0

associated with the risk of losing refinance, there are gains from slippage. The likelihood of these will depend on the extent of such slippage p, the weight attached to the political gains from slippage β and the expected probability of refinance γ. As the subjective likelihood of refinance γ goes toward one (that is the borrower discounts the possibility of punishment) so slippage becomes more attractive. At this stage we treat the cost to the recipient government of complying with the donor's conditions, β, as an exogenous parameter. In reality it will reflect the outcome of a further game between gainers and losers from reform within the recipient's political economy: recipients do not resist conditionality, any more than donors impose it, for its own sake, but rather in order to attain specific economic and political objectives including survival in power, a measure of economic autonomy, and economic development. But I will postpone consideration of this internal game until later in the chapter.

We now move forward to Act 3, and consider the behaviour of the donor in granting or refusing follow-up finance. In the Appendix below I demonstrate that the probability of loan repayment may plausibly be expected to respond to punishment, $(1 - \gamma)$ according to the formula:

$$(6) \quad q = \text{constant} + (be - d \, (DSR) \, (1 - \gamma)$$

where   q = probability of repayment, b, e, d = fixed parameters, of which d depends on the recipient's debt service ratio. Beyond the threshold value of the debt service ratio for which be = d an increase in punishment is counter-productive as it increases the probability that the recipient will default on his current and existing debt to the lender.

We may now consider three possible approaches to punishment in Act 3.

7(a) 'Punishment to suit the crime': the probability of repeat finance in Act 3 depends only on the level of recipient slippage in Act 2, i.e. $Y_{j(3)} = \gamma_1 p_{j(2)}$

7(b) 'Random punishment': the donor uses a random process to punish a fixed proportion $(1 - \gamma_2)$ of those recipients whose Act 2 slippage exceeds a certain threshold amount; the size of the fixed proportion will reflect the weight which the donor places on his disbursement objective, i.e. α.

7(c) Punishment to suit the crime, but with ability to repay debt being accepted as a plea in mitigation, i.e.

$Y_{j\,(3)} = \gamma_3 p_{j\,(3)} + \delta$ (DSR).

Let us first consider the relationship between 7(a) and 7(b). From examination of Table 7.1 it will be clear that the donor's expected utility from its entire lending portfolio will be

$$\gamma_1 \sum_{j=1}^{n} (Y + \alpha p\,(T_{ij} - T_j)$$

in the case of strategy 7(a). Let the 'punishment threshold' for strategy 7(b) be set such that $\gamma_2 = \gamma_1$; in this event, the utility to be derived from each of these strategies in the first round is equal. However, this does not tell the full story, since the donor will wish to use his threat strategy not only to punish past slippage but also to discourage it in the future. It will be apparent from Table 7.3a below that the World Bank has never refused follow-on finance to countries whose slippage levels fall below 50 per cent; it has sometimes, indeed, pardoned higher levels. Recipient countries, observing this behaviour, are likely to infer that they will always get away with a slippage level of up to 50 per cent on future loans; if the donor is to discourage such an assumption, he must punish some recipients with slippage below this level.

In other words, if one imagines two donors, one of whom applies strategy 7(a) in the first period and the other of whom applies strategy, 7(b), and for whom $\gamma_1 = \gamma_2$, such that their utility is equivalent in that period, the second loan will suffer an *increase* in delinquency rates on conditions (p) in the next period as recipients observe that they can get away with any level of delinquency below the threshold, whereas the first donor will not, since by hypothesis he punishes all delinquency at whatever level with probability $(1 - \gamma_2)$. Hence for a *forward looking* donor strategy 7(b) ('random punishment') is a more effective means of reconciling the objectives of disbursement and enforcement of conditionality than strategy 7(a) ('punishment to fit the crime').

We now consider strategy 7(c). Under this strategy the lender observes that for a debt service ratio in excess of some critical value (which is 40 per cent in the arithmetic example of the Appendix) tougher punishment in Act 3 will *diminish* the probability of repayment q, even though, *cet par*, it will increase the rate of compliance with conditions p. If we make the simplifying assumption that the costs associated with non-repayment of adjustment loans dominate the costs associated with non-compliance on the associated conditions, the prescription is simple: in preference to applying strategy 7a, the lender will punish at level 1 − γ only in the case of those countries in which punishment does not have the side-effect of reducing the repayment rate, i.e. those countries with a debt service ratio less than the critical level (40 per cent in Figure 7.3a). If this simplifying assumption is not accepted, then the donor's payoff in the event that he chooses *not* to offer refinance in Act 3 becomes

$$(8) \quad X + \alpha p \, (T_{ij} - T_j) \qquad \text{(Act 2)}$$
$$\quad - t \, \Delta \, q_j \qquad \qquad \text{(Act 3)}$$

where t is the utility loss associated with the increased probability of default, Δq in Act 3 − that is, the Act 3 payoff goes from zero to negative. In this event the utility associated with applying strategy (7c) rather than (7a) for a given level of punishment (1 − γ) is:

$$(9) \quad \gamma \alpha \, \Delta \, p \, (2) + t \, \Delta \, q_j$$

where Δ p (2) is the change in the rate of implementation of conditions in Act 2 associated with strategy 7c rather than 7a (presumed to be negative) and Δ q_j is the change in the probability of default under strategy rather than 7a (presumed to be positive). If, as is likely, (9) turns out positive, (7c) − punishment tailored to the recipient's debt-service ratio − will be the preferred decision rule; but once it is perceived that this decision rule is being applied, this will create moral hazard problems, since the heavily indebted will observe that they will escape punishment for non-observance of conditions only if they remain heavily indebted and thus have an incentive (c.f. Krugman, 1988) to avoid adjustment efforts designed to enable them to escape from that state.

EMPIRICAL FINDINGS

It is time to consider some of the major predictions of the analysis so far in relation to the empirical evidence. These are:

(1) for a borrower not expecting to borrow in Act 3, slippage will be 100 per cent on all 'coercive conditionality', i.e. policy conditions in excess of T_j (p. 135);

(2) for a borrower expecting to borrow in Act 3, (a) slippage will
be positive but less than 100 per cent, (b) the extent of slippage
will reflect his expectation of punishment $(1 - \gamma)$ and his
subjective distaste for the conditions imposed in relation to his
need for finance (β) (p. 139);
(3) punishment $(1 - \gamma)$, being purely an instrument for enforcing
repayment, is likely to be relaxed once the recipient's debt
service ratio d reaches a critical level (p. 142) (further discussion in Appendix below);
(4) random punishment of slippage dominates 'punishment to fit
the crime' (p. 141).

Crime (propositions (1) and (2))

Tables 7.3a and 7.3b show the level of slippage which has so far taken
place on a selection of conditional lending agreements involving the
IMF and World Bank. It is apparent that in the *last* loan of a series of
conditional lending agreements (Thailand II, Bolivia, Kenya II)
slippage was almost total, supporting proposition (1). Throughout
each sequence of conditionality agreements for which we have data,
slippage is positive, though variable, for both World Bank and IMF
loan agreements, supporting proposition (2a). Proposition (2b) is
harder to test with any precision since its parameters β and γ relate to
expectations rather than *ex post* realised values. However, it is
immediately clear from Table 7.3 that the obvious proxies for the
recipient's economic vulnerability and hence his bargaining strength
β – i.e. his end-of-loan period balance of payments and financial
dependence on the donor – have weak explanatory power. There are
numerous cases (Kenya, Ecuador, Malawi, the Philippines under
Marcos) where the recipient exhibited a high level of slippage on
conditionality even though the donor's hold on him was almost total,
in the sense that his economic predicament was desperate and few
alternative sources of finance were available. Our ready-made explanation for this temerity, in terms of the theory so far set out, is that
such recipients, in spite of their vulnerability, do not expect to be
punished (i.e. they expect $1 - \gamma$ to be low) because they are aware of
the financial costs *to the donor* associated with strict punishment. Will
this explanation wash, and does the probability of punishment relate
to the recipient's debt-service position as suggested by equation (7c)?

TABLE 7.3(a) *World Bank refinance behaviour in relation to slippage in previous periods*

Country	First adjustment loan: Title and date	Level of slippage on conditions (%)	Second adjustment loan: Title and date	Level of slippage on conditions (%)	Subsequent adjustment lending by Bank to country
High slippage countries (slippage on initial loan more than 40%):					
Bolivia	SAL I 1980	80		- - none - -	See Note
Guyana	SAL I 1981	80		- - none - -	none
Ecuador	Ag. Sec. Loan 1985	75	Fin. Sector Loan 1988	not known	
Malawi	SAL I 1981	45	SAL II 1983	30	One SAL / One SECAL
Kenya	SAL I 1980	40	SAL II 1982	78	Two SECALS
Low slippage countries (slippage on initial loan less than 30 per cent):					
Jamaica	SAL I 1982	16	SAL II 1983	5	One SAL / Three Export Devt Loans / Two SECALs
Ghana	Export Rehab. 1983	30	Industrial sector credit 1986	25	One SAL / Two SECALs
Philippines	SAL I 1980	30	SAL II 1982	45	One Economic Recovery Loan
Pakistan	SAL I 1982	10	Energy Sector Loan 1985	20	One SECAL / One SECAL
Thailand	SAL I 1982	15	SAL II 1983	40	- - none - - / Three SALs
Turkey	SAL I 1980	0	SAL II 1981	5	Three SECALs

Note: In Bolivia, two Bank reconstruction loans were granted in 1986 and 1987 after a change in government in the previous year. This must be interpreted as a completely separate adjustment episode from that analysed in the table.

SOURCES For slippage data, country case studies in Mosley, Harrigan and Toye (1991), Vol. I, Table 5.2). For balance-of-payments data: IMF *International Financial Statistics*, various issues.

TABLE 7.3(b)   *IMF refinance behaviour in relation to slippage in previous periods*

Country	First adjustment loan:		Second adjustment loan:		Subsequent adjustment lending by Fund to country
	Amount and date	Level of slippage on conditions	Amount and date	Level of slippage	
Sudan	SDR 190m, Feb 1982	80	SDR 170m, Jan 1983	85	Further stand-bys May 1984
Philippines	SDR 410m, 1981	55	SDR 315m stand-by and SDR 183m Compensatory Financing Facility	65	Further stand-by 1984
Jamaica	SDR 120m, May 1978 (Extended Facility)	39	SDR 150m, Mar 1981 (Extended Facility)	45	Further stand-by Jun 1984
Kenya	SDR 1983, Mar 1983	25	SDR 85m, Feb 1985	35	Further stand-by Feb 1988, and ESAF, April 1989

SOURCES   For Sudan, Brown (1990) chapter IV; for other countries, case studies in Mosley, Harrigan and Toye (1991), vol II.

Punishment (proposition (3))

Tables 7.3(a) and 7.3(b) relate the level of slippage in a group of case-study countries to the level of subsequent 'punishment' by the same donor, i.e. refusal of finance or otherwise. Within the sample of countries examined, it is clear that in four of five World Bank cases where follow-up finance was sought, although previous slippage had been high (Kenya, Ecuador, Malawi, Philippines) and in three out of four IMF cases (Sudan, Philippines and Jamaica) that slippage was pardoned in the sense that a follow-on loan was granted. Sandersley, writing in Chapter 4 above, suggests that the implementation record

TABLE 7.4   *Slippage on World Bank conditions and possible determinants*

Country	Slippage 1980–9 (%)	Current account balance as % of GNP 1988–9	World Bank policy-based lending as % of borrower's gross external capital flow 1980–9 (%)	Debt Service Ratio 1988–9 (%)
Six highest slippage countries:				
Bolivia	40	–3.0	11.3	31.3
Guyana	80	–2.6	22.9	. .
Kenya	62	–5.4	20.3	33.3
Malawi	45	–11.6	38.4	28.0
Philippines	38	–3.6	17.0	26.3
Jamaica	37	–13.0	16.6	26.4
Average, high slippage countries	50.3	6.5	21.0	29.0
Five lowest slippage countries:				
Ivory Coast	18	–12.7	12.8	40.9
Pakistan	10	0.0	20.8	23.2
South Korea	25	–5.3	4.5	11.4
Thailand	30	–6.3	11.1	15.9
Turkey	5	–4.5	14.6	32.1
Average, low slippage countries	17.6	5.8	12.8	24.7
t-statistic	3.72**	0.11	1.60	2.63**

** denotes significance at 1% level

on IMF conditionality is actually worse than that on World Bank conditionality; but he is referring to data which covers only the Fund's Structural Adjustment Facility, which constitute only a small fraction of its total lending operations in developing countries. In *all* of these cases except Malawi, the debt service ratio was above the critical 25 per cent level, which gives a clue to why slippage was pardoned; had it not been, the recipient would have had difficulty in servicing (and indeed little incentive to service) his existing loans to that donor, as is formally illustrated in the Appendix. By the side of this threat to the donor's economic viability, the recipient's breach of conditionality pales into insignificance. If conditionality (as we have argued is the case for the World Bank and bilateral development agencies) has little bearing on capacity to repay, this conclusion is strengthened.

We have therefore established:

(1) that slippage on conditionality is substantial across all categories of international finance even in cases where the recipient is financially weak and has little apparent bargaining power;
(2) that such slippage is frequently pardoned;
(3) that this tendency has a compelling financial rationale for the lender, which becomes more compelling as the borrower's financial position deteriorates;
(4) that in spite of this, lenders have strategies available to them which would keep slippage rates on conditions lower.

EXTENSIONS AND CONCLUSIONS

The above analysis, however, only tells a part of the story. In particular, it goes only part of the way towards answering the question which is crucial for lenders: under what circumstances will the imposition of conditionality yield policy reform which will be effective in increasing the yield on that finance? Assuming that the conditions are properly conceived, our answer to this question, as embodied in equation (5), is divided between fear of donor punishment $(1 - \gamma)$, which is often a paper tiger, and 'taste' for reform (β). Although we have given some examination to the former, the latter has remained extraneous to the analysis so far, critical though it is to the outcome of the game. It is, therefore, necessary to drop the assumption prevailing so far that 'the recipient' can be seen as a single homogeneous actor. Rather, it contains, at the least, two groups whose interests in relation to the execution of the conditions imposed by international agencies (p, in the notation used above, p. 135) are in conflict; namely the gainers and the losers from conditionality. The gainers from the type of conditions currently favoured by the IMF and World Bank will typically be, within government, the treasury and central bank, who have an interest in promoting financial inflows from overseas, and outside it, export-oriented farmers and industrialists who will benefit from the removal of controls on production and trade. Opposed to such reforms will be, within government, the ministries of trade, industry and often agriculture, together with urban workers and industrialists who depend on a protected home market for their survival. As pointed out by John Toye in Chapter 5 above, the gainers are typically ill-coordinated and their gains accrue in the long-term, whereas the losers are often highly politicised in defence of their interests against, say, the withdrawal of a food subsidy and their losses accrue immediately any reform is initiated. Hence the weight attached in the recipient's utility function to compliance β is, in the aggregate, negative, and the prospects for reform in the early stages are balanced on a knife-edge.

However, the following actions will tend to make β less negative and ultimately positive.

(1) an increase in the rate of exchange at which the donor offers money for conditions, which will embolden the gainers within government to confront the losers, or else cajole them into acceptance;

(2) following through the logic of (1), compensation payments by the gainers to the losers;

(3) political organisation of some or all of the gainers, for example in an exporters' association or a national farmers' union, or by the same token a weakening in the power of organised groups of losers, notably trade unions;

(4) the very making of a commitment by the gainers to the donor may make it subjectively costlier, through the loss of political reputation, for the gainers to go back on agreed reforms than it would have been in the absence of a conditionality agreement;

(5) the passage of time, which as argued above will allow the benefits of the reforms, if they are well-designed, to come through to the gainers.

By the same token any movement in the reverse direction will strengthen the bargaining position of the losers in relation to the gainers, make β more negative and, according to equation (5), increase the probability of slippage. If β once becomes positive, the game described above collapses, since the political basis for opposition to conditionality has been removed.

The key point to emerge from this bare discussion is that an intelligent strategy for any of the parties involved in the conditionality relationship may involve trying to change the rules of the game rather than to maximise utility given the existing rules. For a loser in a recipient country, measures to make the parameters β (disutility of compliance) more negative, such as strengthening of trade union militancy or creation of local manufacturers' associations, may yield more than overt slippage; and for a donor, measures to increase this parameter, such as those suggested at (1) to (5) above, may yield more than variations in the punishment rule (equation (7)). For a donor trapped on the horns of what we have called the 'disbursement dilemma', this opportunity of escape is likely to prove more than welcome.

NOTES

1. Henceforward we refer to all suppliers of conditional finance as 'lenders' although many bilateral agencies, and the World Bank's IDA (International Development Association) fund, supply it either on grant terms or at highly concessional interest rates. We argue on p. 131 that these variations in financial terms make little difference to the supplier's motivation.
2. In the 1980s, for the first time, the World Bank and IMF, although in principle protected by government guarantees, began to suffer serious arrears on their lending to developing countries. The value of loans to the Bank and Fund 'in nonaccrual status' (i.e. more than six months overdue) at 30 June 1991 was:

TABLE 7.5 *Arrears to IMF and World Bank at 30 June 1991*

Country	Arrears to the IMF (a) US $m	Arrears to the World Bank (b)(c) US $m	Total US $m
Peru	512	884	1396
Zambia	790	9	799
Sudan	956	–	956
Liberia	326	110	436
Panama	146	207	351
Syria	–	312	312
Guyana	115	–	115
Nicaragua	–	224	224

continued on page 150

150   *The Politics of Conditional Lending*

TABLE 7.5   *continued*

Country	Arrears to the IMF (a) US $m	Arrears to the World Bank (b)(c) US $m	Total US $m
Vietnam	125	–	125
Sierra Leone	75	4	79
Somalia	75	–	75
Honduras	–	64	64

Notes:
(a) Arrears of principal and interest on IMF loans as at 30 April 1989.
(b) Debt repayment and interest more than six months overdue as at 30 June 1989.
(c) Countries having sums overdue to World Bank for more than 30 days but less than six months as at 30 June 1991 were Nigeria ($48m), Cote d'Ivoire ($13m), Iraq ($11m), Brazil ($11m), Colombia ($8m), others ($15m).

SOURCE   Faber, M. (1990) 'Debt: New treatment for the chronic but repentant', *Journal of International Development*, 2, April, updated from recent World Bank and IMF data.

APPENDIX: THE LINKAGE BETWEEN LOAN REPAYMENT AND ENFORCEMENT OF CONDITIONALITY

In seeking to determine what punishment it should impose for breach of conditionality, a lender of conditional aid money is subject to two conflicting pressures:

(1) It may be presumed that there is some positive link between compliance with the policy conditionality attached to a loan and the probability that the loan will be repaid – in other words, that the imposition of conditions makes the recipient economy better capable of repaying the loan and thus deputises in some sense for collateral on the loan, as in Figure 7.A1. If there were no such link, indeed, the imposition of conditions would make no financial sense for the lender. (Lenders such as the World Bank may have non-financial motives such as the encouragement of economic development, and believe that the enforcement of conditions is essential to achieve these motives. But if these motives come into conflict with financial imperatives, it is the non-financial motive which is likely to have to give way.)

For purposes of argument, let the link be of the simplest functional form
(1) $q_1 = a + bp$,
where q = probability of loan repayment and p = compliance with conditions.

(2) However, for recipient countries which are debt-distressed there is a negative link between the degree of *punishment of non-compliance* (through refusal of further credit) and the probability that existing loans will be repaid.

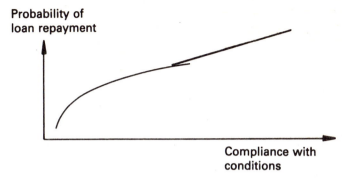

FIGURE 7.A1   *Compliance with loan conditions as collateral*

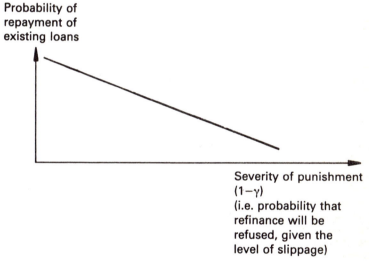

FIGURE 7.A2   *Relationship between severity of punishment and probability of repayment*

Once a recipient government reaches the point where it cannot easily service its loans out of current income, every refusal by a lender to re-lend on account of breach of conditionality increases the probability that he will default on some or all of his existing borrowings from that lender, as in Figure 7.A2. As the size of the debt overhang increases, indeed, not only does the recipient's *ability* to pay diminish but also his *motivation* to do so (Krugman, 1988), because the more he loses access to commercial sources of credit through acts of non-repayment, the smaller the likelihood that he can restore his reputation for repayment, and thus his access to the financial markets, through one act of on-time repayment.

Let this function be of the form

(2) $q_2 = f - d \, (\text{DSR}) \, (1 - \gamma)$,

where $(1 - \gamma)$, is the probability of punishment (see p. 138 above), DSR is the debt service ratio, and d and f are fixed parameters. The slope of the trade-off (d) in Figure 7.A2 will therefore vary with the recipient's debt-service ratio; the higher the debt-service ratio, the steeper the trade-off.

It is not possible to superimpose Figure 7.A1 on Figure 7.A2 directly, because the probability of 'good behaviour' p (compliance with conditions) is not the same thing as severity of punishment for non-compliance $(1 - \gamma)$. However, it is unlikely that there would be much good behaviour in this sense without any punishment for non-compliance, since the political costs of compliance are considerable (p. 129 above) and some countervailing pressure is therefore necessary to make compliance rational. For simplicity we shall assume here that compliance has a positive linear relationship with severity of punishment:

(3) $p = \lambda(1 - \gamma)$

Finally let us suppose that the two components of 'probability of repayment', q_1 and q_2, are additive.

(4) $q = q_1 + q_2$

Hence $q = a + bp + f - d \, (\text{DSR}) \, (1 - \gamma)$ (from (1) and (2))

i.e. (5) $q = (a + f) + (be - d \, (\text{DSR})) \, (1 - \gamma)$ (from (3))

which has a positive slope in relation to punishment $(1 - \gamma)$ as long as $(a + f)$ > $(be - d \, (\text{DSR})) \, (1 - \gamma)$ and a negative slope thereafter. The location of the 'threshold debt service ratio' beyond which punishment becomes counterproductive by raising the probability of default depends on the parameters a, b, e and f and on the nature of the relationship (3) between crime and punishment. Arithmetic examples of the sensitivity of the function to these parameters are given in Table 7.A1. From these estimates a picture emerges in which the 'leverage' of punishment, in terms of the effect on repayment

TABLE 7.A1   *Probability of repayment as debt service ratio and punishment for non-compliance are varied*

Donor's punishment $(1 - \gamma)$	Recipient's Debt Service Ratio (DSR)										
	0	10	20	30	40	50	60	70	80	90	100
0	60	60	60	60	60	60	60	60	60	60	60
10	63	63	62	61	60	59	58	58	58	58	58
20	65	65	64	62	60	58	56	56	56	56	56
30	69	69	66	63	60	57	54	54	54	54	54
40	72	72	68	64	60	56	52	52	52	52	52

TABLE 7.A1   *continued*

Donor's punishment (1 − γ)	Recipient's Debt Service Ratio (DSR)										
	0	10	20	30	40	50	60	70	80	90	100
50	75	75	70	65	60	55	50	50	50	50	50
60	78	78	72	66	60	54	48	48	48	48	48
70	81	81	74	67	60	53	46	46	46	46	46
80	84	84	76	68	60	52	44	44	44	44	44
90	87	87	78	69	60	51	42	42	42	42	42
100	90	90	80	70	60	50	40	40	40	40	40

Note: The values in the table are derived by substituting the following assumptions into equation (5):
   Value of constant $(a + f) = 60\%$
   Value of constant $(be)\quad = 80\%$
   Value of parameter d in (3) as in the following table:

Debt service ratio %	0	10	20	30	40	50	60	70	80	90	100
Value of d	0.5	0.5	0.6	0.7	0.8	0.9	1	1	1	1	1

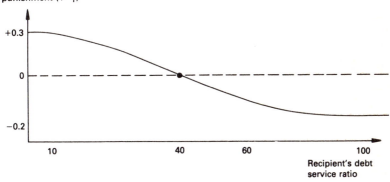

FIGURE 7.A3   *'Effectiveness of punishment' in relation to debt service ratio*

rates per unit increase in punishment, declines as the recipient's service ratio increases and becomes negative after a threshold debt service ratio – which is 40 per cent with the parameter values we have assumed in this exercise – is passed, as in Figure 7.A3. This is the relationship that is used in the analysis at p. 140 above.

Part III
Results

8 Adjustment Programmes and World Bank Support: Rationale and Main Results

Vittorio Corbo and Stanley Fischer

INTRODUCTION

The World Bank (henceforth 'The Bank') introduced adjustment lending in 1979 to assist member countries in their adjustment to the second oil shock. With the debt crisis that emerged in the post 1982 period, adjustment lending grew in importance (Stern, 1983). Increased recognition on the part of many developing countries of the need for structural reforms contributed to the expansion of adjustment lending. The Bank periodically evaluates the effectiveness of the adjustment programmes it supports as well as their design and implementation (World Bank, 1988a and 1990a). It also carries out a continuous research programme on different aspects of the economic development problems facing developing countries. From these evaluations and the findings of its research programme the Bank derives lessons for the design and implementation of programmes.

The typical country initiating an adjustment programme supported by the Bank faces pressing macroeconomic problems that are manifested in the form of a large fiscal deficit, open or repressed inflation, and an unsustainable balance of payments situation. These macroeconomic problems have resulted from expansionary demand policies and large external shocks to the international real interest rate, commodity prices, availability of external financing and the demand for exports. Macroeconomic distortions and institutional weaknesses have exacerbated the situation by severely limiting the capacity of the government to respond to external shocks.

Adjustment programmes have to address the fundamental causes of the problem. Structural reforms to restore macroeconomic balance focus on bringing the level of demand and its composition (tradable relative to nontradable goods) in line with the level of output and the level of external financing that can be mobilised on a sustainable basis. In most cases what is required is a reduction in the fiscal deficit and the realisation of a real devaluation to restore internal and external balance. In countries with acute macroeconomic problems, structural reforms to increase efficiency and to restore growth should be initiated only when enough progress has been made in reducing the macroeconomic imbalances. These type of structural reforms focus on creating more appropriate incentives by deregulating domestic goods markets, liberalising the trade regime, removing constraints on factor employment and mobility, and removing obstacles to saving and investment. The importance of this sequence of reforms – reforms to reduce severe macroeconomic imbalances first and to improve resource allocation and restore growth later – has become increasingly clear with experience but there are also strong analytical underpinnings. It is well accepted by now that the benefits of structural reforms that aim at improving resource allocation through a change in incentives are severely reduced under conditions of macroeconomic instability characterised, on the one hand, by high and variable inflation and on the other, by balance of payments crises (Corbo and de Melo, 1987; Fischer, 1986; and Sachs, 1987). Under high and variable inflation and balance of payments crises the credibility of a sustained change in incentives is low since relative price variability usually increases with the level of inflation.

While reforms that start with low credibility about their sustainability may get current relative prices right, consumers and producers perceive that the reforms will not last and thus intertemporal relative prices will be distorted. The final result is that the responses of consumers and producers can destabilize the whole reform effort (Calvo, 1989). Country studies have also shown that most of the liberalisation attempts that have failed were due to the lack or failure of stabilisation efforts that accompanied the liberalisation (Krueger, 1978 and 1984).

STRUCTURAL REFORMS FOR STABILISATION

Why is Stabilisation Required?

Stabilisation includes the restoration of external (current account) and internal (unemployment) balance, as well as the control of inflation. In countries with a prolonged period of high and variable inflation, stabilisation is not an easy task. Indeed, the success rate of stabilisation programmes for these type of countries is very poor (Kiguel and Liviatan, 1988): from the successful cases it has been learned that the conquest of inflation is a lengthy process. It has also been learned that structural reforms to achieve a sustainable reduction in the fiscal deficit are an important component of successful stabilisation programmes. However, incomes policies, on top of the fiscal adjustment, can also play an important role in stabilising expectations, breaking up inertia, and increasing the political support of stabilisation programmes (Bruno and Piterman, 1988; Dornbusch, 1989; Kiguel and Liviatan, 1990; and Solimano, 1990).

Fiscal adjustment, excluding full Ricardian equivalence, also helps to reduce absorption and thus decrease the non-interest current account deficit towards a level that is compatible with the sustainable level of external financing and interest payments on the external debt.

A real devaluation is also a key component of the restoration of external and internal balance. If the reduction in absorption is not accompanied by a real devaluation, then the demand for both tradable and nontradable goods will be reduced. Lower demand for tradable goods contributes directly to the reduction in the non-interest current account deficit. Lower demand for nontradable goods, without a real devaluation, will reduce the output of nontradable goods, and unemployment and excess capacity will result (Corden, 1981; Dornbusch, 1980).

Structural reforms required for a successful stabilisation programme include tax reforms, substitution of QRs by tariffs, reduction of government subsidies, public enterprise reforms and/or privatisation aimed at reducing the non-financial public sector deficit, adjustment in the exchange rate system to reduce Central Bank losses and to facilitate a real devaluation, and realignment of domestic interest rates with domestic inflation and international interest rates. Some of these reforms, notably tax reforms, public enterprise reforms and privatisation, need to be phased in as institutions have to be put in place and regulatory frameworks established (World Bank, 1988b).

Bank Support for Structural Reforms in Support of Stabilisation

For governments that are fully committed to the pursuit of structural reforms to restore macroeconomic balances, while creating the conditions for long-term growth with a sustained balance of payments situation, balance of payments financing facilitates the phased reduction of the non-interest current account deficit over a period of time. The phased reduction in the non-interest current account deficit, by allowing an expenditure level higher than otherwise, reduces the short run adjustment costs to output, employment and consumption, and contributes to the sustainability of the reforms. An additional reason is that the introduction of some of the structural reforms to reduce the public sector deficit require time for preparation and implementation. This is the case for tax reforms, the restructuring of public expenditures and privatisation. The phased reduction in the overall public deficit made possible by the availability of higher external financing could improve the quality of the fiscal adjustment and in this way maximise the net benefits of the reform.

STRUCTURAL REFORMS TO IMPROVE RESOURCE ALLOCATION, TO INCREASE GROWTH AND TO REDUCE POVERTY

Once inflation has been reduced in a credible way, and progress has been achieved in reducing the non-interest current account deficit, the potential benefits of structural reforms aimed at improving resource allocation and achieving sustainable and 'acceptable' growth is increased. Economic research and country-specific economic and sector work is required for each country to identify the most important distortions that hinder the allocation of resources and limit growth. After the largest distortions have been identified, a central question is the sequence and speed of reforms. We refer to these two points in order.

Sequencing of Reforms

In the presence of multiple distortions, the question of the sequence of reforms is a difficult one to answer because one is working in a world of second- (or higher-) best. In this type of situation the welfare benefits of reforms are case-specific and depend on initial conditions and interrelations across markets (Edwards, 1989b; and the papers in Choksi and Papageorgiou, 1986). However, some general recommendations have emerged. First, reforms should start with large reductions in big distortions. Second, in economies with restrictive trade regimes, widespread price controls, and restrictive domestic competitive practices, goods market reforms should precede asset market reforms. In particular, the liberalisation of the current account should precede the liberalisation of the capital account. This recommendation is based on two arguments. First, the speed of adjustment in capital markets is much faster than in commodity markets and, therefore, to avoid large movements in capital flows and the real exchange rate, capital controls should limit capital flows to the rate at which goods markets adjust to domestic deregulation and foreign trade liberalisation (Frenkel, 1982 and 1983). Second, because asset prices are determined by the expected present value of future income streams, distortions in goods and factor prices result in assets being traded at distorted prices. The final consequence is a misallocation of investment. In countries where there are major impediments to labour mobility and domestic financial markets are almost non-existent, the potential gains from deregulation of goods markets can also be severely curtailed. For this type of economy, reforms in the labour market and the development of a domestic financial market should accompany the goods markets reforms.

Speed of Reforms

On the topic of the speed of reforms, economic arguments suggest the quick removal of distortions in such a way that resource allocation takes place at the right prices sooner rather than later. The faster pace of liberalisation will thus allow higher benefits (Mussa, 1982; Edwards, 1989a and b). It could also be claimed that quick removal of distortions minimises the possibility of opposition to the reforms. What is important, however, is the sustainability of the reform effort. In some cases, the reduction of distortions requires preparation of the appropriate human capital and therefore cannot be implemented too quickly (i.e., financial reforms, trade reforms, etc.). Webb and Shariff (1990) also discuss some of the political economy aspects that affect the speed of reforms. The final conclusion is that specific political economy and initial conditions aspects should determine in a specific country setting the optimal speed of reform.

Sectoral Reforms

Most reform efforts have been centered in these three areas. However, labour market reforms, although of the utmost importance, have been very difficult to carry out due to political economy difficulties. We will examine three areas of reform in greater detail: trade/domestic competition reforms, financial sector reforms, and labour market reforms.

Trade/Domestic Competition Reforms

Small countries with very distorted trade regimes and non-competitive goods markets could obtain large benefits from reducing non-competitive practices and introducing trade liberalisation. Distorted trade regimes generate resource misallocation within import-competing sectors, repress exports and contribute to socially unproductive rent-seeking activities. Structural reforms in the trade area aim at reducing the average level and variance of tariff rates with the ultimate objective of moving towards a more uniform tariff structure. As a practical rule, incentives should not discriminate against export-oriented activities and should promote the development of broadly uniform across-the-board effective incentives for import competing activities (Little, Scitovsky and Scott, 1970; Corden, 1974; Balassa, 1976; Thomas et al., forthcoming).

These recommendations are derived from the standard theory of commercial policy and from the empirical work on commercial policy referred to above. It could be claimed that new developments in trade theory call into question these recommendations and provide a new foundation for differentiated tariffs and, in a more general sense, for an active industrial policy. The new trade theory holds that international markets are typically imperfectly competitive, and that trade is, to a considerable degree, driven by economies of scale rather than comparative advantage (Helpman and Krugman, 1985). A policy implication of this theory is that government should favour industries that generate externalities.

The policy recommendations derived from the new trade theory have met substantial criticism both on the economic and the political economy front. On the economic side, there are difficulties in deriving useful intervention policies given the difficulties involved in modelling imperfect markets. The results are fragile, not robust to changes in model specification and the general equilibrium effects on other sectors are overlooked. On the political economy side, it has been argued that the work on rent-seeking and tariff formation clearly indicate that the final tariff structures are driven more by the pressures of interest groups than by efficiency considerations. A consideration of these criticisms led Krugman (1987, p. 143) to conclude that

> the gains from intervention are limited by uncertainty about the appropriate policies . . . , by the general equilibrium effects that insure that promoting one sector diverts resources from others. . . . Once the expected gains from intervention have been whittled down sufficiently, political economy [factors] can be invoked as a reason to forego intervention altogether. Free trade can serve as a simple principle with which to resist pressures of special-interest politics.

A similar conclusion is arrived at in Helpman (1989), Helpman and Krugman (1989), and Srinivasan (1989).

Financial Sector Reforms

In the area of financial reforms, the objective of the reforms is to improve efficiency in the use of resources, including improvement in the efficiency of investment. Financial reforms include lifting credit rationing and the controls on interest rates, with the intention of allowing them to become market determined. In addition, an appropriate regulatory information and supervision system of financial intermediaries is an essential part of financial reforms. Initial conditions play a central role in the design and implementation of financial reforms. If a large proportion of the assets of financial institutions are held at below market rates or are non-performing, then deregulation of interest rates will create difficulties for existing institutions. In particular, if deposit and lending rates are deregulated simultaneously and free entry into the financial system is allowed, existing banks will be forced to pay market interest rates. They will suffer substantial losses, jeopardising the banking system's solvency. If the government then rescues the banks, a macroeconomic crisis could develop. This implies the need to recapitalise the banks or to allow for a transition phase, in which lending rates are deregulated first, with deposit rates following only gradually (World Bank, 1989). In countries where domestic financial systems are practically non-existent, the creation of a financial system could be a high priority. This point could be especially relevant for Eastern Europe (Calvo and Coricelli, 1990).

Labour Market Reforms

Labour market regulations and institutions play a key role in the efficiency and ultimate success of a structural adjustment problem. In countries that require a large real devaluation to accompany absorption reduction policies, obtaining an initial decline in real wages could make a major difference between getting a large recession with massive unemployment (Chile, 1982) or getting macroeconomic adjustment without a major change in unemployment (Mexico, 1983–9). Labour legislation, in the form of rigid wage indexation rules, is often a major impediment to successful macroeconomic adjustment and the ultimate success of structural reforms aimed at improving resource allocation in goods markets. Success could also be reduced by rigid practices which restrict labour mobility. Large severance payments, lack of flexibility in the real wage structure, the attachment of substantial non-wage benefits, like housing, utilities and education, to employment, and other institutional rigidities to labour mobility are typical impediments to successful adjustment that need to be addressed early on in structural adjustment programmes.

Promoting Economic Growth

Structural reforms that contribute to the reduction of macroeconomic imbalances and the improvement of resource allocation create the foundations for a recovery of growth (Fischer, 1987). Sustained growth generally has four main requirements: stable macroeconomic conditions, an appropriate incentive system, an adequate level of saving, and efficient institutions to turn saving into productive investment. How to achieve the first two requirements was already discussed above. As it is most likely that foreign saving will remain low in the foreseeable future, a major effort to increase national saving will be needed. Empirical evidence, in general, shows that private saving rates are not too sensitive to policies and, in particular, to interest rates (Giovannini, 1985; Schmidt-Hebbel, Webb and Corsetti, 1990). However, private saving rates are very sensitive to the economic cycle as a result of consumption smoothing. If there are no leakages through lower private saving, public saving can contribute to an increase in national saving (see also Summers, 1985). Empirical evidence presented in Corbo and Schmidt-Hebbel (1990) shows that public saving can make a major contribution to an increase in national saving.

The last factor, an increase in the level and efficiency of private investment, is much affected by a stable macroeconomic framework and clear and predictable tax rules and property rights (Rodrik, 1989; Serven and Solimano, 1990a and 1990b). The belief that economic policy and the investment rate are major determinants of economic growth has long been expressed in the writings of economists. It is only very recently, however, that explicit models have been able to capture the link between policy and growth. The new endogenous growth literature, pioneered by Romer (1986, 1990) and Lucas (1988), has created a class of theoretical models in which economic policy can affect investment, human capital accumulation, technological innovation and resource allocation in ways that alter long-run, steady-state growth rates. The ideas underlying these models – economies of scale, externalities, and public goods – have been around for a long time and form the foundation of over three decades of World Bank programmes. Nonetheless, these new models provide a formal environment that may improve our understanding of growth-promoting policies (Easterly and Wetzel, 1989).

The recent growth literature highlights a number of channels through which public policies can affect growth. Recent World Bank papers by Arrau (1989), Romer (1989), and Rebelo (1990) show that carefully subsidising human capital accumulation, or providing the nutritional levels and basic educational skills necessary for augmenting human capital, can both foster growth. Along these lines, Becker, Murphy, and Tamura (1988) show that economies may become stuck in a poverty trap: a situation where low income and low human capital levels create incentives for high population growth and low investment in human capital that perpetuate the state of poverty. Policies that stimulate investment in human capital can break an economy out of this stagnant situation.

The World Bank has been at the forefront of empirical studies of trade policy and growth. Along with large multicountry case studies, recent work by Feder (1983), Balassa (1985), Easterly and Wetzel (1989), Edwards (1989a), de Melo and Robinson (1989), Nishimizu and Page (1990), Dollar (1990), and Levine and Renelt (1990) have carefully examined the cross-country evidence on trade policy and growth. The result of this empirical work indicates that, after controlling for factor accumulation, countries with more open economies have a higher rate of growth.

In terms of fiscal policy, Easterly's 1990 model nicely captures the complicated relationship between fiscal policies and growth. Governments may have positive growth effects by providing essential public goods and designing taxes that close the gap between private and social costs. On the other hand, governments may produce goods that inappropriately compete with private entrepreneurs, waste funds on bloated bureaucracies, or impose taxes and regulations that inefficiently distort investment decisions. Easterly's (1989) analysis suggests that one needs to conduct a detailed study of the composition of government expenditures and the structure of taxes to evaluate the effects of any country's fiscal stance on growth. The complexity of the relationship between fiscal policy and growth is borne out by recent empirical work in Levine and Renelt (1990). They find that broad macroeconomic indicators of fiscal policy are not closely related to growth in a broad cross-section of countries.

The role of financial policy in growth has also been the focus of World Bank scrutiny. Gelb (1989) and Easterly and Wetzel (1989) present preliminary evidence that, after controlling for factor accumulation, financial deregulation has a positive effect on growth.

Alleviation of Poverty

The ultimate objective of Bank lending is to contribute directly and indirectly to economic development and the eradication of poverty. Indeed, the reduction of poverty is the central objective of most Bank country assistance. The strategy to reduce poverty has two components. First, to encourage broad-based economic growth and in this way promote the use of the most abundant factor – labour. Second, to improve the provision of social services demanded by the poor – especially primary education, a social infrastructure and basic health care (World Bank, 1990b). Adjustment from an unsustainable economic situation, following policy mismanagement or adverse external shocks, often has social costs in the short run. Bank-supported lending, which promotes orderly adjustment, is less costly than other forms of adjustment. However, every adjustment programme will have losers as well as winners. The poor, who already have low welfare levels, may find it very difficult to absorb short-term losses. Therefore, adjustment programmes also include an assessment of the short-term effect of policies on the poor as well as specific measures to protect the poor during the transition (Maasland and Van der Gaag, 1990).

World Bank Support: Is it Needed?

It could still be claimed that if the reforms are so favourable, then countries should undertake them themselves without financing from the Bank. However, even very beneficial reforms could have important transition adjustment (and distribution) costs that could make their implementation very difficult. Balance of payments support could make an important contribution to the sustainability and ultimate success of the reforms by reducing the need to cut expenditures and imports while the reforms are being implemented. We will now discuss the rationale for balance of payments support for the different type of reform discussed above.

In the case of trade reforms, balance of payments support could make an important contribution to the financing of a transitory increase in imports while the reforms themselves result in increased export response. As people expect this difference in response, the availability of financing could contribute also to the credibility and sustainability of the reforms. Also, external financing could help to bridge some of the short-term adjustment costs incurred in industries that need to restructure or to disappear altogether.

In the case of financial sector reforms, balance of payments support could contribute to financing transitory increases in government expenditures resulting from capitalisation of banks and the reduction in taxation of financial intermediaries.

Reduction of distortions in goods markets can result in temporary unemployment of resources, although it is most likely that they will be beneficial in the long run. As countries are restricted from borrowing in international capital markets, Bank lending, conditional on the implementation of a programme, helps sustain expenditures while the reforms are being implemented. In general, consumption smoothing, made possible by adjustment lending in support of reforms with adjustment costs, could make an important contribution to sustain a reform effort by sustaining expenditure levels while the benefits of the reforms start to appear.

The World Bank's financial support for adjustment programmes can cushion some of the short-term adjustment costs of reforms and in this way can facilitate their sustainability and ultimate success. Furthermore, to the extent that the Bank brings its expertise to bear, its lending helps member countries to design and implement more effective programmes and, in this way, to adjust more successfully. For the Bank itself, if adjustment programmes are successful, they help restore a country's growth and improve its creditworthiness. Furthermore, in highly distorted economies, the benefits of project lending are severely curtailed. Indeed, with distorted incentives, the increased investment finance may eventually raise capital accumulation in the 'wrong' activities, exacerbating the misallocation of resources. In the extreme, it could even result in immiserising investment.

MAIN CONCLUSIONS OF THE FIRST AND SECOND REPORTS ON ADJUSTMENT LENDING

The First and Second Report on Adjustment Lending are two recent comprehensive efforts at evaluating the Bank experience with adjustment programmes (World Bank 1988a and 1990a). We summarise below the main conclusions of these reports.

The First Report

The main conclusions of the first report were:

Success in Improving Performance

Adjustment lending was moderately successful in improving aggregate economic performance. Despite receiving more serious shocks, the thirty countries that received adjustment loans before 1985 performed better on average than the sixty three that did not. The performance was even better in the twelve countries with three or more adjustment loans before 1987 and in countries that were substantial exporters of manufactured goods. Adjustment lending appeared to have been relatively less successful in the highly indebted countries and in sub-Saharan Africa. Detailed country studies corroborated the statistical findings. The report cautioned, however, that the conclusions were tentative, because it was difficult to isolate the effects of adjustment lending from the effects of initial conditions and external shocks.

Implementation of Conditions

The overall rate of implementation of conditions was good, and conditions were more likely to be implemented when the loan agreement spelled them out precisely. In a sample of about fifty adjustment loans to fifteen countries, 60 per cent of the conditions were met fully during the loan period, and another 24 per cent were substantially fulfilled.

Adequacy of External Financing

Although the sudden cutoff of external financing made some type of adjustment essential, orderly and sustained adjustment required adequate external financing. In some countries unanticipated underfunding of the programme reduced or delayed the benefits. In other instances, however, external adjustment assistance simply delayed the implementation of adjustment measures.

Commitment to the Reform Programme

The governments that best sustained their commitment to reforms were those that 'owned' the programme from the start. Although international agencies often assisted in preparing the programmes, the governments had to be convinced that the operations were the most appropriate way to address the problems facing their countries.

The Second Report

The main conclusions of the second report were:

Aggregate Effects of Structural Reforms

Countries adopting adjustment programmes have on average grown faster than other countries (Corbo and Rojas, 1990). After taking account of the effects of initial conditions, external shocks, and the amount of external financing, the countries that entered full-fledged adjustment programmes (EIAL, or Early Intensive Adjustment Lending countries) had a larger increase in the average rate of GDP growth than other countries. For some of these countries – such as Nigeria, the Philippines, Malawi, Cote d'Ivoire, and Mexico – growth was slower than country characteristics would have predicted. In other countries – such as Korea, Mauritius, Morocco, Ghana, and Thailand – programmes supported by the Bank appear to have stimulated growth by more than the initial conditions, external shocks, and external financing would have suggested. Constant-price exports as a share of constant-price GDP has increased substantially in the EIAL countries, both before and after controlling for other factors.

Controlling for these same factors, investment fell on average as a share of GDP in the EIAL countries. This means, however, that the relative efficiency of investment in EIAL countries rose, because they achieved higher growth with less investment. Both public and private investment declined. Often a decline in public investment was desirable, since its level was unsustainable and some of it had been misdirected. But for countries that have made major progress in reducing macroeconomic imbalances and reducing distortions and institutional weaknesses, resuming public investment in infrastructure is important for restoring growth and for stimulating private investment. The reduction of private investment in the initial years of an adjustment programme was predictable, because incentives were being changed and the credibility of the programme was building. The counterpart of the temporary decline in the investment ratio is that adjusting countries were able to have higher private consumption than otherwise.

Need for a Supportive Macroeconomic Environment

A stable macroeconomic framework contributes to the success of structural adjustment in every major area of the economy (Webb and Shariff, 1990). Adjustment programmes were more likely to fail when a stable macroeconomic framework is not in place, even when the adjustment package focuses mainly on macroeconomic and sectoral policies. So, in a country that starts with high inflation and a large current account deficit, the structural adjustment programme should focus initially on measures to reduce inflation and the current account deficit. The macroeconomic situation will be supportive of the adjustment programme when the inflation rate is low and predictable, real interest rates are appropriate, the real exchange rate is competitive and predictable, public sector saving rates are compatible with the resource mobilization requirements of the programme, and the balance of payments situation is perceived as viable.

Effect of Adjustment on Poverty and Living Conditions

When an economy has to adjust to adverse external shocks or the effects of previous policy mismanagement, some short-run social costs are usually inevitable. Even a well-designed adjustment programme harms some groups, while the majority benefits, since adjustment usually involves changing relative prices and reducing some government expenditures. When some of the poor are among the losers from adjustment, they suffer greatly since they were already at a subsistence level. Although the situation of the poor offers nothing for the Bank to be complacent about, there is no evidence that adjustment lending caused an increase in the overall misery of the poor. On the contrary, orderly adjustment, supported by Bank lending, seems to be less costly for most of the poor and for the general populace than disorderly adjustment without Bank support.

Changes in the available socioeconomic indicators of living conditions do not appear to be systematically related to adjustment lending (Maasland and Van der Gaag, 1990). The rate of growth of private consumption in EIAL countries in 1985–6 increased in total and on a per capita basis, in comparison with other country categories and when controlling for other factors. Current consumption appears to have been protected – relative to other countries – by reduction in investment expenditures. Other short-run indicators, such as nutrition and immunisation, have also improved for the EIAL countries. Long-run indicators of living conditions, such as infant and child mortality, have continued to improve in most countries, with or without adjustment lending. However, the poor quality and the aggregate nature of the data do not point to unqualified conclusions on these issues.

While socioeconomic indicators show continued improvement, the share of central government expenditure on the social sector has fallen slightly on average in countries with adjustment lending. Per capita social expenditures by central governments have also declined in some adjusting countries. It is not certain whether the declines in health and education expenditures caused a deterioration in the total services available to low-income groups, or whether more was paid by local governments and by higher-income clients. The declines in education expenditure have been accompanied by falling primary school enrolment ratios for the EIAL countries. To prevent declines in socioeconomic indicators, most adjusting countries need to increase social sector expenditures targeted toward the poor.

Since adjustment is taking longer in most countries than originally expected, recent adjustment operations supported by the Bank include more detailed analyses of the social impacts of adjustment programmes and more measures to alleviate the short-run costs of adjustment to the newly unemployed and the poor. Such measures include reallocations of social expenditures toward services used by the poor, severance payments and retraining for newly unemployed workers, and public works and employment schemes for unskilled workers. In some cases, several targeted interventions have been assembled into multi-sector compensatory programmes.

Raising Efficiency

Increases in the efficiency of investment can reduce the need for more saving. Distortionary policies, such as trade restrictions and financial repression, hold down the efficiency of investment and thus the rate of growth for a given investment level (Easterly, 1990). Removing these distortionary policies does the reverse: increasing the efficiency of investment and the growth rate of GDP for a given level of investment. Furthermore, the analysis indicates that reform efforts must reach a critical mass to be effective: small decreases in extremely high distortions do not have much effect on growth. To have significant payoffs, reform programmes must usually focus on large reductions in the large distortions.

Increasing Investment

To sustain adjustment and restore growth, countries must not only reduce distortions, they must also create the conditions for the eventual increase in investment (Serven and Solimano, 1990). Some countries, especially in Africa, need more domestic saving and external financing to reach investment levels consistent with the restoration of growth. But in many countries, the prevalence of capital flight indicates that stagnant investment results from inadequate demand for investment rather than from the unavailability of saving. In highly indebted countries, the debt overhang often creates uncertainties about the sustainability of the balance of payments situation and about macroeconomic stability, and thus may thwart the recovery of private investment. Debt and debt-service reductions in the context of adjustment programmes can help reduce these uncertainties.

The eventual recovery of investment requires an appropriate and credible economic environment. Investment does not respond well when investors, foreign and domestic, doubt that the government will sustain its reforms and when legal and bureaucratic impediments are left untouched. Private investors often wait before making irreversible investment decisions, keeping their assets elsewhere. Providing appropriate public investments that complement private investment and getting a few private investors to commit themselves usually helps to overcome the doubts of the majority. But there is no simple way to bring this about. The obvious remedy of investment subsidies is likely to be expensive and at odds with the objectives of leaving decisions to market forces and restoring fiscal balance. An appropriate strategy for increasing investment contains four elements: (1) establishing and maintaining macroeconomic stability, including a predictable and competitive real exchange rate, a low-budget deficit, and low rates of monetary growth and inflation; (2) removing legal and bureaucratic impediments to investment by domestic and foreign firms, and providing clear rules for taxation, property rights, and the regulation of production and trade; (3) expanding public investment that is complementary to private investment; (4) ensuring sufficient external financing to support a sound programme in both the medium and the long terms. In highly indebted middle-income countries committed to sustaining a reform effort, the Brady initiative and other debt-reduction schemes should help improve the viability and credibility of adjustment programmes.

Raising Saving Rates

To sustain desirable rates of investment and growth, the saving rates in most adjusting countries have to increase, especially in typical African countries which started the 1980s with very low saving rates. The most effective way to increase saving in the initial years of an adjustment programme is to increase public saving (Schmidt-Hebbel and Webb, 1990). Private saving, responsive mainly to an increase in the GDP growth rate, starts to increase after growth gets underway. Once real interest rates are positive, further increases of real interest rates on deposits and special tax treatments for savings are unlikely to cause any large increase in saving rates.

Refinements

The findings of the Second Report confirm and extend some of the conclusions of the First Report. The sequence of reform measures is crucial. In countries that start with high inflation and a large current account deficit, structural reforms aimed at restoring macroeconomic balances should be emphasised first. Sectoral reforms should be sequenced in a way that takes account of the linkages among sectors. For instance, trade liberalisation is likely to improve efficiency more if accompanied by measures that improve the functioning of domestic markets for goods and credit, provide needed infrastructure, and reduce controls on domestic investment and impediments to labour mobility. In some low-income countries, barriers to the integration of the domestic economy – poor roads, inappropriate domestic transport infrastructure, lack of domestic financial markets, and so on – are the major impediments to economic growth and should be tackled first.

The data set on conditionality and implementation, with a much expanded sample of loans approved in the financial years 1979–88, showed most of the same patterns found last year and revealed some new ones (Webb and Shariff, 1990). Countries begin implementing their structural adjustment programme before the adjustment loans become effective and frequently continue implementation after disbursement ends. Nevertheless, a uniformly applicable way to measure the progress in implementation is to see what share of conditions in the loan agreements have been implemented by the time of final tranche release. Of all conditions in the loan agreements in the sample, 84 per cent had been implemented at least substantially – better than found in the First Report – and 66 per cent had been implemented fully or more than fully by the time of final tranche release. The implementation rates increased during the 1980s, both for countries that had adjustment lending since the early 1980s and for countries that started more recently. For the loans in the sample that had final tranche release in the financial year 1989, i.e., since the First Report, 99 per cent of the conditions were implemented at least substantially, and 80 per cent of the conditions were implemented fully or more, as originally written in our sample. In the rare cases when a condition does not seem necessary as originally written, the Bank waives the condition, with approval from the Board. Not counting the one loan in the sample for which this occurred in FY89 would raise the proportion of fully implemented conditions from 80 to 88 per cent. Thus, the final tranches were released only when all conditions in the loans were at least substantially fulfilled.

Governments have been more frequently able to develop and maintain political support for structural adjustment when the programme was designed with this aim in mind and when the government was active in explaining the source of the problems addressed by the programme, how the government plans to tackle them, why this is the best option and how people can benefit from the new policy environment. Mobilising beneficiaries to become political supporters usually follows. While technical considerations sometimes cause unavoidable delays in programme implementation, more prompt implementation almost always increases the chances of political support. Awareness of the economic problems that motivated the initial decision for reform will be strongest at the beginning, giving the authorities maximum latitude for reform. The support for sustaining the new status quo then develops as structural reform pays off in growth and higher living standards.

Adjustment programmes need to give greater attention to reforming and developing institutions in several areas: the agricultural sector in sub-Saharan Africa; the financial sector and fiscal management in many countries; and public enterprises in almost all countries. Although adjustment programmes often call for a reduction of resources going into the public sector, it is equally important to strengthen public institutions through improved policies, organisation, and management. Institutional development is essential for both the implementation and the ultimate success of many of the reforms the Bank supports.

9 The Many Faces of Adjustment

Frances Stewart

INTRODUCTION

The 1980s was a decade of adjustment for much of the Third World. At an early stage UNICEF drew attention to the serious human costs of the recession, and subsequently to the impact of stabilisation and adjustment measures on vulnerable groups and the need for special policies to counter these costs (Jolly and Cornia, 1984; Cornia, Jolly and Stewart, 1987). In the latter half of the decade, there were, apparently, very major changes in the international financial institutions in these matters – in their recognition of the social costs of adjustment and of the need for changes in policies.

This chapter is intended to review these issues from the vantage-point of the early 1990s: surveying the extent to which there have, indeed, been social costs during the decade, looking both at macro-performance among adjusting countries and at the changing conditions for human life in the large number of countries subject to external shocks, as well as a more in-depth analysis of six countries; and examining the changes that have taken place in the IMF and the World Bank, in order to assess how far their adjustment policies have in practice been humanised, and whether the changes they have made are enough to deal with the situation, in the light of the evidence presented earlier in the chapter.

The subject is an important one because of the *pervasiveness* of the adjustment problem over time and in terms of the numbers of countries affected – by the end of the 1980s as many countries were seeking adjustment support from the Fund and Bank as at the beginning of the decade, while many countries had had a continuous series of Fund and/or Bank programmes. Thus the idea that a temporary belt-tightening was all that was involved is no longer plausible, and consequently what happens 'while crossing the desert' (to use Bank terminology) is important because the crossing has lasted more than a decade already, affecting not only the immediate

176

wellbeing of hundreds of millions but also their potential for productive activity in the future.

'MACRO' PERFORMANCE OF ADJUSTING COUNTRIES

This review starts with an assessment of the macro-performance of adjusting countries – the growth rate, investment rate and extent of internal and external stabilisation achieved. The macro-performance is of critical significance for the human condition, especially when adjustment processes are prolonged. While design of adjustment programmes can do a great deal to protect the human condition for a temporary period, when the adjustment process is accompanied by falling per capita incomes and reduced investment, it becomes very difficult – even with well-designed programmes – to sustain human conditions over a long period. Thus a major reason behind the deterioration in aspects of the human condition in both Jamaica and Tanzania in the 1980s was that their human-oriented programmes could not be maintained because of prolonged macro-economic failure.

There are many ways of assessing whether the adjustment programmes have 'worked' at the macro-level. (For recent methodological discussions, see Faini et al., 1991, and Khan, 1990.) The objective of most assessments is to compare what has happened with what would have happened in the absence of the programme, i.e. with some counterfactual, which may be approximated in a variety of ways. The results are unavoidably controversial, since the counterfactual cannot be observed and depends on assumptions made. However, for our purpose a more straightforward assessment is relevant, since what we need to know is what the actual macro-performance was in adjusting countries, not whether it was better or worse than some counterfactual.

There has been considerable variation in macro-performance among adjusting countries: on the one hand, there are the experiences of Indonesia, Burkina Faso and Mauritius, for example, which combined adjustment with economic growth and rising rates of investment; on the other, countries such as Zambia and Argentina which have had sharply declining per capita incomes, falling investment, and, despite successive programmes, have not reduced the imbalances in their economies, either budgetary or external.

Despite this variation, in sub-Saharan Africa and Latin America –

the two major adjusting areas – the balance of experience in the 1980s was undoubtedly negative, as indicated in Tables 9.1 and 9.2. In both areas, the region as a whole exhibited falling per capita incomes in the 1980s, falling investment and accelerating inflation. In both, the balance of payments current account showed some improvement (substantial in the case of Latin America) but was still in large deficit, despite rescheduled (and unpaid) debt servicing, and restricted imports. The budget deficit showed no improvement in SSA and a considerable worsening in Latin America. The latter half of the decade was a little better than the first half, from the point of view of GDP growth, but the imbalances (fiscal and current account) which had narrowed in the first half, widened again.

Thus for these two regions taken as a whole the macro-adjustment measures of the 1980s were associated with deterioration in macroperformance, and thus in the basic framework for meeting human needs, while the adjustment process was in no way completed, as indicated by the large imbalances which persisted. While the 1980s is often referred to as a 'lost decade', with the presumption that we begin again with growth as usual in the 1990s, the current state of these regions is such that the 1990s are likely to form another lost decade.

The evidence in Table 9.1 for the regions as a whole includes both adjusting and non-adjusting countries, thus concealing differences between them. To allow for this, Table 9.2 provides data for the 'adjusting' countries only, in the two regions. Among adjusting countries in SSA, three-quarters had falling per capita incomes, over 50 per cent falling investment and half accelerating inflation; in Latin America and the Caribbean, the situation was even worse, with more than four-fifths of the countries having negative performance on per capita incomes and investment. The inflation picture looked a bit better, with improvements in 40 per cent of the countries, but sharp worsening in a few.

In these two regions, then, which are the major 'problem' areas, macro-performance worsened in the 1980s. The adjustment policies did not succeed – except in a minority of cases – in restoring economic growth. Falling investment rates will make growth even more difficult to secure in the 1990s. Moreover, the imbalances persisted in many countries requiring further adjustment in the 1990s. Most oil-producing countries in the Middle East also showed negative macro-performance, but experience elsewhere (Asia and developing Europe) was significantly better, both for the regions as a whole, and

TABLE 9.1 *Macro-performance at regional level*

Sub-Saharan Africa

	1973–80	1981–5		1985–9
Real per capita GDP growth, % p.a.	+0.1*	−1.0		−0.1
Inflation rate, % p.a. (consumer prices)	+6.8	+23.1		+21.1
	1981	1985	1989	
Investment ratio, % GDP	20.9	18.2	17.7	
Govt. deficit as % GDP	−6.9	−5.4	−7.7	
Current a/c balance, $b	−12.9	−3.4	−8.8	

Latin America & Caribbean

	1971–80	1981–5		1985–9
Real per capita GDP growth, % p.a.	+3.1	−1.5		+0.6
Inflation rate, % p.a.	+39.8	+102.8		+260.8
	1981	1985	1989	
Investment ratio, % GDP	22.6	17.5	18.2	
Govt. deficit as % GDP	−4.1	−7.1	−15.5	
Current a/c balance, $b	−43.6	−2.4	−8.9	

* GNP per capita

SOURCE IMF, *World Economic Outlook*, April 1989; October 1990.

for 'adjusting' countries. Thus among the countries outside Latin America and Africa which were adjusting in the 1980s (defined according to the list provided in World Bank (1990b)), ten had positive growth in GNP per capita and only four had no or negative growth.

As noted earlier, the main thrust of reviews of adjustment experience conducted by the international financial institutions themselves has been to compare performance with some postulated counterfactual, represented either by non-adjusting countries' experience, or by some predictions of how the adjusting countries would have behaved in the absence of adjustment policies. For example, *Adjustment Lending: An Evaluation of Ten Years' Experience* by the World Bank, compares adjusting (AL) with non-adjusting (NAL) countries and concludes that 'the average performance of AL countries was

TABLE 9.2   *Macro-performance among adjusting countries[a]*

Sub-Saharan Africa	GNP per cap. % change p. a. 1980–87[b][d]	Investment % change p. a. 1980–88[c][d]	Inflation rate[d] 73–80	80–87
Togo*	−3.4	−1.6	8.2	6.6
Ghana*	−2.0	+4.9	45.4	48.3
Kenya*	−0.9	−1.1	11.6	10.3
Madagascar*	−3.7	−0.7	10.2	17.6
Malawi*	0	−8.3	8.5	12.4
Mauritania*	−1.6	−5.3	8.5	9.8
Mauritius*	+4.4	+14.0	12.5	8.1
Nigeria*	−4.7	−14.5	16.2	10.1
Senegal*	+0.1	+2.0	8.8	9.1
Tanzania*	−1.7	+0.3	15.4	24.9
Zambia*	−5.6	−4.5	8.9	28.7
Cote D'Ivoire*	−3.0	−11.4	16.0	4.4
Burkina Faso	+2.5	+4.3	11.2	4.4
Burundi	−0.1	+8.8	15.4	7.5
Guinea	−0.1	n.a.	n.a.	n.a.
Mali	+0.5	+2.8	10.8	4.2
Niger	−4.9	−10.2	8.5	4.1
Sierra Leone	−2.0	−1.6	14.5	50.0
Zaire	−2.5	−1.6	42.1	53.5
Zimbabwe	−1.3	−1.5	10.6	12.4
Guinea-Bissau	+0.8	+3.8[c]	5.3	39.2
Congo	+1.7	+7.1	9.2	1.8
Central Afric. Rep.	−0.7	+8.8	14.8	7.9
Unweighted average	−1.2	−0.4	14.2	17.1
No > 0	6	10	11[f]	
No ≤ 0	17	12	11[g]	

Latin America	GNP per cap. % change p. a. 1981–89[k]	Investment % change p. a. 1980–88[c]	Inflation rate 1981[k]	1989[k]
Bolivia*	−3.3	−19.5	25.2	1.476
Brazil*	−0.1	0	91.2	21.1
Chile*	+1.2	+0.3	9.5	21.1
Colombia*	+1.7	+0.3	27.5	27.1
Costa Rica*	−0.8	+5.8	65.1	13.9
Jamaica*	−0.7	−1.2	4.8	14.2
Mexico*	−1.2	−6.9	28.7	18.2

TABLE 9.2   *continued*

Latin America	GNP per cap. % change p. a. 1981–89[(k)]	Investment % change p. a. 1980–88[(c)]	Inflation rate 1981[(k)]	1989[(k)]
Argentina	−2.9	−7.7	131.2	3.731
Ecuador	−0.1	3.7	17.9	59.2
Honduras	−1.5	−0.6[(e)]	9.2	10.8
Panama	−2.2	−3.2	4.8	0.1
Uruguay	−0.9	−9.2	29.4	81.9
Guyana	−4.1	n.a.	8.1[(i)]	15.9[(j)]
Unweighted average	−1.1	−3.9[(h)]	34.8	421.9
No > 0	2	2	5[(f)]	
No ≤ 0	11	10	8[(g)]	

Notes: *Countries are 'early-intensively adjustment lending countries'.
(a) Includes countries in SSA + LA adjusting according to World Bank, RAL II.
(b) UNDP, 1990.
(c) World Bank, 1990.
(d) World Bank, 1989.
(e) 1980–87.
(f) no. decelerating.
(g) no. accelerating.
(h) excludes Guyana.
(i) 1965–80.
(j) 1980–8.
(k) ECLA, 1989.

SOURCE UNDP, 1990: *Human Development Report, 1990* (New York: United Nations)
World Bank, 1990: *World Development Report, 1990* (Washington, DC: World Bank)
World Bank, 1989: *Sub-Saharan Africa: From Crisis to Sustainable Growth* (Washington, DC: World Bank)
ECLA, 1989: *Preliminary Overview of the Economy of Latin America and the Caribbean* (Santiago: United Nations)

better than NAL countries: that is, the average improvements in growth and the resource balance was greater for AL countries than NAL countries' (p. 2), despite the fact that on their evidence the majority of AL countries experienced declining per capita incomes and falling per capita consumption levels, a deterioration in performance compared with the pre-adjustment period. The more recent

World Bank review (RAL II) comes to similar conclusions: 'After
taking account of the effects of initial conditions, external shocks and
the amount of external financing, the countries that entered fully-
fledged adjustment programmes . . . had a larger increase in the
average rate of GDP growth than other countries.' (p. 3). However,
the study suggested that lower investment rates were found in adjusting countries than non-adjusting. These assessments are of thirty
countries adopting both Fund and Bank adjustment programmes. An
analysis of 52 countries with Fund or Bank and Fund programmes for
the 1978–86 period, also controlling for the external environment and
initial conditions, found no evidence of any statistically significant
improvement or worsening in growth following the programmes and
some evidence of a decline in the investment ratio (Faini et al.,
1991). A similar methodology, reviewing IMF programmes from
1973–88, found negative growth effects and positive stabilisation
effects of Fund programmes, with stronger effects in the first year
after the programme was initiated than in subsequent years (Khan,
1990).

The data used in these reviews includes not only SSA and Latin
America but also the rest of the world, where performance has
tended to be better, which is one reason why the assessment is less
negative than that suggested above. World Bank, 1988d, notes that
SSA and the highly indebted groups performed less well. Another
reason for the difference in assessment is the 'counterfactual' approach adopted. From the point of view of the effects on human
conditions, the counterfactual methodology is inappropriate, since it
is not performance compared with some postulated counterfactual,
but *actual developments* which are significant. Macro-policies will
only be satisfactory when they lead to sustained growth and rising
levels of investment. This they have failed to do in many countries,
especially in SSA and Latin America.

THE HUMAN CONDITION: EVIDENCE FOR THE 1980s

The mechanisms whereby human development is affected by economic developments are well established: there are three prime factors
(i) through incomes, which are affected by changes in employment,
wages and incomes from self-employment; (ii) through the prices of
basic goods, especially food; and (iii) through the availability of
essential services normally provided by the state – notably health and

education services. A fourth element – usually more difficult to measure – is the demands made on women's time, which affects how well the household can cope in general and, especially, in relation to adverse change.

In *Adjustment with a Human Face* (Cornia et al., 1987) (AWHF), evidence was reviewed of movements in each of these four factors in many adjusting countries in the early 1980s, and of changes in some fundamental indicators of human welfare, including measures of health and nutrition and of educational attainment. While the evidence was partial (because of lack of data) and mixed (showing some improvements, some worsening) the balance was clear: many countries subject to sharp economic shocks and undergoing stabilisation and adjustment showed negative changes in the main indicators. This review will consider whether more recent evidence supports these findings. The review will focus mainly on SSA and Latin America, the two areas most affected by adjustment.

Incomes: Aggregate Performance

Overall trends in GDP and consumption per capita are important indicators. If these are negative, the general deterioration will have been shared by the poor, unless they were specially protected. Conversely, any general improvement in these aggregates is not liable to be associated with a worsening position for low-income groups, unless they have been subject to specially adverse circumstances.

As already noted, macro-performance was poor in most of Latin America and Africa. In Latin America, GDP per capita fell in eighteen countries, 1981–9, and rose, or was unchanged, in five. In SSA, GNP per capita fell in twenty-eight countries and rose or stayed the same in thirteen (1980–7). However, private consumption was relatively protected, with more of the burden of adjustment falling on investment and government expenditure. Nonetheless, in Latin America, consumption per capita fell in fourteen out of twenty-three countries, 1980–8, while in SSA, consumption per capita (1980–7) fell in twenty-five countries and rose in eight. The distributional impact of these aggregate trends depends on changes in incomes and employment in particular sectors.

184 *Results*

Urban Incomes

Real Wages

Adjustment and stabilisation policies tend to depress real wages, as control over money wages is combined with devaluation and price decontrol. Evidence for eleven countries in Latin America shows that average real wages in 1989 (or 1988) were 10 per cent or more below their 1980 level in eight countries. Urban real minimum wages had fallen by more, being over 20 per cent below their 1980 level in eight out of eleven countries.[1] Countries with large cuts in real wages included both 'adjusting' and 'non-adjusting' countries – with Bolivia, Argentina and Jamaica in the former group and Peru in the latter.

In SSA out of eighteen countries for which there is evidence, real wages fell from 1980 to 1986 in sixteen, rising only in Burundi and the Seychelles (JASPA, 1989). In some countries the fall was sharp. For example, in Tanzania, the real minimum wage in 1986 was 35 per cent of its value in 1980, while in Sierra Leone, real wages in 1985–6 were 29 per cent of their 1980–1 value (Weeks, forthcoming). In Nigeria the average wage fell by 25 per cent, 1980 to 1985 and the minimum wage by 45 per cent (Jamal and Weeks, 1988). As in Latin America, the fall in real wages occurred in both 'adjusting' and 'non-adjusting' countries.

Employment

Stabilisation and adjustment policies are likely to lead to reduced employment and real wages in the short run. The hope is that as adjustment proceeds this will be reversed as new efficient job opportunities emerge. However, as the aggregate data for GDP summarised above indicate, GDP growth was not resumed in most countries, so that the short-term negative employment effects generally persisted throughout the 1980s.

The evidence shows that formal sector employment growth slowed down in most countries in both LA and SSA in the 1980s and fell in some; as population increased slowed only slightly in LA and not at all in SSA, this meant increasing un- or underemployment. For Latin America as a whole it is estimated that about four million fewer jobs were created, 1980–5, than would have been created if pre-crisis trends had continued (Albanez et al., 1989). In SSA, wage employment fell significantly in Cote D'Ivoire, Gambia, Niger, Swaziland

and Zambia while in Malawi, Mauritius, Seychelles and Zimbabwe the increase was well below the growth in the labour force (JASPA, 1989).

Unemployment

Urban unemployment rates rose sharply in many Latin American countries in the early 1980s. In a few they fell back significantly in the second half of the 1980s, but in others they remained high, or rose further. Out of sixteen countries, unemployment rates were above the 1980 level in 1989 in ten countries, and the same or lower in six. The data is rather spotty in Africa, but 'the general trend towards a growing prevalence of unemployment in the region is undeniable'. Rising urban unemployment rates were reported for some period in the 1980s in Zimbabwe, Nigeria, Madagascar, Mauritius, Liberia, Cote D'Ivoire, Senegal, Kenya, Togo, Niger, and the Seychelles (JASPA, 1989, p. 16).

Urban Informal Sector

Expansion of numbers in the informal sector was another response to the poor opportunities in the formal sector, although the data is weak. In Latin America, the proportion of non-agricultural employment in the informal sector is estimated to have grown to 32 per cent in 1986 (from 29 per cent in 1980), while in SSA the proportion of the urban labour force estimated to be employed in the informal sector rose from 56 per cent in 1980 to 60 per cent in 1985 (Tokman, 1986; JASPA, 1989, p. 21).

Increasing numbers in the informal sector are liable to lead to depressed incomes, especially when formal sector wage incomes, which provide a market for some informal sector activities, are stagnating. In Latin America, informal sector earnings per capita are estimated to have fallen more sharply than formal sector wages, with a fall of over a quarter for the region as a whole, 1980–5 (Tokman, 1986). But there is no comparable evidence for Africa.

Thus for the urban sector in these countries, the general picture is one of formal sector employment opportunities lagging behind population growth – and in a few cases falling absolutely – rising rates of urban unemployment and an increasing proportion of the labour force in the informal sector. Real wages have fallen in most countries and informal sector incomes are believed to have fallen by as much, or more.

Food Prices

The value of real wages is generally calculated by deflating nominal wages by the consumer price index. But real incomes of the low-income urban population are particularly affected by changing food prices. A number of elements in the adjustment package are likely to lead to rising food prices: these include devaluation (affecting food prices for food-importing countries), rising producer prices for farmers, price decontrol and reduced food subsidies. Detailed investigation of IMF programmes for 1980–4 showed that capping or reduction of food subsidies formed part of thirty two out of seventy eight programmes, while exchange rate reform was in 54 per cent of programmes. There is not comprehensive information for food subsidies or food prices.[2] However, in Latin America, reductions in food subsidies have been noted in Brazil, Mexico, Colombia, Jamaica and Peru. In Africa, an important and universal element in the adjustment policies was a change in the terms of trade in favour of the agricultural sector. Although the biggest change was in export prices, which rose nearly 30 per cent between 1982 and 1986, for thirty-five countries, average food prices rose by 20–25 per cent when deflated by the consumer price index, indicating a *sharp increase* in the relative price of food (1988d, p. 52).

Rural Incomes

As noted above, the adjustment policies were designed to improve the rural/urban terms of trade. The effect on income distribution and poverty thus depends on (a) the extent of this terms of trade change; (b) the location of the poor; and (c) whether the poor in each area are affected differently from the population as a whole. It is often suggested that adjustment policies may on balance *help* the poor because of the terms of trade change and the fact that most of the poor live in the rural areas.[3]

In Africa, it is true that the great majority of the poor are rural. Thus the *World Development Report 1990* estimated that the rural poor account for 80 per cent or more of the total number of poor people in African countries. However, the proportion is less and more variable in Latin America, ranging from just 20 per cent in Venezuela to 66 per cent in Guatemala.[4] In Latin America, therefore, the depressed real incomes of the urban labour force will have adversely affected a large number – in some cases the majority – of the poor, while in Africa the proportion of the poor adversely affected by the large cuts in urban incomes is much smaller (although still, of course, of significance). But it cannot be concluded that the policies have therefore helped the poor in Africa, because they are not distributionally neutral in their effects on the rural sector. In particular, the heavy emphasis on export crop prices and, to the extent that food is included, on foods supplied to the urban sector, mean that rural producers of subsistence crops (as well as rural wage-earners) have not benefited proportionately, and may indeed have lost through curtailment of government services (including fertiliser subsidies). While we do not have systematic evidence on this issue, detailed investigation in the Ivory Coast, confirmed by some evidence for Ghana and Sierra Leone, suggests that even in the rural areas, the poor may have suffered during the adjustment process.

In the Ivory Coast, poverty is particularly concentrated on food producers, the incidence of poverty among this group being estimated at 42 per cent in 1980, as compared with 27 per cent among export crop producers. The Structural Adjustment Loans were mainly focussed on raising export crop prices. All groups in the Ivory Coast suffered a loss in per capita income from 1980–5, but the loss was least (at 1.3 per cent p.a.) among export crop producers and most (4.7 per cent p.a.) among food producers. As a consequence, despite an improvement in the rural/urban terms of trade, poverty incidence worsened significantly, and the poorest groups suffered most. Thus while aggregate per capita incomes fell by 2.6 per cent p.a., poverty rose by 4.8 per cent p.a. and hard core poverty by 7.9 per cent p.a. (Kanbur, 1988).

A similar situation occurred in Ghana. About 80 per cent of the poor are rural and a high proportion are engaged in agriculture. But the rural/urban terms of trade improvement, which focussed on cash crops, especially cocoa, did not reach a high proportion of the rural poor. This is partly because the poor are not so fully in the market economy. For example, the hard-core poor, while accounting for 8 per cent of the population receive only 4 per cent of the revenue from crops. Secondly, the poor are not specialised in export crops. Thus the hard-core poor receive only 2.7 per cent of cocoa-revenue, the rest of the poor account for 21.4 per cent of cocoa-revenue, and the non-poor 76 per cent. Only 16.9 per cent among hard-core poor and 21 per cent (poor in general) of their total revenue from crops comes from cocoa (Boateng et al., 1990). To reach the poor through a terms of trade change, it is therefore necessary to raise the prices of food crops (cassava, yams and cocoyams, maize and rice); altogether food crops account for about three-quarters of the revenue of the poor. Food crop producers in Ghana suffered a net loss because of the removal of subsidies on fertilisers (Mosley, Harrigan and Toye, 1991). However, probably only a small proportion of the poor were affected by this. In Sierra Leone, 'policies which raise crop prices worsen the distribution of income within the rural areas' (Weeks, forthcoming, MS p. 82) because the poorest farmers are net food purchasers.

These three examples show that significant reductions in rural poverty cannot be *assumed* simply because of a shift in the terms of trade that favours the rural areas. In the African context, where the rural poor very often specialise on basic foods, these stories are fairly typical.

Similar mixed results emerge from an analysis by Sahn and Sarris of the impact of structural adjustment on small-holder households, arrived at by modelling some of the policy changes for 'prototypical' low-income rural households in five African countries. (Sahn and Sarris, 1990) Change in non-agricultural income was included, but the methodology does not allow for differentiation among the small-holders, apart from some geographical differentiation. Falling household incomes were shown in Ghana and the Ivory Coast over the adjustment period, a fall in two out of three areas in Madagascar, and sharp falls in Tanzania in the early years of the decade with some recovery in 1989. Malawi gave the best results with an increase in small-holder income of 36 per cent over the decade, more than offsetting a previous 20 per cent fall.

Aggregate Trends in Poverty during Adjustment

The evidence reviewed here shows that urban poverty has increased in most Latin American and African countries, with falling real wages, rising un- and underemployment and falling labour incomes in the informal sector and rising relative food prices. The situation in the rural areas is more ambiguous as there has been an improvement in the rural/urban terms of trade, but the country examples show that this has not necessarily reduced rural poverty – which, indeed, certainly increased in the Ivory Coast and Sierra Leone and probably in Ghana and Madagascar.

According to the World Bank, aggregate evidence on poverty, based on successive poverty surveys, is available for only eleven countries for a significant period in the 1980s. Of the four Latin American countries, three – Brazil (1981–7), Colombia (1978–88) and Venezuela (1982–7) – show unambiguous evidence of rising poverty, while in Costa Rica poverty remained at the same level, 1977–86, increasing in the first six years and decreasing in the last three (World Bank, 1990c, p. 43). There is no comparable data for African countries, but the *World Development Report* concludes: 'With few exceptions, the evidence supports the conclusion that poverty in sub-Saharan Africa is severe and has been getting worse' (p. 42). Elsewhere, reductions in poverty during the 1980s were recorded in India, Indonesia, Malaysia and Pakistan, and large increases in Thailand, Poland, Yugoslavia and China. It must be emphasised that this information is only for a small sample of countries. Less systematic evidence indicates that poverty also increased in most other Latin American and Caribbean countries in the 1980s, in the Philippines, and in Sri Lanka.

Government Expenditure on Social Services[5]

Government expenditure on the social services – here defined as health and education – depends on the total level of government expenditure, and the share going to the social services. Adjustment policies tend to emphasise *decreasing* total public expenditure, rather than increasing taxes as a mechanism for achieving greater fiscal balance. However, in practice there was a variety of experience among adjusting countries in the 1980s, although the balance of experience was of falling real per capita government expenditure. Amongst African countries, total government expenditure per head fell in eleven countries from 1980–7, and rose in seven (staying the same in one); in Latin America, it fell in ten and rose in five; among other adjusting countries it fell in three and rose in five.

The countries which succeeded in raising total government expenditure per head included: (a) those with positive growth in GNP per capita. Botswana, Burkina Faso, Mauritius, Colombia, S. Korea and Sri Lanka were countries with positive growth, which raised government expenditure while improving their fiscal balance. Most raised taxes as a proportion of GNP, but in S. Korea, the revenue ratio was falling. It also included (b) those with falling per capita GNP, who maintained government expenditure by an increased tax ratio. This was achieved by Ghana, Zimbabwe, Argentina and Chile, who each simultaneously *reduced* their budget deficits. Costa Rica and Jordan were in a similar situation, but suffered a moderate increase in the budget deficit.[6]

However, the more common story, when GNP per capita was falling, was for declining government expenditure per head. Falls of over 30 per cent were experienced by Liberia, Sierra Leone, Tanzania, Zambia, El Salvador and Venezuela. How this situation affected government expenditure on health and education depends on changes in the share of these sectors. The sectoral allocation of government expenditure by region is shown in Table 9.3. In aggregate, the share of health and education declined in the two adjusting regions, with a large decline in Latin America. Economic services, general administration, and defence also received a declining share. This was accounted for by a huge increase in interest payments, which rose from 9 per cent to 19.3 per cent of the budget in Latin America and from 7.7 per cent to 12.5 per cent in Africa. Social spending as a proportion of non-interest spending remained broadly constant in SSA (1980–7), but fell in Latin America.

The aggregate effect of the fall in total government expenditure per capita in the two adjusting regions, together with the decline in the share of health and education, was a decline in social spending per head – of 26 per cent in SSA and 18 per cent in Latin America (1980–5). In a sample of thirty-four countries (sixteen which received World Bank SALs, pre–1985 and eighteen which did not), over 60 per cent of the adjusting countries experienced cuts in health and education expenditure per head, 1980–6, while among the non-adjusters the majority showed rises in health and education expenditure (Kakwani et al., 1989). More comprehensive data for Latin America shows that 60 per cent of the countries experienced cuts in expenditure per head on health services in the 1980–6 period (Albanez et al., 1989). In SSA, there was a similar proportion (58 per cent) with cuts in health expenditure per head while 68 per cent of countries cut education expenditure per head.[7] This evidence thus shows more pervasive cuts in per capita expenditure on health and education for Africa for 1980–6/7 than found for 1979–83. For the earlier period, 47 per cent of countries in Africa showed cuts in health and 33 per cent in education; in Latin America, the proportion seems to have remained broadly unchanged at around 60 per cent for both health and education.

Some of the cuts were very large. For example, in Bolivia the cut in per capita expenditure on health, 1980–6, was 76 per cent; in Tanzania education expenditure per capita fell by 64 per cent and health by 44 per cent. But the variety of experience must be stressed. Some adjusting countries succeeded in increasing per capita expenditure on

TABLE 9.3 Regional shares* of total government expenditure by main sector, 1980–1 and 1985–7, and number of countries with shares declining or increasing over same period

	Health & Education 1980–1	1985–7	Economic Services 1980–1	1985–7	General Administration 1980–1	1985–7	Defence 1980–1	1985–7	Interest Payments 1980–1	1985–7	Others 1980–1	1985–7
LATIN AMERICA (9 countries) of which with share	24.4	18.4	19.3	13.6	13.1	9.6	7.7	6.8	9.0	19.3	29.4	33.6
– declining	6		7		6		8		1		3	
– increasing	3		1		2		1		7		5	
– no data	0		1		1		0		1		1	
AFRICA (13 countries) of which with share	20.2	18.9	21.7	20.6	18.8	17.0	12.7	11.5	7.7	12.5	22.6	22.6
– declining	8		6		9		7		1		6	
– increasing	5		7		4		5		11		5	
– no data	0		0		0		1		1		2	
MIDDLE EAST (6 countries) of which with share	14.8	18.9	23.5	20.3	12.5	12.6	27.5	25.0	1.1	1.7	19.2	21.1
– declining	0		4		4		4		1		1	
– increasing	6		2		2		2		3		3	
– no data	0		0		0		0		2		2	
ASIA (10 countries) of which with share	14.9	16.7	30.1	27.4	11.1	11.7	16.7	17.1	8.9	14.1	17.7	14.3
– declining	1		6		6		8		0		5	
– increasing	9		4		4		2		9		4	
– no data	0		0		0		0		1		0	
TOTAL (38 countries) of which with share												
– declining	15		23		25		27		3		15	
– increasing	23		14		12		10		30		17	
– no data	0		1		1		1		5		6	

* Regional averages are the arithmetic average of country shares. Total by line may not add up to 100 because of rounding errors.

SOURCE Elaborations on *Government Financial Statistics* (Washington, DC: International Monetary Fund).

TABLE 9.4   *Increases (+)/decreases (−) in expenditure per head, 1980–86 in education (E) and health (H)*

	E +/−	H +/−
Adjusting, pre-1985	6/10	6/10
Not adjusting pre-1985	15/3	10/8

SOURCE   Kakwani, N., E. Makonnen and J. van der Gaag (1989), 'Structural adjustment and living conditions in developing countries', mimeo (Washington, DC: World Bank).

health and education – for example, Zimbabwe, Burkina Faso, and Thailand.

Intra-sectoral Allocation[8]

In terms of the impact on health and basic education, government expenditure cuts can have very different effects according to the intra-sectoral allocation of resources. There is limited evidence on intra-sectoral allocation of expenditures in health and education. However, information available suggests different trends in the two sectors.

Education

Data on education suggests that primary education has been protected relative to secondary and tertiary education in sub-Saharan Africa, where the share of primary education in total education increased in fifteen out of twenty-two countries (Jespersen, 1990; Berstecher and Carr-Hill, 1990). Much more limited evidence from Latin America suggests mixed experience. For example, in Chile, the share of pre-school and primary education increased from 48 to 57 per cent, 1980–6 (Castanedo, 1987) and in Mexico, primary school enrolments increased at a time of severe cuts in total expenditure (Valero, 1990). But in Costa Rica, the share of expenditure going to basic education fell from 63 per cent of sectoral expenditure in 1980 to 54 per cent in 1987 (World Bank, 1989f). Fees for primary education were introduced in some countries. In Zambia, Mali, Sierra Leone and Togo parental expenditure for a primary school child varied between 7–20 per cent of average GNP per capita around 1986 (Jespersen, 1990).

Health

In contrast to the education sector, data for the health sector for sixteen African and Latin American countries shows very little change over time in the relative shares of hospital and primary health care (IMF, 1990). Despite the overall decline in resources, hospitals have continued to absorb as much as 70–80 per cent of total health expenditure. In contrast, in countries with a strong focus on primary health care (e.g. China), this ratio is significantly less (around 60 per cent in China and only 33 per cent in Myanmar). Nonetheless, there was expansion in low-cost high-impact health care interventions – e.g. child immunisation and oral rehydration therapy – in most countries. The rate of coverage is estimated to have increased by 20–30 per cent p.a., 1981–7. The expansion of these activities is likely to have increased the efficiency of health expenditures.

User Charges for Health Services

This section relies heavily on Creese (1990). These charges were introduced in a number of adjustment programmes – for example, Ghana and Zaire.[9] Studies of the effects on the use of health services in these countries have shown a fall in use which is greater the lower the income of the household. For example, in Zaire prenatal contacts fell from 95 per cent to 84 per cent, with greater falls among the low-income. In Ghana, there was a major increase in fees in 1985. Sharp drops in use of clinics followed; among the urban clinics attendance gradually got back to the pre-1985 level, but the drop in rural utilisation rates was sustained. In Swaziland, charges for government health facilities were raised three to four times. The result was a big shift towards mission facilities and an overall drop in use of modern health facilities of 17.4 per cent. There appeared to be a disproportionate drop in use of modern services among low-income households, and particular declines for sexually transmitted and respiratory diseases. A simulation model using Peruvian data showed that 'price plays a significant role in the demand for health care, and that demand becomes more elastic as income falls, implying that user fees would reduce access to care for the poor proportionately more than the rich' (Gertler et al., 1987).

Aggregate Changes in Health and Education Expenditures

The overall picture is decline in per capita government expenditure
on health and education in adjusting countries in most, but not all,
cases; in some instances the cuts have been very severe. The decline
is due to downward pressure on total government expenditure, and a
declining share going to health and education. Interest payments
have taken a sharply rising share of the budget, more than accounting
for the decline going to the social sector in SSA, and largely accounting for the larger decline in share of the social sector in LA. Intra-
sectoral allocation has helped protect primary education, but has not
protected primary health care expenditures, although special health
interventions have contributed to the maintenance of aspects of
health in the face of deteriorating services. User charges, introduced
in both education and health, have deterred use and imposed a
specially heavy burden on low-income households.

Women's Time

Economic recession and adjustment have exerted increasing pressures on women in each of their four roles – as producers, as home
managers, as mothers and as community organisers.[10] More time has
been needed for each role; but given that many poor women were
already working twelve hours or more, there is an overall time
constraint, and additional time in one activity may be at the expense
of another. In particular, as women spend more time on income-
earning activities outside the home, the time available for maternal
and home management responsibilities lessens, reducing the efficiency with which outside resources are used, and thus the welfare
of the household.

Systematic evidence has not been collected on how the crisis has
affected women. But there is enough for some generalisations:

(1) there has been a definite trend towards greater female participation in the money economy, with rising female participation
rates observed, for example, in Brazil, Costa Rica, Peru, Venezuela and the Philippines, at a time when male participation rates
were stationary or even declining.
(2) decreasing household resources have increased time needed
for household management, requiring adjustment of consumption
habits, sales of assets, negotiation of loans, and increased effort
devoted to subsistence production (see Raczynski in Cornia et al.,

Vol. 2; Moser, 1989). In Lusaka, low-income households acquire almost 50 per cent of their food through female cultivation of vegetable plots (Commonwealth Secretariat, 1989, p. 65).
(3) in some cities, survival efforts have involved cooperative ventures among women for shopping, cooking etc. An example is the *Comedores Populares* in Lima, Peru.
(4) with deteriorating health and health facilities, more time is needed for support of sick children, including travelling to clinics, waiting and for home-cures, such as oral rehydration therapy (Leslie et al., 1986).

A study of low-income households in an urban area of Ecuador, 1978–88, illustrates these developments and their consequences (Moser, 1989). Female participation rates increased over this period from 40 per cent to 52 per cent. Women were working longer hours, and starting to work when the children were younger. Reduced incomes affected diets. For example, the average consumption of milk declined by two-thirds, and there was a marked decline in the consumption of fish and eggs, and a shift from potatoes to platano. The number of meals eaten per day had declined, with one-quarter of the households eating only one meal a day in 1988. Female children are increasingly being called on to substitute for their working mothers in household duties. There was increasing domestic violence, attributed to cash problems. Women are spending more time on community management functions than before, as increasing need for services along with declining state provision has led to more NGO activity, requiring more local participation.

Moser distinguishes three reactions to these pressures: first the 'burnt-out' women, who have given up, more-or-less abandoning families to the streets. This group accounts for about 15 per cent of women. Secondly, those who are 'hanging-on', just managing, while increasingly relying on female children. These are the majority, and are at risk of falling into the first category with further pressures. The third group are the 'copers', who are successfully balancing their roles. About 30 per cent are in this category.

STATUS INDICATORS

The previous section has shown that many adjusting countries suffered severe deterioration in their living conditions, with falling real incomes, reduced expenditures on health and education, and increasing time pressures on women. In each respect the evidence of developments in the mid-1980s confirms the findings of AWHF for the early 1980s. This section reviews how far these worsening conditions have been reflected in the major human indicators – viz. indicators of nutrition, health and education.

Nutrition

Declining real incomes do not necessarily lead to worsening nutrition, since households adjust their consumption patterns to consume low-cost sources of calories. Research by Behrman and Deolalikar (1988) suggests that while average food expenditure declines by 8 per cent for every 10 per cent decline in income, caloric intake declines by only 3 per cent. But even small declines in caloric intake can have serious effects on those who are already on the margin of survival. Nutrition data is rarely collected systematically, so trends often have to be inferred from sporadic surveys or hospital data. However, recently the ACC/SCN has begun to collect international data on a more systematic basis, reporting on thirty-three countries.

Latin America

In Latin America, the ACC/SCN data covers twelve countries. They found rising malnutrition among children under five in four out of the twelve countries (Chile (1984–6), Jamaica (1978–85), Nicaragua (1966–82) and Peru (1984–7)). A sharp but temporary rise in malnutrition also occurred in Venezuela, 1984–5. However, some countries in Latin America showed significant reductions in child malnutrition rates in the 1980s, including Costa Rica, Colombia, Guatemala, and Uruguay.[11] The 1989 nutrition survey in Jamaica also shows a substantial improvement for the 1980s as a whole (World Bank, 1989a). The proportion of babies with low birth weight increased in eight out of fifteen countries, 1979–86.[12]

Africa

In Africa, the ACC/SCN records data for eight countries. Of these there were increases in malnutrition in Niger, Lesotho and Madagascar (1981–7), as well as temporary increases, largely reversed in Togo and Ghana (1982–3) and Botswana (1981–4). Benin showed an increase from 1986–7. Thus of the nine countries covered, seven showed some evidence of rising malnutrition at some point in the 1980s. The two remaining countries showed unchanged rates over this period – in Burkina Faso at a very high level of above 40 per cent of children; and in Rwanda at the still high rate of 30 per cent. Other data shows rising malnutrition among children in Zambia (76–87) (Clarke, 1988), Kenya (79–82) (Ayako, 1990), Nigeria (Adenyi et al., 1990), with no significant changes in Liberia (Jespersen, 1990) and some small improvements in Sierra Leone and Zimbabwe (Kamara et al., 1990; Davies, Sanders and Shaw, 1991). The *World Development Report 1990* reports that 'In sub-Saharan Africa malnutrition is on the rise, and the number of underweight children has grown substantially' (p. 45).[13]

Data for food production per capita for the 1980s (Table 9.5) shed further light on the nutritional situation. Among African countries, twenty-four showed a decline in food production per capita and eleven an improvement (or no change), 1979–81 to 1986–8. In Latin America, fourteen showed a decline and five an improvement. Among other adjusting countries, five showed a decline and six an improvement. Severe declines (over 10 per cent) occurred in thirteen African countries (37 per cent of the countries), five Latin American (26 per cent) and two of the other adjusting countries.

Declining per capita food production occurred among countries with WB adjustment loans as well as non-adjusting countries, at a similar rate (70 per cent of both African and Latin American 'adjusting' countries showed declines in per capita food production and 40 per cent of the 'other' adjusting group). However, the countries receiving WB support showed a lower rate of severe decline in each region. But in Africa, the rate of severe decline remained significant at 30 per cent of adjusting countries.

Food production data is not an accurate indicator of nutritional position because it does not allow for imports and exports, the nature of the food produced and its distribution, and indeed the data itself may be inaccurate. Nonetheless, there is a presumption that a significant decline in food production, especially where food availability is already inadequate, will lead to worsening nutrition. The data suggests that this was the case in around one-third of African countries, and a smaller proportion in Latin American countries – a picture which supports the more spotty evidence coming from direct observation of nutrition status.[14]

TABLE 9.5   *Food production per capita 1979–81 to 1986–8*
(*1979–81* = *100*)

African countries 1986–8			Latin America 1986–8		
	Angola	87	(d), (c)	Argentina	97
	Botswana	69	(c), (a)	Bolivia	95
	Benin	110	(c), (a)	Chile	105
(d)	Burkina Faso	116	(c), (a)	Costa Rica	89
(d), (b)	Burundi	100	(c), (a)	Brazil	108
	Chad	109	(a)	Colombia	100
(d), (c)	Central Af. Rep.	87	(d), (c)	Ecuador	97
(d)	Congo	92	(b)	El Salvador	87
	Cameroon	97	(b)	Guatemala	92
(c), (b)	Côte d'Ivoire	92	(c), (a)	Mexico	93
(b)	Ethiopia	89	(d), (c)	Honduras	76
(d)	Gabon	97	(c), (a)	Jamaica	101
(c), (a)	Ghana	108	(d), (c)	Panama	95
(c), (a)	Kenya	89		Paraguay	106
(d)	Guinea	93	(c)	Peru	96
(c)	Liberia	92		Trinidad & Tobago	71
(c), (a)	Malawi	85	(d), (c)	Uruguay	103
(c), (a)	Madagascar	97		Venezuela	97
(c), (a)	Mauritania	93	(c)	Dominican Rep.	95
(c), (a)	Mauritius	106		Nicaragua	71
	Lesotho	80			
	Mozambique	83			
(c), (a)	Senegal	106			
(c), (d)	Sierra Leone	101		*Other Adjusting*	
(c), (d)	Somalia	100			
(c), (d)	Niger	83	(d), (c)	Bangladesh	92
(b), (a)	Nigeria	103	(d)	China	132
(d), (c)	Mali	97	(d)	Indonesia	117
(c), (a)	Tanzania	89	(c), (a)	Morocco	106
(c), (a)	Togo	88	(c), (a)	S. Korea	98
(c)	Rwanda	82	(c), (a)	Philippines	90
(c)	Uganda	121	(c)	Sri Lanka	79
(c), (a)	Zambia	96	(c), (a)	Pakistan	107
(d), (b)	Zimbabwe	81	(d), (b)	Tunisia	111
(d), (c)	Zaire	98	(d), (c)	Sudan	89
			(d), (c)	Yugoslavia	100

Notes:
(a) Early intensive adjustment lending countries, according to RAL II, defined as receiving 2 SALs or 3 Adjustment operations before 1985.
(b) Countries with IMF programmes in 1 year 1980–7
(c) Countries with IMF programmes in 2 or more years 1980–7
(d) Other countries receiving adjustment lending

SOURCE   World Bank (1990c) *World Development Report 1990* (Washington, DC: World Bank) Table 4.

Health

Health status has been subject to two opposing influences in the 1980s. On the one hand, the deteriorating services in many countries, together with reduced real incomes and in some countries worsening nutrition: on the other, the substantial expansion of life-saving, low-cost interventions – most notably oral rehydration therapy and immunisation – which occurred in the early 1980s.

Accurate data for changing health status in the 1980s is limited. Life expectancy figures, which are a good single index, are not available on an accurate basis, and most published data simply reflects statisticians' extrapolations of previous trends. The same is true of infant and child mortality. Most statements about changes in these fundamental indicators of health are in fact based on extrapolated predictions. However, a few countries have better based data for infant and child mortality rates for two dates between the late 1970s and the late 1980s so that changes can be accurately inferred. But the data for under-five mortality does not necessarily reflect the health of the population as a whole, as it can be greatly improved with a few specific interventions.

Careful analysis of African data reveals only six countries for which data is available for changes in under five mortality rates in the 1980s (Hill and Pebley, 1989). These are Botswana, Ghana, Liberia, Mali, Senegal and Uganda. Of these countries, two – Uganda and Ghana – showed an increase in under-five mortality, and the other four countries continued to show a downward trend at much the same rate as in the 1970s. UNICEF data suggests rising rates of infant mortality also in Ethiopia and Madagascar. In the rest of the world, the Hill/Pebley data records continued progress in reducing under five mortality rates in the 1980s.[15] But a definite slowdown in the rate of progress was recorded in Malaysia, the Philippines, Singapore, Argentina, Costa Rica, Cuba, Dominican Republic, and Panama, whereas the rate of progress speeded up in Kuwait, Brazil, Chile, Colombia, Ecuador, Peru and Uruguay. Particularly high rates of progress were made in Botswana, Kuwait, Colombia, and Costa Rica (despite the slowdown), while very slow progress was made in the 1980s in Bangladesh, Mali, the Philippines, and Honduras, among the countries for which data is available (Hill and Pebley, 1989).

There are no health sector enrolment rates, comparable to education enrolment rates. But declining attendance at public health facilities has been observed in a number of countries – see above – associated with the introduction or raising of charges. Substantial declines in the availability of basic medicines at government clinics is also believed to have reduced attendance in a number of countries, including Zambia and Tanzania.

Education

AWHF showed deteriorating educational performance in many countries in the early 1980s, as indicated by falling enrolment rates and rising drop-outs. More recent data shows that primary school enrolment rates have been dropping in SSA over the 1980s, from an average of 79 per cent in 1980 to 73 per cent in 1986. Moreover, completion rates at primary school fell slightly in SSA (van der Gaag et al., 1990). Secondary enrolment rates continued to rise, on average, but fell in six countries (1980–6). Data for the Bank group of most intensively adjusting countries show a fall in primary school enrolment rates for the twenty-five countries, on average, in contrast to the performance of the less intensive adjusters and non-adjusters (World Bank, 1990a). Outside SSA, falls in primary school enrolments were recorded in Chile, Colombia, Costa Rica, Morocco, the Philippines, and Thailand in the 1980s out of the fifteen non-SSA countries which were in the intensive-adjusters group.

Summary of Findings on the Human Condition

Performance has been mixed. Some adjusting countries have had growing incomes, reduced poverty, rising social expenditures and improved social conditions. But the majority have seen falling incomes; in many cases falling per capita consumption; real wages and incomes in the urban informal sector have been depressed, and unemployment rates rising; the numbers in poverty have increased in a large number of countries. The rural poor have generally not fared as badly, but usually the improved terms of trade have not benefited them proportionately, since they are not heavily involved in cash crop production. In the majority of countries in Africa and Latin America there have been cuts in expenditure per head on education and health. Moreover, the adjustment process has put new pressures on women's time. The impact of these generally adverse changes on human indicators has been mixed. There is evidence of rising malnutrition in quite a few countries in SSA, and in some elsewhere.

Primary school enrolment rates have fallen and other indicators of educational performance worsened in the majority of adjusting countries. Health indicators – notably infant mortality rates – do not seem, on the limited evidence available, to have deteriorated except in a very few countries, but the rate of improvement has slowed down in quite a number of countries. The expansion of low-cost health interventions that took place over these years may have offset other adverse effects.

SOME COUNTRY EXPERIENCES

The previous sections showed that country experience in adjustment has been very varied. Some countries appear to have been successful in protecting the poor during adjustment, while others have been unsuccessful. This section briefly summarises examples of successful and unsuccessful experience in Africa (Tanzania and Burkina Faso), Asia (Indonesia and the Philippines) and Latin America (Chile and Costa Rica), in order to provide some insights into appropriate policy-making.

Indonesia[16]

Unlike most other economies, Indonesia's adjustments only started in 1983 with the fall in oil-price. Until then, Indonesia grew fast, using her oil-revenue to develop infrastructure in agriculture, education and transport. These efforts – and especially expansion of rice output – led to a rapid fall in poverty (the percentage of population falling below the official poverty line declined from 60 per cent (1970) to 40 per cent (1976) to 22 per cent (1984)). Income inequality also declined over this period, and human indicators (infant and child mortality rates, life expectancy, nutrition, and educational attainment) improved.

From 1983, a sharp adverse movement in the terms of trade necessitated adjustment. The adjustment package adopted included severe public expenditure cuts (in real terms of 19 per cent, 1982–3 – 1986–7) and major currency devaluation. The real effective exchange rate fell by 60 per cent from 1982 to 1987. It was thus a broadly conventional package. The Indonesian adjustment was successful, in the sense that the current account deficit was reduced from a peak of over 6 per cent 1983 of GNP to around 2 per cent in 1987. The value of exports fell sharply in 1985 and 1986, but resumed a high growth rate from then. Inflation remained at a moderate level. However, the budget deficit rose as a percentage of GNP, as the revenue ratio fell more sharply than the expenditure ratio, and from this perspective the adjustment package was more expansionary than an orthodox package.

Unlike many countries, during the adjustment period while growth slowed it remained positive. From 1983–7, per capita growth in GDP averaged 2.9 per cent. Per capita consumption rose faster, by 5.0 per cent p.a. 1984–7. Every poverty indicator shows that poverty declined, 1984–7, while inequality lessened with a decline in the Gini coefficient. According to the official estimates of poverty, the percentage of poor declined from 21.6 per cent (1984) to 17.4 per cent (1987), with a larger decline in the rural areas than the urban. Social indicators also continued to improve over this period. The average per capita caloric intake rose by 5.7 per cent, increasing at every level of income; declining rates of protein-calorie malnutrition are reported in both rural and urban areas, 1978 to 1986–7; gross primary school enrolment rates increased (1980–5) and there was a significant increase in immunisation rates; rapidly declining infant mortality rates are recorded (falling from 90 to 70 per 1,000 between 1983–7).

The record thus shows that Indonesia was highly successful in combining adjustment, growth and human development. How was this achieved? Firstly, the considerable *macro* success in maintaining growth of GDP per capita was an important factor. This success was partly due to the balance of macro-policies adopted with considerable emphasis on switching as against disabsorption (associated with the big depreciation and the rising budget deficit); partly to the very favourable supply response – both in terms of expansion of cash crop exports (estate crops grew by 9 per cent p.a., 1984–8, farm non-food crops by 4.3 per cent p.a., which was *not* greatly at the expense of other agricultural products, which continued to expand albeit at a lower rate) and of labour-intensive manufactured exports (manufactures had risen to 29 per cent of the value of exports in 1988 from 8 per cent in 1983). Of course, some of this change is due to changing relative prices. The favourable supply response was in turn due to earlier developments, which had provided Indonesia with extended rural infrastructure, extensive human capital and some industrial and entrepreneurial experience (see Ravallion and Huppi, 1990; World Bank, 1990c).

Secondly, the fact that consumption growth was maintained at a much higher rate than income, protected consumption during the adjustment period.

Thirdly, the growth was relatively egalitarian so that the distribution of additional consumption was favourable from the perspective of poverty reduction. As a result of the changing terms of trade and prior investments, rural consumption rose faster than urban. Within the rural sector, relatively equal land distribution meant that the poor participated in the increased output; while they were not proportionately represented in cash crops, they did participate in their expansion, and also in the expansion of food crops which continued; moreover, non-agricultural rural opportunities expanded. Rural real wages were maintained and employment expanded. Within the urban sector, the focus on labour-intensive manufacturing led to growth in manufacturing employment (manufacturing employment in enterprises with more than fifteen employees is estimated to have expanded by nearly 10 per cent p.a., 1985–8, a considerable acceleration compared with 1982–5) (World Bank, 1990c, p. 20). In both rural and urban areas there was a slight rise in real wages.

Fourthly, the cuts in government expenditure broadly protected the services of the poor (ibid., pp. 20–4). First, the reductions fell most heavily on development expenditures, while routine expenditures were protected (central government routine expenditure grew by over 7 per cent, 1982–3 to 1985–6 while development expenditure fell by 43 per cent); secondly, transfers to the provinces were protected, growing despite the aggregate cuts; thirdly, development expenditures were reallocated to priority areas – thus development expenditures on human resources rose from 16 per cent of the total, 1982–3 to 24 per cent, 1986–7. For the health sector as a whole, expenditure levels per capita increased by 8.7 per cent p.a.; central hospital spending fell from 19 per cent of the total in 1984 (already very low) to 5 per cent in 1987. Health posts were established in more than 70 per cent of the villages (WHO/UNICEF, 1988). However, there is evidence of cutbacks in some preventative health programmes after 1986 (Griffin, 1991).

In summary, both macro and meso policies supported adjustment with a human face in Indonesia. But the process has been accompanied by rising external debt and debt-service ratios which may cause problems in the future.

The Philippines

The Philippines had high levels of poverty (at least 30 per cent of the population), which were not reduced by growth in the 1970s. The Philippines had borrowed a great deal in the 1970s, and in the 1980s suffered from rising interest rates, the cessation of voluntary lending, and adverse terms of trade. The current account deficit rose to over $3 billion in 1982 (8 per cent of GDP) and the fiscal deficit to over 4 per cent of GDP. Stabilisation and adjustment measures were introduced in 1983. Very substantial deflation, through cuts in public expenditure and credit constraint, were the major element, 1983–5, with little change in the real exchange rate. The fiscal deficit fell to 1.8 per cent of GDP in 1985, achieved through expenditure cuts as the tax ratio did not alter. The current account deficit was eliminated by 1985 and was in surplus in 1986, based entirely on cuts in imports as exports fell, 1983–5. From 1986 more expansionary policies were adopted and the real exchange rate was depreciated; government expenditure recovered, the fiscal deficit widened, exports grew but a current account deficit reemerged. Thus Philippine macro policies fall into two phases – deflationary adjustment in the early period, which was effective in reducing imbalances but had major costs, and expansionary adjustment from 1985–6, which led to emerging imbalances, but was associated with positive growth. The two phases were associated with marked differences in social consequences.

The Deflationary Phase

There is evidence of negative social effects arising from the first deflationary phase, which was associated with sharply falling GDP per capita, with a cumulative fall of 17 per cent, 1982–7. Growth has been positive from 1987. Real wages did not change much, but unemployment and underemployment both increased by around one-third, with increases in both rural and urban areas, the sharpest increases being urban. Government expenditure fell sharply – from 15.4 per cent of GDP in 1981 to only 11.6 per cent in 1984. In real terms government expenditure fell by one quarter 1983 to 1986. Real expenditures on both health and education also fell as a proportion of government expenditure (from 5.1 per cent 1983 to 4.7 per cent 1985). Health expenditure per person halved, 1983–5; education expenditure per student fell by 19 per cent.

In terms of protecting basic needs, intrasectoral allocations over this period differed in the two sectors. In health, the share of preventive care fell in the first half of the decade, while that of curative care rose. Health services declined, as measured by nurses, midwives, dentists, nutritionists and sanitary inspectors per patient. (There was a small improvement in the doctor/patient ratio.) In education, primary sector expenditure expanded in line with enrolments, but not secondary schools where expenditure per student fell by nearly 40 per cent, nor tertiary education where it fell by 20 per cent.

Falling incomes and deteriorating health services were reflected in a slow-down in the rate of improvement of infant mortality rates and in rising malnutrition. In 1984 there was a marked increase in the incidence of communicable disease. There was also some worsening in the primary school enrolment ratio and of cohort survival rates in elementary school (Government of the Philippines and UNICEF, 1987).

The adverse effects on the human condition in the Philippines of the 1983–5 stabilisation arose from the macro-policies followed, with heavy emphasis on disabsorption as against switching policies, and on expenditure reductions rather than tax increases. Econometric estimates suggest that disabsorption has adverse effects on the poor, while exchange rate changes are pro-poor in the Philippine context (Blejer and Guerrero, 1990). Meso policies did not, on the whole, help to protect the poor.

The Expansionary Phase

Policies since 1986 have been more expansionary with greater emphasis on switching; special measures have also been taken – notably the Community Employment Development Programme, a two-year emergency employment from 1986–8 – to protect the incomes of the poor. Growth was above 5 per cent in each year 1987–90, although the poor in the Philippines did not participate very fully in resumed growth, because of the prevalent inegalitarian structures, with a high degree of inequality in land ownership. But the urban poor benefited from growth of employment.

It is estimated that the incidence of poverty dropped from 59 per cent in 1985 to 49.5 per cent in 1988. Government revenue per head rose over this period, the combined effect of a rising ratio of taxation to GDP and a rise in GDP per capita. In addition a small rise in the share of government expenditure going to health and education meant that expenditure per head in these sectors rose from 1985, reversing the previous fall (Nuqui, 1991, Fig. 4). There was greater emphasis on preventive health care: immunisation coverage rose from 25 per cent (1985) to 82 per cent (1989), and there was a major increase in disease control programmes. School enrolments rose significantly, reversing the previous fall.

The Philippine adjustment experience thus shows two distinct phases (corresponding to political changes) both in macro and meso policies. In the first half of the decade, both were unfavourable and this showed up in deteriorating human conditions; in the second half, macro policies have been more growth-oriented, while adverse changes in meso policies were replaced by (mildly) favourable ones.

Tanzania

Tanzania is justly famous for the strong emphasis put on human development in the first two decades after independence. But economic performance was less good, and the country started the 1980s with massive imbalances, partly due to poor agricultural achievements and partly to external shocks. The 1980s have seen continual adjustment efforts, at first without, and after 1982 with, the support of the IMF and WB (see Wagao, 1990). Macro policies over these years included expenditure cuts, exchange rate devaluations and price liberalisation. Until 1986, these efforts were associated with declining per capita production, but over the years 1986-9 there was positive growth in GDP and agricultural output per capita. However, the imbalances, which had narrowed in the early years (fiscal and current account) widened again. Over the period as a whole, there was substantial reduction in the real urban wage, leading to a wage-level considerably below any reasonable subsistence minimum.

Total government expenditure per head fell over the 1980s, which was compounded by a slight fall in the share of health and education. Consequently, expenditure per head in education fell by 59 per cent (1978-9 to 1988-9) and in health by 49 per cent. Food availability per head fell sharply until 1985, but was restored to a bit above the 1981 level by 1988.

There is rather limited evidence on the impact of these deteriorating conditions on human indicators, apart from data on primary school enrolment, which fell dramatically – by over a quarter. Anecdotal and partial evidence suggests that many health clinics stopped working at all effectively. A Government of Tanzania/UNICEF analysis finds that

> The conditions of work for health workers, as for others in government service, have deteriorated. Facilities are not maintained. Basic supplies and equipment are lacking. The situation deteriorated so significantly in the maternity wing of Mhimbili Medical Centre, the national referral centre in Dar-es-Salaam, that in 1988 maternal mortality rates were increasing because of lack of supplies and equipment even for blood transfusions (Govt. of Tanzania/UNICEF, 1990, p. 64).

Malnutrition rates remained extremely high throughout the 1980s – although the studies are not precisely comparable (varying in place and season), on average the malnutrition rates in the 1980s (at nearly 50 per cent for underweight underfives) were significantly higher than the average shown by studies completed in the 1970s of around 40 per cent (ibid., Table 2) (Unicef, 1988).

In Tanzania's case, the poor macro-performance was mainly responsible for the sharp worsening in human conditions – meso policies were broadly neutral over the period.

Burkina Faso

Although Burkina Faso is one of the poorest countries in the world, she started the 1980s in a better position than many of her neighbours, from the point of view of economic management, having accumulated relatively little debt (Savadogo and Wetta, 1990). But the 1980s saw some major economic shocks – resulting from the oil-price rise, deteriorating export prices and drought. There was also a succession of political coups in the early years, leading to the establishment of a National Revolutionary Council as government.

Burkina Faso adopted various adjustment measures, but without IMF or WB programmes. Policies included some retrenchment of government employment and wages, measures to increase taxation and incentive prices for agriculture. The share of education in total government expenditure increased sharply (from 15 per cent, 1982–4, to 23 per cent, 1987), while the share of health remained broadly constant. School fees were cut.

Macro-performance showed considerable improvement compared

with earlier decades, with growth of 3.4 per cent p.a. 1983–9. The agricultural sector performed well, especially on food crops. Cereal production increased by 14 per cent p.a., with rising land and labour productivity. Export crop production also rose. There is evidence of marked improvement in human conditions over the decade. The number of health workers rose in relation to population. IMR fell from 148 (1983) to 139 (1987), while the proportion of low birth weight babies fell from 21 per cent to 11.9 per cent. Primary and secondary enrolment rates rose significantly.

Burkina Faso thus stands out in the sub-Saharan African context, seeing positive achievements in macro and meso policies and in human development over the decade.

Chile

Chile's adjustment policies (see Castaneda, 1989; Raczynski, 1987) go back to 1974 when Pinochet initiated a monetarist revolution. In the 1970s, the policies led to severe recession in 1974–5, greatly rising unemployment (from 5.7 per cent at the beginning of the decade to 13.9 per cent at the end) and stagnant real wages (which fell dramatically in 1973 and never recovered their previous level). Per capita income in 1979 was just about at its 1970 level. In the 1980s, Chile faced similar external shocks to other debt-laden and primary producing nations, with worsening terms of trade, reduced capital inflows and rising debt-servicing. The current account deficit amounted to 14.7 per cent of GDP in 1981. In the early 1980s, deflation was the main stabilisation measure, with cuts in government expenditure in 1982 and 1983 and stringent credit controls, and a small real depreciation. From 1984, more emphasis was placed on expanding exports; the real exchange rate fell by 40 per cent between 1984 and 1988. The adjustment/stabilisation measures were successful in reducing the current account deficit – which had fallen to 1.3 per cent of GDP by 1988.[18] In the early period, this was achieved by a drastic cut in incomes (GDP per capita fell by nearly 16 per cent in 1982); but in the latter part of the 1980s, there was a strong expansion of non-traditional exports – exports in 1989 were 69 per cent above their 1980 level. GDP per capita recovered, growing by 1.1 per cent p.a. 1981–9; consumption per capita grew a little slower (0.6 per cent p.a. 1980–8).

Like the Philippines, Chile's experience of adjustment in the 1980s thus falls into two phases – a deflationary phase and a more expansionary phase. Average real wages fell by nearly 11 per cent, 1982–3, and after that recovered a little; minimum wages fell by more, and did not recover over the decade. The unemployment rate rose very steeply to over 20 per cent in 1982–3, recovering to 7.5 per cent by 1989. Public expenditure was cut in 1982 and 1983, but resumed growth after that. Macro policies were thus unfavourable to vulnerable groups in the early phase, and more favourable in the latter phase.

Meso policies, however, have been directed towards protecting the most vulnerable throughout the period, succeeding, for the most part, even during the recessionary phase. Incomes were sustained at minimal levels by very extensive public works schemes. In 1983, almost 13 per cent of the workforce participated in one or other of the employment schemes. During the public expenditure cuts, social sector spending rose as a proportion of total expenditure from 50.4 per cent in 1980 to 59.7 per cent in 1983. Nonetheless, total per capita spending on the social services fell slightly in 1983, back to its 1980 level. Expenditure on both health and education fell from 1982 to 1987 (by 25 per cent in education and 15 per cent in health). However, intra-sectoral allocations did much to protect the most vulnerable.

In education, tertiary levels bore the brunt of the cuts, falling by nearly 50 per cent, while non-university expenditure fell by 16 per cent, 1982–7. The percentage of the educational budget going to pre-school and primary education rose from 48.3 per cent in 1980 to 57.4 per cent in 1986; the secondary education ratio remained broadly constant while the tertiary education share fell from 33.6 per cent (1980) to 29.6 per cent (1983) and 23.8 per cent (1986). (This reflects a longer term trend towards self-financing of university education, see Castanedo, 1989.) As a result of educational reforms the distribution of overall spending on education has become considerably more progressive over time, with the poorest 30 per cent of the population receiving 37.5 per cent of the benefits in 1986, compared with 28.6 per cent in 1974 and the richest 40 per cent receiving 34.5 per cent in 1986, compared with 47.3 per cent in 1974 (Castanedo, 1989)

In health, available statistics do not permit a breakdown of the large expenditure cuts (1982–3) into primary and curative health care. Indirect evidence suggests that basic services were largely protected. Supplies increased their share of total expenditure, and a major cut was taken by investment. Evidence shows rising levels of medical visits per person, and per mother and child, and a rising proportion of births attended by professionals, 1980–3. However, rates of immunisation show some slide from very high levels in 1983 compared with 1982, but rates of 90 per cent still obtained. A series of carefully targeted nutrition programmes did much to sustain nutrition during the recession. Total expenditure on the programmes declined, however, 1982–3 (by 8.5 per cent), with a falling number of meals provided.

While the meso policies thus worked to protect the vulnerable during the 1982–3 recession, despite macro developments, they were not sufficient in some respects, as shown by the evolution of social indicators. Most indicators of health continued to improve – infant mortality rates continued to decline, but not at the remarkable pace previously achieved. Thus from 1982 to 1986, the IMR fell by 18 per cent, compared with a fall of 40 per cent in the 1978–82 period. There was also a slight rise in malnutrition in 1983. Primary school enrolment ratios showed some fall throughout the 1980s, but pre-school and secondary enrolment rose consistently.

Looking at the Chilean case over a longer time period, there was a remarkable combination of almost stagnant incomes spanning the two decades, 1970–89, combined with tremendous advances in standards of health, education and nutrition. Over this period, infant mortality fell from 79.3 (1970) per 1,000 to 19.4 (1986); there was a falling proportion of malnutrition (15.5 per cent in 1975 to 8.7 per cent in 1985 among under-fives); the proportion of low birth weight babies halved; and other indicators of health (maternal mortality, diarrhoea mortality, bronchopneumonia mortality) greatly improved. Thus the twenty-year period can be seen as an almost continuous effort at promoting human development during economic stagnation, which was, despite hiccups in 1982–3, broadly successful in social terms. Success was achieved despite falling real per capita public expenditure on social programmes, by effective targeting and efficient use of public resources. We are not taking into account the costs of political repression, which may have been necessary for the success of the programmes.

Costa Rica[19]

Costa Rica has had a spectacular record in the improvement of human indicators. In 1988, her life expectancy at 75 was at developed country standards; her achievements on infant mortality, adult literacy, and rural/urban disparities put her among the 'top ten' developing countries (UNDP, 1990). But most of this achievement came in the 1970s. The economic crisis of the 1980s was accompanied by a slowdown in progress and some deterioration in human indicators. Costa Rica, like the rest of Latin America, suffered from the debt crisis of the 1980s. In the early 1980s, foreign finance dried up, and GDP per capita fell sharply. Successive administrations have taken vigorous adjustment measures in order to reduce the large budget deficit (7.4 per cent of GDP in 1980) and current account deficit (15.6 per cent of GDP in 1981). The fiscal deficit was reduced through increases in taxes (raising the tax ratio from 18 per cent in 1982 to 25 per cent of GDP in 1988) and a decrease in non-interest expenditures, which fell from 23 per cent of GDP (1980) to 21 per cent (1988). There was a large depreciation of the real exchange rate, which fell by 40 per cent, 1980 to 1988.

The adjustment policies were fairly successful in terms of reducing imbalances. Both budget deficit and current account deficits were cut, and the inflation rate fell sharply. Export values rose by 32 per cent 1980–9. Non-traditional exports rose significantly, accounting for 10 per cent of exports by 1988. But the adjustment was not painless: despite some recovery after a sharp fall in the early 1980s, per capita GDP fell slightly over the decade. Both agricultural and industrial growth was sharply down in the 1980s compared with the 1970s. Average real wages fell significantly in the early years (by 29 per cent, 1980–2), recovering to their 1980 level by 1989. Urban unemployment rose sharply in the early years and then recovered. Real per capita consumption rose by 0.4 per cent p.a. 1980–8, while investment per capita fell by 2.7 per cent p.a. (World Bank, 1990c) There was a big increase in poverty during the crisis years, with the percentage of households classified as in poverty rising from 29 per cent, 1977, to 40 per cent in 1983, the increase being greatest in the urban areas. After recovery, the proportion in poverty fell to below the 1977 level.

Apart from the recession in 1982, macro-conditions thus permitted standards of living to be maintained, but not improved.[20] However, it was the meso-policies which were the main cause of deteriorating performance. As already noted, non-interest expenditure fell as a proportion of GDP. Total real expenditure in the social sectors fell more sharply. Educational expenditures in 1987 were 20 per cent below the 1980 level, while public expenditure in health, nutrition and sanitation was reduced by 35 per cent from 1979 to 1988, and real expenditure per person by 45 per cent. Health expenditure as a proportion of GDP fell from 7.4 per cent (1980) to 5.1 per cent (1988).

Intrasectoral allocation cut further into basic needs. In the health sector, the share of the Ministry of Health, which provides most primary health care, fell from 16.2 per cent of total health expenditure in 1980 to 13.7 per cent in 1988. In the education sector, the share of basic education (which includes primary and secondary) fell from 72.4 per cent in 1975 to 62.7 per cent in 1980 and 53.7 per cent in 1987. The share of higher education rose from 24.4 per cent in 1975 to nearly 40 per cent in 1987. The result was a fall in real expenditure per pre-school and primary school student of 45 per cent, 1980–6, of 25 per cent for secondary pupils and of 10 per cent among tertiary students.

As a consequence of these changes most human indicators show a marked slowdown or even reversal for the 1980s. The infant mortality rate did not improve at all 1980–4, while regional disparities worsened. After 1984, IMR again began to fall. In education, gross enrolment ratios fell in both primary and secondary education, but continued to rise at pre-school and tertiary levels. However, there was an improvement in nutrition.

For Costa Rica, the 1980s as a whole marked progress on most social and economic indicators, with deterioration in the early years broadly offset by the later recovery. Despite its remarkable achievements on social dimensions, Costa Rica did not manage to protect the vulnerable during the recession years. The impact of economic stagnation in the first half of the decade was compounded by meso-policies, which involved cuts in public sector expenditure, cuts in the share of health and education in public expenditure, and cuts in the share of basic health and education within sectoral expenditure. This surprisingly adverse distribution of expenditure cuts appears to be due to institutional factors as much as political intention.

Some Conclusions From Country Studies

This brief review of six country experiences suggests the following conclusions:

(1) Developments on the human condition are the outcome of a combination of macro and meso policies, with good performance (from the point of view of the poor) on one compensating for poor

performance on the other. But clearly the best performance combines good macro and meso policies, as in Indonesia and Burkina Faso, while the worst combines poor performance on both (as in the Philippines, 1983–5).

(2) From this perspective 'good' macro-policies are policies which lead to equitable growth. The design of macro-policies has considerable bearing on this, both with respect to growth and to equity. Disabsorption policies tend to be bad for both growth and equity. Switching policies tend to be good for growth – given appropriate supply conditions, which depends on prior investments and the structure of the economy. But in conditions where agricultural supply is likely to be sluggish, and the manufacturing base is small (as in many African economies), supply response will be smaller and slower and more external finance will be needed, for longer. In certain conditions – especially where the poor participate in cash crops and labour-intensive manufactured exports – switching policies will also be good for equity. But in others, as in Ghana, the Philippines and the Ivory Coast, other policies will be needed to ensure that the poor participate in growth.

(3) Meso-policies can compensate for poor macro-performance, even over a prolonged period, as indicated in the Chilean case. The appropriate design of meso-policies depends on the macro-situation.

(4) Where macro-developments are leading to extreme, but temporary, poverty during the crisis, meso-policies need to support low-income households, by employment programmes, nutrition programmes etc. These schemes must be on a *large* scale, to be effective: i.e. employment schemes should provide employment for all who need it, at a low wage, as in the Maharashtra scheme and effectively in Chile. Similarly, the nutrition schemes need to cover the whole target population. Smaller scale schemes will obviously not provide the necessary comprehensive support.

(5) Where the structure of the macro-economy is leading to persistently high levels of poverty, unrelated to specific crises, longer term measures are needed to incorporate the poor in the economy, including land and credit reform. The Philippines and Ghana are examples.

(6) In all situations, even where the macro-economy is sustaining most primary incomes at satisfactory levels, meso-policies are needed to ensure that the poor have sustained access to basic social services. During expenditure cuts, this can be achieved by intersectoral and

intrasectoral allocations towards basic services. Indonesia was an example of favourable inter and intrasectoral allocations during adjustment; in Chile, the main emphasis was on intrasectoral allocation; Costa Rica, the Philippines and Tanzania failed to use meso-policies to protect the poor, and Costa Rica shifted resources away from basic services during the crisis.

ATTITUDES AND POLICIES OF THE INTERNATIONAL FINANCIAL INSTITUTIONS

Without doubt, there has been a major change in the attitudes of both Fund and Bank to the question of poverty and adjustment. For the first half of the 1980s, both institutions regarded the issue of poverty in relation to adjustment as solely a domestic one, on which they had, and should have, little to contribute.[21] Thus neither institution reported on the poverty implications of their adjustment programmes in country missions before 1985. However, in the last half of the decade there has been a radical change in attitude. A joint Bank/Fund Study prepared for the Development Committee pointed to

declining per capita incomes accompanied by worsening social indicators, particularly in sub-Saharan Africa and Latin America . . . Some of the poor did benefit, but many vulnerable groups were hurt by measures associated with adjustment. By the mid-1980s, it became clear that 'given the time and effort required to turn deeply troubled economies around, it would be morally, politically and economically unacceptable to wait for resumed growth alone to reduce poverty' (IMF/World Bank, 1989, quoting *IMF Survey*, 3 April 1989)

Michel Camdessus, Managing Director of the Fund, acknowledged 'the recognition that macroeconomic policies can have strong effects on the distribution of income and on social equity and welfare. A responsible adjustment programme must take these effects into account, particularly as they impinge on the most vulnerable or disadvantaged groups in society' (Speech to US Chamber of Commerce, 26 March 1990). Each IMF country mission is now required to report on the poverty implications of country programmes.

Since 1987, the World Bank's staff guidelines have required policy framework papers for low income countries to include 'a brief description and assessment . . . of the social impact of the government's intended adjustment program', and all President's Reports supporting structural adjustment to pay particular attention to 'the short-term impact of the adjustment program on the urban and rural poor, and measures proposed to alleviate negative effects' (Zuckerman, 1989).

How Much Action?

Neither Fund nor Bank *have made any significant changes to the basic design of their policies*, as to choice of policy instruments, balance of instruments used (e.g. disabsorption as against switching), or timing and sequencing. As far as the Fund is concerned, statements by the Managing Director indicate that changes in macro-policy are not considered desirable from the point of view of alleviating poverty:

These [Fund] programs involve, first and foremost, macroeconomic discipline, beginning with the reductions of fiscal deficits and monetary measures aimed at achieving prices stability and realistic exchange rates. . . . Macroeconomic discipline goes hand in hand with structural reforms that are designed to promote efficient resource use and to remove the most deep-rooted obstacles to growth. . . . Often, and quite properly, questions are raised about the impact of such policies on the poorest and most vulnerable. *Let me say outright: these policies serve the poor, and we must do our utmost to implement them if we are to be efficient in our fight against poverty.* (Statement by M. Camdessus to the UN Economic and Social Council, Geneva, 11 July 1990)

Recent reviews of Bank policies towards adjustment and poverty, by Bank staff members, agree that 'For the most part, little attempt has been made to identify the possible adverse effects on the poor of specific policy reforms supported by adjustment programs and to redesign the adjustment programs in order to lessen such impacts' (Zuckerman, 1989; Ribe and Carvalho, 1990).

However, although the macro-policy package has not been redesigned, nor have the other aspects of structural adjustment packages, the Bank has supported some specific measures designed to compensate for the adverse effects of adjustment measures (ibid.; and Ribe et al., 1990). The Bank has differentiated between two types of poverty: the new poor, comprising those who have been pushed into poverty by public service retrenchment and others who may fail to find employment because of the contraction in the public sector workforce; and the chronically poor, consisting in people whose poverty predates adjustment, and who may become poorer as a result of the adjustment measures. For both groups, the underlying notion is that of *compensation* of those adversely affected by programmes. This notion is important because it means that compensatory programmes are not usually intended to serve people whose poverty is independent of the adjustment programmes, even though these groups may be poorer than those adversely affected by the programmes. The rather limited nature of the special programmes can be traced, in part, to this principle.

Programmes designed to compensate the newly poor (see Ribe and Carvalho, 1990) include

(i) severance payments, aimed at sustaining living standards of dismissed workers until they find new jobs. These are a common measure and were included in nine programmes (Guinea, Guinea Bissau, Ghana, Senegal, Mauritania, Sao Tome and Principe, Congo, Togo and Gabon) out of thirty SALs undertaken, 1986–8.
(ii) retraining for retrenched workers was included in seven out of thirty programmes. In one the chronically poor were included as well as retrenched workers.
(iii) provision of credit for retrenched workers – nine programmes.
(iv) resettlement of retrenched workers in agriculture, included in four programmes.

Programmes designed both for the newly unemployed and the chronically poor include:

(i) public works schemes, often involved in constructing infrastructure – six programmes.
(ii) nutrition support schemes for children and pregnant women were included in five programmes.
(iii) social expenditure reform aimed at protecting the poor during adjustment (by protecting expenditures on basic services and more generally improving targeting). This is the most common measure; out of 30 SALs, twenty-one made some reference to public expenditure reorientation of this kind.

(iv) targeting food subsidies – these (included in a few SALs) were aimed at protecting the poor (in part or whole) while subsidies are withdrawn. Examples are Tunisia, Morocco and Nepal.

The first set of measures – those designed to compensate retrenched public sector workers – by their nature go to a rather limited number of people, who are almost invariably not among the poorest in society. These measures may be important for the political implementability of the programmes, but are trivial as a device to protect the poor during adjustment. The second set of measures have potentially much wider application. They too are based on the principle of compensation or protection of the poor against adverse effects of adjustment measures; thus if they are 100 per cent successful – that is, they are of sufficient value fully to offset the adverse effects and they reach all those adversely affected – *they will do no more than prevent some of the adverse effects of the adjustment measures*. They do not aim to cover all adverse effects (e.g. resulting from rising food prices; falling real wages; cuts in infrastructure), nor do they attempt to go beyond compensation for adverse effects of adjustment to compensation for other adversities (e.g. from changing commodity prices; recession), or more generally to alleviate poverty irrespective of the cause.

In most cases, the measures to protect the poor included in SALs have consisted in compensation for the 'new poor' (half of thirty SALs 1986–8) and/or some reorientation of public expenditure towards basic health and education (two-thirds of the SALs examined). However, it is not possible to tell how far such reorientation goes without detailed country information. Other measures only occurred in a small minority of cases (see Table 9.6). It is difficult to assess how significant the measures taken were without detailed country investigation, but in those cases where two or less measures were taken it seems likely that the total effect has been small.

However, in a few countries, the Bank has helped to coordinate and finance more general programmes, which simultaneously tackle a number of the aspects noted above. These too are 'add-ons' to a given programme design, but being more comprehensive they have come to be flagships of Bank efforts to be more human in its adjustment efforts. Below we briefly review two of these programmes, in Ghana and Bolivia (Klugman, 1990). These two programmes were the first comprehensive programmes in Africa and

TABLE 9.6 The social content of SALs, 1986-8

	New Poor	Social exp. reallocation	Food subsidies/ nutrition	Employment/ enterprise support	Rural development	No.
Chile I	−	+	−	+	−	2
Malawi III	−	−	−	−	−	0
Senegal II	+	+	−	+	−	3
Guinea I	+	−	−	−	−	1
Niger I	−	+	−	−	+	2
Burundi I	+	−	−	−	−	0
Gambia I	+	−	−	−	−	1
CAR I	−	−	−	+	−	2
Chile II	+	+	−	−	−	1
Panama II	−	+	+	−	−	2
Nepal II	+	−	+	−	+	2
Ghana I	+	+	+	+	+	5
Guinea-Bissau I	+	+	+	−	−	3
Senegal III	+	+	+	−	−	2
Mauritania I	+	−	−	+	−	4
Dominica I	−	−	−	−	−	0
Uruguay I	−	+	−	−	−	0
Zaire I	−	+	+	+	−	2
Sao Tome & P.	+	+	−	−	−	3
Congo I	−	+	−	+	−	2
Chile III	+	+	−	−	−	2
Togo III	+	+	−	−	+	3
Gabon II	+	+	−	−	−	2

Burundi II	–	–	–	–	–	0*
CAR III	+	+	–	+	–	3
Tunisia I	+	+	+	+	–	4
Guinea II	+	+	–	–	–	2**
Honduras I	–	+	–	–	–	1
Morocco I	–	+	+	–	–	2
Costa Rica II	–	+	–	–	+	2
No. 30	16	21	7	9	5	

* Social Action Programme planned.
** Priority Action Programme planned.

+ included in programme
– not included in programme

SOURCE Ribe, H., and S. Carvalho, (1990) 'The treatment of social impact on adjustment programmes supported by the World Bank', mimeo (Washington, DC: World Bank)

Latin America, and have been replicated, with some amendments (or replication is planned), in other countries, including Madagascar, Guinea-Bissau, Chad, Uganda, Egypt, Sao Tome and Principe, Haiti and Guatemala.

Ghana

Following nearly twenty years of mismanagement and illfortune, Ghana introduced an Economic Recovery Programme in 1983, with Fund and Bank support. The programme consisted of the usual package – devaluation, dismantling price controls, reduction in the role of government (with 24,000 public workers sacked), and improved conditions – in terms of prices and inputs – for the major exports, notably cocoa, gold and timber. The programme was, however, unusual in one respect: it was an expansionary programme, involving a large increase in public expenditure, which was made possible by the revival of tax revenue (which had fallen to under 5 per cent of GNP, recovering to over 14 per cent by 1989) and a very substantial inflow of aid (aid rose from 4 per cent to 7 per cent of GDP, 1980–7).

Human conditions in Ghana had deteriorated enormously over the period of stagnation. Real wages for urban workers in 1983 were just 13 per cent of their 1973 level (Pickett and Shaeldin, 1989). In mid-1984, at the worst point when drought compounded recession, the salary of even an upper-level civil servant came to a fraction of the amount estimated to be needed for an adequate diet for a family of five (UNICEF-Accra in Cornia et al., 1987, Vol. 2, p. 98). There had also been dramatic declines in expenditure on the social services: between 1975 and 1982, per capita expenditure on health and education fell by three-quarters in real terms (ibid., p. 100). There were very high rates of poverty throughout Ghana, but the evidence of income levels and social indicators suggests that most of the poor are rural (around 80 per cent) and that deprivation is especially concentrated in the northern part of the country (Boateng et al., 1990). Worsening human indicators were observed between around 1975 and the early 1980s – as noted earlier, the under-five mortality rate has been rising, nutrition rates worsening and primary school enrolment rates falling.

The Recovery Programme has been apparently successful in economic terms, with a sustained growth of GDP of over 5 per cent p.a. over a five-year period. However, some problems are emerging, notably a rising debt problem (the debt service ratio had risen to over

50 per cent from 1985 (Toye, 1990c)), continued specialisation on primary commodities whose prices have been falling, and little sign of a pick-up in industrial investment. In its initial form the programme focussed almost exclusively on economic recovery, paying little attention to social issues. Yet the economic recovery programme – even though relatively successful – did little for the poor, and indeed in some respects (e.g. rising unemployment, withdrawal of some fertilizer subsidies, price decontrol, and the introduction of charges for education and health) caused further hardship. According to one assessment: 'the economic problems of the poor and vulnerable may have worsened in the short run' (Zuckerman, 1989).

The Programme of Actions to Mitigate the Social Costs of Adjustment (PAMSCAD) was initiated by the government in 1987 with international support coordinated by the World Bank, to respond to these social problems. The programme is multidimensional, including twenty-three anti-poverty interventions aimed at assisting both the direct victims of adjustment and the 'structural poor'; target groups include poor farmers, low-income urban unemployed and underemployed and retrenched workers. The projects include urban public-works for slum rehabilitation and repair of urban infrastructure, rehabilitation of schools, credit for small enterprises and farmers, roads, food-for-work for projects in the north, essential drugs, low-cost water and sanitation, and targeted child nutrition support. The estimated total cost is $84 million to be spent over two years, equivalent to 6–8 per cent of the annual cost of international support for Ghana's adjustment effort (Jolly, 1988).

Most of the funds (an estimated two-thirds) benefit the urban sector, despite the fact that the rural poor account for the vast majority of the poor in Ghana. Only 3 per cent of the funds were intended for projects in the north. The largest single allocation (accounting for 22 per cent of the total) was allocated to the 'new poor' for compensation and retraining. There have been serious implementation problems, so that most projects have only recently begun. These are due to the multidonor collaboration, involving numerous complex procedures, as well as local bottlenecks and administrative limitations. Donors earmark funds for specific projects, so some projects are oversubscribed and others not financed. A 1990 Bank review concludes that the project 'at this stage has neither succeeded nor failed' (Ribe et al., 1990)

However, even assuming that the project is successful in its own terms, there are some serious problems with it as a mechanism for

222   *Results*

TABLE 9.7   *Basic elements in PAMSCAD*

	$m. Rural*	Urban*
Community initiative	3.5	3.5
Employment generation		
– urban slum and infrastructure		17.0
– credit for small enterprise and farmers	1.0	1.0
– credit for small farmers	3.0	
– public works in North	2.6	
– feeder roads	3.4	
– other	2.0	6.6
Compensation and training for retrenched		18.6
Basic needs projects	8.2	8.2
Educational support	5.6	5.6
Total**	29.3	60.5

* Rural urban breakdown estimated.
** Total exceeds allotted $84m. because cost recovery is estimated to produce $5.8m.

SOURCE   Jolly, R. (1988) 'Poverty and adjustment in the 1990s', in J. Lewis (ed.), *Strengthening the Poor: What Have We Learned* (Washington, DC: Overseas Development Council)

protecting the poor. First, as noted it has a heavy urban bias. Secondly, the total number of people likely to be significantly affected are a fraction of those in serious poverty in Ghana. While the urban employment programme could provide around 30,000 jobs a year for two years, which would offset much of the loss of employment in the public sector resulting from adjustment, rural income-generating projects are negligible in quantity. The basic needs projects are all desirable, but again small relative to the size of the problem. For example, the nutrition project is intended to cover 15,000 children, yet the number of malnourished children in Ghana is at least half a million (Alderman, 1990). Thirdly, the project is intended to last two years from initiation. Yet, even assuming the adjustment programme continues to be as successful in the future as it has been in the past, there are no indications that the worst affected groups – the urban poor and poor farmers in the north – will be incorporated into the recovery. Thus the need will extend well beyond two years. Finally, the slowness in implementation, combined with the long time-lag before any action was initiated, means that the crisis had been underway for as much as eight years and the recovery programme at least five before any results were felt.

Bolivia

Bolivia is the poorest country in Latin America, with an infant mortality rate of twice the region's average. Life expectancy is only fifty-one years, and malnutrition is widespread, especially in rural areas. In the early 1980s, the economy was characterised as one of 'crisis and chaos', with the collapse of the world tin market, political instability, cessation of international lending, dramatic losses in GNP and per capita consumption and hyperinflation (see Sachs, 1987; Morales, 1990).

An orthodox stabilisation package, introduced in 1985, succeeded in stabilisation as such. The inflation rate fell from 24,000 per cent in September 1985 to 11 per cent in 1987 and to 21 per cent in 1988. But there has been a manifest failure to enter the transition into growth (see Figure 9.1). Meanwhile, cutbacks in government expenditure and investment, with massive redundancies (three-quarters of the

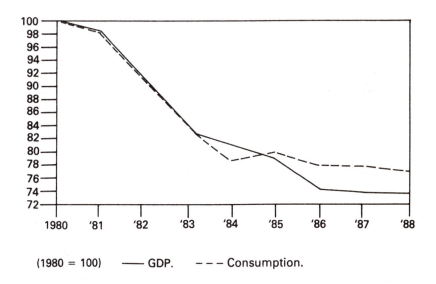

(1980 = 100)   —— GDP.   – – – Consumption.

FIGURE 9.1   *GDP and private consumption per capita in Bolivia, 1980–8*

employees of the state mining company were fired), further worsened the position of the poor: 'data on the determinants of welfare worsened substantially from 1985. Per capita GDP and consumption fell further, and reduced formal sector employment and reduced average incomes. Government social spending, (slashed in 1985), still has not recovered fully, while the population has increased'.[22]

In 1986, a Presidential Decree inaugurated the *Fonda Social de Emergencia* (ESF) to help offset the worst effects and meet 'the most essential and highly deteriorated needs of the people', to provide funds for small labour-intensive projects (Fernando Romero, Executive Director of ESF, in a speech in Paris, 1988). The Fund was conceived as a 'financial intermediary to transfer outside resources to vulnerable people with speed, effectiveness and transparency' (World Bank, 1989e).

The ESF was innovative from an administrative point of view. It was a funding organisation, outside the normal bureaucratic structure, whose only function was to approve and finance projects and monitor implementation. It was of temporary duration, intended for two years (later extended by one); and demand-driven, responding to applications for funds from companies, community groups, NGOs and local governments.

By the end of 1988, ESF had raised over $100 million in foreign currency, one-quarter as much as the current account deficit in that year. (Its ultimate goal was $180m.) 20 per cent of its commitments were to NGOs. Projects included economic infrastructure (38 per cent of committed funds by the end of 1988), social infrastructure (48 per cent), social assistance (8.8 per cent) and production support for micro-enterprises (8.8 per cent). From January 1987 to June 1989, 300 health posts and 415 schools were constructed or refurbished; 10,500 homes built; 1,100 km drinking water and sewerage networks constructed; 287 km of streets paved; and 8,000 km of roads improved. Twenty to thirty thousand jobs were created, at low (3 per cent) administrative costs, and with a relatively small amount of cash ($8 million) provided by the Bolivian government. This employment represents 10 per cent of the unemployed or 1 per cent of the workforce, and roughly offsets the unemployment created by restructuring the tin industry. The employment did not all go to unemployed workers (54 per cent of the workers employed already had a job, and only 39 per cent were actively looking for work). Nor did they all go to low-income groups. A survey showed 25 per cent of ESF household incomes were in the second poorest decile, the majority were in the lower half of the distribution, but 30 per cent were in the upper half. However, the biggest deficiencies from the point of view of reaching the poor were that 99 per cent of the jobs went to males, and it appears most projects were urban.[23]

The Bolivian scheme has raised more money than the Ghanaian, both absolutely and in relation to GNP. The Ghanaian scheme adds up (over its two year duration) to 2.5 per cent of one year's GNP; the Bolivian to 4.5 per cent. However, the major strength of the Bolivian scheme, compared with the Ghanaian, is the *speed* with which it got underway; a large number of projects had been initiated and employment created within three years of the inauguration of the recovery programme. This speed is partly due to the dynamism of the Director of ESF, Fernando Romero, partly to its internal administrative structure (independent of the usual bureaucracy) and also, importantly, to the way donor finance was mainly allocated to the fund as such and not to individual projects.

The major weaknesses of the Bolivian scheme are similar (with the exception of the implementation issue) to those of Ghana's PAMS-CAD: these are that the scheme does not reach the rural poor and does not deal comprehensively with many aspects of poverty and deprivation (e.g. malnutrition); and, while the scheme was intended to be of limited duration, the economy has not picked up in the meantime, so that when the scheme comes to the end of its planned life, the need for protection of the poor will be as great as ever. In Bolivia, the ESF was transformed into a Social Investment Fund (SIF) in 1990 to deal with the long-term problems. The SIF will be incorporated into normal government procedures and will aim to coordinate its work with overall government priorities, as is appropriate for a long-term venture.

Appraisal of World Bank Measures

This brief review of World Bank measures to deal with the social costs of adjustment has suggested some serious deficiencies from the perspective of poverty reduction. To recapitulate, these are:

(1) The 'new poor' measures do not reach the majority of the poor, but often take a large proportion of the funds. For example, in Ghana, measures for retrenched workers were planned to take one-fifth of the funds, but actual implementation of this item has been much speedier than the others and so initially at least they received the bulk of the funds (Jolly and van der Hoeven, 1989).

(2) The 'chronic poor' measures are partial in a number of dimensions:

– in terms of the adverse adjustment measures they compensate for; some countries effectively have no special measures; most countries have programmes directed at just one or two, and only a few countries (like Ghana and Bolivia) have multisectoral programmes (see Table 9.6);

– in terms of the amount of compensation offered (e.g. in Tunisia) the aim is to target subsidy reductions in such a way that the subsidies on foods consumed mainly by the poor are *removed less rapidly* than other subsidies, not completely offset);

– they do not reach *all* the poor adversely affected (e.g. most employment and nutrition schemes only reach a subset of those who have been adversely affected); as noted for Ghana and Bolivia, the rural poor in particular tend to receive disproportionately little from these measures;

– they only compensate for adverse effects of adjustment measures, and do not provide for more general adverse eventualities;

– they are partial in their *time* dimension, in the sense that to date they have only been initiated some years after the adjustment programme – as in Ghana and Bolivia – and they are only intended to last for a limited period of years, even though it appears that the adverse effects are likely to be much more long-lived.

(3) None of the measures are designed to reduce poverty as such – as against offering the poor compensation for adjustment measures – irrespective of its cause. One reason for this is that a prime motive behind the measures is to increase the acceptability of the programmes. Another reason is the argument that poverty reduction should be part of a country's general development efforts, and not be added onto special adjustment policies (Srinivasan, 1988). The problem with this argument is that over the 1980s, and probably the 1990s, for many countries adjustment policies have dominated policy-making, so that there has not been some other 'general development policy' to take care of poverty reduction. For countries with severe adjustment problems, poverty reduction has to be built into adjustment policies if it is to take place at all.

(4) The fundamental deficiency in the approach is the failure to adapt macro and much meso policy design in order to take into account the impact on the poor. Yet it is the design of the basic package that is the major cause of adverse effects. In particular,

the speed of adjustment required, the heavy emphasis on disabsorption rather than switching, the emphasis on expenditure reduction rather than tax increases, price decontrol and wage control,
the requirement of reduction/elimination of food subsidies[24] and
introduction of user charges are all elements in the basic package
which cause major adverse effects. Redesign of this basic package
would obviate much of the necessity for compensatory measures.

(5) The macro-policy design is also defective from the perspective
of long run poverty reduction in two other respects: first, it has
frequently failed (as shown above, pp. 178–9) to reestablish economic growth, and even, often, to eliminate imbalances. As noted
earlier, unless growth is restored the medium term prospects for
poverty reduction will be weak. Secondly, the adjustment package
is not systematically designed to bring about equitable patterns of
productive activity and therefore equitable patterns of primary
income distribution. Yet it is the growth of primary incomes among
low-income households which in the longer run will be most
effective in bringing about poverty reduction. Some aspects of the
usual adjustment package may bring about more equitable growth
(e.g. if employment in labour-intensive exports expands), but
other reforms which are essential for producing equitable growth
(e.g. land reform; credit reform to switch resources to small-scale
and poor producers; technology reforms; products policies) are
generally *not* included in the package of measures. Moreover,
some of the measures which are included in the adjustment package are likely to reduce equity (e.g. the focus on export crops in
countries where exports are produced on estates, as in Malawi;
encouragement of multinationals; cuts in public infrastructure and
education).[25]

CONCLUSIONS

The evidence surveyed in this chapter showed that in many countries
the stabilisation and adjustment policies, together with adverse external developments, have reduced the welfare of the poor, slowing and
sometimes reversing progress in nutrition, health and education.
Moreover, the need for adjustment is ongoing in many countries
because the policies have not succeeded in eliminating imbalances.

Yet some countries have succeeded in combining adjustment,
growth and social progress (as in Indonesia and Burkina Faso), while

others have maintained social progress during a period of adjustment, even without achieving much economic growth (as in Chile). The lessons from these countries are that what is needed is an appropriate combination of macro and meso policies.

The international financial institutions have acknowledged the importance of protecting the poor – or at least compensating for adverse effects – during adjustments. But so far they have not accepted that there is a need to redesign macro-policies in the light of the objective of reducing poverty; nor have they reviewed other aspects of their policy package (including the elimination of food subsidies, the introduction of user charges, or policies towards price decontrol) to avoid adverse effects. Indeed, many of their publications appear to argue that present policies are satisfactory from this point of view and little change is needed. There is, however, acceptance of the desirability of changes in inter and intra-sectoral government expenditure allocations to promote basic services at a time of expenditure cuts. Moves in this direction were the most common way in which recent SALs dealt with social costs of adjustment. Apart from this, Bank policies to deal with the issue consist of add-ons, which in most cases are trivial in magnitude and in the best cases – Ghana and Bolivia – are insufficiently comprehensive and too short-lived. It is clear from the successful cases that adjustment that fully protects the human dimension needs to be incorporated into the basic design of both macro and meso policies. Add-on programmes are very unlikely to be adequate.

The need for macro policies which are successful in bringing about sustained economic growth must be emphasised. This has not occurred in most African and Latin American countries. The World Bank assessments of the experience of the 1980s point to the fact that external shocks were worse than expected and account for some of the poor performance.[26] For SSA and Latin America, a satisfactory growth-oriented adjustment process may not be possible without a change in external conditions – notably in commodity prices, interest rates, the level of debt, and aid and private sector inflows. Thus any review of macro- policies should also consider how to change such external conditions, so a satisfactory outcome is possible, not take them as given and unalterable features of the situation, as most assessments do.

A final question that needs to be considered is *why*, some ten years into adjustment, the IFIs have done so little to protect the poor. One answer is that the poor represent no threat to the interests these institutions represent, which are furthered by the orthodox process of adjustment, and which could be undermined by too radical a change in the basic design of programmes. In particular, a major cause of the macro and meso problems has been the heavy debt burden; for many countries a solution would involve major debt write-off, which the IFIs are not prepared to contemplate. Yet continued failure – particularly at the macro-level – may represent a much greater threat to developed country interests. Another answer is that dominant interest groups in the countries themselves prevent more action, but this is no excuse for not initiating a vigorous dialogue and widening conditionality to incorporate considerations of human wellbeing. A further possibility is that the laisser-faire market paradigm retains such intellectual dominance that no alternative views can gain real ground.

NOTES

In writing this chapter I benefited greatly from discussions with a number of people in the World Bank, the IMF, UNICEF and UNDP, and to comments on an earlier draft from participants at the Manchester Conference. I am very grateful to all of them, but none bears any responsibility for what is written here. A shorter version of this paper was published in *World Development*, December 1991.

1. Evidence from ECLA, 1989. Dominican Republic evidence from UNICEF, *Situation Analysis*; for Jamaica from ILO/PREALC -UNDP-UNICEF-WEP Report, 1988.
2. Pinstrup-Andersen, Jaramillo and Stewart found substantial reductions in food subsidies in the early 1980s in seven out of ten countries. Food prices rose faster than the CPI in almost all the countries studied in AWHF, where data was available (Cornia).
3. For example, according to Serageldin, 'In the short run, the basic shift of incomes from urban to rural population serves to redress the broadest income distribution aspects'.
4. World Bank, 1990c, p. 31.
5. This section draws on Cornia and Stewart, 1990.
6. Some countries raised their government expenditure, despite falling GNP, not by raising taxes but by running an increasing budget deficit. Examples include: Togo, Bolivia, Nicaragua, Brazil, Mali, Nigeria.
7. Jespersen, 1990. Evidence for 1980–7 for some countries; for others 1980–6 or a shorter period.
8. See Cornia and Stewart, 1990, for fuller discussion.
9. World Bank Policy is to place greater reliance on user charges to raise

revenue for the health service. See World Bank, 1987, 'Financing Health Care: An Agenda for Reform', Washington, D.C.: World Bank.

10. For elaboration of these roles and of the impact of adjustment on them, see Commonwealth Secretariat, 1989.

11. World Bank information, reported in World Bank 1990c, is a little different; steady progress is recorded in Chile, Colombia and Costa Rica; halted progress in Uruguay and Venezuela; and worsening in Guatemala and Peru.

12. Albanez et al., 1989. The countries are Barbados, parts of Brazil, Chile, Colombia, Dominican Republic, El Salvador, Surinam and Mexico.

13. Again their data seems to differ from the ACN data. They record a persistent trend of rising malnutrition in Ethiopia, Lesotho, Madagascar, Niger and Rwanda; and rises, then falls, then rises in Benin, Burkina Faso, Ghana and Togo.

14. In SSA in 1982, daily calorie supply was only 91 per cent of requirements, on average. However, in most Latin American countries, average food availability was more than enough.

15. Data from UNICEF Situation Analyses suggests rising rates of infant mortality, however, in Dominican Republic, Haiti and Guyana.

16. Information from this section is derived from World Bank, 1990c; Ravallion and Huppi 1989, 1990; Asian Development Bank, 1990; van der Gaag, Makonnen and Englebert, 1990.

17. The main sources for this section are World Bank, 1988g; Government of the Philippines and UNICEF, 1987.

18. The budget had been in surplus in the early 1980s, a small deficit emerged and was more or less eliminated.

19. Information from World Bank, 1989e, ECLA, 1989 and Jimenez and Cespedes where not otherwise stated.

20. In 1982, the average family would have needed nearly 120 per cent of a minimum wage to purchase a minimum acceptable diet. This percentage had been 76 per cent in 1980 and had fallen to about 85 per cent by 1984.

21. The 1990 *World Development Report* (World Bank, 1990c) comments: 'when structural adjustment issues came to the fore little attention was paid to the effects on the poor', p. 103.

22. World Bank, 1989a. The report concludes, somewhat puzzlingly, 'the actual impact of this on the poor is difficult to estimate'.

23. Information from Newman et al., 1989; Schachter, 1989. According to Schachter 'it is in the poorest rural communities where the ESF has probably had the least effect'.

24. Universal food subsidies often have substantial 'leakages' benefiting the non-poor as much or more than the poor. Nonetheless, they usually form a much larger proportion of the income of the poor, who suffer most when they are withdrawn. For example, World Bank 1990c shows that in Egypt the food subsidy amounts to 10.8 per cent of the income of the poorest rural quartile compared with 2.7 per cent of the richest, even though the richest households actually receive more in absolute terms.

25. The consistency between stabilisation/adjustment measures and aspects of equity is considered in much greater detail in Fitzgerald, and Stewart and Ranis, in Stewart et al. (ed.), 1990.

26. 'The external economic environment, the terms of trade, real interest
rates, and the availability of commercial bank credit turned out to be
substantially worse than was assumed at the start of the 1980s. This
unfavorable environment has made adjustment slower and more difficult than initially expected'. (World Bank, 1988d).

It is ironic that the World Bank blamed domestic policy-making for
worsening performance in the early 1980s and paid very little attention to
the external environment (see e.g. the Berg Report). But for the 1980s as
a whole – when the IMF and the Bank were largely responsible for
policy-making – adverse developments are attributed to external developments.

10 The Social Dimension of Economic Adjustment Programmes: Economic Feedbacks and Implications for Medium and Long-Term Growth

Alessandro Pio

INTRODUCTION

During the 1970s several industrialised countries resorted to IMF-supported stabilisation programmes in order to deal with the impacts of the two oil crises on their external accounts and their internal macroeconomic stability (especially with regard to inflationary pressures). Along with these stabilisation efforts, many countries undertook structural reforms aimed at improving their efficiency and competitiveness through reduced dependency on imported energy sources, rationalisation of the productive structure, greater scope for market forces.

The 1980s have witnessed a similar phenomenon for many Less Developed Countries (LDCs). As a result of the debt burden accumulated in the previous decade and of adverse international conditions (the rise in interest rates associated with anti-inflationary policies in many industrialised countries and the decline in commodity prices), many LDCs were forced to undertake stabilisation policies aimed at reducing their balance of payments deficit. In many cases these measures were accompanied by 'structural adjustment' actions, aimed at removing some of the more deeply-rooted motives of the observed imbalances. Adjustment programmes were often adopted under pressure from international financial institutions as a prerequisite for receiving additional financing. Consistent with their institutional mandate, the IMF typically oversaw stabilisation programmes, while the World Bank negotiated and financially sustained the structural adjustment programmes, though in reality the two institutions cooperated closely in a number of countries devising joint programmes.

After nearly a decade of experience, considerable evidence is available concerning the achievements and shortfalls of this approach, which aimed at promoting market-oriented policies in LDCs using the incentive of external financing. Some of the evaluations regarding the economic results of structural adjustment lending (SAL) are cautiously positive (World Bank, 1989), while others are more sceptical (Harrigan and Mosley, 1990).

One particular line of analysis of SAL focuses on the social impact of stabilisation and adjustment policies, with special attention for the situation of children (Jolly and Cornia, 1984; Cornia, Jolly and Stewart, 1987). The work by Cornia, Jolly and Stewart made a clear and well-exemplified case for 'adjustment with a human face', that is adjustment policies with limited adverse impacts on the poorest segments of the population and on children. This result could be achieved through more gradual and less deflationary policies at the macro level, and through 'meso' policies, that is policies which would cushion the impact on children and the poor through appropriate targeting of social programmes (food subsidies, redirection of health and education expenditures etc). While the literature quoted was rich in examples and policy suggestions, its analytical framework covered only some of the short-term interactions between social and economic variables, concentrating mostly on the household level, focused more sharply on stabilisation than on structural adjustment, and did not attempt to address in depth the long-term implications of adjustment policies.

The debate on long-term economic development has been recently livened by contributions which underline the importance of human capital in the definition of the growth potential of a country (Romer, 1986, Lucas, 1988). In these models, human capital is defined as knowledge (acquired either through schooling or on-the-job training) which spills over, generating positive externalities, thereby increasing the economic system's productivity. With respect to this line of analysis, it seems that a broader definition of human capital should be adopted, to include the contribution of adequate health, sanitation and nutrition to the quality of human resources. By doing so, it

becomes possible to establish a linkage between the short-term social
effects of adjustment policies and a country's long-term development
path.

This chapter is an attempt at linking the social and economic
dimensions of adjustment in the short term and their long-term
development implications. At this stage, the aim is not to present a
formalised model, but rather to identify the key relationships and the
feedback mechanisms which should be included in any such model.
The qualitative analysis of these interrelations can already provide
preliminary policy suggestions for the design of appropriate structural
adjustment packages, which will prove sustainable in the medium and
long-term and conducive to development.

The next section defines the concept of sustainability of economic
policies in a medium and long-term frame, an important criterion for
the evaluation of SAL. The following section analyses the interrelations between macro, micro and social variables in the adjustment
process, outlining both short- and long-term impacts and their most
relevant policy implications, while the final section relates these
impacts to recent theories of long term growth. The main argument
of the chapter is that concern for the social implications of economic
development can pay dividends in terms of long-term growth as well,
sometimes through channels that are normally neglected in economic
analysis.

A MATTER OF SUSTAINABILITY

The concept of sustainability in economic analysis has traditionally
been linked to the matching of real or financial flows over time. Thus,
in cost-benefit analysis a project is viable if the actualised returns
over the life of the project exceed its actualised costs. Temporary
balance of payments deficits can be justified if they allow the import
of capital or intermediate goods which will generate a surplus in later
years through export expansion or import reduction. Public debt has
been defined as sustainable as long as the real growth rate of the
economy exceeds the real interest rate. In recent years the concept of
sustainability has been expanded to express a concern for the environmental impacts of economic development. Development has
been defined as sustainable if it is compatible with a country's
endowment of renewable and non-renewable resources.

For the evaluation of adjustment policies the concept of sustainability should be expanded to encompass four dimensions: political,

social, economic/financial and environmental. A programme can be considered sustainable if it does not trigger reactions in any of these spheres which have a negative feedback superior to the programme's expected positive impacts.

Political

In *political* terms, sustainability implies that the programme will not cause an opposition strong enough to prevent its implementation. This can happen through constitutional changes in power (an opposition party winning elections and adopting a different economic course after the ruling party has become unpopular due to its economic policies), through an armed coup, or through widespread protest which forces the government to repeal the programme. The political sustainability of a programme is usually related to the distribution of the burden of the adjustment. Even though opposition may not be strong enough to cause cancellation of the programme, it can cause partial modifications (typically reintroduction of food or fuel subsidies which had been removed), or it can create a climate in the country which will make its objectives more difficult to obtain (for example, a climate of uncertainty which will discourage foreign investment in spite of favourable legislation and attractive labour costs). While political sustainability is not often declared as an explicit constraint, the maintenance of defence and public security expenditures in the presence of relevant budget cuts in other government functions demonstrates that it is firmly present in the minds of the policymakers. Expenditures on defence and public security functions can be explained by the twin needs (1) to count on an adequate repressive capability in case of social unrest and (2) to avoid alienating the military, which in many LDCs has been an agent of government change through violent takeovers. The rigidity in certain items of public expenditure (food subsidies, defence spending), responds therefore to the need to ensure the political sustainability of a programme, and observation of significant demonstrations of unrest should be taken as evidence of inadequate programme design with respect to the country's socio-political conditions.

Social

Social sustainability has both a short- and a long-term dimension. In the short term, it implies devising ways to cushion the impact of economic adjustment on the most vulnerable groups of the population so as not to cause excessive deterioration of their living standards in terms of nutrition, access to health services and satisfaction of basic needs. This is the approach proposed in the 'adjustment with a human face' literature or in the 'emergency social fund' approach, such as the one implemented in conjunction with the stabilisation package in Bolivia. Long-term social sustainability implies building safeguards into a programme which will ensure the maintenance of those social elements which are conducive to long-term economic growth. The topic will be dealt with more in detail below (pp. 242–3) of the chapter, but a few examples will clarify the concept. While availability of food or curative health services has an immediate impact on welfare, a variety of investments in human capital (education, preventive medicine, etc.) can be reduced with very limited short-term impact. The long-term impact of these actions can however be considerable, in terms of foregone productivity and growth potential for the economic system as a whole, as a consequence of a less educated and healthy labour force. An evaluation of the long-term social sustainability of an adjustment programme implies careful consideration of the feedbacks in terms of economic growth potential of the negative social impacts of the package.

Economic and Financial

The evaluation of *economic and financial* sustainability involves consideration of those parameters traditionally analysed in the economic literature. Falling wage levels result in a decline of public sector revenues from both income and social security taxes, and under some conditions can produce larger rather than smaller budget deficits. In a long-term perspective, a reduction in income levels is usually associated with a decline in the savings rate as consumers try to maintain the previous standard of living, in line with the permanent income hypothesis (Duesenberry, 1952; Friedman, 1957). As a consequence, less endogenous resources become available for investment and hence for growth-generating capital accumulation. If we consider strictly financial aspects, loans contracted to finance structural adjustment policies (reforms of the financial or foreign exchange allocation system) must be repaid out of general revenue funds, and their contribution to the enhancement of national productivity should therefore be sufficient to allow for the servicing of the loan. Cost-benefit analysis should therefore be applied to structural adjustment lending in much the same way that it is applied to project financing, in spite of the considerably harder task of estimating the costs and benefits of the operation.

Environmental

The *environmental sustainability* of adjustment programmes is determined by the survival strategies adopted in response to economic measures. Thus, a reduction in cooking fuel subsidies can result in increased firewood consumption, or an increase in the availability of imported capital goods can result in more energy-intensive production technologies. Environmental sustainability should be measured in the medium and long term, even though some short-term impacts can also be expected, as in the case of sanitation conditions in rapidly expanding human settlements, where water quality can be compromised in a short amount of time by inappropriate disposal of human waste.

The previous discussion indicates that there are two types of feedback mechanisms which should be taken into account in the evaluation of an adjustment programme. The first involves the short-term feasibility of the programme, and is linked to political, social and financial sustainability. The second concerns the long-run impacts on the level and quality of human and physical capital and environmental resources. Both must be taken into account in a comprehensive evaluation of SAL and its impacts. The following two sections of the chapter are devoted to the analytical examination of both short- and long-term impacts.

THE INTERRELATIONSHIP OF MACRO, MICRO AND SOCIAL VARIABLES IN THE ADJUSTMENT PROCESS

Adjustment programmes adopted by LDCs during the 1980s usually consisted of two related components, which can be labelled 'stabilisation' and 'structural adjustment'.

Stabilisation

Stabilisation can be defined as aimed at reducing balance of payments and public sector budget deficits and inflation rates through policies of aggregate demand restraint. For the purposes of our analysis, three types of measures can be associated with stabilisation programmes: reductions in the government expenditure, limitations of money supply or internal credit resulting in higher interest rates, and reduction in real wage levels, achieved either directly through public sector wage cuts and lower legislated minimum wage levels or indirectly through the downward pressure exercised by the rising unemployment associated with falling output levels. Stabilisation programmes address temporary imbalances by reducing the level of economic activity without affecting the system's structural characteristics: equilibrium is achieved through the reduction of demand.

Structural Adjustment

Structural adjustment, on the contrary, aims at balancing the economy through an expansion of supply, achieved by overcoming existing bottlenecks and distortions. Three broad components are present in most structural adjustment programmes:

(1) increased openness of the national economy to international trade, to be achieved through a reduction of export taxes and import tariffs and a more realistic (i.e. devalued) exchange rate;
(2) liberalisation of the price system in order to favour efficient allocation of resources. This step usually involves liberalisation of interest rates, reduction in government subsidies to specific goods and services, as well as the elimination of tariffs and restrictions on the exchange rate;
(3) reform of the revenue and expenditure structure of the public sector, including reduction of price subsidies and international trade taxes, a greater role for direct (income and property) taxation, and a smaller role of the state in both regulation and direct involvement in productive activities, the latter to be achieved through privatisation programmes.

Leaving aside specific measures tailored to the situation of individual countries, six economic policy instruments can therefore be associated with structural adjustment policies: reduction in export taxes, reduction in import tariffs, fluctuation of exchange and interest rates, elimination of price subsidies and increase in direct taxation.
Much of the debate on the social impact of adjustment policies

(and specifically the work by Cornia, Jolly and Stewart, 1987) has focused on stabilisation, more than on structural adjustment programmes. Conversely, the work by Bourguignon, Morrisson and Suwa (1990), which incorporates rather detailed distributional impacts in a model for the evaluation of structural adjustment policies, provides indications on the effects on income distribution but does not extend to the consideration of specific social welfare indicators such as nutrition, school attendance or mortality rates. The purpose of the following pages is to consider both types of adjustment policies, and to extend the conceptual analysis to both economic and social implications, including those whose effects will be felt in the medium and long term.

Methodologically, the assessment of the economic and social impacts and feedbacks requires switching back and forth between the macroeconomic and microeconomic level. As a first step, one must identify the key macroeconomic implications of the adjustment policies analysed: for example a decline in aggregate demand accompanied by reduction in wage rates and depreciation of the exchange agents (households, firms, the government sector etc.) to the macroeconomic changes identified. Households may react to declining income levels by increasing labour force participation of their members and/or by reducing their savings rate and/or modifying their consumption baskets towards lower grade goods (carbohydrates instead of proteins); firms will respond to higher interest and exchange rates by reducing the use of imported capital goods, and so forth. As a third step, the social implications of the microeconomic 'survival strategies' of economic agents must be clarified. Increased labour force participation of school-age children may imply higher drop-out rates, whereas moderate substitution among food groups may not have negative impacts on nutrition rates. As a final step, the feedback of these social and economic impacts on the short- and long-term sustainability of adjustment programmes must be assessed: the short-term reduction in standards of living for some segments of the population may be too severe and result in social unrest which does not allow the programme to reach completion, or the long-term effects on the accumulation of physical and human capital may be so strong as to set the country on a very low growth path, in spite of successful changes in some structural conditions such as export competitivity.

The following discussion will consider separately four types of economic agents: households, firms engaged in production, financial institutions, and the government sector. The analysis will cover three stabilisation policy instruments (reductions in government expenditure, money supply and real wages) and six structural adjustment policy instruments (reduction in export taxes and import tariffs, fluctuation of interest and exchange rates resulting in an increase of both, reduction of price subsidies and increase in direct taxation). Both short- and long-term effects will be outlined in this section, but the latter will be further elaborated upon in the final section.

The Household Sector

Stabilisation policies affect the consumption level of households through their combined effect on (1) disposable income, which depends on the family's endowment of productive factors: labour and real and financial assets and (2) cost of the goods and services provided or subsidised by the public sector.

Labour income is likely to decline as a result of both lower real wages and higher unemployment rates associated with restrictive demand policies and cuts in current government spending. Income obtained from real and financial assets, on the other hand, will vary according to the type of assets held. Low-income families only maintain small cash balances and real assets (dwellings and durable consumer goods in urban areas, small land parcels and animals in rural areas) and therefore receive no monetary returns on such assets. Middle-income families are likely to diversify their portfolio by adding financial assets in the form of foreign currency notes (US dollars) and local bank deposits, while more sophisticated financial instruments (bonds, stock, foreign accounts) will only be held by high-income households. If we focus our attention on low- and middle-income families, we can conclude that stabilisation policies will not affect the asset income of the former group, while the effect on middle income families is uncertain. Restrictive monetary policies will raise interest income on bank deposits, but the reduction in available liquidity and the deflationary expectations generated by stabilisation policies will depress parallel market exchange rates, thus reducing the local currency return of dollar purchases on the parallel market.

Households will respond to this situation through a variety of 'survival strategies'. They will try to raise family labour income levels by increasing labour force participation of females, children or elderly family members; where opportunities for employment are not available, heads of households and family members may turn to illegal activities (for example coca cultivation in the Andean countries). Households will try to maintain living standards by reducing savings rates, and in more extreme cases by mortgaging or selling real or financial assets. They will reduce levels of consumption and substitute goods and services with others of (actual or perceived) inferior quality: tea for milk, carbohydrates for proteins, national for imported goods, as well as reduce demand for those goods and services whose price has increased.

The adoption of structural adjustment measures in addition to the stabilisation effort just described will have further impacts. Reduction of export taxes (typically levied on commodities) will favour producers of agricultural goods or minerals, and hence improve incomes in the non-urban sector. Reduction of import tariffs and depreciation of the exchange rate will have offsetting impacts on the price of imported goods, with the final outcome depending on the net strength of the two effects. Financial liberalisation should lead to an increase in interest rates, thus boosting the incomes of bank deposit holders, while exchange rate liberalisation will reduce the parallel market premium on the dollar, penalising holders of foreign cash balances. Reduction of price subsidies and of public expenditure on social services will significantly worsen the purchasing power of the lower classes, even though in some cases (higher education, but even perhaps the water and electricity supply) subsidies do not benefit middle and upper income groups. The increase in direct taxation is most likely to affect the middle class.

The net outcome of these measures in the short term is likely to be a more unequal income distribution. Lower classes in urban areas will be penalised by price increases in essential goods, not adequately compensated for by possible reduction in import prices. The midddle class will lose subsidisation of some goods and services and in addition be burdened by higher taxation, while its income from financial assets will depend on portfolio choices between domestic bank deposits and foreign cash balances. The upper class is likely to be able to escape from the burden of increased direct taxation and to benefit from the increase in export revenues and agricultural prices. Given the limited bargaining power of labour in a situation of falling real wages and growing unemployment, the owners of land and capital are likely to incorporate most of the gains coming from increased exports of agricultural and manufactured products. The adverse distributional effects of these policies in the short term are confirmed by recent simulations (Bourguignon, Branson and de Melo, 1989 and Bourguignon, Morrisson and Suwa, 1990).

Within reasonable limits the mentioned microeconomic adjustments will not have significant social implications. Their impact will on the other hand be severe if a strongly restrictive policy is adopted. The short-term sustainability of the stabilisation and adjustment programme will be endangered if some of the survival strategies cannot be enacted or are brought to extreme consequences, and specifically:

(1) if unemployment is so pervasive that willing family members cannot find additional employment, or if they find employment by displacing the primary breadwinners at lower wages. In both cases a microeconomic equilibrium will only be reached through dramatic declines in the standard of living;

(2) if the extent of illegal activity to which households must resort in order to meet their income requirements is such that it threatens basic security conditions;

(3) if service cuts and price increases in previously subsidised essential goods are of such magnitude that they cause considerable deficiencies in nutrition and health standards, to the point of affecting current earning potential of employed persons or homemakers' ability to perform household tasks.

Microeconomic reactions to adjustment policies also have significant implications for long-run growth, and precisely:

(1) to the extent that additional income is obtained through labour force participation of children and adolescents, school attendance and performance are likely to suffer, thus resulting in a lower quality work force in the long term. Loss of labour force qualification because of reduced schooling can at least in part be offset by greater specific skills acquired through earlier 'on the job' training;

(2) growth of the illegal sector may require costly public security measures in the long run, and create a climate which will discourage national and foreign investments;

(3) to the extent that health and nutrition conditions are below standards, long-term development and productivity of the labour force will be diminished;

(4) to the extent that female educational levels decline as a result

of increased labour force participation or decline in school attendance, higher future fertility rates and population expansion can be expected, unless higher female participation rates become a stable characteristic of the country;

(5) expenditure cuts in preventive health and sanitation (water supply and sewers) will increase diffusion of communicable diseases, thereby increasing future curative health costs and debilitating the quality of future human capital;

(6) decapitalisation of households resulting from the liquidation of assets (durable goods, vehicles, land, animals) will compromise the recovery potential once the economy starts growing again. Decapitalisation can be particularly severe if it leads to the contemporary sale of similar assets by many families (for example livestock during a famine), since excess supply will further drive down market prices, guaranteeing very limited relief to the sellers;

(7) the process of income concentration should favour capital accumulation by transferring income to social strata with a higher propensity to save. However, this process will benefit the country only to the extent that the surplus is invested internally, and not transferred to international capital markets.

The social impact of the adjustment policies outlined and of the survival strategies enacted by the households can be measured and monitored in economic terms through labour force participation and employment rates, wage levels, and prices of essential goods and services. Social indicators include the degree of malnutrition, weight at birth of children in low income areas, school attendance and drop-out rates, and incidence of communicable diseases.

The analysis of the impact of adjustment policies on households and of their reactions suggests a number of policy implications for the design and mitigation of such programmes.

The search for additional income sources is a relevant survival strategy in situations of adjustment. Short term public employment programmes can therefore provide an important safety valve both economically and socially. To the extent that these programmes also have a training content or contribute to the improvement of the physical infrastructure, their impact goes beyond the short term and becomes relevant for long term development. If no wage employment is available, prospective seekers will 'invent' work in the informal sector, mostly through retail sales (on street corners) or provision of services (self-appointed parking attendants, windshield cleaners etc.) or small illegal activities (theft, gambling, prostitution etc.). To the extent that informal employment takes place in these sectors, it has negligible productivity for the system as a whole, and is basically an informal mechanism of income transfer from formal sector income earners. Informal sector activity in productive manufacturing and services should also increase in times of economic adjustment, as discussed below (p. 246), and there is therefore scope for intervention in support of employment in this sector. Considerable experience and empirical evidence has been accumulated by now in this area (see De Soto, 1987, Levitsky, 1986, Pio, 1990) and the time is now ripe to bring pilot experiences to national scale.

Household living standards can of course be improved through income transfers, provision of public services and selected price subsidies, but these are precisely the target of some of the adjustment measures described earlier. The obvious answer is therefore to reduce expenditure levels while improving targeting and cost efficiency in order to provide a safety net for the truly needy. Considerable attention has already been devoted in the literature to these approaches (Cornia, Jolly and Stewart, 1987). While targeting on the beneficiaries can be costly, self-selectivity can be more efficient: by subsidising food items which are mostly used by the lower classes or small children automatic targeting of subsidies can be achieved. Community involvement in the provision of health and other social services can be an effective way of decreasing costs and improving efficiency, as the UNICEF experience has demonstrated in many parts of the world.

The contribution that the return on real and financial assets gives to household income has received little attention in the design of economic policies. Better knowledge of the portfolio choices of low- and middle-income families would offer the opportunity to target financial reforms to the mobilisation and valorisation of their savings potential and the enhancement of their incomes. Experience in many countries has demonstrated that investment in the construction of the primary dwelling is a very strong motivation for saving even at very low income levels. Saving schemes aimed at purchasing a residence in which the government matches the contributions of low- and middle-income households have proved very successful in Chile. Provisions could be introduced to loan the amount accumulated at any point in time to the owner if necessary due to hardship conditions. A system of public loans against collateral (land, animals, durable goods) at equitable interest rates could help avoid the decapitalisation of many households during times of economic emergency, and would require relatively modest financing, possibly from international aid sources.

While the mitigating measures just outlined address the short-term sustainability of adjustment programmes, maintenance of adequate levels of human and physical capital formation is essential for long term development. Specific initiatives in this sense are discussed in the final section.

Productive Firms

Stabilisation and adjustment policies have an impact on both demand and supply functions at the firm level. The overall demand level will decline in the short term due to contractionary stabilisation policies, while substitution processes in the households' consumption baskets will favour low-cost goods. Whether these low cost goods are of national or imported origin will depend on the extent of openness to international trade and on the net impact on import prices of tariff removal and exchange rate depreciation measures associated with structural adjustment policies. It seems reasonable that local producers of basic goods should be favoured by this process of substitution, though specific demand elasticities should be studied within each national context.

Supply functions will be affected by changes in the relative prices of factors of production. Labour costs should decline as a result of unemployment and depressed wage levels. Financing costs should increase as a result of both monetary restrictions and financial market liberalisation, discouraging the use of capital intensive technologies. The cost of imported goods may increase or decrease, depending on the combined effect of trade liberalisation and exchange rate fluctuations. Exchange rate variability, however, is likely to encourage the use of national inputs, especially in those countries where hedging instruments in the form of forward or future currency markets are not available. As a result of these relative price shifts, labour intensive firms which use local inputs and low-to-medium technologies should be favoured.

The combined analysis of demand and supply conditions suggests that at times of stabilisation and adjustment the modern manufacturing sector should be the hardest hit, unless considerable outlets can be found in the export market, while the potential for traditional manufacturing and the informal sector is relatively better: demand for the goods produced by these sectors should increase, while relative factor prices are more favourable given the characteristics of their production function. This intuition is supported by the modelling analysis of Bourguignon, Branson and de Melo (1989b) which indicates that the impact of adjustment policies falls harder on modern and informal sector urban workers, depending upon where the resulting unemployment is allocated. Further empirical evidence is therefore necessary on the degree of substitution among the goods produced by the two sectors in times of crisis.

In the short term these changes and adaptive responses imply that employment and wages will decline in response to lower aggregate demand, triggering the effects on household income, consumption and living standards discussed on pp. 240–1. In terms of industrial structure, the more favourable position of traditional and informal manufacturers provides significant scope for policies aimed at strengthening these sectors. The provision of credit and technical assistance, the simplification of licensing, accounting and taxation schemes for informal sector producers, the opening of public procurements to small bidders or consortia of small producers, are just some examples of specific policy actions which can be undertaken to strengthen the role of small and micro enterprises. Due to the small dimension of these economic units, the social welfare impact of these measures in terms of income distribution and sustenance of minimum living standards is likely to be substantial, thereby increasing short-term sustainability of the economic programme.

In a long-term perspective, the success of the adjustment programme depends on its ability to increase international competitiveness of local firms. Import tariff and export tax reduction coupled with flexible exchange rates will diminish the extent of protection granted to local industry while stimulating exports. Local firms should be able to count on the same capital and intermediate inputs as their international competitors, and to do so at comparable price levels. At the same time the realignment of relative prices discussed above should bring local firms more in line with the nation's comparative advantages. As a result, the industrial structure of LDCs should undergo a process of restructuring and specialisation. The two key questions then become (1) whether the local 'modern' manufacturing sector will be able to bounce back after the adjustment period and face the competition of the local informal sector for low-grade goods and of foreign producers for high-grade ones; and (2) whether the low capital intensity encouraged by the new structure of relative prices (low wages and high interest rates) will preclude local manufacturers from being able to compete internationally in high technology or capital intensive sectors. Effective responses to these questions at the national level will help shape appropriate industrial policies.

Financial Institutions

Stabilisation pursued through restrictive monetary policies will result in interest rate increases, partly moderated by the falling money demand associated with reduced output levels. Interest rates are also likely to increase as a result of financial liberalisation policies, though the increase will not be uniformly distributed and will more severely affect those sectors of the credit market which were receiving preferential treatment prior to the reforms. Interest rate increases are not likely to significantly affect the operations of financial intermediaries, whose profitability will be maintained by changes in the spread between deposit and lending rates in order to compensate for changing volumes of financial intermediation.

Two other aspects of stabilisation and adjustment policies are likely to affect financial intermediaries more significantly: the impact of changes in income distribution on savings rates and that of exchange rate fluctuations on portfolio choices. The analysis of the household sector has shown that in the short term these policies are likely to result in a more polarised income distribution, favouring high income classes at the expense of the lower and middle class. In an attempt to maintain pre-crisis consumption levels, lower and middle-class households will reduce their savings rates. To the extent that middle-class families are the most significant holders of bank deposits in their portfolio of assets, the supply of credit through the banking system could decline significantly. Conversely, high income families' savings will increase, but it is more likely that they will be invested in other forms of financial instruments or in bank deposits abroad.

Exchange rate liberalisation may exacerbate the problem. In a context of periodically devalued exchange rates, foreign currency cash holdings (typically US dollars) become an attractive hedging instrument against domestic inflation. The middle class will compare capital gains from exchange rate devaluations with domestic interest rates in order to decide how to allocate its portfolio between dollars and bank deposits. Foreign banks deposits or financial instruments, available to the higher classes because of their international connections, will become even more attractive, since they combine positive yields with the capital gains from currency devaluation. The final result can be a significant reduction in financial capital available through local intermediaries, first among them the banking system.

The short-term impact on the sustainability of an adjustment programme is twofold. Firstly, the general decline in economic activity and the restructuring of the financial sector which should accompany a process of financial liberalisation will result in job losses within financial institutions, with the usual effects on households and firms in terms of income and consumption potential. Secondly, adjustment policies can result in a reduction in the amount of financial capital flowing through official intermediaries, and in particular the banking sector, in favour of parallel markets: foreign currency markets or capital markets, such as the '*mercado enterempresarial*' in Argentina. The outcome of this process will depend on some of its characteristics: if financial capital is diverted to foreign markets (bank deposits in Miami or Zurich), the restrictive impact of adjustment will be more severe. If these funds remain within the local economy in parallel markets, there will be a revenue loss for the public sector in the form of taxes on interest earned.

Short-term policies dealing with the financial sector should therefore mitigate these impacts through the design of innovative financial instruments which offer some of the same advantages of the competing parallel markets (for example dollar-indexed deposits). In order to complement the policies discussed above (p. 247) it would be desirable if the financial system would channel part of its resources to the development of the informal and microenterprise sector through the concession of credit. Two obstacles must be overcome for this line of business to develop: the lack of acceptable collateral which these firms can offer (a public guarantee fund could be instituted) and the high fixed cost of processing applications, which makes the concession of small loans unprofitable (a subsidy scheme could be devised, possibly with foreign aid funding).

In a long-term perspective, it becomes essential that local financial intermediaries provide credible alternatives for the local investment of the financial surplus of the higher classes. Reversal (or at least reduction) of capital flight is a prerequisite for long-term development. In part, this reversal depends on the enactment of credible economic policies at the central level, which will restore growth and provide clear rules of the game for the treatment of financial assets. Financial intermediaries can contribute to the process by developing attractive financial instruments, both within and outside the banking system, in order to ensure that at least the supply conditions are met.

The Public Sector

The public sector is of course a primary actor in the stabilisation and adjustment process, since it is responsible for enacting public expenditure and wage cuts, eliminating subsidies, reducing export taxes and import tariffs and increasing direct taxes. The impact of these measures on the other sectors of the economy has already been discussed in previous sections, and the focus of this section concerns the impact on the public sector itself in terms of efficiency, revenues and expenditure structure.

A likely outcome of personnel cuts and wage freezes is the weakening of the administrative structure resulting from the voluntary departure of the brightest civil servants, those with ambition and marketable skills, who will seek employment in the private sector. This process can have a serious impact both in the short and long term for the sustainability and management of the structural reform process.

A second adverse impact, with both short- and long-term consequences, comes from the changing revenue structure resulting from structural adjustment. The reduction of export taxes and import tariffs creates a revenue gap which may be hard to fill, especially in the first years, through increases in direct taxation. The shortfall can be compounded by decreasing revenues associated with the contraction of output levels and the informalisation of the economy, both in the productive and the financial sector.

The third aspect to be considered is the changing structure of expenditure patterns resulting from stabilisation and adjustment. Experience has shown that defence and public security budgets are usually unaffected by expenditure cuts, and that even health and education fare reasonably well. Most of the brunt is borne by maintenance and investment expenditures and reduction in subsidies, and only the latter has significant short-term welfare impacts.

The policy implications of these short-term impacts are fairly straightforward. In terms of personnel policy, the trade-off between quantity and quality must be carefully weighed. A smaller but better-paid civil service will be more efficient than a large but significantly underpaid staff, which has developed survival strategies through the sale of small favours to the public and the search for secondary and tertiary employment outside the public sector, leaving little time, energy and motivation for the provision of public services. The political and social sustainability of this type of choice must of course be carefully considered, since in many cases an oversized public sector is a guarantee of both stability and minimum income levels, acting as a 'safety net' and social buffer in an indirect way.

In terms of revenue structure, improved collection methods are necessary and should be an integral part of the structural adjustment package design. Indexation and prompt collection of revenues to keep pace with inflation, cash flow management to match the timing of major revenues and expenditures, inclusion of informal sector activities through a simplified licensing and taxation system, can all contribute to reduce the revenue gap, and therefore to lessen the expenditure cuts imposed by a balanced budget policy.

Expenditures can be optimised (within the acknowledged political and social constraints) through targeting and utilisation of some of the survival strategies developed by the other sectors of the economy, for example through increased reliance on community organisations for the enhancement of service delivery (promotional efforts in connection with vaccination campaigns, management of food supplement programmes, etc.).

The long-term implications of adjustment policies for the public sector are especially relevant. As already mentioned, the efficiency of the administrative structure can be considerably weakened by a self-selective exodus of qualified personnel as a result of wage cuts. Reduced expenditures on maintenance and new investments will equally affect the quality of public infrastructures, leaving a public sector debilitated in terms of both human and physical capital. The potential for remedial action in the long term is reduced by the changes in revenue structure and level discussed in the previous paragraphs.

In addition to these internal effects, there will be an external impact on national human capital as a result of the spending cuts in health, education, sanitation and food subsidies, which affects the long term growth potential of the country, as discussed in the final section.

Mitigation of these long-term impacts requires some of the same measures discussed previously: a more managerial approach to personnel administration and the design of the public revenue structure, and the cushioning of social impacts through targeting of public expenditure and implementation of emergency social programmes, which can be at least partly financed through coordination of external aid.

ADJUSTMENT AND LONG-TERM GROWTH

Until fairly recently, economic growth models concentrated on three determinants of the growth rate of a country: the state of technology; population growth (as a proxy for labour force expansion); and physical capital (Ramsey, 1928, Cass, 1965 and Koopmans, 1965). The contribution of human capital as a factor of production was considered in purely quantitative terms, measured by the rate of population growth. Literature on human capital was mostly micro-economic, and aimed at measuring the rate of return to individuals of investments in education (Mincer 1974, Becker 1975). Earnings of persons with different levels of schooling were actualised and compared with the actualised cost of education in terms of both tuition and foregone earnings, in order to estimate the profitability of investing in one's skill upgrading.

Recent developments in growth theory (Romer 1986, Lucas 1988) have attempted to include human capital among the determinants of growth. Romer defines human capital as knowledge accumulated through research, which has positive externalities because it allows firms other than the one which developed it to increase their production possibilities, since knowledge cannot be perfectly patented or kept secret. As a consequence, technological change is endogenous and growth rates can vary over time and among countries, as a result of disturbances or of differences in the rate of production of knowledge (which can be higher in larger countries). Lucas defines human capital as the 'general skill level' of workers, which can be increased either by subtracting time from work to devote it to schooling, or by increasing time devoted to work in order to improve skills through 'learning by doing'. The distinction is relevant in terms of policy implications, because in the first case investment in human capital is antagonistic with current production of goods and services, whereas in the second case it is complementary: investment in human capital would be the most productive since it would not imply a reduction in current consumption levels. This contradiction could probably be

reconciled by observing that a certain amount of schooling is necessary to facilitate the acquisition of more specialised skills, and that the
acquisition of skills 'on the job' implies lower productivity during the
learning process.

A human capital framework is particularly useful for the analysis of
the long-term implications of the social impacts of adjustment policies. The concept of human capital simply needs to be expanded to
include a broader definition of the quality of the labour force in terms
of education, health and nutrition levels. Other factors with positive
externalities need to be included in the model in addition to knowledge. The provision of water and sanitation has positive externalities
on the level of public health and hence on the quality of human
capital. Improvements in the organisational capacity of the public
sector or of low income communities also raise the quality and reduce
the cost of the public services delivered, and allow for a fuller
meeting of needs with a limited amount of inputs. While the list could
be extended almost interminably, thereby making modelling infeas-
ible, there is room for inclusion of the most meaningful social
determinants in formalised approaches, and for qualitative consideration of other social effects in the evaluation of adjustment programmes.

The analysis of macro-micro-social interactions in adjustment
programmes carried out above (pp. 242–3) for the main types of
economic agents can be summarised in a few broad trends. At the
household level, stabilisation and adjustment programmes are likely
to result in a polarisation of the income distribution and a worsening
of social indicators, with potential long-term effects on a country's
human capital endowment. At the productive firm level, the process
will favour development of the informal sector, narrowing the field
for 'modern sector', manufacturers and forcing them to enter a
competitive relationship with both local informal producers of low
price goods and international firms in the high quality segment of the
market. In the financial sphere, the process can result in a weakening
of the banking system's role in the intermediation of savings and
capital flows. The public sector, finally, can find itself weakened in
terms of administrative structure (its own human capital) and physical infrastructure, and constrained by a reduced revenue base. In the
medium term, some of these negative connotations of the adjustment
process should be reduced by the positive and growth-inducing
effects of the structural changes. To a considerable extent, in fact, the
negative impact can be ascribed to the stabilisation packages which

accompany them rather than to structural adjustment policies. The ideal condition would therefore be to apply structural adjustment during times of economic growth, when the costs would be more bearable (but the need, unfortunately, much less evident).

In terms of long-term sustainability, adjustment policies should be evaluated in the light of their impact on human capital, physical capital, and environmental quality, and mitigating actions designed to alleviate such impacts. Precise quantification obviously depends on the characteristics of each country's economy, but some general guidelines can be proposed. The following paragraphs only deal with long-term impacts, since short-term policies have already been discussed (pp. 242–3).

Health conditions affect the productivity of workers and hence their contribution to the economy. Long-term improvement of health conditions rests on an emphasis on preventive medicine (e.g. vaccinations) and on environmental conditions (water supply and sanitation) which contribute to the diffusion of communicable diseases. Inclusion of these priorities in public works programmes aimed at temporarily supplementing income can create a linkage between short and long term mitigating measures.

The level of qualification of the work force depends on a mix of basic skills acquired through schooling and specific skills acquired through 'on the job' training. A higher average level of basic skills adds flexibility to the productive structure by facilitating worker mobility between jobs. As we have seen, survival strategies may force children to leave school in order to contribute to the family's income. Maintenance of primary education levels can be encouraged by providing incentives for school attendance. The provision of meals or food packages to school children can obtain the double effect of increasing school enrolments and reducing malnutrition. Training also provides a significant vehicle for the upgrading of human capital, and in this sense cyclical unemployment also has a long-term cost in terms of lost 'learning by doing'. Paid training for the temporarily unemployed can provide both an income supplement and a vehicle for steadier long term growth. Apprenticeship programmes in secondary schools can combine higher levels of schooling with on-the-job experience and a limited amount of income for the participants, with mutually reinforcing effects. They can also provide preferential channels for employment of participants in a training programme.

Organisational capacity can be enhanced by supporting the development of community-based institutions. While considerable responses can be achieved in times of significant social adjustment (creation of communal kitchens, day care programmes, nutrition and health monitoring systems), the permanence of these organisational forms or of their benefits in the long term should be the subject of empirical investigation, since it is possible that they represent only suboptimal choices for their participants, with limited permanence after economic hardship is over.

The enhancement of physical capital accumulation implies as a prerequisite the creation of a macroeconomic environment conducive to investment, and the existence of an efficient financial intermediation system, able to attract and retain local capital. The reduction of capital flight would be a significant step in the satisfaction of the financing requirements of many developing countries.

The long-term environmental sustainability of an adjustment programme depends on the survival strategies triggered in each specific instance. The key evaluation criterion is of course the impact on non-renewable resources and the rate of depletion of renewable ones (which should not exceed their reproductive capacity). Since very few analytical indications have been provided on this topic in the course of this chapter, it does not seem appropriate to attempt suggesting policy actions. This omission, however, should not be interpreted as an attempt to downplay the importance of the issue, but rather of the need for more detailed analysis.

As the preceding analysis has shown, considerable linkages exist between the stabilisation and structural adjustment policies enacted in the short term and their long-term effects on economic growth and development. The argument made here for human capital investments conducive to long-term growth (better levels of health, education, nutrition) is even stronger if we consider that many of them are social goals in their own right.

CONCLUSIONS

The purpose of this chapter was to provide an analytical framework for the analysis of short- and long-term interactions between macroeconomic stabilisation and structural adjustment measures, the microeconomic response of affected economic agents, and their social and developmental implications. The analysis has shown that considerable linkages do exist and can be described qualitatively. On the basis of this qualitative analysis, it is possible to formulate various policy suggestions which should lead both to the mitigation of the social impacts of adjustment policies and to better growth prospects for the long term.

Due to the qualitative character of the analysis, it has often been necessary to include assumptions on the likely outcome of economic processes, especially when countervailing forces were at work (for example on the net effect on import prices of import tariff elimination and exchange rate depreciation). Such assumptions are rather explicit in the text, and it is therefore possible to quickly amend the conclusions reached if empirical evidence is available on the situation of a particular country. As a consequence, not all policy suggestions may be applicable to a given situation. Assumptions in the text are based on the existing consensus in the literature, when one exists, or on personal observations of the author on the reality of developing countries (and specifically Latin America).

The ideal next steps in this research process are the formalisation of the relationships described in this chapter and empirical testing based on the experience of one or more developing countries. Analysis of the voluntary structural adjustments undertaken by industrialised countries in the 1970s can also provide some valuable insights and more reliable data for empirical testing, even though some of the parameters in the reaction functions are likely to be different, because of the different level of development of economic structures in the two sets of countries. Incorporation of human capital in long-run growth models seems to be a particularly promising avenue for the formalised identification of the linkages between short- and long-term effects and of the relationship between social and economic variables. While modelling efforts can never hope to capture the subtleties and institutional constraints of real life, they can provide additional insight into the impact and policy implications of adjustment processes, thereby refining and enriching the present analysis.

Part IV
Conditionality into the 1990s: a Forward Look

11 The International Monetary Fund in Eastern Europe: Lessons of the 1980s and Prospects for the 1990s

Anne Henderson

Historical analysis reveals that the economic development of Eastern Europe has always been influenced by external constraints and pressure. This external pressure was perhaps most evident during the postwar era of Soviet-imposed central planning, but it predated the Soviet presence and outlasted the Soviet dominion over Eastern Europe. Of course, the source and nature of external pressure has changed considerably over time. And during the past two years, the main avenue of outside influence upon Eastern Europe has shifted from the Soviet Union to the Western world.

The ongoing shift in the source and nature of external influence is nowhere more apparent than in the realm of economic strategy. The newly-elected governments of Eastern Europe are struggling to define effective strategies for managing the transition to market economies. In the process, they must decide how to eliminate pervasive subsidisation, abandon full employment, liquidate chronically inefficient enterprises, and stimulate greater competition – all without precipitating economic collapse and political unrest. The Eastern European nations are not grappling with these issues in a vacuum. In fact, their economic strategies are being deeply influenced by pressures from Western corporations and governments, as well as international organisations. These external actors are able to put considerable pressure upon the governments of Eastern Europe, for they control the trade, investment, and financial resources critical to the area's economic recovery.

One of the most influential agents of influence upon Eastern Europe in the 1990s will be the International Monetary Fund (IMF). Every Eastern European country except Albania is now a member of the Fund; and given the combination of economic crisis and fundamental reformism which now characterises the nations of Eastern Europe, it seems inevitable that these countries will come to rely increasingly upon the IMF for financial assistance and economic guidance.

Predictions concerning the IMF's future influence in Eastern Europe cannot be made without reference to the Fund's history of interaction with several Eastern European countries, particularly Hungary, Romania, and Yugoslavia. These countries experienced severe debt repayment difficulties in the 1980s, and turned to the IMF for financial assistance. In return for Fund credits, Hungary, Romania and Yugoslavia accepted standby programmes which committed them to implement market-oriented structural reforms. An examination of the IMF's standby programmes in Eastern Europe in the 1980s can help predict the future course of relations with the Fund and the prospects for economic reform in Eastern Europe. Clearly, the political context of IMF standbys has changed completely since 1989. But many of the economic issues raised in the standbys of the 1980s will remain relevant, and controversial, in the 1990s.

The first section of this chapter will review the main conflicts which shaped relations between the IMF and Eastern Europe in the 1980s. It will develop an analytical model to account for national variations in the outcome of IMF standby programmes. The basic purpose of this section is to identify and analyse the factors which explain why Hungary, Romania and Yugoslavia responded differently to IMF demands in the 1980s. The following section will examine both the continuities and changes in IMF/East European relations in the wake of the democratic revolutions of 1989. The chapter will conclude with an exploration of the future prospects for collaboration between the IMF and the nations of Eastern Europe.

EXTERNAL PRESSURES AND DOMESTIC RESPONSES: A FRAMEWORK FOR ANALYSING IMF RELATIONS WITH EASTERN EUROPE

Through examining IMF relations with Hungary, Romania and Yugoslavia in the 1980s, this chapter will develop a framework for explaining interactions between external pressures and domestic responses in Eastern Europe. More specifically, it will establish whether the causal factors affecting the relationship between the IMF and the countries of Eastern Europe operated at the level of the international system or of domestic politics. Did the IMF shape Eastern European adjustment efforts irrespective of national differences in political structures and processes? Or did those national differences determine how Eastern European countries pursued adjustment and responded to IMF demands?

This study concludes that IMF pressures did influence the adjustment process in Eastern Europe in the 1980s, but those pressures did not fully determine the choice and implementation of adjustment policies. Each country's interactions with the IMF produced different standby outcomes, which reflected differences in the way each country's political system responded to external demands. In other words, international pressures did set constraints upon the actions of domestic actors; yet some leeway to respond to those pressures always existed, and the choice among various response options was determined by the nature of the domestic political system.

Yet precisely which characteristics of the domestic system were most salient in shaping response to external pressures? Several scholars have posited that the critical characteristic determining response to external pressures is the structure of the state (Gourevitch, 1978; Krasner, 1978; Posner, 1978). But although state structure imposes a framework within which policy decisions are made, it does not determine the outcome of specific policy debates. Policy outcomes also depend on the interests of political elites, and the patterns of bargaining and coalition-building among those elites. The interests and composition of elite coalitions cannot be derived from the structure of the state; therefore, they must be considered as a separate factor in the analysis of domestic response to external pressures (Castles, 1982).

It is also important to recognise that domestic responses to external pressures are influenced by factors operating below the level of the policymaking elites. Elite bargaining and coalition-building does not occur in a political vacuum; it is often affected by social pressures and demands. So a full understanding of domestic responses to external pressures must incorporate an analysis of state relationships with society. These relationships define the channels through which social actors participate in the political process, and the means through which the state regulates and responds to their participation.

In sum, three characteristics of the political system shaped domestic response to IMF pressures in Eastern Europe in the 1980s: state structure, political process, and the nature of state/society relationships. For the purposes of this study, state structure was defined along a continuum, with one end associated with central economic planning and extreme institutional concentration of political authority; and the other end characterised by decentralised state economic intervention and a fragmented institutional framework for policymaking. Like state structures, political processes were defined along a continuum, ranging from top-down democratic centralism to bottom-up polycentric bargaining. Finally, the analysis of state/society relationships focused on the state's interactions with managers and workers in public sector industrial enterprises, and placed each country along a continuum ranging from top-down state control over workers and managers to decentralised bargaining. The placement of Eastern European political systems upon this three-fold continuum provided an analytical framework explaining domestic response to external pressure, by demonstrating how national differences in state structures, political processes, and state/society relationships led to divergent responses to IMF demands across countries in the 1980s.

Yet before turning to an analysis of how these factors determined domestic response to IMF demands, it is necessary to outline the nature and content of the Fund's adjustment policies themselves. In analysing the IMF's adjustment strategy in Eastern Europe, it is clearly important to determine whether the IMF's policy demands differed from country to country, and to what extent such differences accounted for national variation in the outcome of standby programmes. Many aspects of the IMF's approach to adjustment were constant across countries and cannot be seen as sources of variation in standby outcomes. In Yugoslavia, Hungary and Romania, the IMF invariably called for stabilisation measures designed to reduce domestic demand and external deficits through restrictive monetary and fiscal policy and devaluation. And in all three countries, the IMF advocated structural adjustment policies, such as price liberalisation, financial reform, and privatisation, which were intended to make the economy more responsive to market signals.

But there were certain variations in the Fund's approach to adjustment across countries. These variations often reflected differences in its degree of financial leverage over standby recipients. The IMF could put forward more stringent demands and adopt a tougher negotiating strategy in a country which was dependent upon IMF credits than in one which had alternative sources of financing. For example, Yugoslavia was unable to obtain loans through channels other than the IMF in the 1980s, while Hungary was able to maintain its access to commercial credits. As a result, the Fund was able to adopt a tougher negotiating strategy in Yugoslavia than in Hungary. In turn, the IMF adopted a stricter negotiating stance in Hungary than it did in Romania, whose decision to forgo all foreign credits after 1983 made it almost impervious to Fund financial pressure.

Differences in the Fund's approach to adjustment in Hungary, Romania and Yugoslavia also reflected the legacy of its divergent historical experiences in each country. For example, the IMF's prior history of interactions with the rigidly anti-reformist Romanian government limited Fund officials' expectations about the prospects for reform in the 1980s. After joining the Fund in 1972, the Romanian government repeatedly rejected IMF proposals for market-oriented reforms; and by the 1980s, this intransigent resistance led the Fund to become disillusioned about the prospects for collaboration with Romania.[1] In Hungary, by contrast, the IMF had no such daunting history to dim its enthusiasm for promoting reform in the 1980s. Reform-oriented elites within the Hungarian leadership had maintained unofficial ties with the IMF since the late 1960s. When Hungary finally joined the IMF in 1982 under the leadership of those reformist elites, the Fund mounted more aggressive efforts to encourage reform than in Romania (Pisulla, 1984). Finally, the IMF's approach to adjustment in Yugoslavia in the 1980s reflected its history of a quarter century of deep involvement in Yugoslavia's stabilisation and reform efforts. Since the IMF had worked closely with the Yugoslav economy throughout the postwar period, it was more aggressive in promoting its adjustment agenda than in Hungary or Romania, where it was on less familiar territory (Jovovic, 1981; Zivanovic, 1979; Kulic, 1982).

Clearly, then, IMF demands had an impact upon the economic adjustment process in Hungary, Romania, and Yugoslavia in the 1980s. But that impact was mediated through domestic factors, most significantly state structures, political processes, and state/society relationships. The following section will develop a framework to explain how the interaction of these factors determined domestic response to Fund policy proposals.

STATE STRUCTURES AND POLITICAL PROCESSES: THREE MODELS OF ELITE RESPONSE TO IMF DEMANDS

State structures and political processes determined the extent of elite debate and the dynamics of elite coalition-building; by doing so, they affected the IMF's capacity to form alliances with domestic elites and influence the outcome of debates on IMF policies. State structures and political processes also shaped the strategy which each Eastern European country adopted during standby negotiations with the IMF. Finally, state structures and political processes influenced each nation's economic development strategy – and development strategy provided a significant reference point which affected elite responses to IMF policy demands.

Centralist Control in Romania

Until the revolution which overthrew the Ceausescu regime in December 1989, Romania's state structure was characterised by highly centralised institutions of political decision-making and economic control. Policy-making authority was concentrated in the hands of Nicholae Ceausescu and a small group of his advisors. Economic authority was also centralised; the state imposed central planning through a hierarchy of top-down bureaucratic control.

Political processes of elite debate and coalition-building took a restricted form in Romania. Since political advancement came through demonstrating loyalty to Ceausescu rather than through challenging his policies, elites had few incentives to initiate policy debates. And since political power was based upon proximity to Ceausescu rather than upon independent institutional power bases, elite coalition-building based on institutional interests was rare. So policy changes were initiated by a signal from Ceausescu rather than through self-generated elite debate; and elite coalitions were assembled by Ceausescu rather than forming through a process of intra-elite negotiation (Jowitt, 1974; Gilberg, 1979).

Romania's centralist state structure and political process both strengthened opposition to IMF demands among the top leadership, and enhanced the leadership's capacity to resist IMF pressure. The leadership's emphasis on strict democratic centralism generated suspicion of any policy proposal which did not originate within its own ranks – a situation which greatly impeded its receptivity to IMF proposals. Furthermore, Romania's state structure and political process concentrated political power in the hands of a small group of top leaders, and enabled those leaders to suppress lower-level policy debates and challenges to their decisions. Therefore, responses to IMF demands were determined entirely by the top leadership, not by a process of debate and coalition-building within the rest of the elite. The top leadership's suppression of elite debate made it impossible for any IMF sympathisers within the elite to articulate their views, form coalitions in support of IMF policies, or influence the leadership's decisions on how to respond to IMF demands (King, 1980; Fischer, 1981).

Romania's distinctive approach to standby negotiations with the IMF also reflected the centralist characteristics of its political system. For instance, the basic goal of Romania's negotiating strategy was to minimise IMF influence; and Romania's centralist state structure and political process were well-suited to achieving this goal. The centralist political system made it possible to confine participation in standby talks to a few ministerial officials whose negotiating positions were specified in advance by the top leadership. Since the negotiators were bound to a predetermined set of positions, they could not represent autonomous institutional interests or take independent positions during negotiations. As a result, the IMF found it almost impossible to play off certain negotiators against others in order to obtain concessions. Instead, it was confronted with a small group of unified negotiators operating under strict central instructions. The centralist negotiating strategy was quite effective in frustrating the IMF's negotiating ploys.[3]

Furthermore, Romania's state structure and political process generated a development strategy which was incompatible with the IMF's adjustment model. The centralist state structure created the institutional framework of a development strategy based upon the centralisation of resource allocation, the suppression of market signals, and the minimisation of linkages between the world market and the domestic economy. Furthermore, the democratic centralist political process meant that changes in development strategy could only be initiated by the top leadership. But since the top leadership was firmly committed to its traditional development strategy and rejected the possibility of reform, Romania's development strategy remained immutable and impervious to IMF pressures for change (Fischer-Galati, 1981; Nelson, 1980a; Chirot, 1980).

Consociational Negotiation in Hungary

Hungary's state structure in the 1980s differed from Romania's in terms of both the institutional framework for policy-making and the nature of state control over the economy. In Hungary, policy-making institutions involved a wider circle of elites and provided greater room for the articulation of competing interests. Political power did coalesce around party leaders in the Politburo; yet policy-making also involved the participation of other party and government officials in the Council of Ministers, the Central Committee and the state ministries, as well as the consultation on non-governmental experts and economists.

Unlike Romania, where the composition of elite coalitions generally reflected the patronage and preferences of the top leader, in Hungary the composition of elite coalitions could reflect organisational interests, as elites attempted to protect or expand their institutional power bases through building coalitions. And also unlike Romania, the elite decision-making process was based on debate and negotiation rather than top-down imposition. But although the Hungarian decision-making process permitted debate, it managed and limited the terms of debate; after debate, all elites agreed to support the final decision even if it diverged from their preferences. Losers in policy debates were given incentives to comply with decisions they originally opposed, in the form of concessions which reflected their policy concerns (Comisso, 1986; Gitelman, 1981).

In contrast to Romania, then, state structures and political processes in Hungary's consociational system diffused policy-making authority among a broader range of elites and permitted more extensive elite debates over IMF policies. Hungary's state structure and political process had mixed implications for elite receptivity to IMF policy proposals. On the one hand, the greater openness of elite debate meant that there were more opportunities than in Romania for elites who supported IMF policies to articulate their views and form coalitions aimed at influencing policy decisions. The openness of elite debate also provided more points of entry into the policy-making process for the IMF, allowing the Fund to locate and form alliances with reform-oriented elites more readily than in Romania. On the other hand, the consociational system's reliance upon compensation-based consensus-building frustrated IMF pressure for rapid adjustment. Since the political process built consensus through avoiding radical change and through providing compensations to losers in policy-making debates, IMF adjustment policies were often delayed and diluted in the interests of maintaining elite consensus.

One basic difference between the Hungarian and Romanian political processes which affected elite responses to IMF demands was the possibility of elite coalition-building based upon institutional interests. In Romania, elites below the level of the top leadership found it almost impossible to develop independent institutional power bases or to form coalitions based on their own organisational interests. By contrast, the Hungarian political process provided greater opportunities for elites to form policy coalitions based on their organisation interests. In fact, Hungarian debates on IMF policies were often shaped by competing organisational interests. Many policy-makers evaluated each IMF proposal in terms of its impact upon the institutions they headed, and were generally more receptive to IMF policies which did not disrupt the operating procedures or reduce the authority of their own organisations. So in Hungary, the outcome of elite debates on particular IMF policies often reflected the relative strength of the institutionally-based elite coalitions which supported and opposed those policies.

The contrasts between Hungarian and Romanian political structures and processes also revealed themselves in the realm of standby negotiation. The goals of Hungary's negotiating strategy differed somewhat from Romania's, since the Hungarian leadership did actually wish to obtain IMF advice on adjustment policies. The nature of the negotiating strategy differed as well. Because of the greater institutional dispersion and flexibility of the Hungarian state structure and political process, Hungary's negotiating strategy was not as centralised or as predetermined as Romania's. Deviations from the pre-set negotiating platform were not uncommon, as representatives of the various ministries involved in standby talks disagreed over adjustment strategy and articulated their own positions. Such divisions within the Hungarian negotiating team allowed the IMF to find allies and win concessions. Yet, it should be emphasised that the extent of division was limited; negotiators maintained a consensus in favour of gradual adjustment and disagreed only over details of policy implementation. As a result, the IMF was able to exploit the differences within the Hungarian negotiating team only to obtain limited concessions.[4]

It is also important to note that Hungary's development strategy was considerably more compatible with the IMF adjustment model than was Romania's. It envisioned a transition towards decentralised market signals in guiding the economy. The main question was not whether the IMF could push elites to reorient their development strategy – which was already moving in the direction of market-oriented reform – but whether the IMF could force elites to accelerate the reform process. This question hinged upon the flexibility of Hungary's development strategy.

Hungary's development strategy was more flexible than Romania's because its consociational political process provided more opportunities for elite debate over changes in development strategy. But the inherent gradualism of the consociational process set limits upon change, because it built elite consensus through tactics of compromise and compensation which ruled out radical revisions in development strategy. Yet although Hungary's commitment to gradualism was well-established, the timing and scope of specific reform initiatives were still the subject of elite debates, and persuaded policy-makers to move slightly faster and further in carrying out the reform (Csaba, 1983; Bauer, 1984). In other words, Hungary's basically coherent, yet continuously evolving, development strategy provided opportunities for limited IMF input into the choice of adjustment policies. So the IMF was able to exert an incremental influence over the transition of Hungarian development strategy towards a more market-oriented approach.

Polycentric Bargaining in Yugoslavia

In the 1980s, Yugoslavia's political system was defined by two mutually-reinforcing characteristics: institutional decentralisation and elite fragmentation. The state structure devolved most political power to republican and local governments. Although the Communist Party was supposed to serve as the unifying agent holding together the decentralised system, it had fragmented into republican organisations which defended their separate interests and had only tenuous links to the central party organisation. The political process reflected this fragmentation of power and interests. Federal policy-making consisted of harmonising the conflicting interests of the various republican elites. Since each republic had a virtual veto on federal policy decisions, policy-making deadlocks occurred frequently and could be resolved only through bargaining processes in which compromises were pieced together through compensating the republican interests which were disadvantaged by particular policy decisions.[5]

The state structure and political process in a polycentric system provided room for even more extensive elite debate over IMF policies than in Hungary, and created even greater opportunities for elite coalition-building. While in Hungary, coalitions on IMF policies were often based on elites' organisational interests, in Yugoslavia they generally reflected regional interests. And while Hungary's consociational political process permitted elite debate but carefully managed its scope, Yugoslavia's polycentric process gave rise to incessant, almost unmanageable debate between competing regional interests (Denitch, 1981; Burg, 1986).

Yugoslavia's polycentric state structure and political process had a rather contradictory impact upon federal elites' responses to IMF demands. On the one hand, the openness of elite debate and the pervasiveness of elite dissension made the Yugoslav political process quite permeable to IMF influence and gave the Fund greater opportunities to affect the outcomes of elite debates than in Romania or Hungary. IMF pressure often played a role in resolving elite stalemates over policy decisions by tipping the balance in favour of market-oriented adjustment policies. On the other hand, the Fund's influence was often transitory. IMF pressure could produce a temporary elite consensus to pursue market-oriented adjustment policies. But elite consensus in Yugoslavia's polycentric system was a fragile commodity; initial agreement on IMF policies often broke down as soon as concrete implementational details had to be worked out.

Furthermore, elite efforts to build consensus through tactics of compensation frequently undermined the impact of IMF policies. As in Hungary, losers on a particular policy issue received some form of compensation in order to ensure their support for the policy agreement. But in Hungary, the level of domestic economic inequality was limited enough so that compensations to regions or sectors which were disadvantaged by adjustment policies could be made without intolerably straining the economic resources of the state or completely undermining the policies themselves. In Yugoslavia, the inequalities were so deep and extensive that compensations to disadvantaged areas entailed insupportably large subsidy costs and sabotaged the whole thrust of the adjustment effort.

Yugoslavia's polycentric state structure and political process gave rise to a standby negotiating strategy which was considerably less effective than either Romania's or Hungary's. Because the state structure institutionalised elite fragmentation, and because the political process encouraged elite dissension, Yugoslav negotiators never managed to agree upon a coherent set of negotiating positions. They were unable to present viable alternative policy proposals to counter IMF demands, and often negotiated on the basis of *ad hoc* positions which did not stand up to IMF pressure. Furthermore, Yugoslavia's negotiating team was characterised by considerable internal conflicts of interest – conflicts which the IMF was able to exploit to win major concessions on standby terms.[6]

In Hungary, policy debates occurred within the context of an overarching consensus on development strategy. But in Yugoslavia, the elite fragmentation which characterised the polycentric political process precluded consensus on development strategy. Elite uncertainty over development strategy increased Yugoslavia's vulnerability to IMF pressure, as the Fund took advantage of Yugoslavia's policy confusion to put forward its own adjustment conceptions (Ognjanovic, 1985). Without a viable alternative to the IMF's policies, Yugoslav elites found themselves accepting IMF proposals by default.

The preceding comparison of state structures and political processes in Eastern Europe in the 1980s can be expressed in the form of an analytical continuum. At one end of the continuum was Yugoslavia's polycentric system, characterised by extreme institutional dispersion of decision-making authority; uncontrollable elite debate; a disunified standby negotiating strategy; and an incoherent development strategy. At the other end of the continuum was Romania's centralist political system, whose characteristics included institutional concentration of authority; top-down suppression of elite debate; a centralised and unified negotiating strategy; and an immutable development strategy. Hungary's consociational political system was positioned between the two extremes of polycentrism and centralism. It was characterised by modest institutional diffusion of policy-making power; managed elite debate; a moderately flexible negotiating strategy; and a coherent yet mutable development strategy. Each country's position on the continuum predicted how its policy-making elites would respond to IMF policy demands. The polycentric end of the continuum was associated with the greatest degree of elite vulnerability to IMF pressure, while the centralist end was associated with the greatest degree of elite resistance to IMF policy demands.

STATE STRUCTURES, POLITICAL PROCESSES,
STATE/SOCIETY RELATIONS, AND THE POLITICS OF
STANDBY IMPLEMENTATION

Although the above-mentioned continuum accurately predicted elite reactions to IMF demands, it remains analytically incomplete. Eastern Europe responses to IMF pressure cannot be analysed solely at the level of elite debate and standby negotiation. In fact, the more concrete response came during the implementational phase, when the terms of the standby agreement were carried out.

The processes of standby implementation in Romania, Hungary and Yugoslavia share certain similarities. In all three countries, the same sets of actors were involved in the implementational process: bureaucrats in the state's economic ministries; subnational government and party officials; and managers and workers in state-sector industrial enterprises. In all three countries, furthermore, these actors opposed IMF policies for the same basic reasons. In all three political systems, for instance, bureaucrats in the state's economic ministries opposed IMF policies which would restrict their power to distribute credits and subsidies to enterprises. Local government officials often resisted the IMF's policies because they had developed similar patron-client relationships with enterprises, and feared that the Fund's policies would disrupt local production, bankrupt local enterprises, and lay off local workers. Furthermore, many enterprise managers in all three countries resisted IMF policies which would force them to compete for investment resources in a financial market, and to accept the market penalty of bankruptcy if they failed to compete adequately. Finally, workers in all three countries opposed IMF policies which would reduce their real incomes through price increases and wage restrictions, and which would threaten their job security through closing down loss-making firms.[7]

Although the identities and motivations of the actors involved in policy implementation were similar in Hungary, Romania, and Yugoslavia, their capacity to obstruct the implementation of IMF adjustment policies varied greatly from country to country. Each country's state structure defined the degree of lower-level bureaucratic freedom to resist central policies, while its political process shaped the patterns of bargaining between central elites and their subordinates over policy implementation, and the nature of its state/society relationships determined the strength of managerial and worker resistance to IMF policies.

Romania's centralist system provided the fewest opportunities for lower-level resistance to IMF policies. For one thing, since the top Romanian leadership rejected most IMF policies outright, lower-level resistance seldom had a chance to materialise at all.[8] Besides, since the party/state thoroughly dominated all economic organisations, local bureaucrats and enterprise managers had limited capacity to challenge instruments, imposing state policies upon the workplace, workers had no institutional channels through which to articulate opposition or protest. In sum, the nature of the state's relationships with social actors made it difficult for enterprise managers and workers to play a role in policy formulation or to challenge the implementation of central policies (Cole, 1981; Linden, 1986; Nelson, 1981b; Gilberg, 1979).

For all these reasons, lower-level resistance to IMF policies seldom had a chance to emerge – it was pre-empted by central elite rejection of IMF policies and suppression of all social dissent. In Hungary, by contrast, central policy-makers did make good-faith efforts to carry out IMF policies, and those policies did generate considerable lower-level resistance. The state's relationship with enterprise managers and workers, and its approach to economic policy implementation, embodied more negotiation and less top-down command than in Romania. For instance, Hungary's political process of negotiated compensation provided opportunities for lower-level bureaucrats and enterprise managers to undermine the IMF's efforts to reduce subsidies and subject the flow of credit to market criteria. The bureaucratic hierarchy was permeated by a network of bargaining relationships through which enterprises negotiated with their superiors for exceptions to IMF policies in the form of subsidies and tax breaks (Tokes, 1984; Bauer, 1985; Lauter, 1972; Robinson, 1973).

Yugoslavia's political system provided even more extensive opportunities for lower-level actors to undermine the implementation of IMF policies. The polycentric state structure allowed republican governments to obstruct the implementation of IMF measures which they felt would have a detrimental impact upon their republics' economies. Furthermore, the federal government had few political mechanisms through which to impose its policies upon enterprise managers. Managers developed much closer ties with local government and party organisations than with the federal government, and the polycentric system encouraged the entrenchment of coalitions between local government officials, banks, and enterprise managers. These coalitions attempted, with considerable success, to sabotage

IMF policies aimed at eliminating interenterprise credits, increasing interest rates, and restricting credit flows to loss-making enterprises (Zarkovic, 1981).

Workers' avenues for resisting IMF policies, and state strategies for dealing with that resistance, differed significantly in Yugoslavia and Hungary. In Hungary, workers had limited capacity to directly resist IMF adjustment policies through strikes. Yet workers' concerns were indirectly represented in the policy process. The state/ worker relationship in Hungary conformed, at least in a limited fashion, to the pattern of negotiated compensation which characterised the rest of the political system. Unions were not charged solely with suppressing workers' grievances; instead, they were provided with some institutional channels to communicate those grievances (Brown, 1984; Pravda, 1983). The union organisation negotiated with central policy-makers for wage and price policy compensations to partially offset the impact of IMF adjustment policies upon the workforce. Furthermore, such union activities were only one part of a broader elite strategy to forestall worker unrest through limiting consumption declines and unemployment. To this end, policy-makers frequently scaled back IMF proposals for consumer price increases and income restrictions (White, 1986; Markus, 1982).

In Yugoslavia, by contrast, the government did much less than its Hungarian counterpart to limit the impact of austerity upon workers through protecting real incomes and maintaining employment. This was in part a conscious policy choice, but it was also a reflection of the weakness of the Yugoslav government's instruments of economic regulation. The government was simply unable to control wage-eroding inflation or to find jobs for all new entrants onto the job market. Partly because the state was unwilling and unable to shelter workers from the impact of adjustment, and partly because it had little coercive power over the workforce, it was often confronted with worker resistance to austerity in the form of strikes. These strikes often resulted in wage gains; yet the gains were generally not substantial enough to compensate for inflation. Essentially, the same polycentrism which gave rise to a relatively loose and non-coercive relationship between workers and the state, and which gave workers the freedom to strike, also made it extremely difficult for the federal government to exercise effective macroeconomic guidance or to limit the impact of adjustment upon the population (Shabad, 1980; Comisso, 1981; Sirc, 1979; Schrenk, 1981; Zukin, 1981).

The incorporation of the sub-elite level into the continuum of political systems typologies adds elements of complexity and apparent contradiction to the analysis of domestic responses to IMF pressures. While at the elite level, the range of responses marked a clear progression from rejection of IMF demands at the centralist end of the continuum to accommodation at the polycentric end, the range of lower-level reactions displayed an opposite progression. The extent of lower-level resistance to IMF policies was lowest at the centralist end of the continuum and highest at the polycentric end. Based upon this observation, it might seem that competing dynamics were at work within Eastern European political systems, as elite and lower-level responses to IMF demands exerted opposing impacts upon standby outcomes.

But this was not necessarily the case. In Romania, for instance, the lack of lower-level resistance to IMF demands by no means contradicted elite-level opposition to those demands. Instead, the lack of lower-level resistance was a direct result of elite-level opposition. It reflected the ability of the centralist system's leadership to pre-empt lower-level reactions by rejecting IMF demands before they reached the implementational phase.

In Hungary, similarly, the existence of lower-level resistance did not so much contradict elite-level responses as it corresponded to them. At both the level of the policy-making elite and the level of policy implementation, responses to IMF demands were shaped by the political process of negotiated compensation. This process limited the IMF's influence by diluting the impact of Fund policies in the interests of compromise and compensation.

Only in Yugoslavia did elite and lower-level responses truly exert opposing influences upon standby outcomes. Elite-level fragmentation and dissension created vulnerability to IMF policy pressure, but lower-level resistance undermined IMF policy implementation. However, this outcome was less an indication of contradictions within the Yugoslav political system than a manifestation of that system's internal consistency. The same polycentric state structures and political processes which generated vulnerability to IMF pressure at the elite level were also responsible for obstructing IMF policy implementation at lower levels. By the same token, the consociational structures and processes which shaped the Hungarian elites' responses to IMF demands also determined the patterns of lower-level resistance. Finally, the same centralist structures and processes which strengthened the Romanian leadership's capacity to reject IMF demands also accounted for the lack of lower-level resistance to those demands. So in each country, the apparent disparities between elite and lower-level responses to IMF pressures did not really represent internal systematic contradictions. Instead, each country's elite and lower-level reactions were separate yet consistent manifestations of a single set of political structures and processes.

STANDBY OUTCOMES IN EASTERN EUROPE: A COMPARATIVE ASSESSMENT

In assessing the outcomes of IMF standby programmes in Eastern Europe in the 1980s, it is necessary to distinguish between the two sets of IMF adjustment measures: those to achieve short-term economic stabilisation, and those to promote long-term structural reform.

The central element of the IMF's stabilisation strategy was restrictive monetary policy. Yet in no Eastern European country did monetary policy function in the manner anticipated by the IMF adjustment model. In Yugoslavia, for example, restrictive monetary policy was not an effective instrument of demand reduction. The federal authorities had no control over the liquidity circulating in the grey credit market, so official monetary restrictions failed to reduce demand as the IMF model assumed (Srebric, 1982; OECD, 1982; Rogic, 1985).[9]

In Hungary, by contrast, the government was capable of exerting stronger central control over the money supply. However, the Hungarian authorities refused to utilise their powers to the full extent; in order to minimise consumption cuts, they resisted Fund pressure for extremely stringent credit restrictions. Because the Hungarian government was determined to limit the impact of austerity upon the population, Hungary never fully achieved its standby targets for consumption reduction (Tarafas, 1985; Tardos, 1987; IMF, 1983a).

Neither reluctance nor inability to reduce consumption was a problem in Romania, where the government imposed strict credit controls. Yet monetary restriction operated through an entirely different mechanism in Romania than in the Fund's model. In the IMF model, monetary restriction reduced demand through market incentives. But in Romania, monetary restriction reduced demand through arbitrary centrally-imposed credit cut-offs which forced enterprises to reduce investment and wages. In fact, Romania's entire demand reduction effort reflected the use of state controls, not market mechanisms. Furthermore, the impetus behind Romania's demand restriction had nothing to do with the IMF. Although the harsh consumption restrictions coincided with IMF standbys, they were an outgrowth of the Romanian government's own stringent austerity programme, not of IMF pressures.[10]

Along with restrictive monetary policy, the second main component of the IMF's short-term stabilisation strategy was devaluation. Unfortunately, the Fund's exchange rate demands were just as economically unworkable and politically unpopular as its calls for market-oriented monetary restriction. In Romania, for example, the exchange rate had no significant impact upon the flow of trade (which was centrally planned) or the prices of tradeables (which were centrally determined), so its usefulness as a stabilisation tool was questionable (Knight, 1983). In Hungary, the usefulness of devaluation was also questionable, as enterprise response to exchange rate signals was impeded by trade controls and subsidies. In addition, strong political resistance to devaluation, reflecting elites' fears of inflation, frustrated the IMF's efforts to bring about major exchange rate adjustments (IMF 1982a; IMF, 1982b; IMF, 1983a; Von Brabant, 1985). The IMF was somewhat more successful in Yugoslavia, where it prevailed upon the federal government to devalue. However, the constant acceleration of inflation, along with frequent governmental lapses from the IMF's exchange rate policy, eroded the effectiveness of devaluation (Bogoev, 1986; Kovacevic, 1986). In sum, the IMF did not succeed in imposing its exchange rate policy upon any Eastern European country, due to a combination of domestic political resistance and the economic unworkability of the IMF's exchange rate model.

In general, the IMF's efforts to impose its short-term stabilisation model in Eastern Europe were not particularly successful. In Hungary, the leadership's commitment to maintaining living standards led it to reject IMF demands for severe monetary and fiscal restrictions. Meanwhile, the Yugoslav federal government's inability to control the activities of lower-level economic and political actors left it incapable of imposing effective fiscal, monetary, or wage restrictions. The Romanian leadership, by contrast, was both willing and able to impose restrictive policies – but its willingness sprang less from responsiveness to IMF pressures than from an independent decision to carry out stringent austerity.

Even when Eastern European governments did agree to carry out IMF stabilisation policies, those policies often played a rather insignificant role in the adjustment process. Adjustment was typically achieved not through the IMF's market-oriented restrictive policies, but through state economic controls such as central import, wage, and investment restrictions. Ironically, the IMF's pressures for demand restriction actually obstructed the achievement of its other main adjustment goal – market-oriented reform. IMF calls for demand reduction encouraged Eastern European governments to impose state controls upon investment, imports, and wages-control which greatly impeded the implementation of decentralising, market-oriented economic reforms.

Another impediment to the Fund's efforts to encourage reform was the fact that its proposals for structural adjustment were simplistic and insufficient. These proposals, which focused on price desubsidisation, interest rate increases, and exchange rate restructuring, were incapable of promoting structural adjustment in the absence of supporting reforms to make the economy more responsive to price, interest rate, and exchange rate signals. The IMF did encourage Eastern European governments to carry out comprehensive market-oriented reform programmes in conjunction with the IMF structural adjustment proposals. But some governments refused to undertake such reforms, which meant that the IMF's structural proposals could not exercise their intended economic effects.

Price rationalisation was invariably a central component of the IMF's structural adjustment strategy. The Fund felt that without a price structure reflecting market scarcities, consumers and enterprises would be unable to make rational consumption and production decisions. In Romania, however, the price realignments demanded by the Fund were not implemented within the context of a market-oriented reform programme; so they had almost no impact upon consumer or producer behaviour. Consumption levels were determined through centrally-imposed rationing, not through prices; enterprise production decisions reflected central plan targets, not price signals (Pisulla, 1984).

In Yugoslavia, the interplay between the IMF's pressures for price liberalisation and the government's fear of inflation led to a vicious cycle of price decontrol and recontrol. The IMF periodically forced the Yugoslav government to free prices, but the government invariably reimposed price controls when inflation accelerated. So although Yugoslavia sporadically adopted a liberalised price system, the transience of Yugoslavia's liberalisations prevented them from contributing to the process of market-oriented reform (Tyson,

Robinson, and Woods, 1985; OECD, 1984).

Only in Hungary did the IMF's proposals for price rationalisation fit into a broader economic reform strategy. The Hungarian leadership never fully embraced the Fund's proposals, fearing that full price liberalisation would exacerbate inflation. But in conjunction with IMF standbys, Hungary did gradually liberalise producer prices and reduce consumer price subsidies, thereby contributing to the broader reform goal of enhancing consumer and enterprise responsiveness to market signals (IMF, 1983a).

Investment rationalisation, as well as price rationalisation, was central to the IMF's conception of structural adjustment. The IMF attempted to promote investment rationalisation through interest rate increases to price capital at a more realistic level. In each country, responses to the IMF's interest rate demands broadly paralleled the responses to its demands for price reform.

In Romania, the interest rate increases which the government carried out were economically meaningless. The interest rate played almost no role in the centrally-planned allocation of credits, and in the absence of market-oriented financial reform, interest rate increases had little impact on investment flows (Tyson, 1984; Jackson, 1986). In Yugoslavia, the government bowed to IMF pressure for interest rate increases, yet repeatedly violated its standby commitments as the economic costs of those commitments mounted. Faced with accelerating inflation and growing enterprise losses, the federal government frequently froze interest rates. Local governments and banks also undermined the IMF's interest rate policy by expanding credit flows and writing off enterprise debts. (Stanovnik, 1985; Tyson, Robinson and Woods, 1984). Finally, in Hungary, the IMF was moderately successful in pressing for interest rate increases. These increases had some potential economic significance, since they were implemented within the context of a broader financial reform programme designed to increase enterprise responsiveness to interest rate signals (IMF, 1983b; IMF, 1983c).

The IMF realised that interest rate increases alone were insufficient to rationalise investment. So it encouraged Eastern European governments to supplement interest rate policy with reforms which would force enterprises to invest more efficiently or else face the threat of bankruptcy. In Hungary, for example, the IMF urged the government to slash industrial subsidies and shut down loss-making enterprises. Yet Hungarian policy-makers proved unwilling to liquidate failing enterprises as ruthlessly as the IMF desired. They were committed to preventing unemployment, and they were under pressure from bureaucrats and enterprise managers to keep loss-making firms afloat through subsidies (IMF, 1983a). Meanwhile, the IMF pressured the Yugoslav government into formulating an ambitious programme for eradicating subsidies and liquidating loss-making enterprises. Yet the federal government lacked the authority to ensure that the programme's policies were carried out at subnational levels. Republican and local governments continued to grant subsidies and debt write-offs to enterprises, and banks continued to extend credits to insolvent firms. So Yugoslavia's financial reform programme never fulfilled the IMF's expectations in even a partial sense (OECD, 1987; Knight, 1984; IMF, 1987).

As part of its efforts to rationalise investment, the IMF also called on its standby recipients to carry out reforms of their banking systems. In Hungary, for example, the IMF pressed the government to replace the system of state credit allocation with a decentralised capital market. Although the banking reform proceeded more cautiously than the IMF would have wished, IMF pressure did contribute to the initiation of a gradual process of financial decentralisation in Hungary.[11] No such claim could be made in Romania, where the IMF's pressure for financial reform was completely unsuccessful. The Romanian government refused to relinquish its central control over credit allocation and rejected IMF proposals for financial decentralisation.

While in Romania and Hungary, the IMF called for financial decentralisation, in Yugoslavia it proposed the opposite. The Fund felt that Yugoslavia's banking system was excessively decentralised, and that the National Bank lacked the authority to impose a nationwide monetary policy. So it called for the strengthening of the National Bank's regulatory powers. But the IMF's proposals to bolster federal policy-making authority became embroiled in an ongoing domestic political conflict over recentralisation, and never received the broad elite support necessary for their implementation.[12]

To summarise, the IMF was least successful in encouraging market-oriented structural adjustment in Romania. The Romanian government categorically rejected the Fund's contention that the adjustment process required reforms to make the economy more responsive to market signals. Instead, Romania tried to resolve the economic crises through strengthening central party control over the economy.

The IMF was more successful in furthering reform in Hungary, partly because Hungary – unlike Romania and Yugoslavia – did have a pre-existing commitment to undertake market-oriented reforms. The IMF was therefore able to work with Hungary to carry out a market-oriented structural adjustment programme. Nevertheless, the fact that Hungary had already decided upon the basic scope and elements of its reform programme in some ways restricted the IMF's influence: the limits of reform were already determined, and the IMF could only exert incremental influence over their implementation. The IMF was never able to catalyse a breakthrough in the reform process from gradualism to radical change.

Of the three Eastern European countries, the IMF exerted the most influence over the choice of structural adjustment policies in Yugoslavia. Unlike Hungary, where the IMF supported an existing domestic reform programme, or Romania, where the IMF confronted intractable resistance to reform, in Yugoslavia the Fund played a significant role in defining the content of Yugoslavia's adjustment programme. But although the IMF managed to impose its policy preferences upon Yugoslavia, it could not force the federal leadership to move decisively in putting the abstract goals of the adjustment programme into practice. Nor could the IMF force subnational governments and enterprises to carry out the federal government's policies.

THE IMF AND EASTERN EUROPE IN THE 1990s: PROSPECTS FOR COLLABORATION AND OBSTACLES TO REFORM

The new era in IMF/Eastern European relations is marked by changes in a variety of areas: in the membership of the Fund, in the IMF's approach to adjustment in Eastern Europe, in the Soviet Union's attitude towards the IMF, and in the political structures and processes which determine Eastern European responses to IMF policy demands.

In previous decades, the IMF's Eastern European membership was limited by both implicit Soviet disapproval of the Fund and by the inherent anti-reformism of several Eastern European regimes. Czechoslovakia, East Germany, and Bulgaria were too suspicious of the market-oriented adjustment strategy espoused by the IMF, and too deferential to Soviet attitudes towards the organisation, to consider joining the Fund. But now the Soviet Union itself has joined the queue of aspirants to Fund membership, and the anti-reformist regimes formerly ruling Czechoslovakia, East Germany, and Bulgaria have been swept from power. These developments have cleared the way for the IMF to play a significant role in overseeing the transition from socialism to market economies throughout the former Eastern bloc. While East Germany has become a Fund member simply by virtue of absorption into the Federal Republic, Czechoslovakia and Bulgaria became members in their own right, and are currently undertaking market-oriented adjustment programmes under the auspices of the IMF.

Meanwhile, the Eastern European countries which were already members of the IMF are entering into a qualitatively new stage in their relations with the Fund. Romania has yet to announce a new standby arrangement, but Poland, Hungary, and Yugoslavia have all embarked upon radical market-oriented reform and restructuring programmes in conjunction with IMF standbys. These standbys have involved the Fund more deeply in the economic reform programmes of its Eastern European members than ever before, and have gone beyond the modest reforms of prior standbys to promote dramatic shifts in the structure of the Polish, Hungarian and Yugoslav economies.

The IMF is ideally situated to influence the economic transition strategies of both its established and new member states in Eastern Europe because these nations are in urgent need of Fund financial assistance and advice. The nations of Eastern Europe have been brought to the brink of economic collapse by a combination of domestic and external economic shocks, which include the dislocations accompanying the 1989 revolutions; the impact of the 1990 oil price increases and the transition to hard-currency trade with the Soviet Union; and the burden of repaying heavy debts to Western banks and governments. Without the assistance of the IMF, most of these countries will be unable to obtain the foreign credits needed to rebuild their economies and meet their external payment obligations. In effect, the Eastern European nations are financial hostages of the IMF, since the Fund's seal of approval upon their economic strategies is critical to their access to Western resources. The actual release of the substantial financial assistance packages pledged by Western governments is contingent upon the finalisation of standby agreements with the Fund.

This is not to imply that the countries of Eastern Europe are averse to IMF supervision; in fact, several of them are eager to obtain the Fund's technical assistance in setting up market-oriented banking and taxation systems. With limited knowledge and experience of the workings of a capitalist economy, the new governments of Eastern Europe are turning to the Fund for advice in making the transition to a competitive market economy.

The potential for IMF influence over Eastern European reform efforts can be explored by utilising the analytical framework developed in the earlier part of this chapter. Obviously, the models discussed earlier applied to the political systems of the 1980s. Nevertheless, the utility of studying state structures, political processes, and state-society relations in analysing responses to IMF demands has not been undermined by the recent changes. Furthermore, the use of a continuum of political models based on these three factors remains a valid approach to the study of IMF/East European relations. Each country's position on the continuum has shifted since 1989; but the continuum itself is still a useful predicator of national response to external pressure.

A preliminary analysis of political processes, state structures, and state-society relations reveals that all Eastern European countries are moving towards political structures based on greater decentralisation and debate. These developments will make it easier for the IMF to gain access to the policy-making process in Eastern Europe, find domestic political allies, and influence the outcome of policy debates on economic reform. Not only will access to potential domestic allies improve, but the prospects for successful alliances with reform-oriented domestic elites will grow as well. The political changes of the past year have brought to power new sets of leaders whose commitment to market-oriented development is considerably greater than before, even in the historically reformist countries of Hungary and Yugoslavia. So both the shift to greater decentralisation and debate in political processes, and the shift to stronger market orientation in development strategy, will augment the prospects for IMF influence over adjustment policy in Eastern Europe.

On the other hand, political decentralisation and the loosening of central controls could exacerbate the problem of lower-level resistance to the IMF's adjustment policies. For instance, many enterprise managers still oppose economic reforms to cut off the flow of subsidised state credits and liquidate loss-making firms. At the same time, workers may attempt to mobilise their recently-revitalised trade unions to block massive layoffs and wage restrictions. Furthermore, privatisation programmes carried out in conjunction with IMF standbys are causing bitter and time-consuming conflicts among the pre-war property owners, the former Communist bosses who now wish to purchase the enterprises they managed, and the workers eager for shares in their firms. In other words, democratisation in the political sphere will not bring a wholesale embrace of IMF-style capitalism in the economic sphere. In fact, the decentralisation accompanying political reform in Eastern Europe will augment the capacity of lower-level actors to resist the implementation of IMF policies. So while Eastern European governments may accept the IMF's market-oriented reforms with unprecedented enthusiasm, they will face considerable difficulties in the implementational phase.

But the prospects for future collaboration between the IMF and Eastern Europe do not depend entirely upon domestic developments within Eastern European societies. The evolution of the IMF's own approach to adjustment will also influence the course of relations with Eastern Europe. In 1990, the Fund announced several modifications of its traditional approach to adjustment in Eastern Europe – modifications which reflected the lessons the IMF had learned from its experiences of the 1980s, as well as its awareness of new opportunities in the 1990s.

For one thing, the IMF established a new Eastern European Department within its organisation, thereby providing an overdue recognition of Eastern Europe's uniqueness and importance. Previously, Eastern Europe had been relegated to a minor position within the IMF's European Deparment, which dealt primarily with the advanced capitalist nations of Western Europe. The Fund did not feel that its few Eastern European members merited a separate Department, or, indeed, a separate approach to adjustment – Fund officials meted out the same advice to their Eastern European standby recipients as they provided to all their other clients. But now, the IMF has acknowledged that the nations of Eastern Europe will be at the forefront of the movement towards economic liberalisation in the 1990s, and will be highly-visible test cases of the IMF's efforts to promote market-oriented adjustment. As such, Eastern Europe is now accorded the status of its own department, and has become the focus of Fund rethinking of its approach to adjustment.

Recent remarks by IMF Managing Director Michel Camdessus and other Fund officials reveal that the IMF has learned several lessons from its experiences in Eastern Europe in the 1980s, and has attempted to adjust its behaviour accordingly.[13] First and perhaps most importantly, the IMF has decided that the gradual, partial reform programmes to which it gave its imprimatur in Hungary and Yugoslavia in the 1980s are unworkable. Now the Fund proclaims that all the elements of a market-oriented reform programme must be introduced simultaneously, in one comprehensive package. The Fund's experiences in Eastern Europe have demonstrated that all elements of economic reform are inextricably interconnected, and that efforts to introduce one component of the reform while delaying another will doom the entire effort to failure.[14]

As a logical corollary of its new resolve to sanction only comprehensive reform, the IMF has also come to the conclusion that there is no such thing as a 'third way' between capitalism and socialism. In the 1980s, the IMF tolerated the Hungarian and Yugoslav experimentation with halfway-house reforms designed to introduce market signals into a socially-owned and operated system. But in the 1990s, the IMF will accept nothing less than a full transition to the market, entailing privatisation of state assets, creation of capitalist financial, legal, and accounting systems, and elimination of the firms which survived only through state subsidisation.

In sum, the IMF's approach to economic reform in Eastern Europe has become considerably more ambitious in the 1990s. This shift reflects the Fund's conviction, based on the unsatisfactory standby experiences of the 1980s, that it *must* demand more in the 1990s; it also reflects the Fund's assessment that because of the Eastern European revolutions of 1989, it *can* demand more as well. Yet along with increased ambition in demanding reform, the IMF has also begun to exhibit increased understanding in dealing with the social dislocations which accompany reform. Now the Fund has recognised that in order to convince governments to implement disruptive reforms, it must sanction compensatory mechanisms. For instance, the IMF now supports the creation of social safety nets to cushion the impact of enterprise liquidations and inflation in Eastern Europe. After years of fruitless pressure for stringent restructuring policies, the Fund has finally realised that the only way to convince governments to carry out such policies is to create social safety nets which will deflect popular pressure for maintaining subsidies.

The new elements in the Fund's approach to adjustment in Eastern Europe do not comprise a fundamental shift in its philosophy or goals. In fact, many elements in the Fund's adjustment model – particularly the emphasis on strict macroeconomic discipline – remain completely unchanged from the 1980s. Nevertheless, it is clear that the IMF has reacted to its standby experiences of the 1980s and to the

Eastern European revolutions of 1989 with a perceptible shift in its tactics. It is now up to the nations of Eastern Europe to respond to that shift.

THE 1990 STANDBYS IN HUNGARY AND YUGOSLAVIA: SOME OBSERVATIONS UPON THE IMF'S EMERGING ROLE IN EASTERN EUROPE

By examining the IMF's 1990–1 standby arrangements in Hungary and Yugoslavia, it is possible to obtain an intriguing portent of future IMF/East European relations. These standby arrangements demonstrate both the tremendous potential for IMF contributions to East European economic restructuring, and the formidable obstacles which continue to impede reform.

In the autumn of 1989, the IMF entered into standby negotiations with Hungary with demands for harsh macroeconomic restrictions designed to force the pace of adjustment. Fund officials felt that previous standbys, by allowing Hungary to avoid stringent stabilisation and delay structural reform, had simply deferred Hungary's pressing economic difficulties rather than resolving them. The Hungarian negotiating team which confronted these stringent IMF demands was in many ways like that which had bargained with the Fund in the past. The same institutional actors were represented in the negotiations as always – the National Bank, the Finance Ministry, the Foreign Trade Ministry, the National Price Office. Furthermore, since free elections were not to take place until March of 1990, the government team was still composed entirely of officials appointed by the Communist regime. Yet beneath the surface stability, Hungary's political processes, development strategy, and state-society relations were changing dramatically – and these changes were affecting the conduct of standby negotiations with the IMF.

Perhaps most importantly, the Communist party had lost its monopoly over the political process, and was competing with a growing range of alternative political organisations. As a result, the party had become more responsive to popular policy preferences. In order to minimise its losses in the upcoming elections, the Communist (now renamed Socialist) party felt it had to devise an economic adjustment programme which would satisfy citizen desires for economic reform without imposing drastic costs upon the population. And the party's leaders now agreed that such an adjustment programme required the abandonment of gradualist reform and the initiation of a much more radical market-oriented approach.

These changes in the Communist party's goals and strategies had two major implications for standby negotiations with the Fund. On the one hand, the party's embrace of comprehensive market-oriented reform facilitated the negotiation process, since Hungary was now officially committed to carrying out the kinds of structural changes the IMF demanded. On the other hand, the party's growing sensitivity to citizen preferences heightened its resistance to the stringent macroeconomic stabilisation policies advocated by the Fund. Meanwhile, the party's fear of antagonising enterprise managers and workers, and of generating massive economic dislocations, meant that Hungarian negotiators would not promise to carry out structural reforms with the speed urged by the Fund.[15]

After months of difficult negotiations, the Hungarian team finally agreed to most IMF demands in December 1989. Yet unlike in the past, this agreement did not represent the end of the standby negotiation process. Because of recent changes in the Hungarian political process and the distribution of power within the state structure, many more actors had become involved in approving the IMF standby. In particular, the Hungarian Parliament assumed a more powerful role in the standby ratification process. Many deputies were suspicious of the stringent IMF standby accord and determined to vote against it. Only after threats of resignation by the Prime Minister and warnings from the government that failure to ratify the standby would bring total financial collapse did the Hungarian Parliament approve the IMF agreement (*Nepzava*, 15 December 1989). In future years, as Hungary's external situation becomes less desperate and as the Parliament grows more powerful and assertive, the process of finalising IMF standbys will become increasingly complex and conflict-ridden.

On 14 March 1990, Hungary drew its first tranche from the 200 million SDR standby and began to implement its commitments to cut wages by 2.5 per cent, slash the current account deficit from $1.5 billion to $550 million, reduce the budget deficit from 50 billion forints to under 10 billion forints, sharply reduce subsidies on public services and housing, devalue the forint, and shut down loss-making enterprises (*FBIS Daily Report*, 3 January and 27 February 1990). And in the first few months of the standby, the newly-elected Hungarian government carried out its obligations admirably, proclaiming a strategy of rapid transition to a market economy and overfulfilling most standby targets.

Nevertheless, it is too early to proclaim a new era of harmonious cooperation between the IMF and Hungary. In some respects, the new government remains more cautious about the transition to a market economy than the IMF. For instance, a substantial faction within the governing coalition wishes to control the pace of privatisation and foreign investment. Fears of foreign exploitation, along with concerns that former Communist party bosses would corner the market on buying state-owned firms, has led the Hungarian government to impose state controls on the pace of privatisation and the sale of assets to foreign investors. Such controls may constrain the reforms which the IMF feels critical to Hungary's transition to a market economy. Furthermore, the government has recently reneged on several standby targets for budgetary subsidies and deficits, and has announced that it will never impose the kind of brutal 'shock treatment' economic strategy sponsored by the IMF in Poland (*Magyar Hirlap*, 16 August 1990).

In fact, the newly-elected government of Hungary seems to share several concerns with its Communist predecessor, particularly the resistance to stringent short-term stabilisation measures and the reservations about a sweeping, immediate transition to the market. Of course, the contrasts are as striking as the similarities – the new regime does endorse a full (if gradual) transition to the market, and it has begun the difficult processes of enterprise liquidation and price and import liberalisation. In addition, the new government has transformed political processes and state-society relations in ways which will have a profound impact upon relations with the IMF. The introduction of new actors into the political process, and the forging of new links between state and society, will both complicate relations with the IMF and enhance prospects for reform-oriented collaboration. Although it is too early to make a definitive judgement, it seems likely that the expanded prospects for IMF involvement in economic reform will outweigh the growing complications of that involvement.

The future of IMF involvement in Yugoslavia's reform efforts is more uncertain, not least because of justifiable doubts about whether Yugoslavia will be able to retain its identity as a single sovereign state. Yugoslavia, like Hungary, has undergone considerable changes in its political processes and state/society relations in the past year. But in Yugoslavia, the effect of these changes has been to drive the country even further towards the decentralised extreme of the political systems continuum. Fissiparous tendencies between republics and within the Communist party have intensified to the point at which several republics have openly declared their sovereignty and the LCY has broken down into regional subparties. Needless to say, these fissiparous tendencies have exacerbated the pre-existing difficulties in negotiating and implementing IMF standbys. As in previous years, the Yugoslavs came to the negotiating table in the fall of 1989 with no clearly-defined programme for economic adjustment. Therefore, they ended up accepting the usual dose of IMF medicine, including commitments to achieve positive real interest rates, limit the money supply and public spending, freeze wages, and free prices (*Borba*, 19 September and 14 October 1989). Meanwhile, the Yugoslav Prime Minister prepared a radical agenda for the transition to capitalism which outstripped all other Eastern European programmes in scope and ambition. If implemented, this programme would fulfil all the IMF's longstanding demands, including import liberalisation, dinar convertibility, fullscale privatisation, the outlawing of government deficit financing through the state bank, and the transfer of control over credit allocation to a market-oriented financial system free from political manipulation.

Yet the prospects for fulfilling these commitments seemed dim in light of the political conditions prevailing in the Communist party and in the Federal Assembly, the two main institutional actors involved in overseeing IMF standbys. In 1990, the Federal Assembly and the LCY moved towards a complete breakdown in internal discipline and policy-making capacity. The Assembly was immobilised by debates over republican sovereignty, while the LCY broke into pieces after a deadlocked party congress which failed to resolve any of the questions concerning the party's role in a newly-defined Yugoslav federation.

Yugoslavia's growing political disarray may have permitted a few determined government officials to push through an unprecedented reform programme; but its accelerating political disintegration will make that reform programme all but impossible to implement. Structural reform can only succeed in Yugoslavia if it is preceded by a recentralisation of regulatory powers in the hands of the federal authorities. Otherwise, the reform programme will once again be derailed by pervasive low-level obstruction. Unfortunately, the present trend in Yugoslav politics is towards decentralisation and disintegration. For example, Slovenia has already in effect seceded from the Yugoslav federation and Croatia is currently (1992) locked in a guerilla war against federal government in general and Serbian political dominance in particular.

In sum, it seems clear that the events of the past year have reinforced pre-existing disintegrative tendencies in Yugoslavia's political structures and processes, thereby adding to the difficulties in implementing IMF standby programmes. Some have faulted the IMF for continuing to finance Yugoslavia's repeated and abortive efforts to carry out market-oriented adjustment. But having set Yugoslavia upon the course of decentralising economic reform as far back as 1952, perhaps the Fund feels an obligation to stand by its oldest and most troublesome Eastern European member.

CONCLUSION

In its relations with Eastern Europe prior to 1989, the IMF provided no solution to a central dilemma of reform in socialist countries: how to shift from planning mechanisms to market signals without causing severe economic disruptions. Since socialist countries themselves never resolved this dilemma after decades of experimentation, the Fund can hardly be faulted for failing to do so. It is to be hoped that the recent changes in both Fund practice and Eastern European politics will prove conducive to more successful reform-oriented collaboration than in the past. However, the revolutions of 1989 in Eastern Europe should not be the cause for misplaced optimism. Changes in leadership do not magically clear the way for an immediate transition from embedded socialist structures to market economies. In some ways, the most difficult phase in the transition from socialism lies ahead.

NOTES

1. Information based on interviews with IMF officials.
2. Development strategy was in some ways a product of the political process, since it reflected the composition and policy orientation of the ruling elite coalition. But development strategy was also shaped by state structures, which created the institutional framework within which development strategy operated and thereby set constraints upon its content.
3. Information obtained from interviews with IMF officials.

4. Information obtained from interviews with IMF officials and with Hungarian National Bank officials.
5. For more on elite fragmentation, political decentralisation, and the implications for policy-making, see Rusinow, 1977; Burg, 1983; Woodward, 1986.
6. Information obtained from interviews with Yugoslav National Bank officials and from 'Najnovija Istkustva i Perspective Regulisanja Odnosa SFRJ sa MMF i Svetskom Bankom' (Belgrade, 1987).
7. It would be an oversimplification to state that all lower-level economic actors opposed all IMF policies. In each country, there were variations in lower-level reactions to IMF policy demands, which generally reflected regional and sectoral patterns of enterprise profitability and creditworthiness. In all three countries, the sectors or regions with concentrations of loss-making and illiquid enterprises were also the focus of resistance to IMF policies.
8. But although lower-level bureaucrats and party officials had little capacity to challenge the centralised chain of command, they were wary of changes in the system and had, in fact, developed interests in its perpetuation. The top leadership was aware of the lower-level opposition to change, and its rejection of IMF proposals stemmed at least in part from its disinclination to disrupt the stability of the centralist system through forcing reforms upon an unwilling party and bureaucratic apparatus.
9. Although Yugoslavia did experience declines in demand during the standbys, these declines were not the result of a conscious government policy to meet standby targets through restricting credit and wages. Instead, real wage erosion was due mainly to uncontrollable inflation. See IMF, 1986.
10. Information based with interviews with IMF officials, as well as IMF survey, 6 March 1980 and 11 July 1981.
11. Information based on interviews with Finance Ministry and National Bank officials.
12. Information obtained through interviews with Yugoslav government officials.
13. For more on the following points, see transcript of remarks by Michel Camdessus, 19 April 1990.
14. For instance, price reform is futile unless it is introduced in conjunction with a series of other reforms to encourage economic actors to respond to price signals. Reforms opening the market to domestic and import competition are necessary to prevent former domestic supply monopolies from engaging in price gouging once prices are liberalised. Furthermore, enterprise managers and workers must be impelled to respond to price signals by forcing them to pay the full costs for failure in the form of bankruptcy, liquidation, and unemployment.
15. The bitterest conflicts emerged over IMF demands for stringent credit restrictions and current account deficit targets. The Fund claimed that strict limits were necessary to reduce demand and force insolvent enterprises out of business, while the Hungarians insisted that the IMF targets would push the Hungarian economy to the brink of import- and credit-starved collapse. (*FBIS Daily Reports*, 10 November 1989, 18 December 1989).

12 Adjusting Structural Adjustment: Getting Beyond the UNICEF Compromise

John Cameron

WHY NEED IS NOT AN ISSUE IN STRUCTURAL ADJUSTMENT THEORY

Structural adjustment policy is constructed on firm foundations in Western liberal philosophy, and neo-classical economic theory. 'Western liberal' for our purpose here, is defined as the philosophy of self-interested individualism, exemplified by Hayek; and 'neo-classical economics' is the school of economic thought that is based on the net-utility-maximising individual. From these perspectives inequality between individuals in potential and outcome is the natural condition of the human species. The underlying primary cause for this innate inequality may be either random genetic mutations or the mysterious ways of a divine creator – not irreconcilable if the divine creator works through what Western science has labelled random genetic mutations. From this perspective, since members of the species are observed to be different they are therefore doomed to be unequal except possibly in the eyes of God and in a structurally adjusted world under laws of voluntary contract.

In Western liberal philosophy, a society based on equal rights to voluntary individual contract is as equal as this imperfect human species can aspire. This is a view of society which is found to be consistent with efficiency, equity and stability in the theorems of neo-classical economics, though these theorems require the addition of assumptions to permit the use of mathematical logic to derive falsifiable predictions which sceptics find hard to accept. These assumptions are not so much defended in themselves by neo-classical economists, but claimed to be only evaluable in so far as they lead to falsifiable predictions about observable behaviour in an open market economy.[1]

The conclusions from such analyses are that societies are best organised for the social good on the basis of individual voluntary contract and open markets. The resulting resource allocation, including inequality in control over resources between individuals, households, and nations, will reflect the unequal abilities and efforts of individuals in contributing to meeting others' desires and the strength of own-preferences for possessing scarce goods and services. The resulting distribution may be said to be equitable in this limited sense, though advocates may extend this judgement to claims that such a distribution is fair and just, and the society has democracy, freedom, liberty and equality.

An immediate response from those who disagree with this view is that a society based on equality of contract must also have equality of opportunity if it is to be fair for individuals within each generation. Many liberals are willing to make concessions on this point and become advocates of equality in access to education, health and meritocratic recruitment procedures. Some may also show concern on the question of the right to inherit material wealth. But sterner liberals will argue that voluntary contract is the dominant principle and restrictions on giving inheritances offends against the right to voluntary contract of the giver. This offence against the primary equality in individual voluntary contract more than negates any gain in a secondary equality in opportunity.

Neo-classical economics also provides a technical supporting argument to the fundamental liberal philosophy position by throwing doubt on the interpretation of all proposed measures of inequality. In the neo-classical world, people choose to allocate their time and energy over numerous potential activities and over an indeterminate period of time. The activities include inactivity and elaborate social rituals, providing they are freely chosen. The period of time will be the individual's expected adult lifetime plus an indefinite period of concern for future generations. What do inequality measures based on a sub-set of activities measured at one point in time tell us about the measurement of inequality over all activities over a whole lifetime? The answer is not much, and what it does tell us is likely to overestimate rather than underestimate any inequality in terms of people's whole lives.

An appeal to claims of immediate poverty demanding common action fares similarly in the arguments of the philosophical liberal/ economics neo-classical alliance. The liberal/neo-classical view does not rule out individual altruistic, charitable actions. Providing information appealing for individual donations does not offend against voluntary contract, neither does appealing for individual donations to support gathering information to strengthen appeals for individual donations for any cause.

But neo-classical economics stresses the difficulty of objectively measuring needs and the impossibility of distinguishing needs from wants above a level of consumption needed for physiological survival (and even the requirements for physiological survival vary widely and indeterminately with circumstances and individuals (see Payne (1988)). Nutrition, water, clothing, shelter, fuel, curative health care, literacy and preventive health measures have all featured in attempts to define basic needs, social indicators, and poverty lines.

In practice, the supporters of the broad project of measuring poverty for policy action have failed to agree on measurable indicators for each factor individually, or how the factors should be weighted and traded-off to give an aggregate indicator. No intervention by neo-classical economists has really been required as these questions have failed to be resolved among the proponents of the principle of welfare intervention.

Thus advocates of structural adjustment policies can draw on well-defended positions in philosophy and economics to justify a lack of concern with inequality and poverty as generally conceptualised and measured by their opponents. They have no need to be drawn into discussions on inequality and poverty issues other than reiterating that voluntary contract in open markets is the best basis on which this very imperfect or fallen species can organise its affairs.

If such a system of resource allocation leaves some people with few resources that is because such people choose to engage in activities which are not socially very valuable. Within their paradigm poverty cannot be measured and if it could be measured it would have no policy relevance.

INEQUALITY AND POVERTY BACK ON THE POLICY AGENDA?

A feature of the late 1980s, as compared with the first half of the decade, was growing discussion of the inequality and poverty implications of structural adjustment in the corridors of, and at academic meetings sponsored by, the World Bank. The academic arguments in favour of structural adjustment have become more sophisticated as a consequence and have opened avenues for empirical appeals to introduce new elements into structural adjustment policy packages.[3] These theoretical arguments demonstrate mathematically that real wage rates for people producing items for local consumption will tend to fall in a market-led structural adjustment process. But assumptions are then added that most people possess non-labour productive assets and produce, or could produce, exportables and the earnings rates from these assets and activities should rise to offset decline in one particular type of earnings. Such assumptions weaken the connection between a falling real rate of earnings on a particular input and the total real income of any specific group of individuals and households.

But the conclusions from such analysis also open up the opportunity for empirical claims against the distributional impact of structural adjustment policy. Empirical identification of a group of people who possess no non-labour assets and have no opportunity to enter production of internationally tradeable items identifies a group of people damaged by structural adjustment. If such people are consumption poor, then advocates can claim they have suffered excessively through no fault of their own. A case that they are candidates for transitional assistance can then be made, though a logical or moral basis for public sector relief/assistance will not be found in liberal philosophy and neo-classical economics.

An apparent modification in the late 1980s of the structural adjustment position that voluntary contract in open markets gives everyone their just deserts, even if that is just a desert for many people, was not an outcome of a rash of non-liberal conscience or intellectual curiosity on the part of structural adjustment advocates. The distributional implications of structural adjustment had been placed on the agenda by the civil disturbances and political instability associated with attempts to implement structural adjustment policy packages.

Civil servants at risk of redundancy, and workers in import-substituting industries at risk of bankruptcy faced insecurity. They also experienced falls in real incomes under structural adjustment programmes even if they were fortunate enough to keep their jobs. The urban young were faced with frustration in obtaining formal sector, regular employment, even if they maintained consumption rights within relatively affluent households. It is these groups that were significant forces in raising the issue of the distributional implications of structural adjustment. These people were certainly rejecting a radical change in distribution against themselves; whether they were rejecting an increase in inequality and poverty for society as a whole is more debatable.

The pragmatic, direct policy response to such claims within the logical framework of structural adjustment was targeted, transitional assistance to people whose positions were under threat. On this argument, they should be encouraged to move into the activities which were more likely to become profitable as a result of structural adjustment. Redundancy payments and vocational training for export-oriented self- or small-scale employment began to figure in structural adjustment policy packages.[4]

The claims of civil servants, factory workers, and the urban young have strengthened, and sometimes forced, the hands of governments in negotiating structural adjustment packages which included an element of distributional concern. This gave other agencies with other constituencies an opportunity to try to widen this ill-defined concern with distributional impact to include people with little or no political influence.

NGOs and some UN agencies entered claims that groups such as landless households dependent upon agricultural labouring to produce non-exported crops, households dependent upon women's earnings, and households dependent upon casual labouring or petty trading were suffering, suffering due directly to structural adjustment policies. As well as drawing on political unrest, such advocates were able to appeal to the World Bank's own theoretical economics literature outlined above. This literature, while attempting to defend the distributional impact of structural adjustment, was not able to dismiss claims for transitional assistance on behalf of the propertyless unable to enter production of internationally tradeable goods.

But such claims still had to overcome the assertion that everyone could move into the production of internationally tradeable items. This assertion set a low ceiling to such claims. Also, the counter-claim had to be accepted that these groups had had very low consumption levels, including consumption of public services, before the implementation of any structural adjustment policies. To say that low levels of consumption during a structural adjustment period were due to structural adjustment and that these groups would have experienced a significant rise in consumption under any other policy framework is not a conclusion which can be asserted with any great confidence.

The literature on 'basic needs' in the late 1970s provided much evidence that the consumption poor were doing badly in the decades before the invention of structural adjustment. If the macroeconomic imbalances on international and government accounts were to be diminished in the 1980s (by everyone except the USA) then there is little evidence that most national governments, given more room for manoeuvre, would have taken the pressure off the poorest as the first priority. It is not without irony that those who opposed internationally-imposed structural adjustment in the 1980s had often produced in the 1970s the most damning evidence that national governments played a crucial role in reproducing poverty however defined.[5]

The problems for the claims being entered by the NGOs and some UN agencies in the 1980s were no different from the 1970s. There was still no agreement on how to define ends, and no more conviction in recommending 'political will' as a means, from the arguments being put forward at the height of basic needs advocacy in the late 1970s. But at that time the claims could be directed, with the support of the World Bank, at reluctant national planners with international bankers queuing up to lend money against government revenues, no matter how collected.

At the end of the 1980s, the claims had to be directed at international ODA agencies. As the effective opinion leader of those agencies, the World Bank had to be re-convinced after a decade of denial that something called poverty was policy operable and should be at the top of its agenda. The case may have been accepted that something must be done about politically disruptive distributional claims and a permissive basically neo-classical economics literature had come into existence; but that only tangentially and indirectly permitted inequality and poverty to creep back onto the international conceptual and policy agendas.

THE UNICEF APPROACH TO PUTTING POVERTY ON THE INTERNATIONAL POLICY AGENDA

The United Nations Children's Fund (UNICEF) is the agency which has done most to place poverty on the international policy agenda in the late 1980s. In the 1970s, it had been the International Labour Organisation (ILO) which had played a similar lead agency role with respect to the concepts of 'informal sector' and 'basic needs'. The current UNICEF approach also has adopted the slogan 'adjustment with a human face'.[6] Central to this position is an acceptance of market-led structural adjustment as an appropriate response to national macroeconomic imbalances. But a rider is added to this acceptance that some resources should be reallocated in order to target children for assistance.

The UNICEF case has to be based on its specific agency concern with children in order to achieve legitimation and limit the risk of USA funding withdrawal. Data on children's changing experience in terms of indicators of mortality, nutritional status, and school enrolment are available for most countries which have had to respond to tightening macroeconomic constraints. From these data, the conclusions were drawn that the 1980s saw either actual reversals in trends in these statistics with rising mortality, declining nutritional status, and falling school enrolments, or, at best, reductions in previous rates of improvement.[7]

In terms of attempting to establish causality and links to policy, the pattern of cuts in public sector spending is shown to have been disproportionately against services which directly impinged on children's nutritional, health and educational status. Recommendations followed that such services should be restored and expanded; but as structural adjustment is necessary this would require changes in national spending priorities, with reduction in armed forces expenditure a preferred option. Internationally, such reductions could release resources for greater 'social sector' official development assistance.

Thus the UNICEF case prioritises the claims of children and juxtaposes their claims, often implicitly, against the demands on resources of armed forces nationally and internationally. The argument for this prioritisation can be couched in terms of children's physiological fragility, including the risk of underdevelopment of mental capabilities, and the non-reversibility of damage done at an early age. This proposition, in turn, leads to an economic case in terms of loss of 'human capital'. This loss of human capital is a reduction in people's capacity to produce in the future as a consequence of failure to allocate sufficient resources in the present for children to fully develop. Future economic growth prospects will be damaged to the extent that children are irreparably damaged now.

Such a line of qualitative argument can be easily admitted in neo-classical economics. Indeed, academic writing supporting structural adjustment has itself put forward the case in principle for greater emphasis on 'human capital' in economies having to economise on importing machinery and other physical inputs as part of bringing the external account into balance. The complementary question of reducing expenditure on armed forces is left open in neo-classical economics. Technically such expenditure is a 'public good' as the effective defence of one person against external attack is the defence of all people residing in that location. Such joint consumption is a problem for neo-classical economics as it is not amenable to a market solution. The defence of liberty to voluntarily contract from external and internal attack is a vital principle but has no clear resource implications.

To support its advocacy, UNICEF has also been active on the operable policy question and has been active in specifying policies and proposing performance indicators. Resource requirements are to be kept down by policy measures amenable to tight targeting. Vaccinate children, resource a Mother and Child Health (MCH) programme, and provide more easily accessible, potable water in a locality, runs the argument, and the local children's chance of survival and healthy development will increase. Build, and as importantly equip and staff, a primary school in a particular locality and children in the locality will have an increased chance of acquiring literacy. Put a meals programme into the school and those children will have an increased chance of not being malnourished and have an incentive to attend the school.

Potential performance indicators include infant and child mortality rates, statistical distribution parameters of anthropometric measurements on children, school enrolment or attendance, and the average results of functional literacy tests or public examinations. Such performance indicators appraise degree of need or can be used in time-series to evaluate policy effectiveness.

Such indicators are not without technical measurement problems in terms of risks of measurement and sampling errors. Also, the links between movements in performance indicators and particular policy actions tend to be indirect and causalities have to be imputed. Nevertheless, UNICEF has developed a basis for monitoring performance of the policies it proposes and the indicators are open to further refinement. The development of these indicators does not solve the problems of measuring poverty but it has been a significant contribution to the general debate on poverty indicators, disaster preparedness and relief management.[8]

The UNICEF approach has been couched in terms broadly compatible with neo-classical economic theory and in principle can be operationalised. The approach has been well publicised and the phrase 'structural adjustment with a human face' has entered the language of development debates. The legitimacy and empirical basis of this advocacy by UNICEF as an agency with a specific concern and little funding of its own for projects and programmes is not disputed. The issue here is whether the UNICEF case is a useful rallying point for those who wish to develop a fundamental critique of structural adjustment as an approach to development after a decade of retreat.

The UNICEF approach provides neither a real critique of structural adjustment as a principle nor a solution to previous problems with conceptualising inequality and poverty. UNICEF can and does extend its claims to include pregnant women and mothers with young children. This is seen as remaining within its agency terms of reference on concern for children. Since such women are also the bread-winners for their children, then the argument can be extended to employment and income-generation for them. It may be just possible to justify a UNICEF concern directed towards men who are low income supporters of mothers and young children. But targeting becomes increasingly problematic and the proposed policy perform-ance indicators more and more indirect as attention moves out through these widening circles of concern.

Policy developments towards the aged, the non-child disabled, the single adult and childless couple assetless and powerless are under-standably left in abeyance by the UNICEF terms of reference. But more importantly, the fundamental human capital argument that integrates the UNICEF claims into the neo-classical economics case for structural adjustment is often irrelevant, and can be counter-productive, for advocacy on behalf of these people. UNICEF advo-cacy has been admirable for those who come within its terms of reference but offers no conceptual basis for extending the critique of structural adjustment to a wider group and deeper principles.

FROM SURGICAL MASK TO HUMAN FACE

The UNICEF approach identifies a specific vulnerable group, young children, who can make a particular type of claim admissible in principle within the framework of neo-classical economics, which constitutes an aspect of a much more formidable philosophical justifi-cation of market-led structural adjustment. The UNICEF approach is characterised here as 'surgical' in that it involves an incision into a wider body of vulnerability and deprivation to isolate a particular type of person for treatment. In defence of the UNICEF position, it is important to state that children as a type of person constitute a very pervasive group, and the proponents of the UNICEF approach do try and stretch coverage to their parents and identify functional types of household where children may be at especially high risk. But the basic limitations remain of having made a case on the terms of market-led structural adjustment. And even this compromised position can be attacked through arguments which Western liberal philosophy and neo-classical economics are willing to mobilise. Thus, if policy concerns are extended to assist parents, then does this not undermine responsibility of parents to care for 'their own' children?[9] And if they have already neglected this responsibility to the extent that their children are at risk of permanent damage, then how likely is it that any extra resources received by the parents will reach the children? These questions tend to push the UNICEF approach to deprivation back towards non-fungible, direct provision to targeted groups of children.

To broaden and deepen qualified criticism into a full critique demands a counter philosophy. In the political and ideological climate of the 1980s, Islam made a strong claim to be the major challenge to the philosophical basis of structural adjustment thinking. The increases in debt burden due to rises in interest rates which have levered open so many economies to structural adjustment cannot be legitimised in Islamic thought. And the individual and collective responsibility of Muslims to relieve poverty through '*zakat*' contributions challenges the view of the inevitable and undeserving poor in Western liberal thinking.[10] But while faith may move mountains, it is less likely to move the World Bank or the billions of non-Muslims.

Within the Western rationalist tradition of philosophy, alongside the liberal stream, there exists a search for the necessary and sufficient conditions for a social order where people act as conscious agents in a collectivity rather than self-interested individuals in markets. Hegel and Marx have been influential figures in this search. Marx himself would have no problem with a critique of structural adjustment. In his analysis, structural adjustment as a concept would constitute an ideological cloak for restructuring out of a profitability crisis in the interests of capital as a global phenomenon. The task would not be to debate ways of modifying the distributional impact of structural adjustment but to use the experience of structural adjustment to raise consciousness of the need to transcend capitalism.

In the 1970s, from a position more central to mainstream Western political philosophy, Rawls put forward a model of conditions for constructing a just social order which attracted much comment but little support.[11] The basic proposition required individuals to select a form of society in which they would choose to live, while accepting that they could not choose which specific positions they would occupy. Rawls then went on to claim that rational individuals would choose relatively egalitarian forms of society with substantial welfare systems. Such conclusions clearly stand in direct opposition to those underpinning market-led structural adjustment.

The artificiality of Rawls' assumptions could hardly be criticised from the perspective of the Popperian falsification theory of scientific knowledge which neo-classical economics uses to defend itself. But the attempt to deduce logically that a particular form of society would result from those assumptions fails. That deduction requires a further assumption that all the choosing individuals are risk averse and fear poverty more than they desire wealth. All Rawls' opponents have to do is to posit that all the individuals involved prefer risk and a totally different form of society would be selected. Rawls' basic model fails to predict a universal desired structure of inequality for all societies, but only sets up a relativistic model where very different desired structures of inequality can be deduced differentiated by 'cultural' attitudes to risk.[12]

A more promising line of philosophical argument in the search for a fundamental critique of structural adjustment which turns the focus towards 'power poverty' rather than 'consumption poverty' has found its source in Kant. Kant was a contemporary of Hegel who lived in the late eighteenth century in a period of momentous times for Europe. It may be no coincidence that his work is entering the development debate[13] at a time when the Hegelian line through Marx appears relatively weak and Europe is again in a process of momentous change. As Poland leads Eastern Europe into a period of formal structural adjustment, the development debate, even more than in the past, must include European experiences alongside those of Africa, Asia, Latin America and the islands of the Caribbean and the South Pacific.

Kant started from the proposition that individual human existence is not a means to some greater purpose but an end in itself. Acting towards people with a view to turning them into better human capital for greater economic prosperity offends against this initial proposition. The definition of development for a neo-Kantian therefore

becomes the extension of individuals' ability to set and pursue ends
freely chosen by themselves for themselves. The terms 'agent' and
'agency' are useful to capture the sense of this principle of conscious,
active beings.

Kant then seeks to identify conditions for a society in which this
definition of development could operate. He claims to identify a
categorical imperative on people who accept the basic proposition
and the definition of development, independent of their cultural
disposition. If they wish to constitute an indefinitely sustainable
society, then they must accept a categorical imperative to create a
social order in which nobody is coerced or deceived. A neo-Kantian
society is constructed to positively avoid undermining anybody's
agency through force or misinformation.

Individual voluntary contract in genuinely open markets may go a
considerable distance towards meeting this categorical imperative.
But what if that voluntary contracting leaves a number of people with
so few resources that their life projects or even their lives themselves
are at risk? If they have no forum to claim resources outside the
market to pursue any of their ends, then development as defined in
neo-Kantian terms suffers. Creating a forum for such claims to be
made becomes a central aspect of the development process; an aspect
which is marginalised, tokenised, ignored or actually repressed in
structural adjustment thinking. Equality of voice is the major component of political equality and poverty should be seen as a process,
not a state.

This basic right to an equal voice contests with the right to voluntarily contract for priority as a basis for social order. Such a right to
equal voice is not the right to appeal as a victim, but the right to
expression as an agent. Open market economics and 'Westminster/
US Constitutional' politics are not antithetical to this right, but are
very partial and limited expressions of the principle. The development challenge is to experiment with democracy, access, participation, accountability to discover what these words can mean in terms
of actually existing human societies now.

This challenge is not any easier or more certain in outcome than
the challenge of increasing growth rates of GNP to over 6 per cent
p.a.; reducing population growth rates below 2 per cent p.a.; raising
the real rate of return to capital to 5 per cent p.a.; or reducing the
proportion of the population below a stated poverty line by 5 per cent
p.a. The neo-Kantian approach does not claim to be easier: rather it
claims to offer a totally different principle of what constitutes devel-

opment and the priorities for achieving development to that principle underlying structural adjustment, and therefore offers the opportunity for a fundamental critique of structural adjustment and its underlying ideology.

Policies for people as ends and agents rather than means and victims/clients require concern with the means and processes of policy formulation and implementation and explicit evaluation of interactions and relationships. With neo-Kantian development, the policy process from identification to evaluation should become more transparent, less opaque, over time. Rights to information and public inquiry procedures become a development issue not a diversion, an optional extra or a nuisance. And beyond such basically defensive mechanisms lies an area of opportunity for investigating positive procedures for engagement of people as agents rather than customers or clients.

From the perspective of structural adjustment, the implicit economics of neo-Kantian development principles are simply unacceptable, as are the implicit politics of structural adjustment to the neo-Kantian. Both will claim that the other view's approach to economics and politics respectively cannot work.

However, both share doubts about bureaucratic allocation of resources and bureaucratic accountability. The structural adjustment approach seeks to marketise away the common problem with bureaucratic economics and politics; the neo-Kantian seeks to politicise it away. Which is the better approach to the critical questions of the 1990s, on conservation of a habitable physical environment, global addictive narcotic production and use, and personal safety, is a crucial issue. The structural adjustment approach to development, which marginalises such issues, is bound to be on the defensive looking towards the twenty-first century.

Many people in organisations concerned with development will suspect the neo-Kantian approach of being politically utopian as much as economically unrealistic. They would argue that day-to-day exercise of power is based on structures where power is concentrated and multi-valent, and any proposal to distribute power equally will meet uncompromising resistance in depth across the whole range of economic, cultural and coercive experience. If this analysis is accepted, which concludes that the agency of large groups of people is structurally denied and their claims undermined and repressed, then the neo-Kantian approach becomes a variant on the Hegel-Marx approach to society and consciousness, in which the process of asserting claims to agency by those to whom it is denied is justifiably assigned a major role.

What are the next steps if market-led structural adjustment is to be eventually displaced from its current position as the dominant development policy framework? A number of parallel activities need to be pursued to build on existing initiatives.

The concepts of democracy, participation, access and accountability need to be problematised and theorised as development keywords and rescued from formalistic use in a bureaucratic paradigm.[14]

The question of agency at a distance needs investigation; an obligation to improve the agency of a remote person is imperfect in the sense that effectiveness of the action is uncertain. This uncertainty is partially due to the expression of that obligation through the channel of some form of organised agency, whose anthropomorphic moral character cannot be assumed. As an example, the desire to stop someone starving to death (an extreme form of undermined agency!) can be seen as an expression of a neo-Kantian obligation, but the delivery of resources to meet that obligation passes through intervening organisations. What rules of organisational accountability are necessary to ensure the obligation results in the planned gain in agency? The words 'accountability' and 'conditionality' need to be investigated and debated in this context.

The numerous practical experiments on a world scale in democracy, participation, access and accountability need to be more widely communicated and distinctions between 'first, second, third and fourth worlds' and degrees of economic 'development' need to be questioned as merely convenient categories with little real significance. Development in a neo-Kantian sense is a question for everyone everywhere.[15]

Technically, there is work to be done in developing means of communication and indicators that allow patterns of whole lives to be understood sensitively at some level of aggregation and omit no sub-group of people. Networks with the ability to communicate patterns of other's lives to people remote from that experience are needed, and universal literacy in, and access to, the written and electronic media is an important objective. Facilitating unstructured cultural contact has a vital role to play. In addition, a more systematic, quasi-quantitative methodology will also be needed to assist policy identification and evaluation.[16]

The neo-Kantian development of universal individual creative agency as the principle of development will require policies which construct networks of conscious, knowledgeable contacts combining varying forms of promoting species-wide mutual responsibility and recognising mutual dependency.[17] If neo-Kantianism has a future, it will be because large numbers of us are willing to recognise the dependent aspect of our being, celebrate cultural differences, and are uncompromising on empowering the power-poor.

If we tear off these masks, if we open ourselves up, if – in brief – we face our own selves, then we can truly begin to live and to think. Nakedness and defencelessness are awaiting us. But there, in that 'open' solitude, transcendence is also waiting: the outstretched hands of other solitary beings. For the first time in our history, we are contemporaries (Paz, 1935, pp. 131–2).

NOTES

1. For a summary of the 'pure' neo-classical economics position see Cole, Cameron and Edwards (1983).
2. A valuable overview of the poverty/social indicators debate and its ultimate indeterminacy can be found in Hicks and Streeten (1979). The technical difficulties of agreeing even the most physiological of poverty lines are well exposed in Dandekar (1981) which summarises a decade of disagreement in India.
3. The World Bank (and IMF) sponsored analyses of the possible distributional impact of structural adjustment are cast in technical economics language inaccessible to non-economists. Warwick University in the UK has been very active in this field, spearheaded by Professor Kanbur. Warwick University hosted an important and inconclusive World Bank financed seminar in November 1987 on the distributional impact of structural adjustment. The OECD and the World Bank supported the 'state of the art' research reported in Bourguignon, Branson and de Melo (1989).
4. The World Bank (1989) report advocates a doubling of spending on education and training and stronger family planning efforts, while maintaining the basic line on government being the development problem which appeared in the World Bank 'Berg' Report in 1981. A maverick view that structural adjustment has not really been implemented due to governments being unable to meet the imposed conditionality requirements can be found in the writings of Professor Mosley of Manchester University (see for instance Mosley, 1987). Such a view clearly causes problems for advocates and opponents of structural adjustment, advocates because they appear incompetent, opponents because they have less to complain about. Mosley himself comes down on the side of more effective structural adjustment.

5. The 'basic needs' approach to development dominated debates between 1975 and 1981 (the year in which the World Bank's World Report focused on basic needs, an apogee rapidly followed by a nadir). Among those who argued that the essential radical message of basic needs, i.e. the question of what processes politically reproduced poverty, had been lost in the reduction of the basic needs challenge to an unanswerable bureaucratic Gap-Target-Delivery question were Blaikie, Cameron and Seddon (1979). This article may be seen as a continuation of that argument, though hopefully in terms more likely to be widely accepted.
6. The UNICEF position appeared in Cornia, Jolly and Stewart (1987) and has received annual expression in *The State of the World's Children* reports. By way of contrast, and warning, the ILO has been very muted following funding withdrawal threats by the incoming USA administration in the early 1980s over the ILO's continuing advocacy of 'leftist' basic needs: see ILO/ARTEP (1987) for evidence of this retreat.
7. Pinstrup-Andersen (1988) mobilises such evidence.
8. The problems of using anthropometry has a literature of its own. Putting to one side problems of actually collecting data, such as (i) which combination of measurements to use out of height, weight, upper arm circumference, skin-folds, age, (ii) taking accurate physical measurements on resisting children of indeterminate age, and (iii) obtaining representative samples in a medically oriented setting, there are controversies around each step in (i) comparing with international or local or time series standards, (ii) interpreting these comparisons as statements about nutritional status and loss of functionality, (iii) relating nutritional status to ultimate causes, and (iv) recommending specific policy action.
   A possible scenario which highlights the argument that a structural adjustment advocate might bring to bear could be as follows:

> The distribution of measurements made on this group of children cannot be compared with international standards as they have a different genetic potential and/or are physiologically adapted to low food intake without loss of function either permanently or seasonally (i.e. they are small but healthy). Even if that is not the case, we do not know if they are small due to low household food availability, low intake of particular or all nutrients specifically by children in the household, or poor food intake utilisation. Therefore we do not know whether policy should concentrate on increasing food production and/or storage, reducing food prices and improving marketing, parental or mothers' education, child feeding programmes, drinking water provision, preventative health services, or curative health services.

Behrman, Deolalikar and Wolfe (1988) is a thoughtful paper written for the World Bank which demonstrates the difficulties of deriving policy conclusions from nutrition data. Professor Payne of the London School of Hygiene and Tropical Medicine is a master of bringing out such problems: for his view of the fundamental conceptual problems see Payne and Cutler (1984) and for a thorough overview of measurement interpretation problems see Payne (1988).

9. The relationship between the atomistic individual in liberal philosophy and neo-classical economics and any collective concept is problematic. It may be useful to see forms of collectives as being more or less permissible as far as the liberal/neo-classical position is concerned. The forms 'family' and 'nation' seem to be permissible as 'natural' collectives, while 'gender' and 'class' are not. Millar and Glendinning (1989) provide insights into the limitations of such a view of 'family' as atomistic unit for understanding women's experience of poverty.

10. Hussain (1987) summarises an Islamic viewpoint of development principles as follows:

> The Islamic system is neither socialist or capitalist, but has its own identity and its own values involving full commitment to human brotherhood (*Mowakhat*) with social and economic justice, to equitable distribution of income, and to individual freedom within the context of social welfare. (p. 7).
>
> Distributive justice in Islamic society after guaranteeing a humane standard of living to all members through the institution of '*Zakat*', allows such differentials as are in keeping with . . . the social value of the services (p. 31).

Ch. Muhammed Hussain is an official in the Pakistan Planning Commission.

11. Rawls (1971) was criticised by a leading member of the 'Straussian' school of philosophy at the University of Chicago in the following terms: 'Rawls' society is a desert. It feeds on false tales – . . . stories that make unequal things appear to be equal' (Bloom, 1975). Not all reviews have been as trenchant but many have been negative.

12. O'Neill (1988/89) dissects Rawls' argument in this way with more destructive impact than Bloom's (1975) bombast.

13. O'Neill (1987) comes from Kantian philosophy towards development; coming from the development side, Professor Amartya Sen has been writing authoritatively on economics and ethics and Riddell (1987) and Toye (1987) attempt to bring morals and ethics into the development debate but perhaps reveal more about the amount of serious thinking to be done rather than advance the argument significantly. Doyal and Gough (1984) clearly did some serious thinking and this article could be a widely accessible starting point for discussion on the principles of an alternative to liberal thinking on social policy.

14. Switching the focus from the 'consumption poor' to the 'power poor' brings into view a mass of literature stretching well beyond what has conventionally been called 'development studies'. Within the fringe of the development literature lies the work of Bernard Schaffer and Raymond Apthorpe to which Cameron (1985) can only claim to be a poor relation. Field (1977) is a provocative analysis of nutrition planning as a muddled outcome of academic and bureaucratic priorities of which Bernard Schaffer may well have approved. On a more abstract plane, the Frankfurt School (see Connerton (ed.), 1976) may have relevance provided they can find an interpreter for the 1990s as influential as Marcuse

in the 1960s. The works of Gramsci and Foucault have much to offer to pursuers of the nature of power and how to change its distribution, the first to the more optimistic and the second to the more pessimistic searcher.

15. *Development Dialogue* (1989) offers an example of writing concerned with power poverty; a concern that journal and the bulletins of the International Foundation for Development Alternatives (Nyon, Switzerland) have consistently advocated internationally throughout the 1980s. Also UNICEF (1989) is written in uncompromising language and proposes the 'seven deadly sins' of development as development without concern for communication, participation, women, the environment, the poor, replicability and mobilisation. No doubt they will be hearing from their sponsors. UNESCO, which has already heard, is active in exposing the growth of illiteracy in the time of structural adjustment. A neo-Kantian view would see literacy as significantly reducing the possibility of deception.

16. Literacy is stressed by UNICEF as an indicator alongside infant mortality and infant/child nutritional status indicators. More work on functional literacy indicators would be useful to escape performance indicators based on school place provision and/or school enrolment. If indicators based on market valuations or public sector outputs are to be superseded, then time budget analysis is a promising alternative. Ayalew (1985) offers a micro-level example of the use of time budgets. At the macro level, Dudley Seers' (1977) advocacy of Active Life Profiles has yet to bear full fruit. Cameron (1983) applies the approach to compare lives of women and men in Fiji, Hong Kong and Malaysia.

17. The challenge is the making of a third philosophically rigorous position beyond the fiercely independent individual of neo-Nietzschean liberalism and the dependent supine victim of bureaucratic welfare paternalism as a model of the species. Professor O'Neill of Essex University has raised the question for this writer of what would be the nature of a society which stressed the reality of human dependence, so clear in infancy, as much, or even more than the reality of our capacity for individual action. The answer, though not necessarily encouraging for a neo-Kantian, may be Japan where 'the *"amae"* mentality could be defined as the attempt to deny the fact of separation that is an inseparable part of human existence and to obliterate the pain of separation' (Doi, 1977, p. 75).

13 Good Governance: Democracy and Conditional Economic Aid

Joan M. Nelson

The 1980s were a decade of intensive experimentation with the use of policy-based lending to promote economic reforms. In the early 1990s many are calling for the use of aid to promote political reforms as well. In the United States there are calls for 'political conditionality' from both the Congress and the Executive Branch. Since mid-1989, high-level officials in the United Kingdom, France, Germany, Holland, and most recently Japan have announced that their aid programmes will give more weight to recipients' observance of human rights and democracy. The World Bank is actively debating ways to improve 'governance' in client nations.

Not long ago the idea that donors should require political reforms as conditions for economic assistance was widely regarded as outrageously interventionist, impractical, and probably unethical. A number of events and intellectual trends have converged to make the idea of political conditionality not merely acceptable, but popular in donor circles.

The most obvious events contributing to this changed outlook are the accelerating spread of democratic openings throughout the poorer nations of the world during the 1980s, and the collapse of the Cold War at the end of the decade. Relieved of Cold War concerns, the industrialised democracies are now much freer to reflect their democratic values in their foreign policies, including foreign aid. The tide of democratic openings in Latin America, Asia, Eastern Europe, and increasingly in sub-Saharan Africa has also greatly reduced concerns that pressing democratic values on other nations might be ethnocentric, that Western-style democracy might be inappropriate or premature for some societies.

Prevailing ideas about the links between democracy and economic

309

growth have also changed. In the 1970s and 1980s, the view was widely held that authoritarian governments were more capable than democracies of taking difficult economic management decisions and promoting growth more generally. Even before the collapse of Communist regimes in Eastern Europe at the end of the 1980s, that view was increasingly discredited. By the late 1980s, there was a growing consensus on two points: overextended, inefficient, and often corrupt governments were perhaps the key obstacle to economic growth in many developing nations. But good government (rather than minimal government) is crucial to development. The best way to ensure better government, many concluded, is to broaden participation and accountability. Democratic political reform is therefore increasingly viewed – above all in Eastern Europe and in Africa but also in Latin America – as not only compatible with but imperative for economic growth.

Pressure for political conditionality is also spurred by the widespread impression that conditions attached to aid, especially by the IMF and the World Bank, were potent instruments for economic reform in the 1980s. As many of the studies in this volume indicate, the real effects of policy-based lending are difficult to assess, and may be more modest than many assume. But the perception that policy-based lending powerfully affected economic reform leads naturally to the thought that conditions should be extended to other goals, including not only democratic reforms but also recipients' efforts to protect the environment, reduce military expenditures, and help the poor.

The push for political conditionality raises many questions. Some of the fundamental premises need closer examination. The links between good government and economic growth are plain, if good government is understood to mean clear laws predictably enforced, reliable information widely available, adequate infrastructure and basic services, and no more than moderate corruption. But there is considerable doubt about the relation between pluralist politics and good government. Many democracies (as well as many authoritarian governments) are inefficient, overextended, and corrupt. And empirical studies of links between democracy and economic growth or economic equality in developing nations have been inconclusive and inconsistent.[1] Industrial democracies may wish to encourage democratic political systems because they value liberty, but they should not do so on the assumption that they are simultaneously and directly supporting economic growth.

Behind this broad point are further questions about the specific kinds of reforms donors seek to encourage. Some advocates of political conditionality emphasise fuller observance of basic human rights. Some stress improved governance, including strengthened legal institutions. Others focus on broadened participation, often including decentralisation. Still others call for establishing or strengthening democratic institutions, including multi-party elections. The various goals overlap, but they suggest quite different priorities for policy reform. Moreover, in specific country settings there are likely to be conflicts as well as complementarities among the diverse items on the political reform agenda.

Not only the priorities and links among goals, but also the choice of means and instruments needs closer examination. Conditionality is only one category of means for promoting desired reforms. Donors have at their disposal a wide array of other techniques and approaches, working through governments and non-governmental organisations, with project and technical assistance, information and networking, persuasion and dialogue. All of these techniques are already being used by bilateral and multilateral agencies to support and encourage better governance and democratic reforms in many countries. The most effective and feasible uses for conditionality, as part of this broader array of techniques, remain to be determined.

One approach to thinking about the potential and the limits of conditionality for promoting political reform is to look for transferable lessons from experience with economic conditionality. Bilateral lenders, but above all the IMF and the World Bank, have accumulated a great deal of experience with using conditions to encourage economic policy reforms. The World Bank, in particular, has analysed its own experience and drawn some conclusions that have clear implications for political conditionality.

The World Bank started policy-based lending in 1980, and by the latter half of the decade roughly a third of its loans were conditioned on economic reforms. Some sixty-one countries had received such loans; many had received multiple loans. If influence is gauged by compliance with conditions, the record suggests substantial but uneven impact. Surveying the record at the end of the 1980s, the Bank concluded that two-thirds of all loan conditions were fully implemented within the period of the loan; 84 per cent were substantially fulfilled. Some kinds of conditions prompted considerably better compliance than others. Exchange rate conditions were fully implemented in three-quarters of all cases where they applied; fiscal policy requirements and financial sector reforms were almost as often observed. Conditions regarding public enterprise and trade policy reforms did less well: 66 and 62 per cent respectively. Social policy conditions were fully observed in 59 per cent of the cases, and wage policy requirements were met within the period of the loan in 45 per cent of the relevant cases.[2]

Why were some kinds of conditions better observed than others? Did governments backtrack or fudge mainly on the most politically difficult measures? Comparatively low compliance on wage policies certainly suggests that link. But some politically difficult categories, such as reduced tariffs or quantitative restrictions on imports, were quite well observed. The Bank's own analysis in 1988 concluded that the degree of institutional change or innovation entailed is more important than political risk as an explanation of low compliance. For instance, in contrast to the good compliance record regarding reduced trade barriers, governments were much more likely to fail to implement requirements for improved export financing. These requirements are often politically popular, but they involve complex institutional changes. In their second assessment of structural adjustment lending, Bank analysts noted also that compliance with conditions was considerably lower in countries struggling with high inflation than in those with less unstable economic circumstances.[3]

More generally, both International Monetary Fund and World Bank experience suggest that compliance is best where the required actions can be authoritatively decided and implemented by a small number of central government officials. The classic examples are the actions typically incorporated in agreements with the IMF: changes in interest rates, foreign exchange rates, and credit ceilings, which can be mandated by the Minister of Finance and the Governor of the Central Bank. Compliance becomes less likely to the degree that the measures entail decisions by a larger number of actors (in the Executive Branch and sometimes the legislature), and where implementation requires cooperation (and especially subsidiary or complementary decisions) on the part of many different agencies or groups. Reforms involving substantial changes in institutional structure and procedures are hardest of all.

Conditionality is less effective with the latter kinds of reforms not only because it is more complex to administer, but also because the inducement offered by the conditional aid is usually irrelevant to at least some of the key groups needed to implement the reform. The

Minister of Finance and the Governor of the Central Bank bear direct responsibility for a gaping fiscal deficit or accelerating inflation. A sizable non-project loan or grant directly eases their burden, and provides a major inducement for them to undertake reforms directly in their control. In contrast, consider a structural adjustment loan requiring a fundamental overhaul of a major state economic enterprise. The reform requires co-operation from both management and workers, but neither will receive any direct gain from the loan; on the contrary, their security and status are severely threatened.

Lessons regarding the kinds of economic reform that are most effectively promoted by conditional aid are directly relevant to potential political conditionality, because the same underlying logic applies. Take the broad goal of promoting fuller participation. Some steps toward the goal can probably be hastened by conditions; others cannot. An aid donor might well insist that a government remove legal and procedural obstacles to reasonable freedom of speech and association: for example, that it revoke or revise laws banning labour unions, forbidding strikes, or tightly restricting media criticism of political leaders or government policies. Such measures are often within the discretion of a small circle of high political authorities, and their removal does not require elaborate implementation. Moreover, the criteria for gauging compliance are fairly clear-cut. In contrast, it is difficult to use conditionality to encourage a more responsible and effective press or unions; support and persuasion are more appropriate approaches. Similarly, a condition requiring installation of channels for central government consultation with local citizens' committees on local projects is not likely to be effective. Implementing such a condition requires extensive institutional innovation, sensitivity and commitment on the part of central and local officials, and cooperation from local citizens. Such requirements cannot be created by a central decree, nor are they easy for outsiders to monitor objectively.

The relevance of IMF and World Bank experience with conditionality extends beyond the choice of kinds of reforms most likely to be amenable to conditions. Their experience also sheds light on the whole process of providing conditional aid over a period of many years in order to promote a series of interlinked changes. For the Bretton Woods agencies, specific conditions are means to the broader goals of altering patterns of government behaviour and promoting economic stabilisation and growth. Simple compliance with conditions is a very partial gauge of these broader objectives. Indeed, compliance is only loosely linked to actual influence over reforms and to outcomes of reforms.

It may seem paradoxical to state that compliance has little relationship to actual influence. Yet clearly one expects the fullest compliance from governments already largely committed to reforms. In such cases, however, the government would probably have pursued similar reforms without the conditions – although external financial support may well accelerate or broaden reform decisions and facilitate implementation. High compliance, in short, does not necessarily imply strong influence. Conversely, poor compliance does not necessarily imply lack of influence. Even failed conditions may push some officials and groups to seriously consider options that had not been on the policy agenda previously. Those options are likely to resurface later, if the same economic difficulties persist.

The links between compliance with conditions and the desired outcomes also tend to be loose. For instance, a more realistic foreign exchange rate should encourage exports, but many other factors will affect the speed and scope of producers' responses. Some conditions appear to lead almost automatically to their proximate goals: lowering subsidies seems virtually certain to reduce the government deficit. Even in this case, however, the expected outcome can be defeated either by the absence of complementary policies (such as failure to contain pressures for other expenditure increases) or by exogenous factors (like bad weather or falling international prices that shrink revenues from taxes on key agricultural exports). Many specific reforms will have little effect – or possibly perverse effects – unless they are part of a broader package of measures, not all of which can be specified by aid conditions.

Parallel problems confront the use of conditions to promote political reforms. The risks of sham compliance with requirements for, say, multi-party systems are obvious. Conditions requiring specific political reforms may have little, or even negative effects on outcomes, if they are not buttressed by appropriate supporting measures, or if they prompt unexpected and adverse reactions. Decentralisation, for example, might turn out to empower local notables far more than ordinary citizens.

In short, the complex and evolving processes of restructuring economies and political systems cannot be directed by outsiders. Outsiders' pressure can often make a difference, but there is no substitute for genuine conviction by the government and/or coherent demands from domestic groups. By the late 1980s, World Bank documents were stressing the need for 'government ownership' of economic reform programs, and the principle was well-recognised (though not necessarily consistently observed) in international development circles more generally.

Indeed, where governments are not committed to reforms but badly need external finance, and where donors feel under some obligation to provide funds, the process of conditionality can degenerate into a charade. Without ownership, extensive use of conditions is likely to produce elaborate games of superficial or partial compliance, failure to adopt key supplementary measures to make the reforms effective, or a trail of reform efforts launched and abandoned. These games are worse than frustrating. They destroy the credibility of the reform process within the country concerned, and they obstruct dialogue and persuasion between the government and external donors or creditors.

A more positive note regarding the process of conditionality may partly counterbalance the risks sketched above. The judicious use of conditions can contribute to the broader process of altering perceptions and attitudes and building commitment to reforms within initially resistant governments. Requiring specific conditions can focus serious top-level attention on measures that have previously been beyond the limits of political debate within the country.

The 1980s saw a major shift in the parameters of debate regarding economic policy in much of the developing world. The risks of loose fiscal and monetary management, the costs of severely overvalued and rigid exchange rates, and the inefficiencies and distortions of detailed government price regulation are far more widely recognised than was the case in 1980. The costs of high protection and inefficient import-substitution, and the need to integrate more fully into the international economy are generally accepted in Latin America and are under serious consideration in Africa, although the speed and thoroughness of opening the economy are bitterly debated.[4] This partial convergence of assumptions and prescriptions in the realm of economic policy is a result of many forces too complex to be considered here. The relevant point is that in many countries the imposition of conditions undoubtedly furthered the process of rethinking old assumptions, even though the conditions themselves were resented and may have been implemented only partially or not at all.

In the 1990s, a similar reassessment is underway in much of the world regarding the role of governments and their relations to their citizens. As with the economic reassessments of the 1980s, some kinds and degrees of conditionality, directed to political rather than economic reforms, may well contribute to the rethinking process in some countries. But that contribution will be modest at best, and must be weighed against possible costs and risks.

In sum, the extensive World Bank and IMF experience with using conditions to promote economic reforms makes clear that the links between conditions and effective reform are much less simple, direct, and powerful than many observers assume. Conditionality is no quick fix, no short cut to altering the webs of policies and institutions that block both economic recovery and political liberalisation in many nations. The use of conditions to promote reform is instead part of an extended process of persuasion, pressure, and support. It is a subtle and complex process, with risks to both recipients and donors. For all its limitations, it has been valuable in the economic realm. The challenge is to learn from that experience in order to design effective and appropriate uses in the political realm.

NOTES

1. For a recent survey, see Sirowy and Inkeles, 1990, pp. 126–57; also Huntington, 1989, pp. 11–28.
2. World Bank, 1990b, Table 4.3, p. 44 and text pp. 41–3. The data are based on an analysis of ninety-seven SALs and SECALs in thirty-two countries. The figures given are those for implementation of conditions appearing in the loan agreement itself. Most loans also involve additional 'expected actions' which are not part of the legal loan agreement; observance of these actions was somewhat lower than fulfillment of legal conditions.
3. Ibid., Table 4.4, p. 45; and World Bank 1988d, pp. 61–2.
4. On Latin America, see Williamson, and Iglesias, both in John Williamson (ed.), *Latin American Adjustment: How Much Has Happened?* (Washington, D.C.: Institute for International Economics, 1990). For the evolving debate over appropriate policies in Africa, see Organization of African Unity, 1986; the annual reports of the Economic Commission for Africa, and World Bank, 1989d.

Bibliography

Addison, T. and L. Demery (1987) 'Alleviating poverty under structural adjustment', *Finance and Development*, 24, December.

Adeniyi, E.O. et al. (1990) 'Structural adjustment policies in Nigeria: a preliminary overview', mimeo (Florence: UNICEF).

Administrative Committee on Coordination (ACC/SCN) (1989) *Update on the Nutrition Situation: Recent Trends in 33 Countries* (New York: UN).

AID (1989) *US Assistance for Africa: The Development Fund for Africa – An Action Plan* (Washington, DC: AID).

Aghazadeh, P. and D. Evans (1988) 'Price distortions, efficiency and growth', unpublished paper (IDS, University of Sussex).

Albanez, T., E. Bustelo, G.A. Cornia and E. Jesperson (1989) 'Economic decline and child survival: the plight of Latin America in the Eighties', *Innocenti Occasional Papers* 1 (Florence: UNICEF).

Alderman, H. (1990) 'Nutritional status in Ghana and its determinants', Social Dimensions of Adjustment in Sub-Saharan Africa, Working Paper 3 (Washington, DC: World Bank).

Arrau, P. (1989) *Human Capital and Endogenous Growth in a Large Scale Life-Cycle Model*, World Bank PPR Working Paper No. 342.

Asian Development Bank (1990) *Asian Development Outlook* 1990 (Manila: ADB).

Ayako, A. (1990) 'Structural adjustment in the 1980s: Kenya case study', mimeo (Florence: UNICEF).

Ayalew, S. (1985) 'Time budget analysis as a tool for PHC planning (with examples from Ethiopia)', *Social Science of Medicine*, 21.

Balassa, B. (1976) 'Reforming the System of Incentives in Developing Countries', *World Development* 3, 6.

Balassa, B. (1985) 'Exports, Policy Choices, and Economic Growth in Developing Countries After the 1973 Oil Shock', *Journal of Development Economics*, 18.

Baldwin, David (1985) *Economic Statecraft* (Princeton, NJ: Princeton University Press).

Bandow, Douglas (1989) 'What's still wrong with the World Bank', *Orbis*, Winter.

Bates, Robert (1981) *Markets and States in Tropical Africa* (Berkeley: University of California Press).

Bates, Robert (1986) *Government Policies Towards Agriculture in Africa: The Prospects for Reform*, Duke University Program in International Political Economy, Working Paper No. 4.

Bauer, T. (1985) 'Reform policy and the complexity of economic policy', *Acta Oeconomica*, no. 3–4.

Becker, G.S. (1975) *Human Capital*, 2nd edition (New York: NBER).

Becker, G., K. Murphy and R. Tamura (1990) 'Economic Growth, Human Capital and Population Growth', *Journal of Political Economy*.

Behrman, J.R., A.B. Deolalikar and B.L. Wolfe (1986) 'Nutrients: impacts and determinants', *World Bank Economic Review*, 2.

Behrman, J.R. and A.B. Deolikar (1988a) 'Health and nutrition' in H. Chenery and T. Srinivasan (eds) *Handbook of Development Economics* (Amsterdam: North Holland).

Behrman, J.R. and A.B. Deolikar (1988b) 'How do food prices affect individual health and nutritional status? A latent variable fixed effects analysis', mimeo (Philadelphia: University of Philadelphia).

Belgrade, Centre for Strategic Studies (1987) 'Najnovija Iskustva i Perspektive Regulisanja Odnosa SFRJ sa MMF i Svetskom Bankom'.

Berg, E. and A. Batchelder (1985) 'Structural Adjustment Lending: A Critical View' (Washington, DC: World Bank).

Berstecher, D. and R. Carr-Hill (1990) *Primary Education and Economic Recession in the Developing World since 1980* (Paris: UNESCO).

Bienen, Henry and Mark Gersovitz (1985) 'Economic Stabilisation, Conditionality and Political Stability', *International Organization*, 39, 4.

Blaikie, P.M., J. Cameron and J.D. Seddon (1979) *The Struggle for Basic Needs in Nepal* (Paris: OECD Development Centre).

Blejer, M.I. and I. Guerrero (1990) 'The impact of macroeconomic policies on income distribution: An empirical study of the Philippines', *The Review of Economics and Statistics* LXXII, 3.

Bloom, A. (1975) 'J. Rawls vs. the tradition of political philosophy', *American Political Science Review*, 69.

Boateng, E.O., K. Ewusi, R. Kanbur and A. McKay (1990) 'A poverty profile for Ghana', Social Dimensions of Adjustment in Sub-Saharan Africa, Working Paper 5 (Washington, DC: World Bank).

Bogoev, K. (1986) 'Platnobilansne Prilagodjavanje Jugoslavije' in *Yugoslavija U Medjunarodnim Finansijama* ed. B. Babic (Belgrade: Institut za Medjunarodnu Politiku i Privredu).

Boomgard, James (1989) *AID Microenterprise Stocktaking: Synthesis Report* (Washington, DC: AID).

Bourguignon, F., W. Branson, J. de Melo (1989a) 'Macroeconomic adjustment and income distribution: a macro-micro simulation model', Technical Paper No. 1 (Paris: OECD Development Centre).

Bourguignon, F., W. Branson, J. de Melo (1989b) 'Adjustment and income distribution: a counterfactual analysis', Working Paper no. 2943 (Cambridge, Mass.: NBER).

Bourguignon, F., C. Morrisson, and A. Suwa (1990) 'Structural adjustment packages: a CGE-counterfactual analysis applied to Morocco', mimeo, March. Reprinted in abridged form in Chapter 8 of Mosley, Harrigan and Toye (1991).

Bovard, James (1986) *The Continuing Failure of Foreign Aid* (Washington, DC: Cato Institute).

Brown, Robert (1984) 'Conditionality: A New Form of Colonialism' *Africa Report*, September.

Brown, Richard (1990) 'Sudan's debt crisis: the interplay between international and domestic responses, 1978–88', PhD thesis, Institute of Social Studies, The Hague.

Bruno, M. and S. Piterman (1988) 'Israel's Stabilisation: A Two-Years'

Review' in M. Bruno et al. (eds) *Inflation Stabilisation* (Cambridge, Mass.: MIT Press).

Burg, S. (1983) *Conflict and Cohesion in Socialist Yugoslavia* (Princeton, NJ: Princeton University Press).

Burg, S. (1986) 'Elite conflict in Post-Tito Yugoslavia', *Soviet Studies*, April.

Callaghy, Thomas (1988) 'The State and the Development of Capitalism in Africa', in D. Rothchild and N. Chazan (eds), *The Precarious Balance* (Boulder, Colorado: Westview Press).

Callaghy, Thomas (1990) 'Lost between state and market', in J. Nelson (ed.) *Economic Crisis and Policy Choice: The Politics of Adjustment in the Third World* (Princeton, NJ: Princeton University Press).

Calvo, G. (1989) 'Incredible Reforms' in G. Calvo et al. (eds) *Debt, Stabilisation and Development* (Oxford and Cambridge, Mass.: Basil Blackwell).

Calvo, G. and F. Coricelli (1990) 'Stagflationary Effects of Stabilisation Programs in Reforming Socialist Economies', PRE Working Paper (Washington, DC: World Bank).

Cameron, J. (1983) 'Active Life Profile Analysis: a comparison of lives in Fiji, Hong Kong and Malaysia' (Paris: OECD Development Centre).

Cameron, J. (1985) 'Destitute allowance vs. family assistance: conflict over welfare labels in Fiji', *Development and Change*, 16.

Cass, D. (1965) 'Optimum growth in an aggregative model of capital accumulation', *Review of Economic Studies*, no. 32, July.

Castanedo, T. (1989) *Innovative Social Policies for Reducing Poverty: Chile in the 1980s*, mimeo (Washington, DC: World Bank).

Castles, F. (1982) 'The Impact of Parties on Public Expenditure', in F. Castles (ed.) *The Impact of Parties: Politics and Policies in Democratic Capitalist States* (Beverly Hills, Calif.: Sage).

Chenery, H. and A. Strout (1966) 'Foreign Assistance and Economic Development', *American Economic Review*, 56, 4.

Chirot, D. (1980) 'The Corporatist Model and Socialism: Notes on Romanian Development', *Theory and Society*, 2.

Choksi, A. and D. Papageorgiu (eds) (1986) *Economic Liberalisation in Developing Countries* (Oxford: Blackwell).

Clarke, J. (1988) *Debt and Poverty: A Case Study of Zambia* (Oxford: OXFAM).

Cole, J. (1981) 'Rural workers in contemporary Romania', in D. Nelson (ed.) *Romania in the 1980s* (Boulder, Colorado: Westview Press).

Cole, K., J. Cameron and C.B. Edwards (1983) *Why Economists Disagree* (London: Longman).

Comisso, E. (1979) *Workers Control Under Plan and Market: Implications of Yugoslav Self-Management* (New Haven, Conn.: Yale University Press).

Comisso, E. (1986) 'State Structures, Political Processes and Collecting Choice in CMEA States', *International Organization*, Spring.

Commonwealth Secretariat (1989) *Engendering Adjustment for the 1990s* (London: Commonwealth Secretariat).

Connerton, P. (ed.) (1976) *Critical Sociology* (Harmondsworth: Penguin).

Corbo, V. and J. de Melo (1987) 'Lessons from the Southern Cone Policy

Reforms', *World Bank Research Observer* 2, 2.

Corbo, V. and M. Goldstein and M.S. Khan (1987) *Growth-oriented adjustment programmes* (Washington, DC: IMF and World Bank).

Corbo, V. and P. Rojas (1990) 'Country Performance Effectiveness of World Bank-Supported Programs', manuscript (World Bank).

Corbo, V. and K. Schmidt-Hebbel (1990) 'Public Policies and Saving in Developing Countries', *Journal of Development Economics*.

Corbo, V. and Stanley Fischer (1990) *Adjustment Programs and Bank Support: Rationale and Main Results*, unpublished manuscript (Chapter 8 of this volume).

Corbo, V. and Steven Webb (1990) 'Adjustment Lending and the Restoration of Sustainable Growth', paper presented to conference on 'Policy-based lending: experience to date and prospects for the 1990s' (University of Manchester) September.

Corden, Max (1974) *Trade Policy and Economic Welfare* (Oxford: Clarendon Press).

Corden, Max (1981) *Inflation, Exchange Rates, and the World Economy*, 2nd edition (Chicago: University of Chicago Press).

Corden, Max (1990) 'Strategic Trade Policy: How New? How Sensible?', PRE Working Paper No. 396 (Washington, DC: World Bank).

Cornia, G.A. (1987) 'Economic decline and human welfare in the first half of the 1980s', in Cornia et al.

Cornia, G.A., R. Jolly and F. Stewart (1987) *Adjustment with a Human Face: Protecting the vulnerable and promoting growth* (Oxford: Oxford University Press).

Cornia, G.A. and F. Stewart (1990) 'The fiscal system, adjustment and the poor', *Innocenti Occasional Papers* 11 (Florence: UNICEF).

Creese, A.L. (1990) 'User charges for health care: a review of recent experience', Strengthening Health Services, Paper 1 (Geneva: WHO).

Csaba, L. (1983) 'Adjustment to the world economy in Eastern Europe', *Acta Oeconomica*, no. 2.

Dandekar, V.M. (1981) 'On measurement of poverty', *Economic and Political Weekly*, XVI.

Davies, R., D. Sanders and T. Shaw (1991) 'Liberalisation for development: Zimbabwe's adjustment without the Fund', paper for University of Witwatersrand Economics Initiatives Conference, Capetown, March.

De Melo, J. and S. Robinson (1989) 'Productivity and Externalities: Models of Export-Led Growth', manuscript (World Bank).

Denitch, B. (1981) 'Yugoslav Exceptionalism', in Jan Triska and Charles Gati (eds) *Blue Collar Workers in Eastern Europe* (London: Allen and Unwin).

De Soto, H. (1987) *El Otro Sendero* (Bogota: Oveja Negra).

Development Dilemmas (1989) Issue No 1 (Uppsala: Dag Hammarskjold Foundation).

Doi, L.T. (1977) *The Anatomy of Dependence* (Tokyo, New York, San Francisco: Kodansba International).

Dollar, D. (1990) 'Outward-Oriented Developing Economies Really Do Grow More Rapidly: Evidence from 95 LDCs', manuscript (World Bank).

Donaldson, T. (1990) 'The Ethics of Conditionality: International Debt and

the Problem of "Good Medicine"', mimeo.
Dornbusch, R. (1980) *Open Economy Macroeconomics* (New York: Basic Books).
Dornbusch, R. (1989) 'Credibility and Stabilisation', manuscript, (Massachusetts Institute of Technology).
Doyal, L. and I. Gough (1984) 'A theory of human needs', *Critical Social Policy*, 4.
Duesenberry, J. (1952) *Income, saving and the theory of consumer behaviour* (Cambridge, Mass.: Harvard University Press).
Easterly, William R. and D. Wetzel (1989) 'Policy Determination of Growth. A Survey of Theory and Evidence', World Bank PRE Working Paper No. 343.
Easterly, William R. (1990) 'Endogenous Growth in Developing Countries with Government Induced Distortions' (World Bank).
ECLA (1989) *Preliminary Overview of the Economy of Latin America and the Caribbean 1989* (Santiago: United Nations).
Edwards, Sebastian (1989a) 'Openness, Outward Orientation, Trade Liberalisation, and Economic Performance in Developing Countries', World Bank PPR Working Paper No. 191.
Edwards, Sebastian (1989b) 'On the Sequencing of Structural Reforms', NBER Working Paper No. 3138 (Cambridge, Mass: NBER).
Faber, M. (1990) 'Debt: New treatment for the chronic but repentant', *Journal of International Development*, 2, April.
Faini, R. J. De Melo, A. Senhadji-Semiali and J. Stanton (1991) 'Growth-oriented adjustment programs: a statistical analysis', *Ricerche Economiche*.
Feder, Gershon (1983) 'On Exports and Economic Growth', *Journal of Development Economics*, 12.
Federal Government of Nigeria (1986) *Structural Adjustment Programme for Nigeria 1986–88* (Lagos: Government Printer).
Field, J.O. (1977) 'The soft underbelly of applied knowledge: conceptual and operational problems in nutrition planning', *Food Policy*.
Fischer, M. (1981) 'The Origins and Future of the Ceausescu Cult', in D. Nelson (ed.) *Romania in the 1980s* (Boulder, Colorado: Westview Press).
Fischer, S. (1986) 'Issues in Medium-Term Macroeconomic Adjustment', *World Bank Research Observer*, 1, 2.
Fischer, S. (1987) 'Economic Growth and Economic Policy', in V. Corbo et al. (eds) *Growth-Oriented Adjustment Programs* (Washington, DC: IMF/World Bank).
Fischer-Galati, S. (1981) 'Romania's Development as a Communist State', in D. Nelson (ed.) *Romania in the 1980s* (Boulder, Colorado: Westview Press).
Fitzgerald, V. (1987) 'The impact of macroeconomic policies on small-scale industry – some analytical considerations', in Cornia et al (1987).
Frenkel, J. (1982) 'The Order of Economic Liberalisation: A Comment' in K. Bruner and A.H. Meltzer (eds) *Economic Policy and World of Change* (Amsterdam: North-Holland).
Frenkel, J.A. (1983) 'Remarks on the Southern Cone', *IMF Staff Papers*, March.

Friedman, M. (1957) *A theory of the consumption function* (Princeton, NJ: Princeton University Press).

Gates, Scott (1989) 'Micro Incentives and Macro Constraints on Development Assistance Conditionality,' unpublished PhD, University of Michigan.

Gelb, Alan (1989) 'A Cross-Section Analysis of Financial Policies, Efficiency and Growth', manuscript (World Bank).

Gertler, P., L. Locay, W. Sanderson, A. Dor and J. van der Gaag (1987) 'Health care financing and the demand for medical care', LSMS Working Paper, 37 (Washington, DC: World Bank).

Gilberg, T. (1979) 'The Communist Party of Romania', in S. Fischer-Galati (ed.) *The Communist Parties of Eastern Europe* (New York: Columbia University Press).

Giovannini, A. (1985) 'Savings and the Real Interest Rate in LDCs', *Journal of Development Economics*, August.

Gitelman, Z. (1981) 'The Politics of Socialist Restoration in Czechoslovakia and Hungary', *Comparative Politics*, January.

Goldstein, Morris (1986) *The Global Effects of Fund-supported Adjustment Programmes*, IMF Occasional Paper 42 (Washington, DC: IMF).

Good, Kenneth (1989) 'Debt and the One-party State in Zambia', *Journal of Modern African Studies*, 27, 2.

Gordon, David F. and Joan C. Parker (1984) 'The World Bank and its Critics: The Case of Sub-Saharan Africa', *Rural Africana*, Spring.

Gourevitch, P. (1978) 'The Second Image Reversed: The International Sources of Domestic Politics', *International Organization*, Autumn.

Government of the Philippines and UNICEF-Manila (1987) *Situation of Children and Women in the Philippines* (Manila: Government of the Philippines and UNICEF).

Government of Jamaica and ILO/PREALC-UNDP-UNFPA-UNICEF-WFP (1988) 'Sustaining the incomes and standard of living of the poor during adjustment: An action programme for Jamaica 1988–92', mimeo (New York: UNICEF).

Government of United Republic of Tanzania and UNICEF (1990) *Children in Tanzania: A Situation Analysis* (Dar-Es-Salaam: UNICEF).

Green, R.H. (1988) 'Ghana: Progress, Problematics and Limitations of the success story', *IDS Bulletin*, vol. 19, January.

Green, R.H. (1989) 'Medium term constraints to growth: Ghana', a paper for WIDER project on medium constraints to growth.

Griffin, C.G. (1991) 'The need to change health care priorities in LDCs', *Finance and Development*, March.

Haggard, Stephan (1986) 'The Politics of Adjustment: Lessons From the IMF's Extended Fund Facility', in M. Kahler (ed.) *The Politics of International Debt* (Ithaca: Cornell University Press).

Haggard, Stephan and Robert Kaufman (eds) (1992 forthcoming) *The Politics of Economic Adjustment: International Constraints, Distributive Politics and the State* (Princeton, NJ: Princeton University Press).

Harrigan, Jane (1988) 'Modelling the Impact of World Bank Policy-Based Lending: A Case Study of Malawi', unpublished paper, Institute for Development Policy and Management, University of Manchester.

Harrigan, Jane and Paul Mosley (1991) 'World Bank Policy-based Lending 1980–87: an Evaluation', *Journal of Development Studies*, April.

Harsanyi, John C. (1977) *Rational behaviour and bargaining equilibrium in games and social situations* (Cambridge: Cambridge University Press).

Heclo, Hugh and Aaron Wildavsky (1974) *The private government of public money* (London: Macmillan).

Helleiner, G. (1986) 'Outward orientation, import stability and African economic growth: an empirical investigation', in Sanjay Lall and F. Stewart, *Theory and Reality in Development* (London: Macmillan).

Helleiner, G.K. (1989) 'Structural Adjustment and Long-Term Development in Sub-Saharan Africa', unpublished paper presented at conference on 'Adjustment in Sub-Saharan Africa', Oxford, December 1989.

Helpman, E. and P.R. Krugman (1985) *Market Structure and Foreign Trade* (Cambridge, Mass.: MIT Press).

Helpman, E. and P.R. Krugman (1989) *Trade Policy and Market Structure* (Cambridge, Mass.: MIT Press).

Hemphill, W. (1974) 'The effect of foreign exchange receipts on imports of less developed countries', *IMF Staff Papers*, 21.

Herbst, Jeffrey (1990) *Labour in Ghana under Structural Adjustment: the Politics of Acquiescence*, unpublished manuscript.

Hicks, N. and P. Streeten (1979) 'Indicators of development: the search for a basic needs yardstick', *World Development*, 7.

Hill, K. and A. Pebley (1989) 'Child mortality in the developing world', *Population and Development Review*, 15, 4.

Humphreys, Charles and John Underwood (1989) 'The External Debt Difficulties of Low-Income Africa', in I. Husain and I. Diwan (eds) *Dealing with the Debt Crisis* (Washington, DC: World Bank).

Huntington, Samuel P. (1989) 'The Modest Meaning of Democracy', in R. Pastor, *Democracy in the Americas: Stopping the Pendulum* (New York: Holmes and Meier).

Hussain, Ch. M. (1987) *Development Planning in an Islamic State* (Karachi: Royal Book Company).

IBRD (1989) *Sub-Saharan Africa: from crisis to sustainable growth* (Washington, DC: IBRD).

Iglesias, Enrique (1990) 'From Policy Consensus to Renewed Economic Growth', in Joan Williamson (ed.) *Latin American Adjustment: how much has happened?* (Washington, DC: IIE).

ILO-ARTEP (1987) *Structural adjustment: by whom, for whom?* (New Delhi: ILO-ARTEP).

IMF (1982a) *Hungarian Peoples' Republic: Staff Report for the 1982 Article 4 Consultation* (Washington, DC: IMF).

IMF (1982b) *Hungarian Peoples' Republic Request for Standby Arrangement* (Washington, DC: IMF).

IMF (1983a) *Hungarian Peoples' Republic: Recent Economic Developments* (Washington, DC: IMF).

IMF (1983b) *Hungarian Peoples' Republic Letter of Intent* (Washington, DC: IMF).

IMF (1983c) *Hungarian Peoples' Republic Standby Arrangement* (Washington, DC: IMF).

IMF (1986) *Yugoslavia: Staff Report for the 1986 Midyear Consultation Under Enhanced Surveillance* (Washington, DC: IMF).

IMF (1987) *Yugoslavia: Recent Economic Development* (Washington, DC: IMF).

IMF/World Bank (1989) *Strengthening Efforts to Reduce Poverty* (Washington, DC: World Bank).

IMF (1990) *Government Financial Statistics* (Washington, DC: IMF).

Jackson, M. (1986) 'Romania's Debt Crisis: Its Causes and Consequences', in *East European Economies: Slow Growth in the 1980s* (Washington, DC: Joint Economic Committee of the US Congress).

Jamal, V. and J. Weeks (1988) 'The vanishing rural-urban gap in sub-Saharan Africa', *International Labour Review*, 127, 3.

Jespersen, E. (1990) 'Household responses to the impact of the economic crisis of the 1980s on social services in Sub-Saharan Africa', mimeo (New York: UNICEF).

Jimenez, R. and V.H. Cespedes (1990) *Costa Rica: Politica Economica, Cambio Estructural y Situacion Social Durante la Crisis y La Recuperacion*, mimeo (San Jose, Costa Rica).

Jobs and Skills Programme for Africa (JASPA) (1989) *African Employment Report* 1988 (Addis Ababa: ILO).

Jolly, R. and G.A. Cornia (1984) *The Impact of World Recession on Children* (Oxford: Pergamon Press).

Jolly, R. (1988) 'Poverty and adjustment in the 1990s', in J. Lewis and contributors, *Strengthening the Poor: What Have We Learned* (Washington, DC: ODC).

Jolly, R. and R. van der Hoeven (1989) 'Protecting the poor and vulnerable during adjustment: the case of Ghana', unpublished paper (UNICEF, New York).

Jovovic, D. (1981) 'Saradnja Jugoslavije sa MMFom', *Medunarodna Politika*, March.

Jowitt, K. (1974) 'Political Innovation in Romania', *Survey: A Journal of East/West Studies*, no. 4.

Kahler, Miles (1989) 'International Actors and the Politics of Adjustment', in J. Nelson (ed.) *Fragile Coalitions: The Politics of Economic Adjustment* (New Brunswick: Transaction Books).

Kahler, Miles (1990) 'External Influence, Conditionality and the Politics of Adjustment', mimeo (San Diego: University of California).

Kakwani, N., E. Makonnen and J. van der Gaag (1989) 'Structural adjustment and living conditions in developing countries', mimeo (Washington, DC: World Bank).

Kamara, S., M.T. Dahniya and P. Greene (1990) 'The effect of structural adjustment policies on human welfare in Africa South of the Sahara: Sierra Leone', mimeo (Florence: UNICEF).

Kanbur, S.M.R. (1988) 'Poverty and the social dimensions of structural adjustment in Cote D'Ivoire', mimeo (Washington, DC: World Bank).

Khan, M. (1974) 'Import and Export Demand in Developing Countries', *IMF Staff Papers*, vol. 21.

Khan, M.S. and M. Knight (1985) 'Fund-supported Adjustment Programmes and Economic Growth', *IMF Occasional Paper* 41.

Khan, M. and M.D. Knight (1988) 'Import compression and export performance in developing countries', *The Review of Economics and Statistics*, vol. LXX, no. 2.

Khan, M.S. (1990) 'The macroeconomic effects of Fund-supported adjustment programmes', mimeo (Washington, DC: IMF).

Khan, M., P.J. Montiel and N. Ul Haque (1990) 'Adjustment with growth: relating the analytical approaches of the IMF and the World Bank', *Journal of Development Economics*.

Kiguel, M. and N. Liviatan (1988) 'Inflationary Rigidities and Orthodox Stabilisation Policies: Lessons from Latin America', *The World Bank Economic Review*, 2.

Kiguel, M. and N. Liviatan (1990) 'Nominal Anchors, Stabilisation and Growth' manuscript (Washington, DC: World Bank).

Killick, Tony et al. (1984) *The Quest for Economic Stabilisation: The IMF and the developing world* (London: Heinemann Educational).

King, R. (1980) *A History of the Romanian Communist Party* (Stanford, Calif.: Hoover Institute Press).

Klugman, J. (1990) 'Adjustment with a human face – rhetoric or reality?', Essay submitted for MSc in Development Economics, University of Oxford.

Knight, P. (1983) 'Economic Reform in Socialist Countries' (Washington, DC: World Bank Staff Working Paper).

Knorr, Klaus (1975) 'The Power of Nations' in his *The Political Economy of International Relations* (New York: Basic Books).

Koopmans, T. (1965) 'On the concept of optimal economic growth', in *The Econometric Approach to Development Planning* (Amsterdam: North Holland).

Kovacevic, R. (1986) 'Spoljnotrgovinske Performanse i Perspektive Zaduzivanja Jugoslavije do 1990 godine' (Belgrade: Foreign Trade Institute).

Krasner, S. (1978) *Defending the National Interest: Raw Materials Investment and US Foreign Policy* (Princeton, NJ: Princeton University Press).

Krueger, Anne (1978) *Foreign Trade Regimes and Economic Development: Liberalisation Attempts and Consequences* (Cambridge, Mass.: Ballinger Press).

Krueger, A.O. (1984) 'Problems of Liberalisation' in Arnold C. Harberger (ed.) *World Economic Growth* (San Francisco: ICS Press).

Krueger, Anne, C. Michalopoulos, and V. Ruttan (1989) *Aid and Development* (Baltimore: Johns Hopkins University Press).

Krugman, P.R. (1987) 'Is Free Trade Passe?', *Journal of Economics Perspectives*, vol. 1, no. 2.

Krugman, Paul (1988) 'Forgiving vs. financing a debt overhang', *Journal of Development Economics*, vol. 29, November.

Kulic, S. (1982) 'Saradnja Jugoslavije s Medjunarodnim Finansijskim Organizacijama', *Ekonomski Pregled*, no. 11/12.

Kydd, Jonathan and Adrian Hewitt (1988) 'The effectiveness of structural adjustment lending: initial evidence from Malawi', *World Development*, vol. 14.

Lal, D. (1983) *The Poverty of 'Development Economics'* (London: IEA) Hobart Paperback 16.

Landell-Mills, Pierre (1981) 'Structural Adjustment Lending: Early Experience', *Finance and Development*, January.

Lauter, G. (1972) *The Manager and Economic Reform in Hungary* (New York: Praeger).

Legum, C. (1990) 'The Coming of Africa's Second Independence', *The Washington Quarterly*, Winter.

Leslie, J., M. Lycette and M. Buvinic (1986) 'Weathering economic crises: the crucial role of women in health' (Washington, DC: International Center for Research on Women).

Levine, R. (1990) 'Stock Markets, Growth, and Policy', *World Bank PRE Working Paper* No. 484.

Levine, R. and David Renelt (1990) 'A Sensitivity Analysis of Cross-Country Growth Regressions', manuscript (World Bank).

Levitsky, J. (1986) *World Bank Lending to Small Enterprises: a review*, Industry and Finance Series, vol. 16 (Washington, DC: World Bank).

Linden, R. (1986) 'Socialist Patrimonalism and the Global Economy: the case of Romania', *International Organization*, Spring.

Lipton, M. (1977), *Why Poor People Stay Poor: Urban Bias in World Development* (London: Temple Smith).

Little, I., T. Scitovsky and M. Scott (1970) *Industry and Trade in Some Developing Countries* (London: Oxford University Press).

Loxley, J. (1991) 'Ghana's Recovery: An Assessment of Progress, 1987–90', mimeo, University of Manitoba, for the North-South Institute, Ottawa.

Lucas, Robert (1988) 'On the Mechanics of Economic Development' *Journal of Monetary Economics*, 22.

Maasland, A. and J. Van Der Gaag (1990) 'World Bank Supported Programs and Living Conditions', manuscript (World Bank).

MacGaffey, Janet (1987) *Entrepreneurs and Parasites: The Struggle for Indigenous Capitalism in Zaire* (Cambridge: Cambridge University Press).

Machiavelli, N. (1968) *The Prince* (London: J.M. Dent, Everyman edition).

Maddala, G.S. (1988) *Introduction to Econometrics* (London: Macmillan).

Malloy, James M. (1989) 'Democracy, Economic Crisis and the Problem of Governance: The Case of Bolivia', unpublished manuscript, University of Pittsburgh, August.

Markus, M. (1982) 'Overt and Covert Modes of Legitimation in East European Societies', in T.H. Rigby and F. Feher (eds) *Political Legitimation in Communist States* (New York: St. Martin's Press).

Michaely, M. (1987) 'Trade Liberalisation Policies: Lessons of Experience', manuscript (World Bank).

Michalopoulos, C. (1987) 'World Bank programs for adjustment and growth', in Corbo, Goldstein and Khan.

Middlebrook, Kevin (1989) 'The Sounds of Silence: Organised Labour's Response to Economic Crisis in Mexico', *Journal of Latin American Studies* 21.

Millar, J. and C. Glendinning (1989) 'Gender and Poverty', *Journal of Social Policy*, 18.

Mincer, J. (1974) *Schooling, Experience and Earnings* (New York: NBER).

Mistry, Percy S. (1988) *African Debt: The Case For Relief For Sub-Saharan Africa* (Oxford: Oxford International Associates).

Mkandawire, T. (1990) 'Growth exercises in Zambia', a paper for WIDER project on Medium Term Adjustment Strategy (Helsinki).
Moore, M.P. (1984) 'Political Economy and the Rural-Urban Divide 1767–1981', *Journal of Development Studies*, 20, 3, 5–27.
Morales, J.A. (1990) 'The transition to sustained growth in Bolivia', mimeo (Bolivia: Univ Catolica Boliviana).
Moran, C. (1990) 'Imports under a foreign exchange constraint', *The World Bank Economic Review*, vol. 3, no. 2.
Moser, C. (1989) 'The impact of recession and structural adjustment policies at the micro-level: low-income women and their households in Guayaquil, Ecuador', in UNICEF, *Invisible Adjustment*, vol. 2 (New York: UNICEF).
Mosley, Paul (1980) 'Aid, Savings and Growth Revisited', *Oxford Bulletin of Economics and Statistics*, 42.
Mosley, Paul (1985) 'On Persuading a Leopard to Change his Spots: A Study of World Bank Structural Adjustment Lending', *University of Bath Papers in Political Economy*, No. 35.
Mosley, Paul (1987) *Conditionality as Bargaining Process: Structural Adjustment Lending 1980–86* (Princeton, NJ: Princeton Essays in International Finance, 168).
Mosley, Paul and L. Smith (1989) 'Structural Adjustment and Agricultural Performance in Sub-Saharan Africa 1980–87', *Journal of International Development*, 1, July.
Mosley, P., J. Harrigan and J. Toye (MHT) (1991) *Aid and Power: The World Bank and Policy-Based Lending in the 1980s*, 2 vols (London: Routledge).
Mudge, James (1984) 'Implications of the Agenda for Aid Policies and Priorities in Agriculture', *Rural Africana*, Spring.
Mussa, M. (1982) 'Government Policy and Adjustment Process' in J. Bhagwati (ed.) *Import Competition and Response* (Chicago: University of Chicago Press).
Ndulu, B. (1990) 'Macroeconomic constraints to growth. An empirical model for Tanzania', a paper for WIDER Project on Medium Term Adjustment Strategy (Helsinki).
Nellis, John (1989) *Public Enterprise Reform in Adjustment Lending* (Washington, DC: World Bank).
Nelson, D. (1981a) 'Development and Participation in Communist Systems: the Case of Romania', in D. Schultz (ed.) *Political Participation in Communist Systems* (New York: Pergamon).
Nelson, D. (1981b) 'Vertical Integration and Political Control in Eastern Europe: The Polish and Romanian Cases', *Slavic Studies*, no. 2.
Nelson, Joan (1989) *Fragile Coalitions: the Politics of Economic Adjustment* (New Brunswick, NY: Transaction Books).
Nelson, Joan (ed.) (1990) *Economic Crisis and Policy Choice: The Politics of Adjustment in the Third World* (Princeton, NJ: Princeton University Press).
Newman, John, Steen Jorgenson and Menno Pradhan (1989) *How Did Workers Benefit from Bolivia's Emergency Social Fund?*, World Bank draft staff study, November.

Nishimizu, M. and J. Page (1990) 'Trade Policy, Market Orientation and Productivity Change in Industry' in J. de Melo and A. Sapir *Trade Theory and Economic Reform: North, South and East.*

Nunberg, Barbara (1988) *Public Sector Pay and Employment Reform,* (Washington DC: World Bank).

Nuqui, W.G. (1991) 'The health sector and social policy reform in the Philippines since 1985', *Innocenti Occasional Papers,* 12 (Florence: UN-ICEF).

OECD (annual) *Economic Survey of Yugoslavia* (Paris: OECD).

OECD (1991) *Development cooperation: efforts and policies of the Development Assistance Committee* (Paris: OECD).

Ognjanovic, V. (1985) 'Spoljni Dugovi Jugoslavije i Politika Savladjavanja Problema', *Finansije,* no. 3/4.

Olsen, M. (1982) *The Rise and Decline of Nations: Economic Growth, Stagflation and Social Rigidities* (New Haven, Conn.: Yale University Press).

O'Neill, O. (1987) *Faces of Hunger* (London: Allen and Unwin).

O'Neill, O. (1988/89) 'Constructivism in ethics', Presidential Address to Aristotelian Society, *Proceedings* Volume LXXXIX, London.

Organisation of African Unity (1986) *African Submission to the Special Session of the United Nations General Assembly on Africa's Economic and Social Crisis,* ECM/2XV/E/ECA/ECM.1.1., March.

Otani, I. and D. Villanueva (1989) 'Determinants of Long-Term Growth Performance in Developing Countries', IMF Staff Working Paper (WP/88/97) and *World Development,* 18.

Oyejide, A. and M. Raheem (1990) 'Macroeconomic constraints and growth programming: empirical evidence from Nigeria', paper for WIDER Project on Medium Term Adjustment Strategy, Helsinki.

Pante, F. (1990) 'Health policy research and development in the Philippines', mimeo (Manila: Philippine Institute of Development Studies).

Papanek, G. (1972) 'The Effect of Aid and Other Resource Transfers on Savings and Growth in Less Developed Countries', *Economic Journal,* 82.

Pastor, M. Jr. (1987) 'The Effects of IMF Programs in the Third World: Debate and Evidence from Latin America', *World Development,* 15, 2, February.

Payne, P. and P. Cutler (1984) 'Measuring malnutrition, technical problems and ideological perspectives', *Economic and Political Weekly,* XIX.

Payne, P. (1988) 'Undernutrition: measurement and implications', mimeo (London: London School of Hygiene and Tropical Medicine).

Paz, O. (1985) *The Labyrinth of Solitude* (Harmondsworth: Penguin).

Pennant-Rea, Rupert (1986) *The African Burden* (New York: Twentieth Century Fund).

Pickett, J. and Shaeldin, I. (1989) 'Agriculture, industry and development in Ghana', mimeo (Glasgow: David Livingstone Institute).

Pinstrup-Andersen, P., M. Jaramillo and F. Stewart (1987) 'The impact on government expenditure', in Cornia et al.

Pinstrup-Andersen, P. (1988) 'Macroeconomic adjustment and human nutrition', *Food Policy.*

Pio, A. (1990) 'Piccole e medie imprese ed economia informale: l'appropriabilita' di un modello', *Dimensioni dello sviluppo*.

Pisulla, P. (1984) 'Der Internationale Wahrungsfonds und Seine Bedeutung fur die Osteuropischen Lander', *Osteuropa Wirtschaft*, no. 2.

Please, Stanley (1984) *The Hobbled Giant: Essays on the World Bank* (Boulder, Colorado: Westview Press).

Pravda, A. (1983) 'Trade Unions in East European Communist Systems', *International Political Science Review*, no. 2.

Przeworski, Adam (1990) 'The Political Economy of Adjustment', unpublished manuscript.

Putnam, Robert (1988) 'Diplomacy and Domestic Politics: the Logic of Two-Level Games', *International Organization*, Summer.

Raczynski, D. (1987) 'Social policy, poverty and vulnerable groups: Children in Chile', in Cornia, Jolly and Stewart, vol. 2.

Ram, R. (1985) 'Exports and economic growth: some additional evidence', *Economic Development and Cultural Change*, vol. 33, no. 1.

Ramsey, F. (1928) 'A mathematical theory of saving', *Economic Journal*, 38, December.

Rattso, J. and R. Davies 'Growth Programming for Zimbabwe', a paper for WIDER Project on Medium Term Adjustment Strategy (Helsinki).

Ravallion, M. and M. Huppi (1989) 'Poverty and undernutrition in Indonesia during the 1980s', Policy, Planning and Research Working Papers (Washington, DC: World Bank).

Ravallion, M. and M. Huppi (1990) 'Poverty in Indonesia during an adjustment period: a case study in methodology', mimeo (Washington, DC: World Bank).

Ravallion, M. (1990) 'Does undernutrition respond to incomes and prices?', mimeo (Washington, DC: World Bank).

Rawls, J. (1972) *A Theory of Justice* (Oxford: Oxford University Press).

Rebelo, Sergio (1990) 'Growth in Open Economies', manuscript (World Bank).

Remmer, K. (1986) 'The Politics of Stabilisation: IMF Standby Programs in Latin America 1954–84', *Comparative Politics*.

Ribe, H., S. Carvalho, R. Liebenthal, P. Nicholas and E. Zuckerman (1990) 'How adjustment programs can help the poor: the World Bank's experience', World Bank Discussion Papers, 71 (Washington, DC: World Bank).

Ribe, H., and S. Carvalho (1990) 'The treatment of social impact in adjustment programs supported by the World Bank', mimeo (Washington, DC: World Bank).

Riddell, R.C. (1987) *Foreign Aid Reconsidered* (Baltimore, Johns Hopkins University Press).

Rimmer, D. (1990) 'Alternatives to structural adjustment and the future of the Nigerian economy', paper for Conference on Democratic Transition and Structural Adjustment in Nigeria, Hoover Institution, Stanford, August 26–9.

Robinson, Brandon (1990) 'Collaborative Sector Analysis: A Foreign Assistance Technique for Improving LDC Sector Management', *World Development*, July.

Robinson, W. (1973) *The Pattern of Reform in Hungary* (New York: Praeger).

Rodrik, D. (1989a) 'Promises, promises: credible policy reform via signalling', *Economic Journal*, 99, September.

Rodrik, D. (1989b) 'Policy Uncertainty and Private Investment in Developing Countries', NBER Working Paper No. 2999 (Cambridge, Mass: NBER).

Rodrik, D. (1990) 'How should structural adjustment programs be designed?', *World Development*, July.

Roemer, Michael (1982) 'Economic Development in Africa: Performance Since Independence and a Strategy for the Future', *Daedalus*, Spring.

Rogic, Z. (1985) 'Analiza Efikasnost Restriktivne Monetarno-Kreditne Politike u Razdoblju 1979–84', *Jugoslovensko Bankarstvo* February.

Romer, Paul (1986) 'Increasing Returns and Long-Run Growth', *Journal of Political Economy*, 94, 5.

Romer, Paul (1989) 'What Determines the Rate of Growth of Technological Change?', *World Bank PPR Working Paper* No. 279 (Washington, DC: World Bank).

Romer, Paul (1990) 'Endogenous Technological Change', *Journal of Political Economy*.

Roxborough, Ian (1989) 'Organised Labour: A Major Victim of the Debt Crisis', in Barbara Stallings and Robert Kaufman (eds) *Debt and Democracy in Latin America* (Boulder, Colorado: Westview).

Rusinow, D. (1977) *The Yugoslav Experiment* (Berkeley: University of California Press).

Sachs, J. (1986) '*Conditionality and the Debt Crisis: Some Thoughts for the World Bank*', unpublished manuscript, Harvard University.

Sachs, J. (1987) 'Trade and Exchange Rate Policies in Growth-Oriented Adjustment Programs', in V. Corbo et al. (eds) *Growth-Oriented Adjustment Programs* (Washington, DC: IMF-World Bank).

Sachs, J. (1987) 'The Bolivian Hyper-Inflation and Stabilisation', *American Economic Review: Papers and Proceedings*.

Sachs, J. (1989) *Efficient Debt Reduction* (Washington, DC: World Bank).

Sahn, D.E. (1987) 'The prevalence and determinants of malnutrition in Cote D'Ivoire', mimeo (Washington, DC: World Bank).

Sahn, D.E. and A. Sarris (1990) 'Structural adjustment and rural smallholder welfare: a comparative analysis', unpublished paper (Washington, DC: Cornell University Food and Nutrition Program).

Sandbrook, Richard (1986) 'The State and Economic Stagnation in Tropical Africa', *World Development*, 14, 3.

Savadogo, K. and C. Wetta (1990) 'The impacts of a self-imposed adjustment policy: the case of Burkina Faso', unpublished paper (Florence: UNICEF).

Schacter, M. (1989) 'Bolivia's "Emergency Social Fund": Historical notes and impressions', mimeo (Washington, DC: World Bank).

Schmidt-Hebbel, K.S., S. Webb and G. Corsetti (1990) 'Household Saving in Developing Countries', manuscript (Washington, DC: World Bank).

Schrenck, Martin (1981) 'Managerial Structures and Practices in Manufacturing Enterprises: A Yugoslav Case Study', *World Bank Staff Working Paper* 455 (Washington, DC: World Bank).

Seers, D. (1977) 'Life expectancy as an integrating concept in social and demographic analysis and planning', *Review of Income and Wealth*, 23.

Sender, J. and S. Smith (1990) *Poverty, Class and Gender in Rural Africa: A Tanzanian Case Study* (London: Routledge).

Sepheri, A. and J. Loxley (1990) 'Medium Term Constraints to Growth: Uganda', paper for WIDER Project on Medium Term Adjustment Strategy (Helsinki).

Serageldin, I. (1989) *Poverty, Adjustment and Growth in Africa* (Washington, DC: World Bank).

Serven, L. and A. Solimano (1990) 'Investment Determinants', manuscript (Washington, DC: World Bank).

Serven, L. and A. Solimano (1990) 'Private Investment and Macroeconomic Adjustment in LDCs: Theory, Country Experiences and Policy Implications', unpublished paper (Washington, DC: World Bank).

Shabad, G. (1980) 'Strikes in Yugoslavia', *British Journal of Political Science*, July.

Sirc, L. (1979) *The Yugoslav Economy Under Self-Management* (London: Macmillan).

Sirowy, Larry and Alex Inkeles (1990) 'The Effects of Democracy on Economic Growth and Inequality: A Review', *Studies in Comparative International Development*, 25, 1, Spring.

Smith, P. (1990) 'Nigeria's New Adjustment Strategy', *Africa Recovery*, 4, 1, April-June.

Solimano, A. (1990) 'Inflation and the Costs of Stabilisation: Historical and Recent Experiences and Policy Lessons', *World Bank Research Observer* 5, 2.

Srinivasan, T.N. (1988) 'Structural adjustment, stabilisation and the poor', Economic Development Institute Working Paper (Washington, DC: World Bank).

Srinivasan, T.N. (1989) 'Recent Theories of Imperfect Competition and International Trade: Any Implications for Development Strategy?', *Indian Economic Review*, 24.

Stanovnik, J. (1985) *Svet U Dugovima i MMF* (Novi Sad: Dnevnik).

Stern, E. (1983) 'World Bank Financing of Structural Adjustment' in J. Williamson (ed.) *IMF Conditionality* (Cambridge, Mass.: MIT Press/ Washington, DC: IIE).

Stewart, F. and G. Ranis (1990) 'Macro-policies for appropriate technology: a synthesis of findings', in F. Stewart et al.

Stewart, F., H. Thomas and T. de Wilde (eds) (1990), *The Other Policy* (London: Intermediate Technology Publications).

Summers, L.H. (1985) 'Issues in National Saving Policy', NBER Working Paper No. 1710 (Cambridge, Mass: NBER).

Tarafas, I. (1985) 'The Possibility and Conditions of Anti-Inflationary Economic Policy in Hungary', *Acta Oeconomica*, no. 3–4.

Tardos, M. (1987) 'The Role of Money in the Hungarian Economy', *European Economic Review*, February/March.

Taylor, Lance (1988) *Varieties of stabilisation experience: towards sensible macroeconomics in the Third World* (Oxford: Oxford University Press).

Taylor, L. (1988) 'Medium Term Development Strategy', unpublished paper, Massachusetts Institute of Technology.

Taylor, L. (1989) 'Gap disequilibria: inflation, investment, saving and foreign exchange', unpublished paper, Massachusetts Institute of Technology.

Thomas, V. et al. (forthcoming) *Strengthening Trade Policy Reforms in Developing Countries* (Washington, DC: World Bank).

Tinguiri, K.L. (1990) 'Structural adjustment and satisfaction of basic needs: A Case Study using experience of Niger (1982–9)', mimeo (Florence: UNICEF).

Tokes, R. (1984) 'Hungarian Reform Imperatives', *Problems of Communism*, 9/10.

Tokman, V.E. (1986) 'Ajuste y empleo: los desafios del presente', mimeo (Santiago: PREALC).

Toye, J. (1987) *Dilemmas of Development: Reflections on the Counter-Revolution in Development Theory and Policy* (Oxford: Basil Blackwell).

Toye, J. (1990a) 'Is There a New Political Economy of Development?' in C. Colclough and J. Manor (eds) *States or Markets? Neo-Liberalism and the Development Debate* (Oxford: Oxford University Press).

Toye, J. (1990b) 'The Year of Liberal Revolution: A Survey of 1989', *World Economic and Business Review* (Oxford: Blackwell Reference).

Toye, J. (1990c) 'Ghana's economic reforms and World Bank policy-conditioned lending 1983–88', mimeo (Brighton: Institute of Development Studies).

Tyson, L. (1984) *Economic Adjustment in Eastern Europe* (Santa Monica, California: Rand Corporation).

Tyson, L. (1985) 'Conditionality and adjustment in Hungary and Yugoslavia' (Berkeley: University of California).

UNDP (1990) *Human Development Report 1990* (New York: Oxford University Press).

UN Economic Commission for Africa (1989) *African Alternative Framework to Structural Adjustment Programs for Socio-Economic Recovery and Transformation* (New York: United Nations).

UNICEF, Dominican Republic (1986) *Situation Analysis of Women and Children in the Dominican Republic* (Santo Domingo: UNICEF).

UNICEF, Accra (1987) 'Adjustment programmes to protect children and other vulnerable groups in Ghana' in Cornia et al., vol. 2.

UNICEF, Manila (1987) 'Redirecting adjustment programmes towards growth and the protection of the poor: The Philippine case', in Cornia, Jolly and Stewart, vol. 2.

UNICEF, Dar-es-Salaam (1988) 'Annual report: Tanzania and the Seychelles', (Dar-es-Salaam: UNICEF).

UNICEF (1989) *The State of the World's Children* (Oxford: Oxford University Press).

Valerio, F. (1990) 'Country case study on education in Mexico', mimeo (Florence: UNICEF).

Van der Gaag, J., E. Makonnen and P. Englebert (1990) 'Trends in Social Indicators', mimeo (Washington, DC: World Bank).

Von Brabant, J. (1985) 'East European Exchange Rates and Exchange

Policies', *Jahrbuch Der Wirtschaft Osteuropa* (Munich: Gunter Orzog Verlag).
Vries, A. de (1987) *Remaking the World Bank* (Washington, DC: Seven Locks Press).
Wagao, J.H. (1990) 'Adjustment policies in Tanzania, 1981–89: the impact on growth, structure and human welfare', *Innocenti Occasional Papers*, 9, (Florence: UNICEF).
Waterbury, John (1989) 'The Political Management of Economic Adjustment and Reform' in J. Nelson (ed.) *Fragile Coalitions: The Politics of Economic Adjustment* (New Brunswick N.Y.: Transaction Books).
Webb, S. and K. Shariff (1990) 'Designing and Implementing Adjustment Programs', manuscript (Washington, DC: World Bank).
Weeks, J. (forthcoming) *A Case of Maladjustment: Decline and Impoverishment in Sierra Leone* (London: Macmillan).
Westphal, Larry (1990) 'Industrial Policy in an Export-Propelled Economy: Lessons from South Korea's Experience', *Journal of Economic Perspectives*, Summer.
White, S. (1986) 'Economic Performance and Regime Legitimacy', *World Politics*, April.
Whitehead, Laurence (1989) 'Democratisation and Disinflation: A Comparative Approach', in J. Nelson (ed.) *Fragile Coalitions: The Politics of Economic Adjustment* (New Brunswick, NY: Transaction Books).
WHO/UNICEF (1988) 'The world economic crisis and its impact on health and health services: evidence and requirements for action', mimeo (New York: UNICEF).
Wildavsky, Aaron (1964) *The politics of the budgetary process* (Boston: Little, Brown).
Williamson, John (1983) *IMF Conditionality* (Washington, DC: IIE).
Williamson, John (1990) 'What Washington Means by Policy Reform', in John Williamson (ed.) *Latin American Adjustment: How Much Has Happened?* (Washington, DC: Institute for International Economics).
Woodward, S. (1986) 'Orthodoxy and Solidarity: Competing Claims and International Adjustment in Yugoslavia', *International Organization*, Spring.
World Bank (1980) *World Development Report 1980* (Washington, DC: World Bank).
World Bank (1981) *Accelerated Development in Sub-Saharan Africa: An Agenda for Action* (Washington, DC: World Bank).
World Bank (1983) *Ninth Annual Review of Project Performance Audit Results*, Operation Evaluation Department (Washington, DC: World Bank).
World Bank (1986) *Structural Adjustment Lending: A First Review of Experience*, report No. 6409, Operations Evaluation Department (Washington, DC: World Bank).
World Bank (1987) *Nigeria: Country Economic Memorandum*, Report No. 6716, June (Washington, DC: World Bank).
World Bank (1988a) *Annual Report* (Washington, DC: World Bank).
World Bank (1988b) *Report on Adjustment Lending*, report no. R88–199,

document presented to Executive Board (Washington, DC: World Bank).

World Bank (1988c) *Interim Report on Adjustment Lending*, report no. R88–15 (Washington, DC: World Bank).

World Bank (1988d) *Adjustment Lending: An Evaluation of Ten Years of Experience*, Policy and Research Series No. 1 (Washington, DC: World Bank).

World Bank (1988e) *World Development Report* (Washington, DC: World Bank).

World Bank (1988f) *Turkey Economic Memorandum: Towards Sustainable Growth* (Washington, DC: World Bank).

World Bank (1988g) *The Philippines: The Challenge of Poverty* (Washington, DC: World Bank).

World Bank (1989a) *Annual Report* (Washington, DC: World Bank).

World Bank (1989b) *World Development Report* (Washington, DC: World Bank).

World Bank (1989c) *World Debt Tables 1989–90* (Washington, DC: World Bank).

World Bank (1989d) *Sub-Saharan Africa: From Crisis to Sustainable Growth: A long-term perspective study* (Washington, DC: World Bank).

World Bank (1989e) *Project Completion Report (ESF)* (Washington, DC: World Bank).

World Bank (1989f) *Costa Rica: Public Expenditure Review* (Washington, DC: World Bank).

World Bank and UNDP (1989g) *Africa's Adjustment and Growth in the 1980s* (Washington, DC: World Bank).

World Bank (1990a) *Report on Adjustment Lending II: Policies for the Recovery of Growth*, Report R90–49, document presented to Executive Board (Washington, DC: World Bank).

World Bank (1990b) *Adjustment Lending Policies for Sustainable Growth*, World Bank Country Economics Department, World Bank Policy and Research Series No. 14, March (Washington, DC: World Bank).

World Bank (1990c) *World Development Report* (Washington, DC: World Bank).

World Bank (1990d) *Indonesia: Poverty Assessment and Strategy Report* (Washington, DC: World Bank).

Zarkovic, V. (1981) 'Striving for Economic Stabilisation', *Socialist Thought and Practice*, October.

Zivanovic, N. (1979) 'MMF i Jugoslavia', *Jugoslovensko Bankarstvo*, September.

Zuckerman, E. (1989) 'Adjustment programs and social welfare', *World Bank Discussion Papers*, 44 (Washington, DC: World Bank).

Zukin, S. (1981) 'The Representation of Working Class Interests in Socialist Society', *Politics and Society*, no. 3.

Zulu, J. and S. Nsouli (1985) *Adjustment Programs in Africa: The Recent Experience*, *IMF Occasional Paper* No. 34 (Washington, DC: International Monetary Fund).

Index

336 *Index*

 markets
endogenous growth, *see* new growth
 theories
enrolment rates, in schools, 200
European Bank for Reconstruction and
 Development, 1, 101–2
European Community, 5
exchange rates, 43, 64–6, 247, 276; *see
 also* black economy
'exploitative behaviour' by recipient,
 136
export prices, 19
externalities, 162

Faber, Michael, 150
farmer associations, as interest group,
 94–6
financial institutions, 247–9
financial markets, 35–8; *see also* interest
 rates
financial sector reform, 163–4, 278–9
food subsidies, 230
France, 14

Ghana, 4, 65, 70, 91–8, 108, 187–8, 193,
 220–3
'governance', 105, 309–16 *passim*
gradualism, 4, 63, 71
growth theory, 251

health, government expenditure on,
 190–1, 193, 199–200, 298
 Costa Rica, 212
 Indonesia, 202–3
 Philippines, 204–5
 Tanzania, 206–7
Helleiner, G.K., 26
human capital, 233–55
Hungary, 260–90 *passim*
hybrid loans, 22

implementation, of policy conditions,
 see conditionality
income distribution, 241
Indonesia, 177, 201–3
industrialists, as interest group, 97–8
inflation, 67–8
informal sector, 244, 246
initiation, of reform, 108–16
interest groups, 88
interest rates, 68, 278, 300; *see also*
 financial sector reform

International Labour Organisation
 (ILO), 296
International Monetary Fund (IMF)
 adjustment programmes, 1, 9
 approach to Africa, 31
 Structural Adjustment Facility (SAF
 and ESAF), 59–60, 72
 implementation of conditionality, 72
investment, 28, 35, 76, 170, 172–3
irrigation projects, 19
Islam, 300, 307
Ivory Coast, *see* Cote d'Ivoire

Jamaica, 109–10, 177
Jolly, Richard, 239, 244, 306

Kahler, Miles, 38, 104
Kanbur, Ravi, 305
Kant, Immanuel, 302–5
Kenya, 37, 92–7
Killick, Tony, 37
'knife-edge problem', 87, 99, 148
Krugman, Paul, 151, 163

labour markets, 161–2, 164, 184
labour unions, *see* trade unions
Lal, Deepak, 88, 100
learning by doing, 251
legal conditions, 16
leverage, *see* conditionality,
 effectiveness of
liberalisation (of import restrictions), 2,
 66–7; *see also* trade policy reform;
 structural adjustment
Lipton, Michael, 86

Machiavelli, Nicolo, 2, 87–8
macroeconomic imbalance, *see*
 stabilisation
maize, 95
Malawi, 92–7, 146
malnutrition, 207
Mauritius, 177
meso policies, 209–11
Mexico, 107, 109–10, 119, 164
military expenditure, 297–8
Moi, Daniel arap, 92
moral hazard, 29, 130
Moser, Caroline, 195
Mosley, Paul, 305
Mozambique, 48
multinationals, 2

Nelson, Joan, 3–4

This book is to be returned on
or before the date stamped below

20. MAY 1997

21. JUN 1997

CANCELLED

31st Oct 97

-CANCELLED

1 3 JAN 2000

2 5 OCT 2002

− 1 MAY 2003

1 6 JUN 2003

1 5 JAN 2004